# A Historical Geography of Ghana

# A Historical Geography of Ghana

**KWAMINA B. DICKSON**
*Department of Geography,*
*University of Ghana*

**CAMBRIDGE at the University Press 1971**

Published by the Syndics of the Cambridge University Press
Bentley House, 200 Euston Road, London NW1 2DB
American Branch: 32 East 57th Street, New York, N.Y.10022



Library of Congress Catalogue Card Number: 69–19375
International Standard Book Numbers
0 521 07102 X cloth edition
0 520 09657 X paperback

First published 1969
Paperback edition 1971

First printed in Great Britain at the University Printing House, Cambridge
Reprinted in Great Britain by Lewis Reprints Limited, London and Tonbridge

*To my Mother*

# Contents

# *Maps and diagrams*

# Tables

# *Preface*

The desire to write this book arose out of the conviction that ignorance of the past confounds any attempt to understand the contemporary human geography of Ghana. While it is true that the importance of the historical perspective in the elucidation of geographical problems in Ghana has never been lost sight of, as may be seen in several of the geographical publications on the country, what is clearly needed now is a coherent and consistent account of at least the main outlines of historical geography.

In all the book consists of fourteen chapters. Chapters 1 and 2 are introductory, seeking to identify the forces behind the evolution of the cultural landscape from earliest times to the end of the seventeenth century. Chapters 3, 4, and 5 form a cross-sectional study of the country's human geography around the year 1700. From this point onward the major component topics of human geography, except the growth of towns of which it is not possible to give a coherent account before 1850, are discussed one after the other—chapters 6 to 11—within the period from about 1700 to the mid-nineteenth century, and then (this time including the growth of towns) from the mid-nineteenth century to 1936. The mid-nineteenth century is regarded as an important landmark in the evolution of the cultural landscape, and if a cross-sectional account has not been written for that date, it is because of the absence of a detailed and coherent body of the relevant source material. Chapters 12 and 13 present the final period picture of the country's human geography on the eve of the Second World War, that is, between 1937 and 1939. The final chapter is meant to sum up, through an examination of the changing vegetation cover and the cultural landscape substituted for it, the salient features of man–land relationships from earliest times to 1937–9. The terminal period is 1937–9 because it is considered that by then nearly all the major elements of the country's human geography up to independence in 1957 had appeared.

There is perhaps much to criticize in this method of presentation. There is, for one thing, always the risk of a certain amount of repetition if, in a cross-sectional study after a narrative, it is attempted to present more than a bare descriptive account. Also, the development of each of the major elements of human geography is not narrated in a single chapter or in a number of consecutive chapters. But it is hoped that such breaks in continuity are not so serious as to obscure the nature of this cross-section-

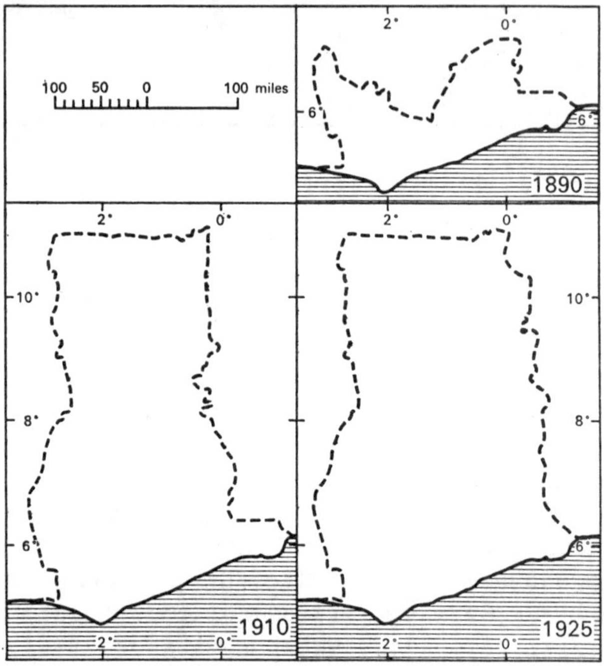


1*a* The Gold Coast

narrative method of presentation, whereby significant time periods are identified with reference to the total human geography, and within them the development of each of the major elements of human geography is narrated with emphasis on their inter-relatedness.

The name Ghana has been used throughout, instead of the old name Gold Coast. It is realized that for the period covered in this book the name Ghana did not exist, but from the practical point of view it is much more convenient to use that name. Gold Coast is, for the period under review, a

---

1*b* Ghana, administrative units. The regions are U.R.—Upper Region; N.R.—Northern Region; V.R.—Volta Region; B.R.—Brong-Ahafo Region; A.R.—Ashanti Region; E.R.—Eastern Region; W.R.—Western Region; C.R.—Central Region.

The following districts are given by the corresponding number on the map: 02 Ahanta-Shama; 03 Sekondi-Takoradi; 04 Komenda-Edina-Eguafo-Abrem-Asebu; 05 Cape Coast; 06 Mfantsiman; 08 Swedru; 09 Agona (Southern Ghana); 10 Nyakrom-Kkum; 11 Breman-Ajumako-Enyan; 13 Denkyira-Twifu-Hemang; 15 Tarkwa-Abosso; 18 Sefwi-Anhwiaso-Bekwai-Bibiani; 21 Accra; 22 Tema Development Corporation; 30 Western Akim; 32 Nsawam; 33 Akwapim; 35 Akwamu-Anum-Boso; 36 Manya-Yilo-Osudoku; 37 New Juaben; 39 West Akim Abuakwa; 40 Oda Swedru; 41 South Kwahu; 51 Keta; 64 Kumasi; 65 Kumasi South; 71 Sunyani; 84 Tamale; 91 Kassena-Nankani

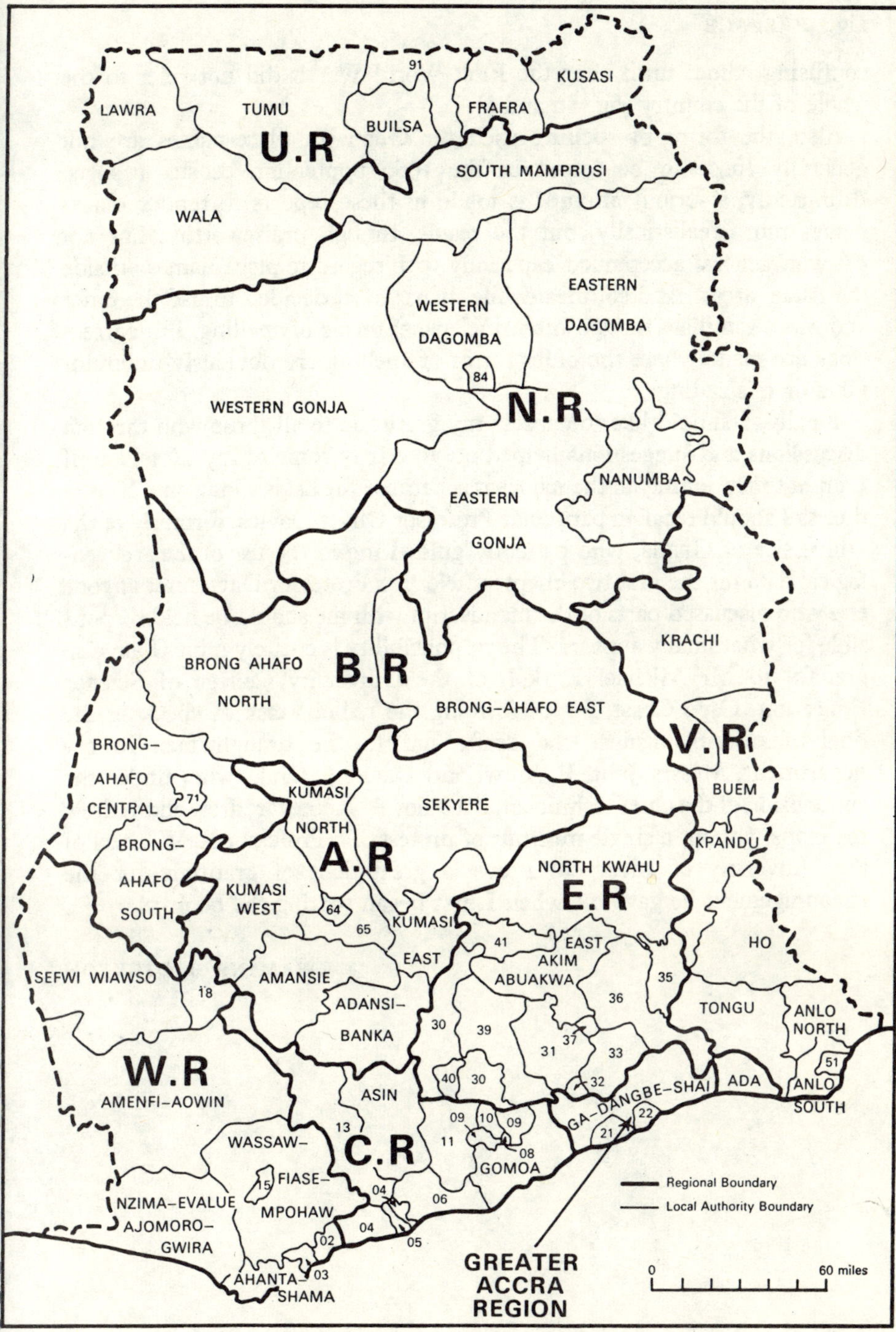


*1 b* Ghana, administrative units

confusing name: until after the First World War it did not refer to the whole of the country (fig. 1 *a* and *b*).

Also, the forms of spelling used for Ghanaian place-names are not generally those to be found in the 1960 population census reports. Admittedly, a serious attempt is made in these reports to render place-names more realistically, but the result, though praiseworthy, has not yet won general acceptance, especially with regard to place-names outside the Akan areas. And so, meanwhile, it has been decided to use the older and more familiar (though often inelegant) forms of spelling. But corrections are made where the older forms of spelling are obviously unintelligible or misleading.

Finally, I should like to express my gratitude to all those who through discussions and suggestions helped me to clarify some of my ideas, and if I am not mentioning all the names it is because the list is a long one. Nevertheless I should recall in particular Professor Oliver Davies, formerly of the University of Ghana, who patiently guided me in the use of the archaeological data for the first two chapters. Neither Professor Davies nor anyone else who discussed parts of the manuscript with me should be held responsible for what finally appears. The responsibility is entirely mine. I am also grateful to Mr Michael Darkoh of the University College of Science Education, Cape Coast, for performing the tedious task of checking the final manuscript against the draft, and to the draughtsmen in my department, Messrs John F. Antwi and David J. Drah, who, under the supervision of the chief technician, Mr Pilot A. Kemevor, drew and redrew the maps without a single murmur of protest. To Professor R. W. Steel of the University of Liverpool I owe a great debt of gratitude for the encouragement he gave me when I first began writing the book.

KWAMINA B. DICKSON

PART I

# *Introduction: from earliest times to the end of the seventeenth century*

# 1. The peopling of the land and the crystallization of tribes and states

## SETTLEMENT: EARLIEST TIMES TO 1200

Situated not far from the midway point on the coast of Guinea and stretching from about latitude 5° N. to just beyond latitude 11° N., far enough to belong at once to the two great generalized regions of West Africa—forest and savanna—Ghana has, since the earliest times, been in the path of the currents and forces that have shaped the culture history of West Africa.

Archaeologists in West Africa divide the Palaeolithic, the earliest period in the cultural evolution of man, as seen in the evolution of types of stone implements, into two major stages, to which they have given the distinguishing names of Early Stone Age and Middle Stone Age. There is no Late Stone Age in West Africa.[1] The two main stages in the West African Stone Age are each characterized by groups of culture complexes, and each culture complex belongs to a definite phase of Pleistocene climatic variation, consisting of pluvials or periods of heavy rainfall and excessive moisture, separated by interpluvials or periods of reduced rainfall or drought. The pluvial periods sometimes had their own variations of subpluvials and sub-interpluvials. The archaeological evidence suggests that this rhythm of climatic variation, involving the alternation of wet and dry phases, has been of paramount importance in the peopling of Ghana and of West Africa as a whole, for peoples moved to and fro, in conformity with climatic rhythm, between the Niger Bend and the Sahara on the one hand and the wooded savanna and forest in the south on the other. The reason for this alternation of movement centred on the probability that man's material culture in Stone Age times enabled him to live more easily in open savanna areas than in the difficult forest and desert environments.[2] Increases

[1] Except where otherwise stated, the first part of the chapter on prehistoric population is based on the following publications by Oliver Davies: (*a*) 'The Stone Age in West Africa', *Ghana J.S.* III, 1 (April 1963); (*b*) *Archaeology in Ghana* (Thomas Nelson and Sons Ltd, 1961), pp. 1–4; and (*c*) 'The Distribution of Stone Age Material in Guinea', *Bulletin de l'I.F.A.N.* XXI, Sér. B, 1–2 (1959). The terms employed for the phases of Pleistocene climatic variation were originally used for East Africa. An explanation of these as well as of the archaeological nomenclature employed is to be found in J. D. Clark, *The Prehistory of Southern Africa* (Penguin, 1959), pp. 37–42.

[2] The rarity of pebble tools in the forest poses a problem. It may be a result of the fact that High terrace gravel deposits are rare in the forest.

in rainfall would result in a northward extension of the forest and the conversion of desert to savanna; the opposite would occur with the onset of a dry phase. This was so from Palaeolithic to Neolithic times.

To the Early Stone Age of the Palaeolithic belong the pre-Chellean or pebble tool culture of the first interpluvial (Kageran–Kamasian I), the Chellean which may be assigned to Kamasian I–II, and the Acheulian which is typologically late and possibly belongs, with the Sangoan, to the Kamasian II–Gamblian interpluvial.[1] The Sangoan, a derivative of the Acheulian, is transitional between the Early Stone Age and the Middle Stone Age. The Middle Stone Age begins with Sangoan derivatives, which are succeeded by Kalinian and Early Lupemban cultures belonging to the Gamblian pluvial. Then, in what may correspond to the post-Gamblian dry phase, come the Late Lupemban, Guinean Aterian or quasi-Magosian, and Ultimate Middle Stone Age cultures, which complete the Middle Stone Age and the Palaeolithic. After the Palaeolithic are the Mesolithic culture, possibly contemporary with post-Pluvial III in the Near East, and the Neolithic which came not long after the Mesolithic.

The artefacts belonging to the various Palaeolithic culture complexes and found near the coast of West Africa as a whole are associated with some raised beaches, apparently with three well-defined river terraces—the High, Middle and Low terraces—and with pedological sections. Thus examples of the simple and irregular pebble choppers and flake tools, belonging to the pre-Chellean of the Early Stone Age and presumed to represent man's first essays in tool manufacture, have been found sporadically in the High terraces of rivers rising far north in the savanna, and also of the Birim where the terraces have been exposed through mining activities. One of the most significant sites for these tools is Yapei on the White Volta where, from High terrace gravel on the east bank, over ninety 'more or less convincing rolled pebble tools' have been collected. Other more or less convincing specimens have been collected at Kamba Bridge on the Black Volta, at Bato on the Oti, and at a place on the Volta three miles north of Kete Krachi. All the sites are in fairly open savanna country. The forest and the coastal bush and scrubland have on the other hand yielded pebble tools whose identification is more difficult, and among the most convincing specimens found so far are two or three uniface quartz choppers from a gravel deposit at Akim Oda. Elsewhere the few pebble tools collected, as at Senya Beraku, belong to the hand axe Chellean.

Rigid tests have been applied for the identification of pebble tools in

[1] The correlation of Ghana's climatic phases with those in East Africa must strictly be regarded as being no more than approximate.

Ghana. Pieces are not regarded as pre-Chellean unless they are rolled and occur in a suitable geological horizon (usually a High river terrace). Sites have been recorded as doubtful if the assemblage of possible pebble tools in the right horizon is too small or if the pieces occur in an area where the High and Middle terraces cannot be distinguished; and heavily rolled pieces found together with unrolled Sangoan tools have been rejected. On the basis of these criteria it has been asserted that there is sufficient evidence for a pre-Chellean rolled industry in the country. The known sites are shown in fig. 2 which indicates that the pre-Chellean industry or population may have spread in an uncoordinated manner southward and westward along the rivers.

There are many questions on this earliest culture that are as yet unresolved and will perhaps always be argued. One of these is the rationale of the distribution of pre-Chellean man. One conclusion is nevertheless clear; the pre-Chellean population was attracted to the watercourses.

Also outstanding is the question of whether pre-Chellean man came from somewhere else or originated in the country. The only suggestion so far is that if the pebble tools in Ghana belong to the Kageran–Kamasian interpluvial, then they occur fairly late in the series established for other parts of Africa. It could presumably then mean that this early culture did not develop independently in Ghana.

After the pre-Chellean came the Chellean whose remains in the form of rolled stone tools (hand axes, unspecialized flake tools) are found on the Middle terrace. The terrace corresponds to an old beach at a height of about 75 feet, in which pre-Chellean material is also found. It seems that the Chellean population, apparently from the lower middle valley of the Niger not far from Niamey, penetrated through the Volta Region along the foot of the Togo–Atakora Ranges and along the Dayi and Volta rivers to the Accra Plains, and from there followed the coast and into the Birim valley, where the vegetation was probably much thinner then. The Chellean invasion and occupation appear to have been weak, and did not extend into the Western Region (fig. 2).

The end of the Kamasian I–II sub-interpluvial and the reversion to more pluvial conditions probably drove the Chellean population north from the Guinea forest, as well as driving an Early and Middle Acheulian population south into the Sahara and across it to about latitude 9° N. in places; but it was not until the end of the pluvial period that a Late Acheulian population was able to penetrate to the Guinea coast. Stone tools of the Late Acheulian culture, often heavily rolled, are found on the Low terrace together with unrolled Sangoan, and their distribution demonstrates the importance of

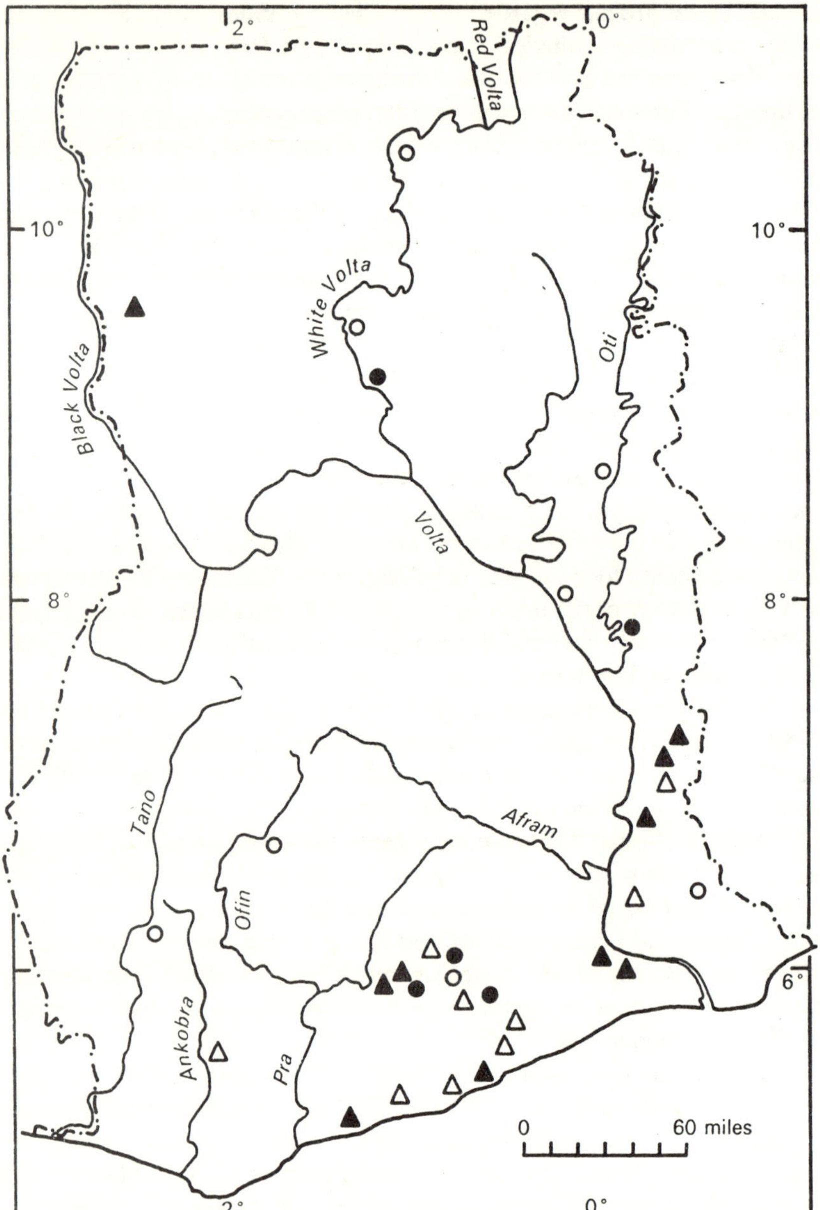


2 Pre-Chellean and Chellean sites (after O. Davies). Pre-Chellean: ● certain, ○ doubtful; Chellean: ▲ certain, and △ doubtful

the route of penetration along the Togo-Atakora Ranges at whose foot there would probably have been springs in the dry interpluvial. The Acheulian occupation was, like the Chellean, weak and did not extend over much of the country. Only thirty-six sites, half of them doubtful, have been recorded as Acheulian, and they are almost all confined to the Volta, Eastern, and Central Regions (fig. 3).

Much more widespread was the Sangoan population which came south independently but apparently in the same interpluvial as the Late Acheulian. More than 240 Sangoan sites have been recorded (fig. 4). The route of Sangoan penetration was, it would appear, the same as the Acheulian: along the foot of the Togo-Atakora Ranges, except that from where the Togo-Atakora Ranges approach the Volta a branch route turned northwest up the Black Volta to Kamba bridge. There are also some Sangoan sites on the Red Volta but they do not indicate any clear line of approach. It would seem that the Sangoan population pushed its way westward along the coast and up into the Akim and Ashanti forest as far as the Pra and the Ofin rivers, but perhaps not very much north of Kumasi.

Starting about 40,000 years ago, the Gamblian pluvial once more probably made much of the country uninhabitable for Sangoan men, except perhaps the coast where the woodland vegetation that would have resulted from the increased moisture would have been open enough to permit settlement. The pluvial phase apparently also drove, in a generally northwestward direction, bearers of Kalinian culture from the Congo or Central Africa who spread along what was then probably wooded savanna between a wetter Sahara, occupied by an Aterian population originally from North Africa, and the Guinea forest which probably extended farther north than it does now. It seems the Kalinian population generally avoided Ghana, for only one Kalinian site is known in the extreme north of the country.

After the pluvial phase, which lasted about 20,000 years, came a period of severe aridity during which men moved from the Sahara and the Sahel to the more genial environment in the south. Bearers of the Lupemban culture, a developed form of the Kalinian, retreated south to Ghana where products of their industry have turned up in a good many places, including the coast. The Lupemban population was followed by Aterian (quasi-Magosian) refugees, from north of the Niger Bend, who occupied mainly the wooded savanna and as far south as Kpong. They did not quite reach the coast. The remains of the culture have been located on basal gravel, deposited in valleys presumably in the dry phase which ended the era of valley rejuvenation in the Gamblian pluvial. The gravel is now covered first by ferruginized grits and then by silt deposited at a later wetter period

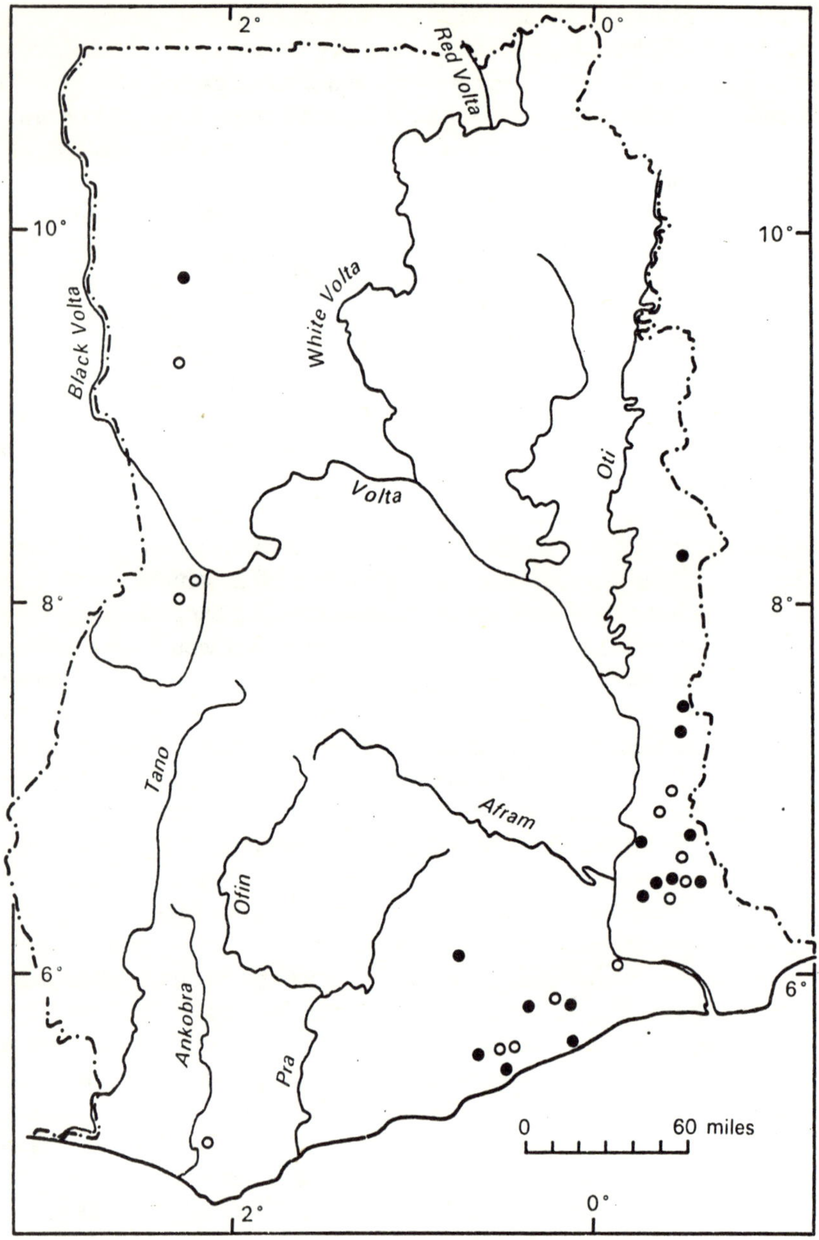


3 Acheulian sites (after O. Davies). ● certain; ○ doubtful

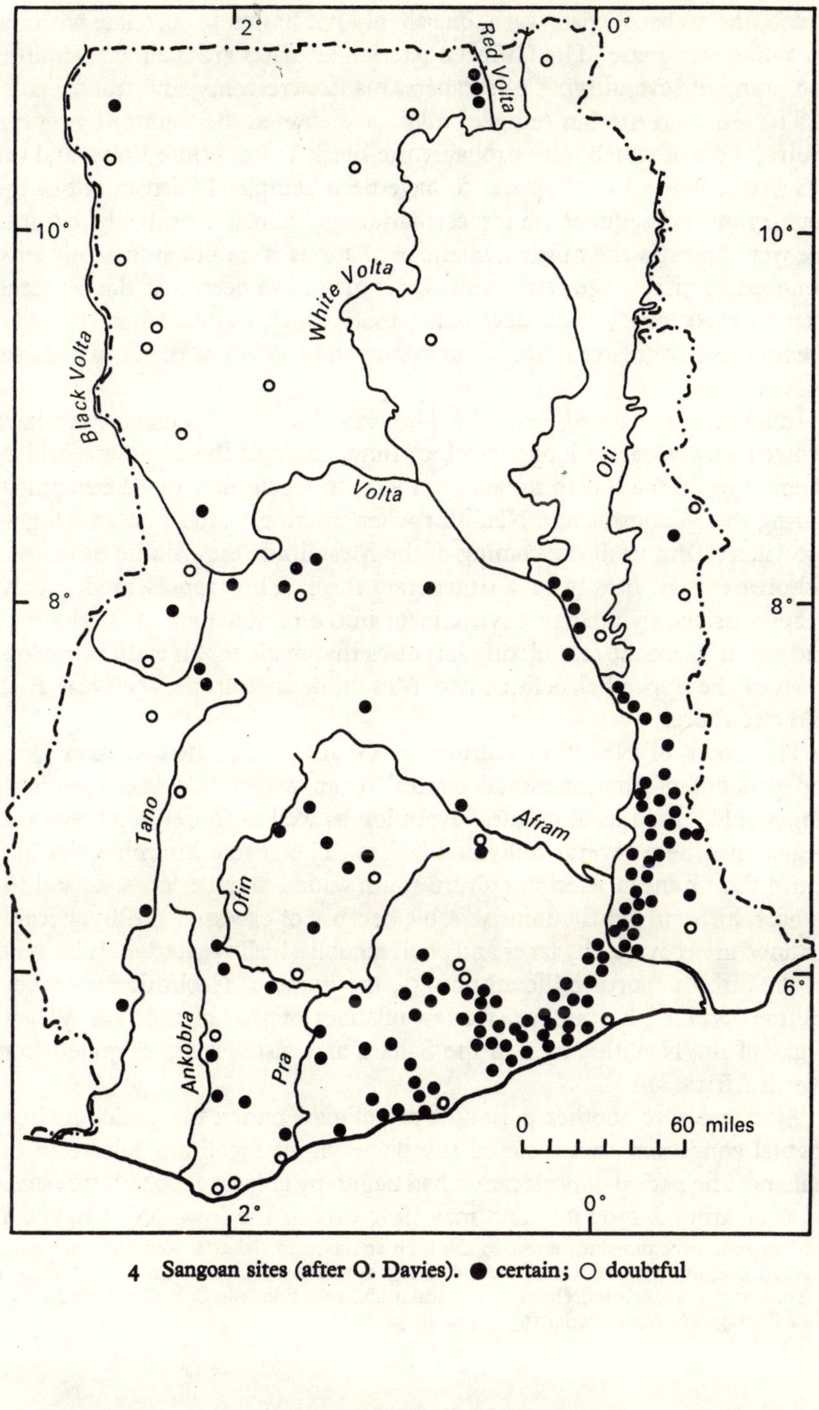


4 Sangoan sites (after O. Davies). ● certain; ○ doubtful

which, the archaeologists warn, one should not hasten to correlate with the Makalian wet phase. The Guinean Aterian artefacts are mainly microliths consisting of several types of scrapers, blades, crescents, and tranchets.

The Guinean Aterian refugees may have entered the country by several routes, three of which were probably the Black Volta, White Volta, and the Oti rivers. They do not appear to have been completely driven out of the country by subsequent minor oscillations of climate, probably because the wet phases in the minor climatic oscillations were not sufficiently pronounced to discourage settlement. Or it may have been that the Guinean Aterian men were slowly developing tools which enabled them to adapt themselves to a greater range of environmental conditions than was hitherto possible.

Industries associated with the Guinean Aterian in Ghana may have evolved slowly over a long stretch of time, through the Ultimate Middle Stone Age, in the fourth millennium B.C., to reach their full development during the Mesolithic and Neolithic when microlithic tools became highly specialized. But until the coming of the Mesolithic, the Middle Stone Age cultures existed mostly in a degenerate form. They represented, partly, peoples driven by a harsh environment into a remote part of West Africa and cut off from the stimulating impulses that made for an earlier development of the upper Palaeolithic and Mesolithic in Europe, the Near East, and elsewhere.

The roots of Neolithic culture in Ghana, which helped man to be independent of environmental control to an extent that was previously impossible, lay in local cultural evolution as well as in developments that began elsewhere several millennia before. The severe interpluvial which drove the Guinean Aterian culture south ended about 6000 B.C., and the Sahara, hitherto mostly uninhabitable because of excessive aridity, became a humid area covered by lakes and pools among a lush vegetation. It became, in the fifth or fourth millennium B.C., the home of Neolithic man whose culture, typified by pottery, was an offshoot of that of the Nile Valley.[1] Some of the Neolithic men in the Sahara may also have immigrated from North Africa.

A reversion to another period of dry climate ended the genial environmental conditions that fostered the flowering of Neolithic culture in the Sahara. The period of desiccation had begun by at least 2600 B.C. It reached its peak around 1300 B.C. and may have caused the invasion of Egypt by

[1] Numerous cave drawings attest to the high standard of Saharan Neolithic culture. A comprehensive presentation of these drawings is in Henri Lhote's *Tassili Frescoes* (New York, 1959). A less comprehensive but still useful selection is in E. F. Gautier's *Le Passé de l'Afrique du Nord* (Paris, 1937), pp. 48–9.

Saharan peoples, some of whom also fled south towards the more humid forest. Somewhere around 1000 B.C. some of the south-moving refugees entered Northern Ghana and penetrated to the edge of the forest where, cut off from the mainstream of Neolithic civilization around the Mediterranean, they lost most of their Neolithic arts, except their stone techniques, and reverted to a Mesolithic culture of which there were already traces in the country.

As the dry phase began to tail off, some time after 900 B.C., two further groups of Neolithic peoples arrived in the country. The first group would seem to have come from the east or northeast—from the Congo or Central Africa—to the south-east coastal plains. From there, perhaps under pressure from waves of newly arriving immigrants, they entered the Closed Forest a little later. The generally westward movement of these peoples did not end in Ghana but continued as far as Conakry, in the Republic of Guinea, and beyond. Although many of their cultural remains have been found on the Black Volta, these Neolithic people on the whole seem to have preferred and kept to the more humid south. It was these people who apparently showed how it was possible to occupy and exploit the tropical forest in West Africa.

Soon after came the other Neolithic culture, probably from somewhere near the Niger Bend. It has been named 'Kintampo culture'. Its general appearance is northern and its bearers may have been the first to introduce the knowledge of pottery into Ghana.[1]

Sites have been found in the Accra Plains showing a fusion of the older Neolithic with the Kintampo culture, which may have arrived there with incomers from the north. The fully developed Neolithic culture in Ghana is generally associated with pottery with impressed decoration, a large variety of stone hoes, axes and celts, biconically pierced quartz discs and pebbles, and with products of a lithic industry consisting of lunate microlith scrapers, backed blades, micro-tranchet, arrowheads, etc.

The stone axes or celts have a fairly general distribution, although there are a few areas where they seem to concentrate; but it should not be assumed that these concentrations indicate higher densities of population.[2]

[1] O. Davies, 'The Invaders of Northern Ghana', *Universitas* (University of Ghana, Legon), IV, 5 (March 1961). The report is curiously abbreviated in spite of the historical importance of this culture: 'It is characterized by wattle-and-daub houses, village agglomerations usually in remote and sheltered situations, very fine stone tools, stone bracelets, small polished stone axes, coarse pottery stamped with square-toothed combs, polishers for small beads probably of shell or ostrich eggshell, stone net-sinkers, and by curious scored objects of terra cotta which look like flattened cigars. The last are the most noticeable objects of this culture...'

[2] C. T. Shaw, 'Report of Excavations carried out in the Cave known as "Bosumpra" at Abetifi, Kwahu, Gold Coast Colony', *Proc. Prehist. Soc.* X (1944).

Neither should the general distribution of the implements be taken to mean that Neolithic people were to be found in every part of the country, since the practice of shifting cultivation by the Neolithic people would entail the discarding of useless tools wherever the ground was temporarily cultivated. Moreover, it is not only Neolithic people who should be associated with stone celts, for the tools also lasted well into the Iron Age. Concentration of the celts in the gold-mining areas of Tarkwa, Obuasi, and Akrokeri should not be vested with any significance since artefacts are much easier to find in mines, where pedological sections are clearly displayed.

The next major landmark in the peopling and culture history of the country was the coming of iron users. It is generally believed that a regular knowledge of iron-working techniques came to Neolithic West Africa around the dawn of the Christian era from Meroe in the Nile Valley and south from across the Sahara. West Africa did not know an intermediate Copper or Bronze Age except, as far as is known, in western Mauritania where the culture was based on the copper mines at Akjoujt.[1]

So far the archaeological evidence collected in Ghana favours the suggestion that iron technology came there some time between about A.D. 500 and 1000 with an invasion from the Sahara, probably from somewhere north of Gao.[2] The evidence was revealed in a small excavation conducted at Ntereso on the Black Volta near the western boundary of the country, which showed, among other things, bone harpoons and fish hooks of exquisite workmanship. The invasion was probably brutal: the finds from the excavation did not demonstrate stages of fusion of Neolithic with Iron Age cultures, but showed two distinctive cultures, the older elements of which belonged to the Kintampo culture while the newer elements bore no relationship to the former.[3] Apparently it was these invaders who first brought the knowledge of iron-working into Ghana.

After this invasion, iron technology spread to other parts of the country. The excavated upper levels of Bosumpra cave at Abetifi[4] showed that in due course Neolithic people came to fashion iron objects and made a more sophisticated type of pottery decorated with grooves. Iron-working did not entirely replace the stone industries but existed side by side with them until a few centuries ago, as may be seen from the association of celts with tuyere at several sites, from the tradition that in the late sixteenth century pieces

[1] R. Mauny and J. Hallemans, 'Préhistoire et Protohistoire de la Région d'Akjoujt Mauritanie)', *Prehistory—Third Pan African Congress, 1955*.

[2] See footnote 1 on p. 11.

[3] Ibid.

[4] Shaw, op. cit.

of iron were used as currency in Ashanti,[1] and from the fact that celts were found in excavated sixteenth-century sites at Sekondi.[2]

Archaeological research has not reached the stage where it can suggest a distribution pattern of the Early Iron Age population, but a few observations are possible. It appears that the forest country in the south with its overwhelming vegetation was as well populated as the more open country in the north, and one well-defined area of population concentration, it has been suggested, was the wetter zone immediately north of the forest along the Black Volta.[3] Water was obviously the controlling factor there. Similarly, in the south, the watercourses and areas with high water table attracted settlement, especially in the Accra Plains where water was generally not so plentiful.

The population would not be static, for the practice of shifting cultivation would entail continual search for fresh soils and perhaps the displacement of people already living in the newly found area. Such a practice does in itself contain a temporary stabilizing factor, which arises from the fact that the possibility of being evicted from their lands would induce many people to live together in large nucleated settlements, or perhaps in a scatter of small settlements, looking to one another for protection. In heavily populated areas where such permanent and perhaps fortified settlements would be common, agriculture would gradually cease to be migratory and develop into the more stable bush fallowing. But as settlements increased in size with a corresponding increase in the pressure of population on the land, search for new lands would become necessary once more, and migration and the founding of new settlements would then result. Wars and plagues of all kinds must also have caused population movements.

The process just described involving population movements and the founding of large nucleated settlements is necessarily conjectural; but it may very well have occurred throughout the country in those early times. Similar events occurred in later centuries even when societies were more stable and tribal boundaries were fixed. Large groups of Lobi tribesmen for example migrated, as late as the eighteenth and nineteenth centuries, from Wa and Lawra districts and crossed the Black Volta to the Ivory Coast, searching for fresh land for cultivation.[4]

[1] R. S. Rattray, *Ashanti* (O.U.P., 1923), pp 324–7.

[2] O. Davies, 'Native Culture in the Gold Coast at the time of the Portuguese Discoveries', *Congresso Internacional de Historia dos Descobrimentos* (Lisbon, 1961).

[3] Personal communication from Oliver Davies.

[4] H. Labouret, 'Les Tribus de Rameau Lobi' (*Mémoire de l'I.F.A.N.*, 1958), pp. 24–35.

## SETTLEMENT: 1200–1700

### Tribes in Southern Ghana and Ashanti–Brong Ahafo

It was in Iron Age times that the foundations for the basic structure and composition of Ghana's present-day African population were laid. The first Iron Age invasion, which took place over a thousand years ago, involving the immigration of foreign peoples and radical alteration of the material culture of the local population, was the last of its kind. Since then it has mainly been the imposition of different political systems upon the local population by small groups of better armed warriors, who were eventually absorbed by the local population.

The view expressed here is not new. It was the conclusion reached and amply demonstrated by Rattray in the 1920s, but the point was largely ignored in subsequent years. Instead, theories were advocated of mass immigration of alien or culturally different peoples from elsewhere into a virtually empty country since the thirteenth century or so.[1] Rattray stated his point of view as follows:[2]

I have for some time past been inclining more and more to the opinion that we were on the wrong lines in talking of, and seeking for, origins and lines of migrations for the people who today we call the Ashanti, in terms of a compact or composite tribe...The forest belt had probably been their habitat from time immemorial. Their later barbaric civilization and the more striking features of their constitution, the reshuffling of tribal units and the formation of territorial groupings, these are the origins we have to trace. We have been confusing...the migration of a few families of a higher and more civilized type, who produced these changes, with the migration of a people.

Rattray's statement has since been reiterated by Goody, and the anthropological evidence upon which Rattray based his conclusions reinforced by arguments based on linguistics. Goody's statement also read thus:[3]

For example, the Ashanti speak one of the Kwa languages which extend through the forest belt of the Ivory Coast, Dahomey and Western Nigeria, and which shade into the Gur group through the Guang languages, and one cannot accept stories of migration from quite a different area as applying to the entire population when the linguistic continuity has to be accounted for...Given that these stories may contain an element of historical fact which can be cross-checked against the tradi-

[1] Elaborate statements of the mass immigration theory are to be found in W. E. F. Ward, *A History of Ghana* (London, 1958), chapters III and IV, and E. L. R. Meyerowitz, *The Akan Traditions of Origin* (London, 1950), *passim*.

[2] R. S. Rattray, *The Tribes of the Ashanti Hinterland* (O.U.P., 1932), I, xx.

[3] J. Goody, *The Ethnography of the Northern Territories of the Gold Coast, West of the White Volta* (Colonial Office, London, 1954), p. 6.

tions of other peoples, the linguistic situation indicates that there must have been an existing Akan-speaking population from whom the immigrants acquired the language. The tendency for the traditions of the ruling lineages to be adopted by those of subordinate rank would explain the uniformity throughout the society of these migration stories.

For an alternative to the mass immigration theory it is not necessary to postulate a static situation in which the Early Iron Age population was left alone in isolation to increase and multiply. There were immigrations of small groups of people, sometimes speaking languages similar to those of the local inhabitants. There were social upheavals and revolutions resulting from the adoption of new ideas from politically superior but numerically inferior groups of alien people. It is in this light that the peopling of the country from about the twelfth or thirteenth century should be viewed.

Figure 5 shows the large number of tribes in the country. It is possible, using linguistic and cultural criteria, to place those in Southern Ghana and Ashanti–Brong Ahafo, nearly all of whom belong to the Kwa linguistic group,[1] into four groups (fig. 6): the Akan group, including those speaking the Twi-Fanti, Anyi-Baule, and Guan dialect clusters; the Gã-Adangbe group, including the Gã, Adangbe, and Krobo; the Ewe group, including the Ewe people only; and the Central Togo group, of which the Togo Remnant Languages group forms a part.[2]

## The Akan group

Akan-speaking peoples are organized into seven clans—there appear to be eight clans in Ashanti—and all persons belonging to a clan, irrespective of their tribal allegiances, their prejudices, their local dialects and customs, believe that they are descendants from a common ancestress.

There is nevertheless the question of whether the Brong are to be classed with the Akan and regarded as having a single origin with the Fanti and Ashanti. The basis of the problem was the discovery by Rattray that the Brong at Techiman, whom he referred to as the 'pure Brong', were apparently wholly ignorant of the Fanti and Ashanti clan names, and that equivalent exogamous divisions among them took their names from streets or quarters in the towns.

Rattray himself put forward two possible explanations. The first was that the Brong, the Fanti, and the Ashanti had a common origin, and that they all used the Brong system of organization by streets. The Fanti and the

[1] D. Westermann and M. A. Bryan, *The Languages of West Africa* (O.U.P., 1952), pp. 76–94.

[2] Ibid. p. 96.

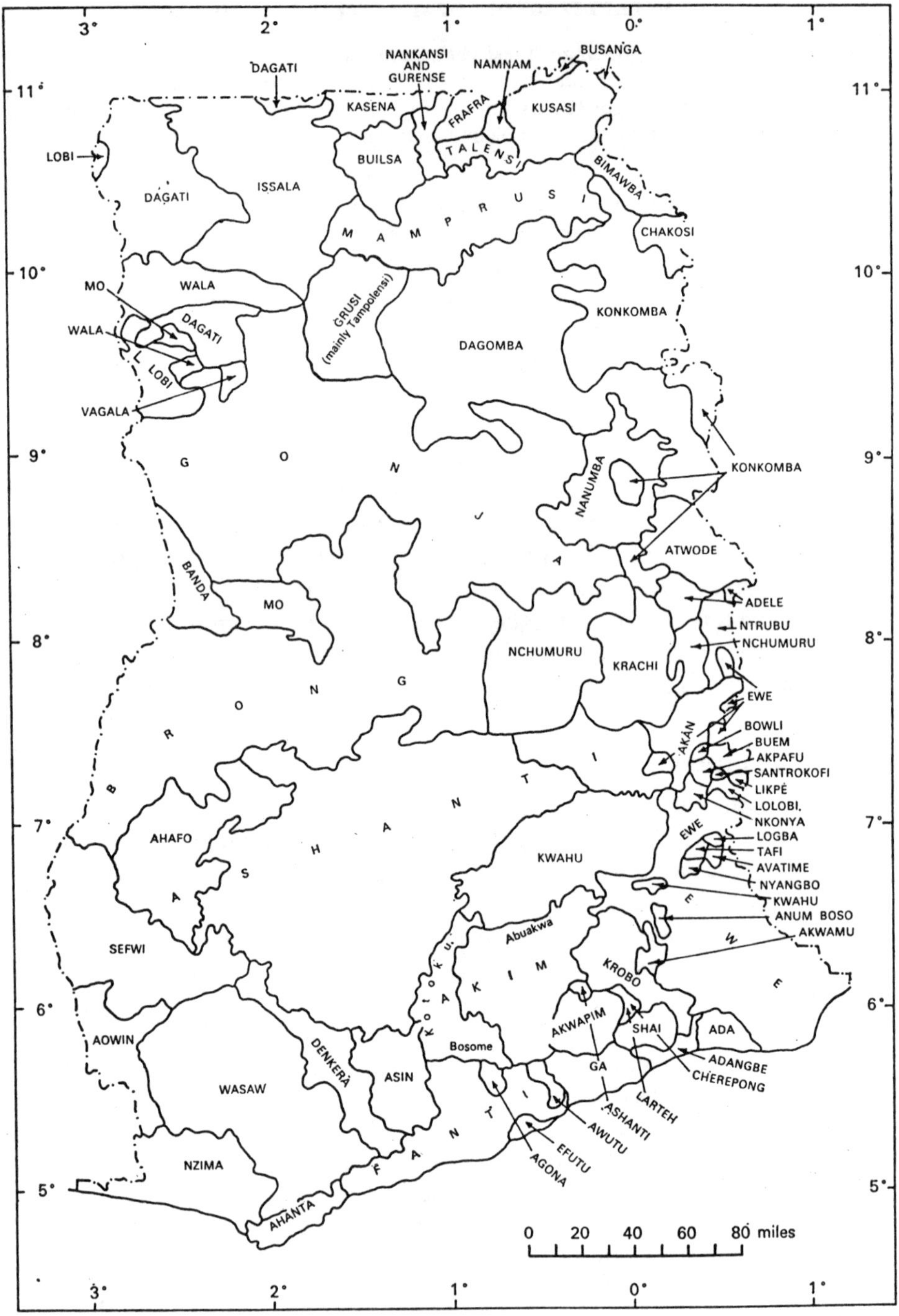


5 Tribes (from Atlas of Population Characteristics, Accra, 1964)

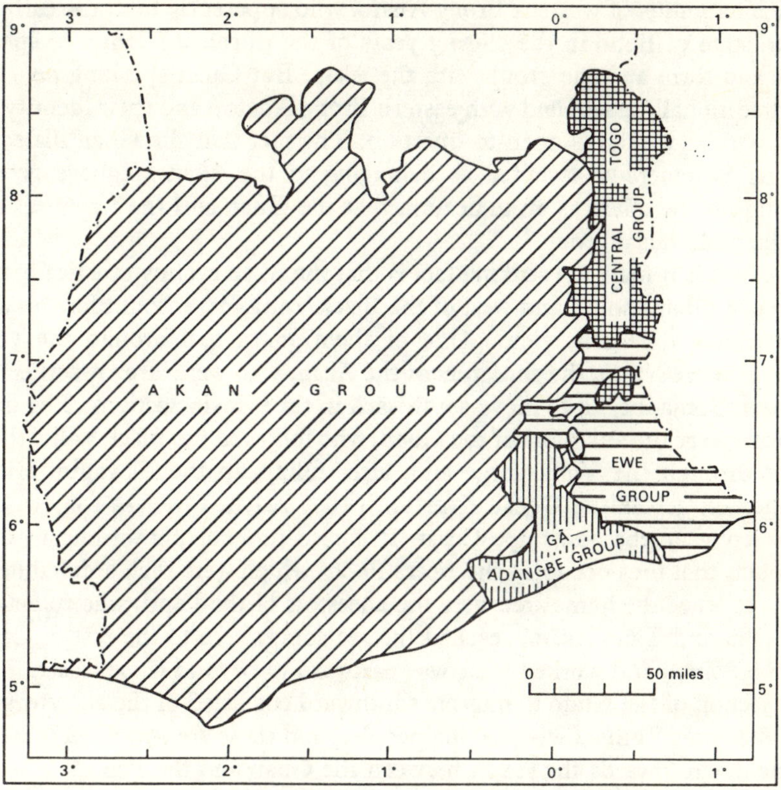


6 Culture groups in the Kwa linguistic area in Ghana

Ashanti then broke away from the parent stock, migrated southward and possibly came into contact with another culture from which they borrowed their present totemic organization. Alternatively, the Ashanti may have been an alien race 'who overran the Brong, bringing with them their own clan organization and passing southward, and settled down, ousting or exterminating or absorbing the local Brong inhabitants, and later, to strengthen their position, which was that of mere usurpers in the land, they encouraged the fiction of a common descent from the real proprietors...'[1]

The earlier of the two suggested explanations raises the difficult problem of the possible identity of the culture from which the dynastic ancestors of the Fanti and the Ashanti may have borrowed their totemic organization. The second suggestion raises fewer problems but makes the dubious assumption that the Brong are, as a whole, an alien race from the Akan.

[1] R. S. Rattray, *Ashanti Law and Constitution* (O.U.P., 1929), pp. 64–5.

The inhabitants of western Brong Ahafo, who apparently built the earliest Akan state of Bono in the closing years of the thirteenth century,[1] speak Twi and form a single group with the Akan. But Guan-speaking peoples are traditionally associated with eastern Brong Ahafo,[2] and their identity of race with the Akan is open to question. The fact that the Guan dialect-cluster is generally accepted as belonging to the Akan language group should not be taken as an indication that the Guan and the Akan belong to the same racial group.[3]

Be that as it may, the striking fact is that the Akan occupy practically the whole of Ghana south and west of the Black Volta. To account for this are two widely divergent views. One of them states that around the year A.D. 1200 the Ntafo, the ancestors of the Akan, who were already settled in or near Gonja, began to move southward in three main sections. The first to leave were the ancestors of the Guan, who followed the Black Volta, then went through the Volta gorge and, after filling up the Akwapim Hills, pushed on across the Densu river until they reached the sea somewhere between Winneba and Cape Coast. It is also probable, according to this account, that they occupied the Accra Plains which were then uninhabited. Next to leave the home area were the ancestors of the Fanti, who followed the Ofin and Tano rivers, reached the sea somewhere to the east of Cape Three Points, and worked their way eastward to beyond Cape Coast. The last section of the Ntafo to migrate southward consisted of the ancestors of the Ashanti and the Twi-speaking peoples, and these are supposed to have come down towards the sea in between the Guan and the Fanti.[4]

One underlying assumption in this account is that the forest country was uninhabited at the time the Ntafo moved in.[5] If that was so, then it would be necessary to account for the absence of the Neolithic and Early Iron Age

[1] Meyerowitz, op. cit. p. 29.

[2] J. Goody, 'Ethnological Notes on the Distribution of the Guang Languages', *J. Afr. Lang.* II, 3 (1963).

[3] H. Baumann and D. Westermann, *Les Peuples et Les Civilizations de l'Afrique* (Paris, 1948), p. 345. The distinctiveness of the Guan shows even more clearly in their music. See A. A. Mensah, 'The Guans in Music' (unpublished M.A. thesis, University of Ghana, 1966).

[4] Ward, op. cit. pp. 51–2. The date A.D. 1200 is a little later than that suggested by E. L. R. Meyerowitz. See below, p. 19.

[5] Often presented as proving the contrary is the legend among the Akan themselves that when they first arrived at their present home they encountered Stone Age *mboatia*—literally meaning dwarfs but indicating Negrilloes or people of the Pygmoid race. These were, according to the legend, unfamiliar with fire or iron. But this legend of *mboatia* is nothing more than a piece of unsubstantiated oral tradition, for no remnants of Negrilloes survive in Ghana or along the Guinea coast today. The Gagu of the Ivory Coast, formerly considered to be a possible remnant of a Pygmoid race, are now regarded as true Negroes, in spite of their relatively short stature. See G. P. Murdock, *Africa: Its Peoples and their Culture History* (New York, 1959), p. 49.

population that was undoubtedly present in the country before the Akan. There is no archaeological or other evidence that the country was empty; neither does the geological evidence suggest violent climatic fluctuations such as could have driven men out of the country since the Neolithic.

More acceptable is the view, already put forward,[1] that it was the ancestors of Akan aristocracy who migrated into the country, not in a single massive wave, but in a series of disjointed groups, and succeeded in establishing themselves and their rule over the autochthones, thanks probably to their possession of superior iron weapons. The earliest Akan-speaking peoples in the country were the Guan. They may have been widely distributed throughout the whole of the southern half of Ghana, as is suggested by the oral tradition that nearly all the aboriginal peoples inland from, and along the whole length of, the coast 'belonged to the Guan, Kyerepong, Le, and Ahanta tribes, speaking different dialects of the Ahanta, Obutu, Kyerepong, Late (Le) and Kpesi languages',[2] all of which are related. Indeed it would not be far-fetched to suggest further the possibility that the Guan, in view of their possible countrywide distribution, could have been direct descendants of the Neolithic population. Neither would it be out of place to speculate on the possibility of the Guan having introduced or acquired iron technology before the Akan arrived, for it may not be for nothing that Gua, a senior god of the Kpesi (Guan) in the Accra Plains, is the blacksmith and thunder god.

It is thus probably incorrect to restrict the original home of the Guan to the 'eastern forest and adjacent plains', which they are supposed to have infiltrated and settled after having migrated from Mossi, the whole process of migration and settlement stretching over a period of some two hundred years, beginning from about A.D. 1000.[3]

[1] See above, pp. 14–15.

[2] E. J. P. Brown, *Gold Coast and Asianti Reader*, Book 1 (London, 1929), p. 100. Christaller confirms this tradition: see Baumann and Westermann, op. cit. p. 345.

[3] Meyerowitz's explanation for the restricted home of the Guan is that the Anyi (Brosa) people from somewhere in the savanna and semi-desert area to the north were filling up the western and central forest region at about the same time as the Guan immigration (op. cit. p. 130). But Meyerowitz seemed to admit the possibility of the former large extent of Guan territory when she wrote on p. 103 of the same work: 'The majority of the Kumbu people who migrated into the Gold Coast spoke Twi, a language that spread right through the forest region once the Twifo, or Twi people, were dispersed after the collapse of the three states founded by them—Twifo-Heman, Akwamu and Doma. The languages Twi superseded were Guan and Bono, of which Brong is regarded by Christaller as a Twi dialect...Today the Akan people in the forest region are often referred to as Twi people, particularly the Asante.'

Presumably Twi superseded Guan and Bono while spreading *right through the forest region*. Nevertheless J. Goody is rather sceptical of the former large extent of Guan territory. See footnote 2, p. 18.

There is no doubt, on the other hand, that the areas where Guan is spoken today in one form or another lie within a stretch of territory which extends along the Black Volta, through the Afram Plains and the Volta gorge and swings westward to the coast beyond Cape Coast, after skirting the eastern margins of the Closed Forest. On the assumption that the Guan once occupied the forest country, spilling over into the parkland zone immediately to the north of the Black Volta, the distribution of present Guan-speaking areas could be accounted for by postulating absorption of the Guan by later groups of Akan-speaking peoples who infiltrated into Guan territory from the Ivory Coast and fanned out in all directions. Thus the circumferential distribution of Guan-speaking areas with respect to the forest area would indicate, not the route for Guan immigration, but remnants of Guan people displaced and engulfed by newcomers from the west. The operation would have taken many centuries, beginning from about the end of the twelfth century, if not earlier.

A possible motive for the intrusion of Akan peoples into Guan territory may have been overpopulation in their original homeland, resulting in famine and making it necessary to search for fresh hunting grounds or for new areas for cultivation. It is not unlikely that the westernmost section of the Akan group in the Ivory Coast, the Baule, borrowed the Sudanese agricultural complex from the agriculturally advanced Mande (Malinke) or possibly through the Senufo. Then, after the original forest vegetation would have been largely destroyed and useless lateritic soils formed or exposed over wide areas, the Baule may have pressed on their neighbours the Anyi (Agni) who themselves, needing plenty of room for bush fallowing or for migratory agriculture, would have pushed into Ghana. The Baule country today forms part of the impoverished West African Middle Belt, and is characterized by generally lateritic and sandy soils covered by Guinea Derived Savanna.[1] A similar sort of pressure may have been brought to bear on the Brong to move in a generally southward or south-eastward direction by the Voltaic-speaking peoples to the north of them.

After migration into Ghana, not by whole masses of people but by individual families which scattered throughout the forest country, a slow process of rearrangement and consolidation of separate family groups from the same clan into new tribal units, members of which spoke the same languages, would have occurred. The process of tribal formation perhaps followed the pattern suggested by Rattray: various family units coming, in course of time, under the authority of one family unit, then expanding into a larger territorial group consisting of many such units, and eventually

[1] R. J. Harrison Church, *West Africa* (Longmans, 1961), p. 347.

coming under a single head. The enlarged community became a clan and then a tribe. It was probably in this way that the large territorial or tribal units which ultimately came to form the Ashanti nation under one head, the Ashanti King, were formed.[1] Thus also the remaining Akan tribes may have been formed. The process of expanding family or tribal units was a never-ending one, for members of some kindred group in a tribe would not infrequently migrate to other parts of the country for such reasons as over-population, wars, plague in the home territory, and the desire to join up with other groups of the same clan prospering elsewhere. The period roughly up to the end of the seventeenth century was one of very frequent internal migrations, of the formation of tribal units, and of struggle for territorial expansion.

### *The coastal Akan*

On the coast the Fanti became the most powerful and largest of the tribes. According to oral tradition, Borbor Fanti originally consisted of five main groups which first lived together as a nation[2]—the Abura, Kurentsi, Ekumfi, Nkusukum and Enyan groups, and Fanti as well as Brong traditions insist on a connection between them and Techiman (Brong) or Kong in the Ivory Coast or the Western Sudan in general. It has been argued, for example, that confirmation of a connection between the Brong, on the one hand, and Fanti and some other coastal tribes, on the other, is to be found in the fact that the *Apo* ceremony of the Brong was the same ceremony observed and described by Bosman at Axim in the early eighteenth century.[3] It is not impossible, indeed it is practically certain, that several family units, some of which may later have formed ruling dynasties, migrated from Brong country to the coast. One such migration of some Brong to kindred peoples in Gomua country (Great Akron) on the coast took place in the early eighteenth century after the Ashanti sacked Techiman.

The new Fanti nation fought and defeated the Gomua, formerly called the Akraman, whose territory extended westward beyond its present boundary; the Fanti then founded and settled at Mankesim (literally 'in the great country') after leaving some of their people at Kwaman, their earliest major settlement near the coast. Mankesim was then divided into five wards, one for each of the five great groups constituting the Fanti nation; and it was from here that the Fanti dispersed to conquer fresh territory along the coast as well as inland. A section of the Abura people,

[1] R. S. Rattray, *Ashanti Law and Constitution* (O.U.P., 1929), pp. 62–3.
[2] Brown, op. cit. pp. 53–4.
[3] R. S. Rattray, *Ashanti* (O.U.P., 1923), p. 151.

after routing the Asebu, founded the town of Abura; it was reputed to be very large, consisting of seventy-seven wards. Another section of the Abura founded Egya, Anomabu, and other villages in the immediate interior. The Nkusukum group built most of the settlements between Saltpond (which originally consisted of the three villages of Nankesidu, Bakadu and Okukudo) and Cape Coast. They later founded more settlements west of Cape Coast, including Akitakyi or British Komenda, and extended their territory right up to the eastern banks of the Pra. The Enyan group settled to the north and north-east of Mankesim, founding such settlements as Enyanmanmu, Esiam, Denkera, and Abasa. All these splinter groups maintained contact with Mankesim, the parent settlement.[1] The main period of Fanti expansion ended roughly at the close of the seventeenth century.

### *The forest Akan*

In the forest country the earliest centralized kingdom was that of Akwamu, whose ruling dynasty 'was in origin an intrusive group of northern and probably Mande origin which, like that of Gonja, came to speak the language of the autochthones over whom it established its supremacy'.[2] The seeds of the empire were sown in the early sixteenth century and the progress of the empire builders from Gonja followed a trajectory through Wam or Dormaa, Twifo, Asamankese, Nyanoase, and along the coast to beyond the Ghana–Togo border, taking some two centuries in all.[3] The origin of the Akwamu royal house explains the tradition of migration of all Akwamu from Kong, and a similar explanation may perhaps be offered for those traditions which place the original home of some of the Akan peoples in the Western Sudan.

Another early Akan forest state was apparently Adansi, which may have been founded somewhere in the middle of the sixteenth century or much earlier. It was older than the Akwamu empire, but lacked the sophisticated political and military organization of the latter. The name Adansi itself could mean 'house building', which would imply, according to one tradition, that the Adansi were the first people to build wattle-and-daub houses in Ghana.[4] The interpretation is improbable, for wattle-and-daub houses were known in Ghana long before the sixteenth century. The name Adansi is also capable of another interpretation, according to a different tradition,

1 Brown, op. cit. pp. 61 ff.

2 I. Wilks, *The Northern Factor in Ashanti History* (Institute of African Studies, University of Ghana, 1961), p. 9.

3 Idem, 'The Rise of the Akwamu Empire, 1650–1710', *Trans. Hist. Soc. Ghana*, III, 2 (1957).

4 Ward, op. cit. p. 52.

which says that the name means 'the beginning of change'.[1] Whatever the etymological possibilities of the name Adansi, it is fairly certain that the Adansi were settled in their traditional area in the forest by the end of the sixteenth century. Their settlements were sited, for purposes of defence, on the Kwisa and Moinsi hills between the Fum and Oda rivers, and the capital was Adansimanso which was close to the modern village of Mansia between Fomena and Akrokeri.

The Adansi were hemmed in by the Denkera in the west, by the Akwamu in the east and south, and by the Ashanti and Brong in the north. In the war between Adansi and Denkera around the beginning of the seventeenth century, Adansimanso was destroyed; the Adansi then built a new capital at Dompoase, not far from the old capital. Eventually, around the middle of the seventeenth century and under Denkera rule, they moved eastwards to settle near the Pra river. There they remained until the early part of the eighteenth century when they returned to their old home and built a new capital at Fomena. One result of the Adansi–Denkera war was a piecemeal migration eastwards of some Adansi who, joined later by more refugees from an Ashanti war, were to ally themselves with the local people (Guan and Akwamu?) in their place of refuge between the Pra and Birim rivers and set up three military organizations called Akim Abuakwa, Akim Kotoku, and Akim Bosome.[2] The Akim were also to take over large portions of Akwamu territory in the early eighteenth century.

The decline of Adansi was matched by the rise of Denkera which became, within the last forty or fifty years of the seventeenth century, the most powerful kingdom in the forest country. The Denkera conquered Sefwi, Wasaw and Twifu, thus carving out for themselves a rectangular kingdom stretching from a point on the Ghana–Ivory Coast boundary across the river Bia eastward to the Anum river, then southward along the Pra to about halfway between the sea and the Pra–Ofin confluence, and westward to the middle Tano. The Ashanti were also under Denkera overlordship until they destroyed the latter in 1701.

Of the forest kingdoms the one that came to acquire the greatest fame and power was Ashanti. At the time of the Denkera conquest of Adansi, Ashanti consisted mainly of a group of settlements around Lake Bosumtwe and others scattered in the forest country immediately to the north and north-west of the lake. The Ashanti fished in the lake and cultivated its environs. The name now given by the Ashanti to the lake region is Amanse, meaning 'the home of nations', and their most important settlement,

[1] Meyerowitz, *Akan Traditions*, p. 94.

[2] M. J. Field, *Akim Kotoku: An Oman of the Gold Coast* (London, 1948), p. 4.

Ashanti tradition affirms, was Asantemanso which grew to be a large town with seventy-seven streets.[1] It is not known when the Ashanti first came to settle around the lake, but one reason for settling there seems fairly clear: the happy combination of good soils and an abundance of freshwater fish. There are possibly other and more important reasons which will only come to light or be stated with a tolerable degree of precision when the mystery surrounding the earliest period of Ashanti history is penetrated and dispelled. All one has to go by at the moment is the intriguing Ashanti tradition that they came out of a hole in the ground at Asantemanso. The tradition may simply indicate the antiquity of their settlement around Lake Bosumtwe, or the reluctance on the part of the Ashanti to uncover something that they would, for various reasons, rather be silent on. Legends of people having originally emerged from a hole in the ground, of having come down a stout rope from the skies, etc., are common throughout the country, and no straightforward interpretation could be put on them. There is another tradition, a popular one, according to which the immediate home of the ancestors of Ashanti aristocracy was Bouna, in north-eastern Ivory Coast and close to the Ghana boundary; they fled from there to seek refuge in the lake region and founded Asantemanso. There is nothing improbable in the story. Yet another tradition recorded by Bowdich has it that some of the ancestors of the Ashanti originally lived near Winneba on the coast; but Bowdich himself was sceptical: 'there is nothing to countenance the report', he opined.[2]

It was within the first half or around the beginning of the second half of the seventeenth century, while they were still under Denkera overlordship, that the Ashanti began to emigrate from Asantemanso in a generally northern direction to settle in the forest country beyond the lake. The emigration was of varied degrees of magnitude. It was sometimes a case of small kindred groups leaving to found their own settlements like Kumasi (originally called Kwaman). There were also cases where whole settlements broke up and their inhabitants emigrated *en masse* to settle in new areas. In this way such settlements as Mampong, Nsuta and Kumawu were founded: Mampong by migrants from Adansi, and Nsuta and Kumawu by people from Asantemanso.[3] Several reasons may have accounted for the migrations from the lake region: the growing pressure of population on the land resulting partly from the large influx of Adansi refugees from their war with Denkera; a desire to be nearer the ancient trade route skirting the northern

[1] Rattray, *Ashanti Law and Constitution*, p. 61.

[2] T. E. Bowdich, *Mission from Cape Coast Castle to Ashantee* (London, 1819), pp. 228–9.

[3] Rattray, *Ashanti Law and Constitution*, pp. 72–3.

edge of the forest and ending up at Jenne on the Niger through Begho;[1] the increasing tyranny of their Denkera rulers; the lure of the fame of the Ashanti Chief Oti Akenten's military prowess in the wars he fought with the Doma people who lived just to the north of his capital, Kwaman.

Whatever factor or factors operated most powerfully in causing the exodus from the Lake Bosumtwe region, the colonization and settlement of the forest to the north of the lake was a fact of prime importance to subsequent patterns of trade and economic development in much of Ghana. It was not very long after the migration that Osei Tutu, the successor of Oti Akenten, welded, with the active help of Okomfo Anokye of legendary fame, all the independent Ashanti tribal groupings together to form the Ashanti nation. Ashanti was to become perhaps the most illustrious of the forest empires in West Africa, and was, for a long time, to shape the economic life and future of Ghana.

## The Gã-Adangbe group

Since about the eleventh century the Accra Plains, like the forest country and home of the Gã-Adangbe, have not known large-scale immigration of peoples but sporadic intrusions of small groups of people from neighbouring areas. The evidence for this is archaeological. Up to the early seventeenth century, or late sixteenth century, the evolution of pottery design in the Plains was uninterrupted, and whatever new styles appeared were based on those preceding them. Then came the seventeenth century when a revolutionary change in the design of pottery occurred. Relics of the new type of pottery have been found along three ancient trade paths leading from the interior to European trading posts on the coast.

An explanation of this revolutionary change in pottery design with reference to conquest by masses of foreigners would have to make the highly unlikely assumption that three large groups of culturally homogeneous immigrants arrived at about the same time to settle on the three trade paths and nowhere else. Even if a case could be made for the possibility of small significant immigrations, the fact should be reckoned with that there is no known archetypal culture in other areas along the Guinea coast on which the new pottery cultures found on the three trade paths could have been based.

A more likely explanation would be twofold: first, that seventeenth-century pottery designs were inspired by, and not a direct copy from, the new art forms and artistic ideas exhibited and suggested in imported brass-

[1] See below, p. 29.

ware bought from European traders at the coast and traded along the main routeways leading into the interior. Secondly, that the presumed development of centralized mass production in the crafts, after the powerful stimulus given to trade and general economic activity by Europeans, made for new conceptions of pottery styles. In support of these explanations is the fact that older characteristics appear in seventeenth-century pottery styles. This shows that the newer cultures were not from extraneous sources but were closely connected with the older ones.[1]

Nevertheless it is not being implied that individual families or small kindred groups of people never came from elsewhere to live in the Accra Plains; but there were aborigines of the Accra Plains, the Kpesi people who are a branch of the Guan. They intermixed, since perhaps the sixteenth century, with the later immigrants who were neither numerous nor powerful enough to impose radically new cultures on the autochthones. Proof of longstanding settlement in the Plains by the Kpesi before the arrival of other groups is to be seen in the fact that when the Gã 'towns' were formed the Kpesi were recognized as true owners of the land, and their priests the only ones able to propitiate the Earth Gods.[2]

On the founding of the seven Gã towns which are, from west to east, Accra, Osu, Labadi, Teshi, Nungua, Tema, and Kpone, M. J. Field has collected a great deal of information.[3]

> The towns themselves are of curious constitution. The people of each one narrate that it was founded by what seems to have been a harried gang of refugees fleeing easterly lands and travelling probably along the beach, a natural highway still carrying much foot traffic. The gangs appeared at different times and each consisted of 'a few men and their sons and brothers and many wives and children.' Each gang seems to have first fortified one of several hills, now uninhabited, on the boundaries of the plain—Legon, Okakwei, Adzangote, Lanma, etc. and to have removed later to the coast and settled there permanently, deciding that coastal sites were safer as they needed protecting on one side only.
>
> The first care of each of these little coastal settlements was to keep up its numbers, for only so could it defy inland raiders. For this reason it seems to have been the habit of all the Gã towns to allow any friendly band of outsiders to attach itself to the town and receive all its benefits and protection in return for military help.
>
> Thus it came about that each town today consists of several so-called 'quarters'.

This satisfactorily explains how the Accra Plains were peopled by the Gã, while dismissing the persistent tradition of a solid phalanx of Gã marchers moving in from somewhere in Nigeria to people the empty Accra Plains.

[1] P. Ozanne, 'Notes on the Early Historic Archaeology of Accra', *Trans. Hist. Soc. Ghana*, VI (1962).

[2] M. Manoukian, *Akan and Gã-Adangbe Peoples of the Gold Coast* (O.U.P., 1950), p. 67.

[3] M. J. Field, *Religion and Medicine of the Gâ People* (O.U.P., 1937), p. 2.

Shai (Adangbe) settlements, which may have been earlier, were apparently founded under roughly the same circumstances as the Gã settlements. According to one tradition, the refugee ancestors of the Krobo and Shai originally lived together at Tagulogò, near Lolovo Hill. After a dispute the Shai moved in two main tribes, Hiowe and Mla, to Ada, then to the Shai Hills where at the western end of the summit stretch the Hiowe built their chief settlement of Hiowe as well as Salom, Bonase, Nangala, Laga, Kayikpon, Gblaka, Drawe, and Minawe. The Mla on the eastern end built Mla, the largest of their settlements, together with Yoma, Abotia, Lekpedze, Lenodze, Kpofu, Asinidze, Manya, and Magbiem.[1]

There is a similar tradition on the founding of Krobo settlements, and discrepancies between this account and the Shai tradition just cited, where they both concern Krobo and Shai together, are simply matters of detail. It appears, from the Krobo tradition, that the Krobo migrated from Lolovo to Ada with the Shai, then left them behind to emigrate into the Accra Plains where they settled on top of Krobo Mountain.[2] They later received refugees from all over Southern Ghana and Ashanti whom collectively they called 'Afutu Bleku'.

## The Ewe and Central Togo groups

Here again the traditional stories feature mass migrations of the Ewe, who occupy more than threequarters of the Volta Region, and of the other tribes in the Togo–Atakora Ranges.[3] Apparently the westward displacement of the Adja-Ewe people from their original home at Ketu was caused by a Yoruba movement which generally unleashed a series of migrations whose waves rolled out successively for about two centuries.[4] One group of Ewe refugees under the leadership of Afotche crossed the Mono river and founded Nuatja (Notsie) in the republic of Togo. Some of these later fled from Nuatja around the beginning of the eighteenth century because of the cruelty of Agokoli, Afotche's successor, and travelled to Ghana in three groups. The first group went in a north-westward direction to found Kpandu, Kpalime, Leklebi and Wodze among others; the second group

[1] S. W. Saxton, 'Historical Survey of the Shai People', *Gold Coast Rev.* I, 1 (June–December 1925), 127–45. According to another account, referred to in footnote 2, a settlement by the name of Drawe was the capital of the state of Ladoku, founded by the Gã.

[2] Noa Akunor Aguae Azu, 'Adangbe (Adangme) History', *Gold Coast Rev.* II, 2 (July–December 1926), 239–70. For the names of original Krobo settlements, see appendix 1.

[3] The Ewe oral traditions were first recorded by Jakob Spieth in his *Die Ewestamme* (Berlin, 1906).

[4] R. Cornevin, *Histoire du Togo* (Paris, 1959), pp. 47–57.

travelled westward and founded Ho, Adaklu, etc.; and the third group went south to form the state of Anlo (Awuna).

There is nothing improbable in this tradition of Ewe immigration, provided it is regarded as a slow process extending over many years and referring to small family or kindred groups coming in at different times to join those that had arrived before them. The only questionable point is the date of arrival of the immigrants, which has been variously put at 1720 and not later than the early years of the seventeenth century.[1]

It should not be assumed that the Togo–Atakora Ranges were uninhabited at the time of the piecemeal Ewe immigration. With the exception of their southern end where internal dissensions provoked the Ewe-Adja immigration, the Togo–Atakora Ranges have on the whole not known any significant or large-scale invasions from the west or east. The stories of campaigns current there were probably brought by refugees from elsewhere.[2]

In sum, the Ewe country, like the rest of the southern half of Ghana, has known a long period of settlement. If the rest of Southern Ghana including the dry Accra Plains was possibly the original home of the Guan who may have been there before the thirteenth century, then it is inconceivable that the superb defensive sites offered by the Togo–Atakora Ranges, the attractive well-watered intermontane lowlands, and the lower end of Volta Region with its splendid opportunities for fishing and cultivation would have been ignored by earlier settlers and left empty until groups of Ewe people arrived.

North of Ewe country and still forming part of the Togo–Atakora Ranges is Buem-Krachi or the Central Togo group area whose peopling followed the lines described for the Ewe. There are no fewer than six—possibly more—individual languages spoken in Buem, unrelated to one another and obviously brought to the area by refugees who continued to stream in from elsewhere many years after the end of the seventeenth century. Wars in the late seventeenth century and after among the Ashanti, Gonja, Akwamu, Dahomeyans and many others all drove refugees at one time or another to seek asylum in the mountain fastnesses of Buem country. The region was by no means uninhabited when the refugees arrived, for all the evidence[3] points to the existence of indigenous groups of people who accepted the refugees and gave them land to live on.

Thus the peopling of Southern Ghana and Ashanti–Brong Ahafo may be described. What is yet to be accounted for is the grouping of different

[1] Cornevin, op. cit. pp. 47–57.

[2] Ibid. pp. 27–8.

[3] See for example Cornevin, p. 29.

peoples into states and the territorial expansion of some of the states. The motives were many and of varied degrees of importance, but one that should be underscored is the economic motive. The mechanics of tribe and state formation were set into motion by the need for people to come together for mutual protection from more powerful neighbours and for establishing the necessary atmosphere of security within which trade with the coast or the interior could be successfully prosecuted. It was for such motives that the Gã, for example, who had hitherto lived in small, scattered and isolated communities came, in the late seventeenth century, to form a state with a centralized government and set up military organizations which they copied from the neighbouring Fanti and Akwamu.[1] The need for mutual protection among the Gã arose not only from the fact that they were threatened with extermination by the incessant slave raids carried on by the Akwamu but also from the desire to organize themselves to trade more effectively with the European trading posts, for which their territory was a hinterland.

Similarly, a major reason for the territorial expansion of Denkera, and perhaps even more so in the case of Akwamu, was the desire to trade directly with the Europeans at the coast and eliminate the coastal peoples who acted as middlemen between the European traders and the interior. The desire was not unnatural since the coastal people came to gain a reputation for sharp dealing and unscrupulous treatment, not excluding outright robbery, of merchants from the interior. European goods were highly prized, especially firearms, which was all the more reason for merchants from the interior to want to have direct access to the source of supply. Thus the Akwamu came to settle at Nyanoase in the late sixteenth century, from where they controlled all the trade routes leading from the interior to the European forts at Accra and Osu and held a monopoly of the trade with the Europeans. Thus also the Denkera pushed their way southward and in the late seventeenth century controlled practically all the trade with Europeans in the Western Region.

The operation of the economic motive is seen even more clearly in the case of Ashanti. The rise of the Ashanti kingdom after emigration from Asantemanso is probably largely accounted for by the ambition of the Ashanti to control the flourishing trade on the famous route from Adansi through Tafo, Begho, Kong to Jenne on the Upper Niger. It was this routeway that directed the expansion of the kingdom to as far as Kong and beyond. It may be also significant that Kumasi, the town chosen by Osei Tutu to be capital of the new Ashanti kingdom, was located about 3 miles south

[1] Manoukian, op. cit. p. 67.

of Tafo on the Niger–Begho trade route. Even long before the seventeenth century, the migration to the Adansi area of groups of Akan peoples, who were later to press northwards and form the nucleus of the kingdom of Ashanti, was largely determined by the fact that the Niger–Begho trade route extended also to Adansi.[1]

## TRIBES IN NORTHERN GHANA[2]

As in the case of tribes south of the Black Volta, explanations of the origins of the Gur-speaking tribes north of the Black Volta need not include stories of large-scale migrations of people coming from elsewhere to occupy empty land.

Settlement in Northern Ghana goes back to very ancient times. Among the indigenous tribes were the Konkomba and the Nanumba, whose original home was in the valleys of the Oti and Daka and the neighbouring plains,[3] and possibly the Lobi and the Grunsi (Gurunsi). The Grunsi form the substratum of Isala (Sisala), Kasena (with the Fra or Awuna), Tampolem, Builsa, Vagala, Degha, and Chakelle populations.[4] The land stretching across the whole width of the country immediately north of the Black Volta may have been originally inhabited by Guan-speaking peoples—the Gonja (called Ntafo by the Twi), Dompo, Choruba, Beri, Nawuri, Nchumuru, Krachi, etc.;[5] the Ntribu in Krachi district, with Breniase as their principal settlement, are also autochthonous but speak a language belonging to the Tem–Kabre group.[6]

The dislocation of the indigenous peoples, particularly in the eastern parts of the country, and their subsequent tribal reorganization was caused by the invasion of bands of warriors who came from the north-east, probably around the middle of the fifteenth century, and settled in the first instance at Gambaga. It was these invaders who imposed their rule over the indigenous peoples and founded the sister kingdoms of Mossi (now Upper Volta), Mamprusi, and Dagomba.[7] The influence of the Mamprusi covered the whole of the north-eastern corner of the country, where the heads of the Nankese, Talense, Nabdam, and Kusase tribes all claim that their ancestors originally came from either the old Mamprusi capital of Gambaga

[1] Meyerowitz, *Akan Traditions*, op. cit. chap. IX.

[2] One could not hope to discuss adequately the origins of all the tribes in Northern Ghana; such is their variety and complexity.

[3] Cornevin, *Histoire du Togo*, pp. 31–2.

[4] Rattray, *The Tribes of the Ashanti Hinterland* (O.U.P., 1932), I, viii–ix.

[5] Goody, *Ethnography of the Northern Territories*, map 2 on p. 184.

[6] Cornevin, op. cit. pp. 38–9.

[7] Rattray, *Tribes of the Hinterland*, p. xii.

or from nearby Nalerigu.[1] Mamprusi influence also extended westward to cover part of the Grunsi-speaking areas in eastern Wa. In all these areas the local Earth Priests (Tindana) retained their position and handled all matters concerning land and religion, while the invaders became secular kings and political overlords. In Dagomba the establishment of political authority by the invaders was accompanied by much violence towards the indigenous population. In eastern Dagomba the Konkomba were driven from their lands on the right banks of the Oti river and to the north of it, and in western Dagomba the Earth Priests were killed. At the height of its power the Dagomba kingdom extended westward as far as the Ghana-Ivory Coast boundary.

There was a certain amount of dispersal of the original inhabitants in Dagomba, as well as in Mamprusi, towards the west and south-west, to Wa and western Gonja. This may explain, for example, the scattered distribution of the Kasena, Sisala, Vagala, and Tampolem tribes, all of which are unanimous in claiming a common ancestry and a common origin in Mamprusi territory. A similar movement southward may have been caused by other bands of Mossi warriors who arrived from the north perhaps a little later than the Mamprusi and Dagomba rulers, came as far south as Wa and, after mixing with the indigenous population, gave birth to a new series of tribes.[2]

After the Mossi conquest came the invasion of western Gonja from Mali by Mande-speaking peoples under the leadership of Nabaga around the mid-sixteenth century.[3] These nevertheless were not the first Mande peoples in western Gonja, which indeed had been within the commercial ambit of Mande peoples (Ligbi) as far back as the fifteenth century because of the gold trade there. Also, when Begho, a Mande outpost on the north-western limits of the Ashanti forest, was torn by a civil war within the first half of the sixteenth century, some of the Ligbi elements in its Mande population moved to Bole in western Gonja where they were absorbed into the indigenous population.[4] Bole again became the headquarters of the Mande invaders under Nabaga and it was from there that Jakpa, a grandson of Nabaga, and his followers set out on their expedition of conquest.[5] They extended their influence eastward across the White Volta, capturing the important salt-making centre of Daboya and defeating the Dagomba and others in a number of major engagements. By the end of the seventeenth

[1] Ibid. [2] Baumann, and Westermann, *Les Peuples...de l'Afrique*, p. 404.

[3] Personal communication from Ivor Wilks.

[4] Goody, *Ethnography of the Northern Territories*, p. 12.

[5] See also D. H. Jones, 'Jakpa and the Foundation of Gonja', *Trans. Hist. Soc. Ghana*, VI (1962).

century they had founded Gonja kingdom. It stretched latitudinally, just north of the Black Volta, beyond the Togo–Atakora Ranges. Further north Gonja did not extend eastward far beyond the White Volta, for the lands east of this river formed the heart of the Dagomba kingdom.

The spread of Gonja power scattered, to some extent, the indigenous Guan population as well as the Konkomba and the Nanumba, and those nearest Togo sought refuge there. Thus significant proportions of the populations of such villages as Aniagan and Bassari in the republic of Togo are of Guan origin.[1] The conquerors of Gonja, like those of Mamprusi before them, simply imposed their authority over the local people, whose women they married and whose language they adopted.

In conclusion, the origins of most of the peoples in Northern Ghana go back into remote antiquity, and it is these indigenous peoples who form the substratum of the tribal organizations that came into being after invasions by foreign soldiers of fortune. The invaders were superior militarily, not numerically, and they imposed new political systems over the local peoples: the former became rulers, the latter commoners. The sphere of influence of the invaders was confined mainly to the north-east and south-east, and to the west and south-west. The central portions of the country were areas of marginal influence, where the aboriginal Earth Priests continued to rule undisturbed until the arrival of the British in the late nineteenth century.[2] The economic motive for the establishment of these centralized political systems should be given prominence; such systems were essential for creating the necessary framework for successful trade. Northern Ghana, and indeed Ashanti, were already within the wider framework of Western Sudan's commercial life, and significant events in the peopling of the whole of Ghana are attributable as much to the country's geographical position or space relations as to its having been, by virtue of its gold, ivory, kola and slave resources, within the vast network of West African and European trade.

[1] Cornevin, *Histoire du Togo*, p. 63.

[2] Rattray, *Tribes of the Hinterland*, p. xvi.

# 2. The changing human geography

## FROM EARLIEST TIMES TO 1200

In Ghana there is not the wealth of archaeological and other evidence that could support reasonably confident statements on early economies, their variations and mutations, their spatial distribution, and their significance to the look of the landscape. The indications are few and not always precise. This is particularly true of the earliest period of man's existence in the country.

It may be surmised, after consideration of relevant conclusions on the way of life of early man in similar environmental conditions and at roughly the same cultural stage,[1] that the earliest attempts by man to wrest a living from the physical milieu that surrounded him in Ghana may have taken the form of food collecting and the hunting, wherever possible, of small animals. The vegetable world presented to early man a readily available source of food, the collection of which required either no tools or the most rudimentary of tools for digging up root crops. The earliest stone tools used by man could have been artefacts or simply pieces of stone suitably shaped by natural agencies.

The unit of settlement was perhaps the family household, a number of which would constitute the local group, based on an association of family units more or less loosely related by blood ties or merely showing a common interest in livelihood in the same area. The population would be necessarily nomadic, making use of natural shelters like caves and rock overhangs. The population density may also have been rather low, for that stage of cultural development would mean the most elementary and least efficient forms of exploitation of the physical environment, and therefore would probably have been incapable of providing enough food for a large population. The influence of this culture on the look of the landscape would be negligible, as man did not apparently possess such tools as would make him an active factor of change. It would seem that fire, the great modifier of the natural landscape, was not yet in deliberate use in the country. The landscape may therefore have presented large expanses of natural vegetation broken here and there by small, isolated cells of settlement among which there would be little communication.

[1] H. Bobek, 'The Main Stages in Socio-Economic Evolution from a Geographical Point of View', in *Readings in Cultural Geography*, ed. P. L. Wagner and M. W. Mikesell (University of Chicago Press, 1962), pp. 218–47.

By slow degrees man improved his stone tools, giving them a finer cutting edge, making them lighter, varying their sizes and shapes, hafting them or shaping them in such a way as to give a firmer grasp. As the varieties of stone tools increased, so presumably did the range of man's livelihood forms. The simple food-collecting economy would be gradually diversified, while hunting of big game, which requires more skill and more sophisticated weapons, would slowly acquire greater importance. Man was presumably able to interfere more and more with the natural landscape, plundering the vegetation for food and other materials perhaps for building or making an enclosure of a kind, and possibly burning the vegetation repeatedly to flush game, although it is not certain that fire was used deliberately in Ghana before Neolithic times.

So man went up the scale of cultural development within the Early Stone Age, starting from the most primitive pre-Chellean or pebble tool culture through the Chellean to the Acheulian, with which are associated stone cleavers and hand axes. In Sangoan times the presumed pattern of settlement was perhaps basically the same as has been described for the earlier cultures, except that the units of settlement would probably have been larger in Sangoan times, since man was presumably capable then of exploiting the physical environment more effectively. He possessed stone hand axes, picks, and blade tools; he was a hunter, fisherman, and food gatherer. It is also likely that he practised elementary navigation on rivers and probably along the coast, perhaps using rafts or floating logs but not necessarily dug-outs.[1] From Sangoan times to the Ultimate Middle Stone Age man developed greater skills in making a living with the aid of smaller, finer, and more specialized tools.

In Mesolithic times there was possibly a certain amount of proto-cultivation, that is, the raising of crops through chance and unpremeditated scattering of seeds collected from the wild. This may have been the case on the basis of the possibility that the gathering of grains, root crops, and fruits was a well established livelihood form. It should then be inevitable that seeds or portions of root crops lying around a settlement should germinate, reach maturity and yield a harvest. This is a phenomenon commonly assumed to have occurred in the time of Mesolithic men before they progressed to Neolithic culture. The predominance of trees like the kola, shea butter, baobab, and oil palm in certain vegetation associations may have come about through selection and proto-cultivation.[2]

[1] O. Davies, 'The Distribution of Stone Age Material in Guinea', *Bulletin de l'I.F.A.N.* XXI, Sér. B, 1–2 (1959).

[2] R. Schnell, *Plantes Alimentaires et Vie Agricole de l'Afrique* (Paris, 1957), pp. 122–5.

The establishment of Neolithic culture with all its social, political and economic implications was not a sudden event. It was the culmination of a long process of development resulting from diffusion and adaptation of ideas from both within and outside the country, from the Congo basin and the Sahara. Of the two levels of Neolithic culture in Ghana the one originating from the Congo basin is the older, while the one from the Sahara was of greater significance to the human geography of the country.

With the Neolithic culture came the art of cultivation. A broader issue in connection with Neolithic culture in West Africa as a whole is how Neolithic men acquired crops and the knowledge of cultivation. There are some who, relying on many kinds of evidence, declare that agriculture was invented independently in West Africa and give long lists of crops that were ennobled in West Africa.[1] There are others who, also relying on similar types of evidence, cast the West African Negro in the role of a ready recipient of crops and agricultural techniques from elsewhere, and a ready modifier of or experimenter with these to make them suited to the environment he lived in. It is not denied that agriculture has a long tradition in West Africa, but it did not originate there.[2] Whatever the truth of the matter, it is not of particular relevance to Ghana, since it has in no instance been considered even as a possible secondary centre of agricultural origin. Porteres recognizes four such centres in West Africa, including Benin in the forest of Western Nigeria, and Ghana is not one of them.[3]

Little is known of the crops cultivated by Neolithic man in Ghana, but yam (*Dioscorea* sp.), of which there are several varieties indigenous to the country, is generally considered to have been one of them. It is both a forest and savanna crop easily cultivated by removing the eyes from the tubers and planting them in plots cleared from the forest or bush. It is perhaps significant that in many West African, as indeed in East African, languages the word for yam contains the undoubtedly indigenous element 'ku' which is the same as the common West African verb meaning 'to dig'.[4]

The rudimentary form of cultivation practised existed side by side with the established occupations of hunting and food collecting and was for centuries subordinate to them. Neolithic culture nevertheless had far-reaching consequences on the natural landscape. The small rude clearings

[1] For example, G. P. Murdock, *Africa: Its Peoples and their Culture History* (New York, 1959), pp. 68–70.

[2] See, for example, H. G. Baker, 'Comments on the Thesis that there was a Major Centre of Plant Domestication near the Headwaters of the River Niger', *J. Afr. Hist.* III, 2 (1962).

[3] Schnell, op. cit. pp. 144–7.

[4] C. Wrigley, 'Speculations on the Economic Prehistory of Africa', *J. Afr. Hist.* I, 2 (1960).

of previous times that were like tiny islands in a vast sea of waste increased in size and significance in the natural landscape as cultivation became more established and settlements presumably larger and permanent.

Cultivation meant a radical change in man–soil relationship. It was no longer the wild food plants and game that were laid claim to in a given area but the soil itself, since control over or attachment to the soil is a necessary prerequisite for the raising and caring of plants. Individual ownership of land, accompanied by a less regularized form of bush fallowing, would possibly be the rule at the beginning. The practice of constantly changing farm plots would be arrived at through empirical means, but such a practice would only ensure good, regular yields if there were communal regulations on the choice of plots for farms and on the length of the fallow period. It would thus presumably be inevitable that land should be owned and controlled communally so that its exploitation could be conducted effectively and yields maximized. A communal system of land tenure is characteristic of practically all rudimentary and simple agricultural systems, and it breaks down only when the related social, economic, and technological conditions change.

It is not in any doubt that Neolithic men in West Africa and the Sahara kept livestock, and there is a great deal of evidence that the animals were cattle, sheep and goats. But there is hardly any archaeological or other evidence for animal rearing by Neolithic men in Ghana. The possibility must, on the other hand, not be entirely ignored. It appears that the breed of cattle first domesticated or kept in West Africa or the Sahara was the diminutive *Bos brachyceros*; then followed cattle of the larger breed, *B. primigenius*, which had formerly roamed freely in the great rolling grass plains of the Sahara, and which became the ancestor of the present Hamitic longhorn or Ndama cattle.[1] At a later stage domesticated cattle arrived in the Western Sudan from two source areas and possibly also penetrated to favourable locations on the Guinea coast. Men and their cattle came southward from the Sahara as the drying-up process was intensified, and cattle from the Nile Valley also arrived which travelled westward along the great savanna corridor linking the Indian Ocean with the Atlantic coast of West Africa.

The reason for stating that *B. brachyceros* was the earliest breed of cattle to be domesticated rests mainly on the fact that the animal was not milked in ancient times and is still not milked wherever it is found in West Africa today. Yet this animal should be easier, because of its small size, to handle and milk than the larger *B. primigenius* which is now reared for its flesh and

[1] J. L. Stewart and M. D. W. Jeffreys, *The Cattle of the Gold Coast* (Accra, 1956), pp. 1–7.

milk. Man in the earliest stages would domesticate animals merely to save himself the trouble of hunting them, and the animals were no use to him until they had been killed. In later stages man would be able to use them while they were alive, although he also killed them. In the ultimate stages he would use the animals only while they were alive. In other words, man kept cattle for the flesh and hide until he eventually acquired the highly skilled art of keeping dairy cattle exclusively for their milk.[1] A few Dwarf Shorthorns (*B. brachyceros*) are to be found in remote areas in the country and had by all accounts been there before the arrival of Europeans in the fifteenth century. The question of whether Neolithic men in Ghana kept sheep and goats cannot similarly be answered with certainty in view of the present state of knowledge.

Cultivation and possibly animal rearing were not the only features of economic life in Neolithic times. Trade, in the form of barter, would also be another feature. Exchange presupposes specialization in economic activities, and it is not hard to see the possibility of early trade resulting from the development of a primary division of labour between fishing communities on the one hand and cultivators on the other. The commodities involved in trade would be not only products of fishing, cultivation, and of the chase, but also stone tools and probably suitable rock material for tools and ornaments. Stone tool manufacture became a specialized occupation, and there is evidence that there were many stone tool 'factories' in the country.[2] Similarly, a certain degree of regional, or at least local, specialization in the manufacture of pottery and in the working of gold into ornaments would have developed. Gold objects have not so far been found in association with Neolithic material in the country, but it would be surprising if gold-working, already known in Gambia and elsewhere in West Africa in the sixth century B.C., according to Herodotus, was not also known in Ghana around the same time.

Trade in Neolithic times was at two levels; internal, which has been described above, and international. Ghana was in uninterrupted contact with neighbouring regions, for there were no political boundaries in West Africa to prejudice the continuous free movement of men as they explored new regions, searched for new livelihood areas, or sought to join kindred groups elsewhere. Such movements naturally brought different regions into contact, forging links between them. The invasion of Ghana by Neolithic peoples from the Niger Bend was not an event whose significance simply

[1] Ibid. p. 27.

[2] A summary of the evidence will be found in C. T. Shaw, 'Report on Excavations carried out in the Cave known as "Bosumpra"..., *Proc. Prehist. Soc.* x (1944).

ended with the introduction of Saharan Neolithic culture; the invasion was also significant because it forged a line of communication along which men and commodities travelled between the Western Sudan and Ghana. Uninhibited circulation of men makes for exchange of goods and, more important, for diffusion of ideas, and this may partly explain the remarkable similarities that exist among certain Neolithic artefacts in West Africa.

Ghana may also have been in touch with overseas countries. It is said that Phoenicians as far back as the seventh or sixth century B.C. embarked on the incredible adventure of circumnavigating Africa, and that the return journey took three years. The sole object of the adventure was to search for gold, and it is believed that the Phoenicians did stop on the West African coast for the precious metal.[1] It may well be, although it cannot be proved, that the Ghana coast was among the stopping places, for it was not impossible that Ghana's wealth of gold should have been known by the avid gold-seekers from the Mediterranean.

But the matter is not so easily settled. Raymond Mauny for example agrees on the probable antiquity of gold-mining in West Africa, and suggests that gold could have been one of the items of traffic between western Mauritania and Morocco and between the Fezzan and the Niger Bend within the first millennium B.C. He also refers to Herodotus's account of the gold trade conducted within the second half of the first millennium B.C. Nevertheless he argues that this early maritime trade in gold in West Africa must have been of negligible importance, because apart from the text of Herodotus there is no other mention of it until well into medieval times, although European merchants were in the meantime desperately in need of gold for the purchase of luxuries from the Far East. 'This eloquent silence of the texts is remarkable,' Raymond Mauny concludes; 'it confirms to our satisfaction the falseness of the hypotheses advanced by several authors who claim that the ancient navigators came as far as the Gulf of Guinea, and even speak of Morocco as a "Punic market for gold" from the Sudan.'[2] But perhaps the silence of the texts should not be invested with importance of such magnitude. The extent of Carthaginian gold trade in West Africa may well have been kept a secret in conformity with the known Carthaginian policy of falsifying information or covering up their activities in order to discourage trade rivals.[3] The more lucrative the trade, the more anxious, it may be thought, the Carthaginians would be to keep it a secret.

[1] C. H. V. Sutherland, *Gold* (London, 1959), pp. 56 and 115.

[2] R. Mauny, *Tableau Géographique de l'Ouest Africain au Moyen Age* (I.F.A.N.–Dakar, 1961), p. 299.

[3] E. F. Gautier, *Le Passé de l'Afrique du Nord* (Paris, 1937), p. 44.

Early Iron Age culture was not clearly characterized by the use of iron as an agricultural implement for, as noted earlier, the two cultures, Neolithic and Iron Age, existed side by side for many centuries and it was not until comparatively recent times that iron completely replaced stone as material for implements. The significant features of the Early Iron Age that were to make a great deal of difference to the natural landscape only began to develop at a faster pace after the Akan and other tribes became established in the country.

## 1200–1700

For the early part of this period, the most significant features were the crystallization of Akan and other related tribes in the southern portions of the country, and the military invasions of Northern Ghana from the Western Sudan which were to change the social organization and cultural attributes of the people. Later within the period, those events and features that truly characterized the Iron Age developed more fully. These were the growth of overlordship, changes in trade and communications, changes in cultivation, fishing and navigation, in population size, and in types and numbers of settlements.

### Development of overlordship

Effective overlordship becomes possible only when men have entered into a stable relationship with the soil, settling on it and deriving their sustenance from it. Thus among the outstanding events in post-Neolithic times in Ghana was the development of overlordship or chieftaincy. The earliest form of authority or overlordship would arise from a claim to be mediator between the Earth God and men; it would, in other words, arise from religion. The office of Tindana in Northern Ghana, for example, is known to be ancient, preceding the institution of secular authority. The power wielded by the priests was limited, and it was not until alien warriors invaded Northern Ghana in the fifteenth century and imposed centralized systems of government over the sedentary population that overlordship, in the true sense of power and command over men and their goods, was established. Elsewhere in the country too the role of outsiders in the development of secular authority was considerable. Mande peoples, for example, were instrumental in the setting up of centralized military-type governments among some of the Akan peoples,[1] and the name Caramansa,

[1] Akwamu government was for example Mande-inspired.

by which the King of Elmina was known at the time of the first Portuguese visit in 1471 may, it is believed, very well be derived from *Karah*, a known personal name among the Mande, and *Mansa* which is the Mande word for ruler.[1] Similarly Batimansa, the name of a Senegal chief Cadomosto met in 1456, shows Mande influence. There is no doubt in this case because Cadomosto himself indicated that Batimansa's government was Mande in conception.[2]

The formation of societal groups, like tribes, under a centralized authority is of geographical significance. One aspect of this is the tendency towards a steady population increase as a result of organized defence and the guaranteeing of peaceful conditions. Another aspect is the organization of economic activities leading to systematic development of the cultural landscape. In the sphere of agriculture, permission had to be granted before any piece of land could be cleared for cultivation, and it was not impossible for chiefs to order the clearing of specified areas for farms. Similarly, chiefs could order the building of new villages, the cutting of pathways, and so on. There were already several independent kingdoms on the coast before 1600, which were strictly ruled by chiefs. The royal court consisted of treasurers, tax officials, executioners, etc.,[3] and the whole set-up was not dissimilar to that of later times.[4]

The power of chiefs penetrated ultimately through several intermediaries to the lowest stratum of society, consisting of slaves. The intermediaries themselves enjoyed well-defined powers and privileges according to the stratum of society to which they belonged. At the bottom of the social ladder were domestic slaves whose lot, if later nineteenth-century evidence is anything to go by, was not always an unhappy one. It was the institution of export slavery that introduced an odious element into the concept of slavery by inculcating the idea of slaves being mere objects and trade commodities and not human beings worthy of humane treatment. The age-old institution of domestic slavery, on the other hand, was a fully accepted social practice that, unlike export slavery, had no disruptive effect on society. Domestic slavery was also an important part of the country's

[1] I. Wilks, *Ghana Notes and Queries*, no. 3 (Sept.–Dec. 1961). Nevertheless Caramansa is capable of other interpretations, the most popular of which is that it is a corruption of the Akan name Kwamina Ansa.

[2] G. R. Crone (ed.), *The Voyages of Cadomosto* (London, 1937), Hakluyt Society, Second Series, LXXX, 67. In the same way the River Casamance or Casamansa is 'River of Chief Casamansa' (p. 75).

[3] N. Villault, *A Relation of the Coasts of Africk called Guinea* (London, 1670), pp. 223–37. The work was published three years after Villault's return from the Guinea coast.

[4] Compare Villault's account with that of Ashanti by Rattray in his *Ashanti Law and Constitution*.

economic system. One relevant aspect of its importance rested on the fact that the life of domestic slaves was ruled by unquestioning obedience to their masters, so that they could be put to work and made instruments for the acquisition of wealth, and for the execution of works that also added variety to the cultural landscape.

## Changes in trade and communications

The establishment of strong secular authority also provided the necessary framework for trade. There was already a certain amount of internal trade in Neolithic times, and this presumably gained in volume and stability as society became better organized and better regulated, and as a greater variety of goods became available. Regional specialization also developed to a greater degree, as a result of several factors. Two examples will suffice. There were peace-loving sedentary tribes or peoples who were wholly devoted to cultivation, while other tribes disdained an agricultural existence and struck terror into their neighbours by occasionally fighting and capturing them to sell into slavery. The warlike tribes normally depended on the sedentary agricultural ones for their food supplies. Thus the warlike Akwamu, who lived at Nyanoase behind Nsawam and made their military superiority felt wherever possible, depended on their neighbours for agricultural produce. Again, as the gold trade increased in magnitude, the inhabitants of certain areas directed much of their energy to gold mining and therefore paid little attention to cultivation of the soil. And so the Akim, who devoted themselves to the lucrative occupation of gold mining, bought quantities of foodstuffs from neighbouring Gomua and Winneba territories where the people were fully dedicated to agriculture.

Superimposed over the complicated cross-currents of internal trade were three major directions of trade: the south–north trade between the whole country and the Western Sudan; the coast–interior trade based on the exchange of slaves, gold and ivory from the interior of the country for goods, especially firearms, obtainable from the forts and trading posts built by Europeans on the coast; and, thirdly, the sea trade between the coastal settlements of Ghana and Nigeria, which the Portuguese exploited to their advantage by acting as middlemen.[1] It would not be unreasonable to suggest the possibility that this coastwise trade between Ghana and Nigeria came into being or was stimulated in response to Mande trading activities on the coast of Ghana, just as merchants from Dahomey came to

[1] I. Wilks, 'A Medieval Trade-Route from the Niger to the Gulf of Guinea', *J. Afr. Hist.* III, 2 (1962).

trade their wares in the late eighteenth century at Anomabu, which was then one of the largest markets on the Ghana coast.[1] It is not known if Mande traders also penetrated the coastal forest of Nigeria, although Northern Nigeria was one of the major rendezvous for Western Sudan merchants partly because of the apparently sizeable quantities of alluvial gold obtainable there.[2] It would not therefore be inconceivable that Western Nigerian traders crossed the distance to Accra, shorter than that from, say, Benin City to Katsina in Northern Nigeria, in order to share in the prosperous trade there. On the other hand, it is also probable that it was Benin goods, and not Benin traders, that found their way to the coastal settlements of Ghana through intermediaries from Dahomey and Togo.

### *Trade with Western Sudan*

There was, by the fifteenth century, a definite trade route linking the coast and the forest of Ashanti with Jenne and other commercial emporia on the middle Niger in the Western Sudan. The forging of this link was the work of Mande-speaking peoples whose trading activities encompassed most of West Africa.

Perhaps the earliest Mande settlement to be founded in the country was Begho, which was situated in a gap in the Banda Hills, on the northern fringes of the Ashanti forest. It is not definitely known when the Mande first came to Begho, but it appears that the main Mande colonization of the town took place in the early fifteenth century.[3] It was apparently a walled town with a cleared area outside it where the Mande conducted their trade with the local inhabitants living to the south of them. In later centuries the Mande built quarters for themselves in several towns at the northern edge of the Ashanti forest in order to collect and transmit to the Western Sudan the riches of the forest. The Mande did not confine their trading activities to the interior towns; they also ventured to the coastal areas where apparently they were actively trading before the Portuguese first arrived. The Portuguese themselves reported in the 1480s that the Mande were buying Congo and Benin slaves at Elmina.[4]

The intensification of Mande trading activities, which found expression in the colonization of Begho and, later, of other settlements, may have been touched off by the increased demand for gold in Europe which, by the

[1] P. Labarthe, *Voyage à la Côte de Guinée* (Paris, 1803), p. 71. He actually visited the West African coast in 1788.

[2] K. M. Buchanan and J. C. Pugh, *Land and People in Nigeria* (London, 1958), p. 188.

[3] I. Wilks, *The Northern Factor in Ashanti History* (Ghana, 1961), pp. 1–13.

[4] Crone, op. cit. p. xxix.

beginning of the fifteenth century, had been greatly denuded of precious metals by the demands of a rapidly increasing foreign trade and by a series of expensive and disastrous wars. Europe looked to Africa for fresh supplies, particularly to the markets of the North African coast which must in turn have transmitted the demand for gold along the great caravan routes to the trading centres of the Western Sudan.[1]

Through contact with the Mande the country was able to add much to its material culture, as may be seen in the fact that several cultural terms and the names of certain articles in common use in the Twi language today are thought to be Mande in origin. The Twi names for camel (*Yoma*), horse (*oponko*), box (*adaka*), sack (*kotoku*), snuff (*asre*), tobacco (*tawa*), gold-mine (*nkoron*), lion (*gyata*) correspond to the Mande names *nyoroma*, *ponko*, *laka*, *kotoku*, *sara*, *tawa*, *kolo* which means mineshaft, and *gyata* respectively.[2] It is possible that some of the crafts and objects, the names of which are of Mande origin, may well have been introduced by the Mande. It has been suggested, for example, that tobacco-smoking, or more accurately the smoking of New World tobacco, spread from Senegambia where it had probably been introduced by the Portuguese, eastward to the Western Sudan, from where it was transmitted southwards by the Mande in the early seventeenth century into Akan-speaking areas.[3]

Although the Mande also introduced Islam in the sixteenth and seventeenth centuries,[4] with its cultural associations like the weaving and wearing of garments, it is very probable that the wearing of cotton cloth or garments preceded Islam since the Mande reportedly wove and sold cloth at Begho.[5] It is fairly certain that it was the Mande who originally introduced the present-day technique of weaving and making kente cloth by means of joining the sides of several narrow strips of woven cloth. This mode of clothmaking was also observed by Cadomosto in the fifteenth century in Senegal which was at the time under strong Mande influence.[6] Nevertheless it was not until the end of the seventeenth century and after, when Islam took firm root and Mande communities lived and propagated new

[1] Ibid. pp. xiii–xv.

[2] I. Wilks, 'The Mande Loan Element in Twi', *Ghana Notes and Queries*, no. 4 (January–June 1962).

[3] Ibid. Another oft-quoted example of Mande innovation in the country is thought to be indicated by the close similarity of the Twi and Mande words for gold mine: the Mande are supposed to have introduced certain techniques of gold mining. The example is a dubious one for the evidence, based as it is on linguistics alone, is inconclusive.

[4] I. Wilks, 'Islam in Ghana History', *Ghana Bull. Theol.* II, 3 (December 1962).

[5] See footnote 3 on p. 42. See also *Dutch Map of the Gold Coast, 1629*, Furley Collection, Balme Library, University of Ghana, Legon.

[6] Crone, op. cit. pp. 31–2.

ideas everywhere in the kingdom of Ashanti, that the art of cloth weaving with an awareness of the indigenous local cotton as a natural resource, became widespread. In support of this is the tradition among the Ashanti that they learned the art of cloth weaving about the time of one of their early chiefs, Oti Akenten, who lived in the second half of the seventeenth century.[1]

The Jenne–Begho trade route forged by the Mande was not the only link between Ghana (Gold Coast) and the Western Sudan. An earlier kola nut route already existed, according to the *Kano Chronicle*, between Gonja and Katsina in Northern Nigeria in the fifteenth century although the kola trade along the route was probably of little importance. In the seventeenth century in the time of Jakpa, another kola route came into being, and its direction from Ashanti through Salaga and Yendi was determined after Jakpa transferred the market at Buipe to Salaga.[2] There may have been other routes across the savanna country of Northern Ghana to the Western Sudan, routes that may have persisted and came to be fully described in the nineteenth century.[3]

### *Trade with Europe*

Ghana looked not only north to the Western Sudan but also south to the European establishments on the coast for trade. The first European traders to reach Ghana since the thirteenth century were the Portuguese who, driven by a desire for gold, had been systematically exploring the Guinea coast of Africa under the distinguished patronage of Prince Henry the Navigator since the early fifteenth century. King Alfonso, continuing Prince Henry's policy of exploration and discovery, leased the Guinea trade to Fernão Gomes in 1469 for five years on certain conditions, one of which was that Fernão Gomes should undertake to explore a hundred leagues of new coastline every year. It was under the terms of this contract that one of Gomes' men, Soeiro do Costa, discovered a river 'near the house of Axem where the factory of the gold trade is', and which was named after him. This is the River Comoe in Ivory Coast. Later, in January 1471, two agents of Fernão Gomes discovered the gold trade at Shama and Elmina which they named 'the village of two parts'.

In 1481, ten years after the discovery of the gold trade, King João II

[1] Rattray, *Religion and Art in Ashanti* (O.U.P., 1927), p. 220.

[2] Mahmoud El-Wakkad (translator), 'Qissatu Salga Tarikhu Gonja—The Story of Salaga and the History of Gonja', *Ghana Notes and Queries*, no. 3 (September–December 1961).

[3] J. Dupuis, *Journal of a Residence in Ashantee* (London, 1824), pt. II and T. E. Bowdich, *A Mission from Cape Coast Castle to Ashantee* (London, 1819), pp. 162–72.

wanted a fortress built 'to be the first stone of the oriental church...in praise and glory of God for the possession he took of that which he had discovered and which remained to be discovered...' In reply to protests from his councillors against the distance involved, the debilitating climate and the certainty of high mortality rate among Europeans on the West African coast, the king 'considered that the possibility of getting even one soul to the Faith by baptism through the Fortress outweighed all the inconveniences. For he said that God would take care of them, since the work was to His praise, that his subjects would win profit, and that the patrimony of this kingdom would be increased.'[1] Clearly, the economic motive was no less important than the religious. Thus in January 1482 Diogo de Azambuja arrived at Elmina and built a stone fortress there. It was christened São Jorge da Mina. The Portuguese, wishing to monopolize the coastal trade, lost no time in building other smaller forts at Axim, Shama, and Accra.

The Portuguese monopoly was challenged half-heartedly and unsuccessfully by several other European nations through the greater part of the sixteenth century. It was not until the very close of that century that the Dutch, following the conquest of Portugal by Philip II of Spain and their rebellion against Philip, seriously began to interfere in the Portuguese Guinea trade. In spite of stout Portuguese opposition and of atrocities perpetrated against any of the coastal peoples who traded with the interlopers, the Dutch succeeded in 1598 in establishing trading posts under the shelter of small fortresses built of earth at Mouri, Butri, Kormantin and Komenda. Nevertheless the Portuguese still had control over most of the coastal trade. They even succeeded, in 1623, in building a fort (Fort Dumas) at a place about fifteen miles up the Ankobra river where they worked a gold mine until both the mine and the fort were destroyed by an earthquake in 1636.

In 1631 the English, who had so far shown fleeting interest, joined in the international rivalry for the Guinea trade in order to obtain slaves for their sugar cane plantations in the West Indies. To facilitate their trading operations, they built a fort at Kormantin. The Dutch meanwhile enlarged their trading posts at Mouri, their principal settlement at the time, and converted it to a stone fort. Their bitter rivalry with the Portuguese culminated in their capture in 1637 of the principal fort of the Portuguese at Elmina. Five years later, in 1642, they also captured the Portuguese fort at Axim, which was the residence of the vice-president of Portuguese

[1] The account of early Portuguese contact with the coast is based on that in *The Asia of João de Barros*, which is Book Two of Crone (ed.), *The Voyages of Cadomosto*, pp. 108–23.

settlements in the country. Although the Portuguese lost all their important forts to the Dutch, they maintained their trading interests on the Slave Coast east of Keta and even for a brief period of three years, beginning from 1679, regained control of Christiansborg.

From about 1650 to the end of the century the rivalry for the booming Guinea trade reached a new level of intensity as Sweden, Denmark, France, and Brandenburg joined in it. Battles and squabbles accompanied trade on the coast, and forts changed hands with remarkable rapidity as one European power gained superiority over, or lost it to, the other. Sweden, France, and Brandenburg, after some initial successes, failed to gain a firm foothold on the land, while Denmark, England, and Holland succeeded in establishing themselves. By the end of the seventeenth century, the length of the coastline of Ghana was dotted with forts, big and small, belonging to the Danes, the English, and the Dutch.[1]

The impact of European contact, especially contact with the Portuguese, on the human geography of the coastal areas was tremendous. Just as the Mande introduced ideas and techniques from the Western Sudan that contributed significantly to the cultural capital of man in Ghana, so did the Portuguese introduce innovations that played an important part in the evolution of the man-made landscape of Ghana.[2]

### Changes in fishing and navigation

There were major changes in fishing gear but not necessarily in fishing methods. Locally made cords and nets, iron fish hooks, and lead sinkers were part of the coastal fisherman's equipment by the beginning of the seventeenth century.[3] The changeover from bone to metal fishing tackle could have occurred before the Portuguese arrived.

Dug-out canoes were used for fishing as well as for transport purposes. It is not known when dug-outs became popular in the country. A typical transport canoe was 35 feet long, 5 feet wide, and 3 feet high, and it appears it was transport canoes and not those for fishing that carried mast and sail.[4] The Portuguese used cloth sails while the local people used sails of rush

[1] Accounts of European trade rivalries on the Ghana coast will be found in published histories on the country, such as those by W. W. Claridge and W. E. F. Ward.

[2] For the moment it will suffice to mention only the Portuguese loan element in the Akan language. A list of such words is given by the Rev. J. G. Christaller in *A Grammar of the Asante and Fante Language* (Basel, 1875), pp. 48–50.

[3] Pieter de Marees, *Description et Recit Historial du Riche Royaume d'Ore de Gunea* (Amsterdam, 1605), pp. 48–50. This is a key source material for the early seventeenth century.

[4] Ibid.

mats. A baffling problem is how the idea of using sails originated among the local people. It is possible that the rush mat sails were the result of an attempt to copy the cloth sails on the Portuguese ships; but it may be wondered why cloth sails did not replace those of rush mat before 1600, unless the Portuguese did not make sail cloth available to the local people. Or perhaps the observation that rush mat sails were used should be interpreted to mean that they were still to be seen on some parts of the coast. This would then imply that the local people, with perhaps a few exceptions, had generally changed over to cloth sails. It would also imply the possibility that the idea of using sails was indigenous and not suggested by their use on Portuguese ships. By the beginning of the eighteenth century sails of rush mat had completely disappeared.

### Changes in agriculture

In the sphere of agriculture there were no spectacular changes in the method of cultivation, which continued generally to be bush fallowing, except that iron implements had completely replaced stone ones along the coast by the beginning of the seventeenth century. Stone implements were still used in the interior.

The principal development in agriculture was the introduction of certain domesticated animals and a large variety of food crops from the New World by the Portuguese. Most of the items introduced are easily gathered from the work of de Marees who visited the country in 1601.[1] His visit was at a time when the Portuguese were at the height of their power, controlled much of the country's overseas trade, and had earned the wholehearted enmity of the Dutch. De Marees, a Dutchman, was thus very critical of whatever the Portuguese did in the country, and enlarged on the atrocities inflicted on his countrymen and on the local people by the Portuguese. But his outraged opinion of the hostile attitude of the Portuguese did not prevent de Marees from writing an unbiased assessment of the Portuguese contribution to the making of the country's agricultural landscape.[2] The Portuguese, he said, had done much for the country, even if the primary motive was dictated by self-interest. They had brought into the country for the first time several kinds of animals like pigeons, hens, pigs, and sheep; then maize 'for the relief of the country', and, 'for their own refreshment', sugar cane, pineapple which they brought from San Thome, and banana or Congo banana, so called because the Portuguese introduced it from the Congo. The crops, de Marees said finally, were first of all very new to the

[1] Op. cit.

[2] Ibid. pp. 86–8.

local people who therefore paid exorbitant prices for them; but they had become so common in the country by the time of his visit that they fetched a low price.

There is general agreement on the crops listed by de Marees as having been introduced by the Portuguese, with the possible exception of maize. The controversy over the source and date of arrival of maize in West Africa as a whole has been a lively one. Briefly, there is the contention that maize reached West Africa directly from the New World. Against this is the view that the crop reached West Africa from the Arab world before Columbus's discovery of America in 1492, and was being cultivated at Elmina when the Portuguese first arrived there. This argument rests partly on the identity of the crop the Portuguese named *milho zaburro*. *Zaburro* is supposed to be derived from the Akan name for maize, *aburow*, which would suggest that maize was known and cultivated at any rate at Elmina where the Portuguese had their first major contact with Ghana in 1482. But it is also argued that the Portuguese writer Valentim Fernandes who used the name *milho zaburro* frequently in his work on the Guinea coast applied it generally to cereals including millet and sorghum and not to maize in particular, and that *milho zaburro* should, if anything, be identified with sorghum and not with maize, which was introduced by the Portuguese after 1492.[1]

On the whole the arguments in favour of maize being originally a New World crop are too weighty to be easily brushed aside, in spite of other persuasive arguments supporting the contrary. A satisfactory conclusion would be that maize, originally of New World provenance, was brought by the Portuguese and other Europeans across the Atlantic to West Africa, and that the New World crop also reached the interior of West Africa by an overland route from Egypt, to which the crop had been transmitted from the Mediterranean.[2] De Marees was emphatic on how maize came into Ghana. It was brought originally by the Portuguese, he wrote, from the West Indies to San Thome and from there to Ghana. 'Before the arrival of the Portuguese the inhabitants here did not know it. The Portuguese sowed and distributed it among the savages, so that the country is now full of it, and it grows in abundance everywhere at present.'[3]

The list of crops introduced by the Portuguese and cultivated in the country at the time of de Marees' visit could be extended to include sweet potatoes, oranges, lemons, red pepper and tobacco, which were

[1] A brief outline of the controversy on the introduction of maize into West Africa is given by Bruce F. Johnston, *The Staple Food Economies of Western Tropical Africa* (California, 1958), p. 26, and by Raymond Mauny in his *Tableau Géographique*, pp. 240–2.

[2] Johnston, op. cit. p. 175.

[3] Marees, op. cit. p. 44.

present in Ghana before the end of the seventeenth century.[1] Groundnut, known to have been brought to West Africa by the Portuguese to feed slaves on their way to the New World, was also in the country before the end of the seventeenth century.

Two other crops cultivated in the country at the time of de Marees' visit were ginger and rice, but there is no indication of their origin. The original home of ginger is believed to be South-West Asia;[2] of the date of its introduction into Ghana nothing is known. Rice may have referred to the two species *Oryza glaberrima* and *O. sativa*. The former is indigenous and its cultivation in West Africa is estimated to go back over 3,000 years; by the sixteenth century it had spread along the West African coast as far east as Axim. *O. sativa* is Asian rice introduced by the Portuguese and readily accepted in areas of indigenous rice cultivation in West Africa.[3]

## Changes in population and settlement size and distribution

Although the period from about the thirteenth to the end of the seventeenth century saw remarkable changes in population and settlement size and distribution, the roots of the changes went further back in time than the beginning of the thirteenth century. One of the factors that may have accounted for a probable increase in population in Early Iron Age times was the arrival of Malaysian food crops—Asian yam, taro, and plantain, which added to the range of food crops available in the forest and presumably made it possible for the latter to support a larger population. It is not being argued here that the introduction of these food crops resulted in a population explosion,[4] for such probably was not the case. There is no evidence for it. But there may have been some increase in the size of the population, the extent of which cannot be placed within any definite limits. Settlements may also have increased in size with the rise and recognition of leadership and authority which in those troubled times organized the defence of the peasantry.

It should not be inferred from what has gone before that the country was in those early times teeming with people, for it appears that even in the late fifteenth century there were wide open spaces in which men could move about and build new settlements whenever they wished. King Caramansa of Elmina, in a famous reply to Diogo de Azambuja's request for permission

[1] William Bosman, *A New and Accurate Description of the Coast of Guinea* (London, 1705), Letter XVI.

[2] Murdock, op. cit. p. 23.

[3] Schnell, op. cit. p. 147; also Johnston, op. cit. p. 26.

[4] Murdock, op. cit. p. 245.

to build a castle at Elmina in 1482, warned that the Portuguese would have themselves to blame if after building the castle they should behave treacherously to his people, 'because the land was great, and he and his men could build another abode elsewhere with a few sticks and branches, of which they had plenty'.[1]

A major factor that accounted for changes in population and settlement numbers from the sixteenth century onwards was the Atlantic slave trade, which deprived the whole country of part of its population and sapped its vitality. It is not possible to give a reliable estimate of the numbers sold into slavery from Ghana, but it is not hard to see that the frequent battles waged deliberately to provide cargo for the slave ships must have left many areas in the country practically empty.

If changes in settlement numbers were striking, equally so were changes in settlement distribution, particularly from about the sixteenth century onwards. Before the arrival of European traders and the establishment of their trading posts on the coast, there was a line of small seaside fishing settlements which were offshoots of much larger settlements in the immediate interior. The opening of the European trading centres modified the pattern of settlement size distribution by calling into being a line of fair-sized settlements on the coast which for some time continued to be subject to their parent settlements in the immediate interior. Paramount chiefs lived in the latter and stationed in the former governors, tax collectors and other government officials, and slaves to trade for them.[2] Accra was one of the few coastal settlements which grew at an extraordinary rate in subsequent years. Its growth was greatly stimulated by the break-up of its parent settlement, Ayaso,[3] and the transfer of the Ayaso population to Accra after an Akwamu war around the mid-seventeenth century.

In Northern Ghana the eastward push by the Mande in Gonja in the mid-seventeenth century also caused shifts in population and in settlements, especially in Gonja itself. Jakpa, the conqueror of Gonja, established a line of fortified settlements, each with an Imam, from Bole eastward to Northern Togo and in the process altered or confirmed the geographical values of settlements in that part of the country.[4] A few settlements in northern Gonja and in Dagomba territory also gained in, or suffered diminution of, importance according as Jakpa did or did not select them to be major settlements in his new kingdom. Thus Daboya, the ancient salt-making centre and market, flourished even more after Jakpa's recognition

[1] Crone, op. cit. p. 122.
[2] Marees, op. cit. p. 30.
[3] Referred to as Greater Accra in some early European records.
[4] Mahmoud El-Wakkad, op. cit.

of its importance to the economy of his new kingdom. Salaga, the zongo of Kpembe, also grew to be a large commercial centre after Jakpa transferred to it the market functions of Buipe. In the heart of Dagomba territory, on the other hand, the locations of some settlements were displaced as the population dispersed in the face of Jakpa's advancing armies. The Dagomba capital, for example, was moved from its original site at Dipali some thirty miles north of Tamale and near the modern village of Diari, which lies on the main Tamale–Bolgatanga road, to its present and more easily defensible location at Yendi.

Along with changes in population density and in distribution of settlements came changes in architecture and settlement forms. There is no means of knowing what shapes the earliest building types took, but the possibility could be depended on that the simplest types of buildings may have been round huts consisting of sticks in the ground with their upper ends bound together to make them cone-shaped. Or they could have been circular arrangements of upright poles covered on the outside with woven mats and roofed with thatch. Such buildings would have had the advantage of being easy to construct. Perhaps the suggestion put forward here may have confirmation, first, in the tradition at Winneba that buildings in the town were 'in earliest times' low and oven-like or circular in shape and were grouped in a compact mass for purposes of defence and security; and, second, in the fact that traditional huts built for gods throughout the country are generally circular in shape. Tradition plays a large part in religious affairs, so that the form of fetish huts probably points to the style of ancient architecture.

It is most probable that by the fifteenth century the buildings in Southern Ghana and Ashanti-Brong Ahafo were of the Guinea forest house type, that is, rectangular, gable-roofed, and of wattle-and-daub. But there is no direct evidence for this, except the claims of oral tradition and what may be gathered from late sixteenth-century prints of settlements on the coast.

It was not until 1605 that detailed descriptions of buildings and settlements on the coast were published.[1] De Marees' first comment on the buildings was uncomplimentary: they looked like pig sties to him. He then went on to describe in detail how a rectangular wattle-and-daub house was built and its gable roof covered with oil-palm leaves. A household consisted of a number of the rectangular huts connected to one another by cane or mat walls and arranged in a square with a courtyard in the centre. The houses were small in size except the chief's palace, which was built some distance from the rest of the town (Cape Coast) and consisted of a group

[1] Marees, op. cit.

of buildings a little taller and bigger than ordinary. There were no sugges-tions on the possible origin of the house types. But just over a century later one writer observed:[1]

> The great commerce they have had with the Europeans having learned them the art of building, the officers and great merchants of the country have followed their directions and built themselves houses, with high and lofty roofes, several apart-ments, with one chamber opening into another...

This will explain the touch of sophistication that came to be applied to the architecture, and not the provenance of the basic design which may probably be indigenous.

It appears the Guinea forest house type was originally common to the whole of the Kwa linguistic area, but was steadily displaced in the south-east coastal plains, from perhaps the sixteenth century, by the circular house type until by the end of the seventeenth century the circular type was definitely established in place of the rectangular one. The circular house was probably one of convenience hurriedly adopted by the immigrant groups which came to populate the south-east coastal plains.

In Northern Ghana the situation was entirely different. Northern Ghana was part of the Western Sudan, sharing in its trade and cultural charac-teristics and benefiting from novel ideas from the undoubtedly more culturally advanced peoples of the Niger Bend and elsewhere in the Western Sudan. The countryside of Northern Ghana, of which there were pre-sumably no written descriptions before the seventeenth century, would therefore have had marked similarities with the general countryside of the Western Sudan where, by the fifteenth century, round huts with conical or flat roofs, grouped together within a circular wall, was the typical home-stead. The huts were built of wood or of layers of earth.

The building of circular compound homesteads was a response to a combination of physical, social, and economic conditions differing from what prevailed in Southern Ghana and Ashanti–Brong Ahafo. The home-stead was built like a fortress to provide safety in an area where wars and conflicts were frequent, and consequently included grain silos and enclosures for livestock. A normal homestead would be built in this manner because Northern Ghana consists of extensive flat areas or undulating surfaces covered with savanna vegetation too open to afford seclusion to settlements. Also, the circular compound homestead was essential for preserving cohesion and unity among members of the extended family.

It was probably in the late seventeenth century that a new house type from the Western Sudan, where it had been introduced from the Maghreb,

[1] Villault, op. cit. pp. 154–5.

either first arrived in Northern Ghana or became more noticeable there. It consists of a number of rectangular structures with flat earth roofs enclosing an interior courtyard and having an exterior wall of mud or sun-dried brick often surmounted by a crenellated parapet.[1] Its introduction into Northern Ghana could not have been much earlier than the seventeenth century; archaeology has so far been unable to turn up conclusive evidence pointing to the contrary.[2] Besides, this house type appears to have been rare in the Western Sudan, excluding the Saharan and sub-Saharan areas, in the period from the eighth to the sixteenth century.[3]

As far as recorded evidence goes, it appears that one of the earliest towns in Northern Ghana to be built exclusively in Western Sudanese style was Larabanga in western Gonja in the second half of the seventeenth century.[4] The town consisted of the rectangular flat-roofed buildings (the Moroccan house type), and had a mosque. It was long after this date that reports of this type of settlement in the country became frequent.

[1] This may be the unspecified type of architecture that was supposed by Bovill to have come to the Western Sudan under Moorish influence, presumably in the late sixteenth century or perhaps a little later. See E. W. Bovill, *The Golden Trade of the Moors* (O.U.P., 1961), p. 178.

[2] Excavations at the site of the old Dagomba capital of Dipali, near Diari on the Tamale–Bolgatanga road, have revealed evidence of rectangular architecture of indeterminate antiquity.

[3] Mauny, op. cit. pp. 490–503.

[4] Mahmoud El-Wakkad, op. cit.

## PART II

# *From the beginning of the eighteenth century to about 1850*

# 3. William Bosman's Gold Coast: population and settlements

The end of the seventeenth century marked a beginning of change in the development of the country's human geography. After about 1700 a series of struggles occurred among tribes with ambitions for territorial aggrandisement. Such events were known before, but the emergence of the Ashanti nation from the confusion of inter-tribal warfare as the most formidable power in the land acted as a catalyst that completely altered the character, speed and magnitude of the change of events. The human geography of Ghana took a new turn with the rise of Ashanti.[1]

## POPULATION

In appearance the countryside was one vast wilderness of uniformly thick forest and savanna vegetation relieved in only a few places by clearings for settlements and farms. But hidden within the forest and the savanna, and never seen by Europeans, were a vast number of rural settlements in which most of the country's population lived.

Of the total size of the population no estimate can be made. It could not have been very large in view of the frequent inter-tribal wars since the final decade of the seventeenth century in which large numbers of people lost their lives or fled to neighbouring countries. Ahanta, for example, was seriously depopulated through the fatal war with Adom which began in 1690 or 1691 and continued for four years. The few that survived the war

[1] It is fortunate that there is a case for a period picture at the beginning of the eighteenth century, as there is for the purpose the brilliant account of the country's human geography by William Bosman. His work, *A new and Accurate Description of the Coast of Guinea*, was written originally as a series of letters between 1700 and 1702. It was first published in book form in Dutch in 1704 and was followed by an accurate English edition a year later. Bosman left the country on 27 July 1702 after a stay of fourteen years. He was chief factor for the Dutch, and his trading interests took him to most parts of Southern Ghana. Bosman's work is easily the most reliable of the major works on the country produced in the eighteenth century. It thoroughly covered Southern Ghana which was fairly well known to Europeans, but was hardly concerned with Ashanti, Brong Ahafo, the inland sections of Volta Region, and Northern Ghana, about which Bosman and other Europeans only had scraps of information collected from local Ghanaian merchants. It is nevertheless possible to make good the deficiency from other sources. Unless otherwise stated, the basic material for this chapter comes from Bosman's work.

in Ahanta sought protection under the Dutch fort at Butri, while the greatest part of the land lay wild and uncultivated. Yet before the war the countryside of Ahanta 'regaled the eyes with the pleasant prospect of numerous villages well peopled...'[1] The same was true of the states of Axim, Ankobra, Abocroe, and Egwira (fig. 7 on p. 62) which together could provide just over 3,000 armed men.[2] Denkera also was completely sacked by the Ashanti in 1701 after a prolonged deadly war, and the looting, accompanied by indiscriminate slaughter of the Denkera, occupied the victorious Ashanti for fifteen days.[3] Again, the Akwamu, through a series of wars begun towards the close of the seventeenth century, destroyed and caused considerable depopulation of the middle Densu basin and the Accra Plains.[4] Similar reductions in population size must have occurred in Northern Ghana and elsewhere as a result of the many tribal wars. The death rate among those wounded in the wars was also high because of inadequate medical facilities. On the other hand Ashanti, which had suffered no crippling conquests and invasions, must have had a larger population than many areas of the country.

Equally devastating were the numerous epidemics that periodically swept over the country. The two most deadly were smallpox and guinea worm disease, which Bosman referred to as 'national diseases'.[5] Within the last two decades of the seventeenth century thousands of men perished through an epidemic of smallpox. Guinea worm disease, which as far as Bosman could observe appeared to be endemic on the whole coast, also contributed significantly to the high death rate, and there was no certain cure for either of the two diseases.

Life expectation appears to have been low. 'It is observable', wrote Bosman, 'that there are several grey-headed people who look as if they were old, but indeed are not so; this perhaps may be owing to their too early and excessive venery, by which they do enfeeble themselves, that a man of fifty (a good old age here), seized by any sickness, generally leaves this world.' Although Bosman's explanation of 'too early and excessive venery' may not be valid, it was probably true that the life span for most of the population was short. It is further possible that women lived longer than and outnumbered men because of the latter's frequent involvement in war. Birth as well as infant mortality rate may also have been high.

[1] Bosman, op. cit. Letter II.

[2] West India Company (W.I.C.) 97, 'Report on St. Anthony, Axim', dated 15–16 November 1701.

[3] Bosman, op. cit. Letter VI.

[4] Ibid. Letters V and XVIII. Also Christiansborg Diary, entry dated 2 March 1702 (Furley Collection).

[5] For the section on diseases and vital statistics, see Bosman, op. cit. Letters VIII and IX.

Forming an insignificant proportion of the coastal population were Europeans, who were confined to their forts, and mulattoes, the offspring of marriage or liaison between European men and African women. The mulattoes, who also lived mainly in the coastal settlements, constituted a social problem for they were accepted by neither Europeans nor Africans. Some of them were merchants, but the majority served the Dutch as soldiers. The death rate among the resident European population, which by any estimate could not have numbered more than three hundred, was high because of malaria and sunstroke, against which they had no efficacious remedies. New arrivals on the coast were more prone to malarial attacks and other discomforts, but once they survived their first few months they no longer faced the prospect of certain death through those ailments. Bosman made some shrewd observations on the need for Europeans to adapt their clothing to suit the climate, and to desist from excessive indulgence in drinking alcohol, although he conceded that Europeans at Kormantin and Apam were prone to infection by guinea worm because of the foul water they were obliged to drink there.

## RURAL SETTLEMENTS

It is impossible to reconstruct, in the absence of suitable data, an accurate distribution of the African population and settlements, the majority of which were rural, about the turn of the eighteenth century. It would be unrewarding and fruitless, except in a few cases, to attempt the reconstruction from later known distributions, since settlement sites changed frequently within the eighteenth century as a result of the need for regular readjustments of population and settlement distribution to the ever-changing political conditions in the country. The persistence over a long period of time of the name of a settlement did not mean permanence of location, as it was usual to transfer the name of an older and moribund or deserted settlement to a newer and different one built by settlers from the former.

### Southern Ghana and Ashanti–Brong Ahafo[1]

Nucleated settlements were the rule in the time of Bosman. Their sites were generally chosen on the basis of ease of defence, and ranking among them were hilltop sites. Such settlements were common in the Accra Plains

[1] Here and subsequently the term Southern Ghana is used to cover Volta Region as well. It is a matter of convenience.

where the tops of large inselbergs like Shai, Krobo, Osudoku, and Ningo provided excellent defensive sites and were preferred to low-lying areas. Where settlements were built on lower and more vulnerable sites, the controlling factor was the availability of water, for the Accra Plains have an anomalously low total annual rainfall of about 30 inches. But water and considerations of defence as factors in the siting of settlements in the Accra Plains did not always pull in opposite directions, for the reason that an inselberg often had a high water table at its base which, together with the rainwater collected in rock basins at its summit, satisfied the water requirements of villages perched on top of it.

Other areas of important hilltop settlements were the Togo–Atakora Ranges in Volta Region and the Akwapim Mountains. The Togo–Atakora Ranges offered suitable defensive sites, while the well-watered intermontane valleys could be cultivated by the settlers on the tops of the Ranges. Similarly, in Akwapim, some of the settlements like Akropong and Abiriw, originally in the low-lying Densu basin, came to be sited on top of the Akwapim Mountains for the sake of security, and their inhabitants farmed, whenever possible, in the valleys and plains on either side of the hills. Granaries were essential elements in these settlements, just as they indeed were throughout the rest of Southern Ghana.[1] They would have been needed above all to ensure that the settlements did not easily succumb to a siege through starvation.

Elsewhere in the forest country settlements were also sited wherever possible on hilltops, as in Kwahu or Ashanti–Akim. Nevertheless most of the large settlements, because of the rareness of high inaccessible mountains, were sited on lower ground but often away from the main routeways for purposes of isolation and security. This, observed by Barbot in the 1680s,[2] was still true in the early nineteenth century when the country was frequently in the turmoils of inter-tribal war. Marshy, swampy places, accessible only by some narrow crooked paths, also attracted settlements.[3] River islands, particularly those in the Volta and the Ankobra, similarly provided suitable sites for settlements.[4] Little wonder Bosman lamented that 'the negroes, in building their villages, have not the least regard to the pleasantness of the situation. They choose a dry and disagreeable place to build on, neglecting the well-planted hills, charming valleys, and beautiful rivers

[1] John Barbot, *A Description of the Coasts of North and South Guinea* (London, 1746), pp. 252–3.
[2] Ibid. [3] Ibid.
[4] The Rev. Riis saw examples in the Volta River in 1838. See 'Digest of Basel Mission Archives on Ghana (Manuscripts), 1828–1851', I, EC 1/33, National Archives of Ghana (NAG).

...'[1] Walled settlements were unusual, Labadi east of Osu being a rare example.[2]

Although compact nucleated settlements were the rule, there were also a few isolated hunters' camps which not infrequently became the basis for a future larger settlement. Hunters' camps could exist in isolation in those unsettled times because of the hunters' peculiar knowledge of the terrain and his skill in evading the enemy. The town of Sunyani in Brong Ahafo, originally sited a few miles west of its present location, apparently began as a small camp for elephant hunters, to which the rich rewards of hunting soon attracted large numbers of people. In support of the tradition is the name Sunyani itself which implies skinning of elephants.

Settlements in Southern Ghana and Ashanti–Brong Ahafo were characterized by two principal house types: the Guinea forest or rectangular gable-roofed type and the circular type with conical roof. The former had a wide distribution while the latter was restricted to the south-east coastal plains. A variety of the rectangular type had, not the thatched and inflammable gable roof, but a flat roof of compacted earth introduced mainly into the coastal settlements west of Accra in order to eliminate the possibility of the houses being destroyed by fire during wars. Relics of this variety are still to be found in Biriwa, Egya, and Cape Coast, among others.

## Northern Ghana

In contrast with Southern Ghana and Ashanti–Brong Ahafo, with their nucleated settlements, was Northern Ghana, an area of generally dispersed settlements[3]. Dotted evenly over the grassy plains of Northern Ghana and possibly culminating, where population density was high, in a nebular nucleation without any recognizable centre, were circular compound homesteads, the smallest self-contained units of settlement. They may have existed side by side with, or were probably replaced by, the Moroccan house type in parts of western Gonja. It is possible that the Moroccan house type was originally found eastward, beyond its present limit, in eastern Gonja and southern Dagomba, and that it gave way there, probably in the early years of the eighteenth century, to the older and more common circular compound homestead after the Dagomba freed themselves from Gonja domination and reasserted their authority.

Northern Ghana was a livestock country where animals were grazed extensively on individual land holdings, and the dispersion of homesteads

[1] Bosman, *Guinea*, Letter IX. [2] Barbot, op. cit. p. 185.

[3] Settlements in Dagomba were probably nucleated, as they are today.

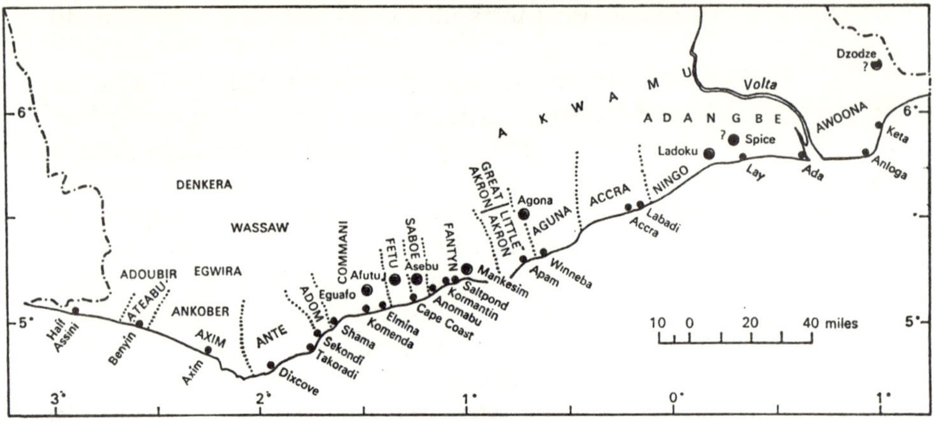


7 Some major coastal and sub-coastal settlements, *c.* 1702. ⊙ Sub-coastal settlement, ● coastal settlement, . . . approximate tribal boundaries

was due to the traditional practice of building the family house in the middle of its land holding. Although the homesteads were physically scattered, they were grouped into communities on the basis of kinship ties and the need for mutual protection.

## Distribution of rural settlements

### *Southern Ghana and Ashanti–Brong Ahafo*

It appears there were four groups of rural settlements in Southern Ghana and Ashanti–Brong Ahafo: parkland settlements between the northern edge of the forest and the Black Volta, including the Afram Plains, and stretching in a line from north-west to south-east; forest settlements; a broken horizontal line of settlements a few miles from the coast; and, finally, coastal settlements (fig. 7).

Some of the parkland settlements may have existed before the seventeenth century in connection with the trade route that skirted the northern edge of the forest on its way from the Volta gorge to Begho. Others may have served as major stopping centres on trade routes between Northern Ghana and Ashanti. Wenchi, Techiman, Atebubu, Nkoranza, and Banda were, in addition to Begho, some of the important pre-1700 settlements. All these settlements, presumably with colonies of Mande traders attached to them, were congregated in western Brong Ahafo, the economic heart of Brong Ahafo region. Eastern Brong Ahafo apparently had fewer major settlements, probably because of the relative newness of the trade routes that passed through the area, connecting Kpembe/Salaga with Kumasi. Krachi or Odente was no more than a transhipment point on the Volta, and its importance derived mainly from its possession of a powerful fetish with countrywide prestige. It appears that Kete, which in later years formed a twin settlement with Krachi, was not yet founded.

It becomes apparent from the list of known major parkland settlements that the latter avoided the immediate environs of the Black Volta. Indeed, parts of Brong Ahafo immediatedly south of the large convolutions of the Black Volta belonged to what had become a sparsely populated area referred to in nineteenth-century literature as the Desert of Ghofan and now part of the Middle Belt.[1] It would appear that the physical conditions in the Desert of Ghofan were as they are today. In the wet season much of the ground is flooded and near impassable, while in the dry season the soil becomes parched and broken up by fissures. Also, hard concretionary laterite appears on the surface over wide areas. The Afram Plains, with similar physical environmental conditions, may also on the whole have been sparsely populated, as they were in the early nineteenth century.

The presence of surface laterite in the Desert of Ghofan could have been due to human agency. Most tropical soils have sub-surface horizons of concentrations of sesquioxides. These undergo a process of irreversible crystallization and become true laterite or duricrust only when they are exposed to the atmosphere, particularly in regions of pronounced drought.[2] It would thus seem that the exposure of duricrust over large areas in what is now referred to as the Middle Belt resulted from soil erosion which would have been caused or accelerated after the vegetation cover had been removed through shifting cultivation and regular burning.

It may be assumed that in the forest of Ashanti–Brong Ahafo villages congregated around major settlements like Kumasi, Juaben, Kokofu, Mampong, and others of the newly constituted Ashanti nation, and that rural settlements became fewer with increasing distance from these regional centres. The assumption is based on the fact that rural settlements in Ashanti, as in Fantiland, were traditionally offshoots of larger primary settlements, one of whose functions was to protect the former. Consequently, it should be expected that the inhabitants of the secondary or subordinate settlements would not, in those times of frequent warfare, normally choose to live where they could not easily flee, if need be, to seek refuge with the larger settlement. It would nevertheless be an over-

[1] See below, p. 280.

[2] K. W. Butzer, *Environment and Archaeology* (London, 1964), pp. 81–2.

simplification to explain the distribution of rural settlements solely in terms of distribution of large primary or regional centres. It would be nearer reality to present a picture of a hierarchy of settlements each of which, except for those at the very bottom of the scale, was a focus for a smaller number of rural settlements, just as there was a group of intermediate Chiefs between the smallest Chief and the King of the nation.

This arrangement of rural settlements may also have applied to the forested Gyaman territory of western Brong Ahafo, which could not have had a large population except, perhaps, in the neighbourhood of trade routes. At the beginning of the eighteenth century, settlements like Odumasi and Berekum in western Brong Ahafo were new, having been founded by refugees from Doma which, situated about 5 miles north of Kumasi, was sacked by the Ashanti King Osei Tutu.[1] Similarly, Denkera, Wasaw, and Sefwi could not have been heavily settled since they engaged at the turn of the eighteenth century in a series of deadly wars with the Ashanti, in one of which—that with Denkera proper—over 130,000 men were reportedly killed, of whom 100,000 were Denkera and the rest their Akim allies.[2] Similarly, those parts of the Birim basin now the home of Akim Kotoku and Akim Bosome could not have been densely settled since they were then in the process of being colonized, unlike Akim Abuakwa which was already well colonized and was strong enough to demand a tribute from the powerful Akwamu.[3] Asin country, not having fully recovered from the shattering defeat it suffered at the hands of the Denkera, was still sparsely populated, like the present Krobo country which was then thickly forested and had not been colonized by the Krobo. In the forested part of the Volta Region rural settlements may have been more frequent in the traditionally long-settled area between Hohoe and Ho, with the arrangement of the settlements possibly following a pattern similar to that in Ashanti. Buem may have been less densely settled, and the settlements may also have decreased in frequency, as they later were, from south to north.

The existence, immediately behind the coast, of a line of larger settlements parent to the smaller ones fronting the sea is attested to by every major European work on the country written in the late seventeenth or early eighteenth century. Nevertheless it is not being argued that all the coastal settlements depended on larger parent ones in the immediate interior, since

[1] Sir Francis Fuller, *A Vanished Dynasty, Ashanti* (London, 1921), pp. 10–11. For a slightly different tradition on the founding of Berekum and other towns in western Brong Ahafo, see Meyerowitz, *The Akan Traditions of Origin* (London, 1950), pp. 121–3.

[2] Bosman, *Guinea*, Letter VI. Bosman, although he agreed that the Ashanti–Denkera war was fought on a large scale, thought the reported casualty figure was exaggerated.

[3] Ibid. Letter V.

the position was the other way round in a few cases. Little Accra or Dutch Accra, Axim, 'Coto' (Ketu?) and Anloga were examples of coastal settlements to which some villages in the immediate interior were tributary. Otherwise the majority of the coastal settlements were not the seats of paramount chiefs and therefore not the principal settlements of the kingdoms or states to which they belonged.

There is a number of possible explanations, each of limited application, for the siting, inland, of the capitals of the maritime states. Some may have been sited to exploit the natural advantages of position on the border of two contrasting types of physical environment, forest and coastal bush and grassland. Some may have been originally drawn inland as a distant response to the pull of the Western Sudan markets to which the trade of Southern Ghana was directed before the Europeans established their trading posts on the coast. Yet others may have been sited inland to avoid the danger of being driven into the sea in the event of an attack.

Information on these inland capitals of maritime states is scanty and covers only a few of them. The principal settlement of the state of Fetu (Afutu), bearing the same name, lay inland and controlled a number of coastal villages of which Cape Coast was the largest. The village of Afutu, a few miles north of Cape Coast, may be the present successor of the old capital. Fanti kingdom possessed about nine major maritime outposts including Anomabu, Egya, Kormantin and Abadze, while 'the capital town of Fantin, from which the country has its name, lies five leagues up the inland, where there are many other villages scattered about it'.[1] The kingdom of Saboe (Asebu) whose subordinate maritime settlements were Ekon and Mouri, a few miles east of Cape Coast, was ruled from the principal settlement of Asebu, lying 'about two leagues and a half up the inland, being a populous place'. There was also Eguafo, 'the metropolis of Great Commendo..., the usual residence of its king, being a large and populous village or town seated on a hill, four leagues up the inland from Little Commendo' or Akitakyi which stood on the coast. The relatively large settlement of Elmina on the coast was subordinate to Eguafo. Ladoku was also an example of the inland capitals of maritime states. It belonged to a state of the same name, and ruled a number of important coastal trading posts including Great Ningo, Lay, and Cincho.[2]

While the sub-coastal settlements were referred to vaguely by European authors, seaside settlements received much attention and were described in

[1] Barbot, *North and South Guinea*, pp. 175–6. The capital for the whole of the Fanti nation is traditionally Mankesim, probably the 'Cabes Terra' of European writers.

[2] The identity of the settlement of 'Spice', the seat of an important chief and a large market lying a few miles inland from Lay and Cincho, is not certain.

some detail. They were all clustered around or behind the European forts and castles.

The larger and more prominent of the coastal settlements included Axim, Shama, Komenda, Elmina, Cape Coast, Anomabu, Great Kormantin, and Accra. The rest of the settlements were either normally smaller than those listed or were, if formerly large, reduced by wars to an insignificant size. Winneba, for example, was normally a tiny fishing village containing perhaps not more than fifty houses, while Sekondi, formerly one of the richest and largest of the coastal settlements, was entirely destroyed in the Adom–Ahanta war which began in 1690 or 1691. 'The few slight dwellings which are here at present were built since, and others are daily building, so that ere long, it may grow to be an indifferent village; but to reinstate it in its flourishing condition requires several years.' The same was true of Takoradi which was so mercilessly routed 'that it is at present inhabited by a few inconsiderate people only'.[1]

Of the larger settlements it was, paradoxically, Axim, an important gold market that Bosman was very familiar with, which was most poorly described. Shama, containing some two hundred houses, was 'so seated as to form three small villages together'; and although its population was said to be large it was the poorest among the larger settlements on the Western Region coast. Akitakyi or Little Komenda was, like Shama, divided into three parts, containing a total of about 150 houses. Much of the village was accidentally destroyed by fire 'not long ago', with the result that part of its population migrated to nearby Ampenyi.

East of Komenda was Elmina, the seat of the Dutch Administration. Barbot described it thus:[2]

> The town is very long, containing about twelve hundred houses, all built with rock-stones, in which it differs from all other places, the houses being generally only composed of clay and wood. It is divided into several streets and lanes very irregular, crooked, and dirty in rainy weather, the ground being low and flat, and the streets and lanes close and very narrow; and more particularly, it is very dirty and sloppy at the time the river Benja (Benya) overflows and fills it with water.
>
> Most of the houses of the town are one story high, and some two, all very full of people: for they contain above six thousand fighting men, besides women and children, who are very numerous, every man generally keeping two, three, or more wives, as is usual in Guinea.
>
> The town is divided into three distinct parts, as if it were three large villages near one another[3]...it is fortified at the west end, toward the country of

[1] Bosman, Letter II.

[2] Barbot, *North and South Guinea*, p. 156.

[3] In the late fifteenth century Elmina, as well as Shama, was divided into two and not three distinct quarters. See above, p. 44.

Commendo, with a strong rock-stone wall, in which is a gate, defended by some iron guns, and a large ditch. The wall begins at the sea shore, and ends at the river side.

The description was true of normal and prosperous Elmina such as it was in the early 1680s; for around 1700 the settlement was only about one-eighth the size of what it was 'about fifteen or sixteen years past'. Its population was, after the 1680s, so reduced by an epidemic of smallpox and by the Komenda wars that hardly fifty fighting men were left. The majority of those who survived the epidemic and the wars deserted the settlement because of 'the tyranny of their governors'[1] and, it must be added, the harsh treatment they were subjected to by the Director-General J. van Sevenhuijsen, his chief factor William Bosman, and their assistants.[2] When Wilhelm de la Palma took over the reins of government from Sevenhuijsen in May 1702, he estimated the number of fighting men to be a thousand, an improvement over the figure given by Bosman but still far short of that for the early 1680s.

Cape Coast, the headquarters of the British, contained about 500 houses, divided by narrow crooked lanes, just as it was a century earlier at the time of de Marees' visit. The settlement extended inland as far as the foot of the hill on which Fort William stands and 'looked like an amphitheatre from the coast'.[3] Cape Coast was much smaller than Elmina, and the 500 houses it was supposed to contain in the early 1680s must have been heavily reduced in number during the Komenda wars. Besides, many of the inhabitants regularly joined English merchant ships sailing to Whydah in Dahomey to assist in the purchase of slaves, after which they generally remained at Whydah, presumably to pursue the profitable occupation of middleman between Dahomey slave dealers and European merchants. The effect of this, combined with the effect of the Komenda wars, was to reduce the size of Cape Coast, 'so that at present the village is half wasted, and the houses are in a ruinated condition'.[4]

The busy Dutch port and market of Mouri was described as being smaller, in physical extent, than Elmina but more populous. The village lay on rising ground behind Fort Nassau and, if Bosman's estimate that four or five hundred fishing canoes put out to sea every morning is to be depended on,[5] its population could have been between four and six thousand at least. This assumes two men to a fishing canoe, each of whom would have, at a rather conservative estimate, a family of five persons.

[1] Bosman, op. cit. Letter III.

[2] W.I.C. 97, letter dated 26 June 1702 from Director-General W. de la Palma, Elmina, to the Association of x, Amsterdam.

[3] Barbot, op. cit. p. 168.  [4] Bosman, op. cit. Letter IV.  [5] Ibid.

Anomabu was a large village. It was primarily a fishing settlement and its population, calculated on the basis of not fewer than a thousand fishermen resident there, may have exceeded six or seven thousand. The settlement was by itself capable of fielding more armed men than the whole state of Asebu or Komenda. European merchants were always impressed by the size and military strength of Anomabu. It was apparently so powerful that it was not unusual for the English governor of the fort there to have to submit to the indignity of being forcibly put aboard a canoe and paddled to Cape Coast on compulsory transfer by the people of Anomabu, if they were displeased with him. Almost as large and powerful was Great Kormantin lying on the seaward-facing slope of a low hill and important both for trade and fishing.

Accra was the blanket name for the three separate villages of Soko (or Chorkor, the name now given to a quarter of Accra about three miles west of James Fort), Little Accra and Orsaky (Osu), respectively under James Fort (English), Fort Crevecoer (Dutch, and now called Ussher Fort), and Christiansborg Castle (Danish). Accra was so severely damaged by the Akwamu in the war of 1680–1 that Little Accra, which was described before then as 'pretty handsome and commodious, being a market town well govern'd and much resorted to', was reduced to a small village of about sixty houses.[1] Osu suffered a similar fate and many of its inhabitants, as well as others from Little Accra, fled to Whydah and Fetu. Soko, which was spared by the Akwamu, also received some of the refugees; it became one of the largest and most important settlements on the whole coast, as well as a major market for the English.[2] By 1700 Little Accra and Osu were rebuilt and were enjoying a certain measure of prosperity.

### *Northern Ghana*

The pattern of rural settlement distribution in Northern Ghana around 1700 is not clear, but it was probably different from today. Settlements were, wherever possible, attracted to points of water supply, as may be seen in the case of the Red Volta whose banks, now deserted because of wars in the nineteenth century followed by the simulium fly and river blindness, are known to have been once inhabited. Another area, served by a number of streams and rivers, that is now sparsely populated but may have been more heavily settled in the early eighteenth century is that large expanse of land roughly bounded by the Nankong–Tumu–Han road in the

[1] Barbot, op. cit. p. 176.
[2] Ibid. p. 448.

north, the Han-Wa road in the west, the upper Sissili river in the east, and in the south by a line from the lower Kulpawn river to Wa.

Political and social factors also had a part to play in fashioning the general pattern of settlement and population distribution. Wars, dynastic quarrels, shortage of land—all at one time or another set into train population movements of differing magnitude. Against these were certain other social and religious observances, like the custom of living close to land in which ancestors had been buried, which made for stable settlement in some areas. Strong stable political regimes also favoured increased population and permanent settlement, and for this reason it is most probable that the core areas of Mamprusi–Dagomba and Gonja kingdoms and Wa–Lawra districts were among the more heavily settled areas.

Among the sparsely populated areas were probably north, central, and south-east Gonja, so determined on the basis of evidence that is partly botanical and partly historical. The botanical evidence derives from the recent discovery that the grass *Andropogon schirensis*, normally present in undisturbed soils but nearly always absent in areas that are or have been heavily cultivated, was abundant along the Sawla–Damongo–Yapei road while it was absent or rare in the heavily populated north-east and north-western corners of the country. The grass was also absent in the present low-population-density areas which include parts of Lawra–Tumu and Wa districts and were defined earlier as a large expanse of land bounded on the east by the upper Sissili and lower Kulpawm rivers. The inference may be that the area around the Sawla–Damongo–Yapei road in the northern part of western Gonja could not have known a large population in the recent past.[1] The area is still sparsely populated and forms part of the Middle Belt.

The historical evidence is more direct.[2] When Jakpa, blazing a trail of conquest eastward from Bole, reached Tulwe after an off-route northerly excursion to Daboya, he was informed of the existence of 'a large populous town' in front of him to the east but which he was advised not to attack for fear of ambush 'in the desert'. There water was scarce and, it may be inferred, population density low; besides, the area was ideal for guerrilla warfare, according to Jakpa's informants. Jakpa invaded and conquered the area, and built the settlement of Zugu Kolo among others. This sparsely populated area is likely to have been part of the Desert of Ghofan.

[1] R. Rose-Innes, 'An Ethno-botanical Problem', *Ghana Notes and Queries*, no. 3 (September–December 1961).

[2] Mahmoud El-Wakkad (translator), 'Qissatu Salga Tarikhu Gonja—The Story of Salaga and the History of Gonja', *Ghana Notes and Queries*, no. 3 (September–December 1961).

## Towns

Although the country's population was predominantly rural, and rural settlements were accordingly numerous, there were some settlements, including many that have already been classed as rural, which appear not to have been entirely so in characteristics and function. They belonged to two categories: state capitals, or seats of paramount chiefs, and major trading centres. Examples of settlements in the first category included Kumasi, Gambaga, Little Accra, Bole, and Yendi, to mention but a few, while to the second category belonged Anomabu, Cape Coast, Great Kormantin, Elmina, and Salaga, among others.

The state capitals were primarily administrative and cultural centres, although most of them were in addition centres of craft industry and commerce. Bearing in the Akan areas the generic name of *ahenkurow*, they were traditionally regarded as true towns; indeed some of them already stood in a special relationship with the surrounding countryside and discharged functions that were more than purely administrative or cultural. The state capitals occupied different positions in a hierarchy, according to the varying nature and importance of their extra-administrative and cultural functions. Kumasi for example must have occupied a high position in the hierarchy. Kumasi under Osei Tutu became the premier settlement and nerve centre of the powerful, tightly knit kingdom of Ashanti, as well as a major market whose sphere of influence embraced a large part of the country. Kumasi's population, which increasingly acquired a cosmopolitan nature after 1701, also included powerful merchants, nobles and captains of war who employed slaves to cultivate their country estates. Serving as a contrast was Little Accra which was itself under the rule of the king of Akwamu and was nowhere near as important as Kumasi.

Of the settlements which owed their position in the rural–urban category to their function as major trading centres, those on the coast were especially important, as they were the most effective points of contact between European merchants and local merchants from the interior. Some of them derived additional importance from their position as administrative headquarters for the Europeans. In this respect Elmina deserves special mention for serving as administrative headquarters for over two centuries, first for the Portuguese and then the Dutch. As early as 1486 it was granted the privileges of a city by a decree issued by the king of Portugal on the fifteenth of March of that year, and since then it dominated much of the life on the coast. Also deserving special mention for being perhaps the most illustrious of the major trading centres was Kpembe/Salaga, where an Arab scholar refugee from Northern Nigeria built the 'Learned Man's Compound', one of the earliest Islamic schools in the country;[1] and as an educational centre it attracted scholars from neighbouring countries. Its population was truly cosmopolitan, while its market was, by all accounts, the largest in Northern Ghana and the principal resort of kola nut merchants.

[1] See footnote 2 on p. 69.

# 4. William Bosman's Gold Coast: primary and secondary occupations

## PRIMARY ECONOMIC ACTIVITIES

From the point of view of primary occupation, the population of Ghana was grouped into seven classes engaged in collecting, farming, livestock rearing, fishing, hunting, salt making, and gold mining. The divisions were by no means strict, as it was normal for an individual or a community to be engaged in more than one occupation.

### Collecting

The collecting economy, based on the immense variety of wild food and other plants that grew in the surrounding vegetation and closely supplementing cultivation, was never practised entirely on its own. While contemporary written sources are generally uninformative on this mode of living, relics of it in present-day life and oral traditions testify to its importance in the past.

Each of the two great vegetation formations, of savanna and forest, had its characteristic wild food plant resources. In the savanna of Northern Ghana some of the more important wild trees, from the point of view of food collecting, were shea butter (*Butyrospermum parkii*), baobab (*Adansonia digitata*), tamarind (*Tamarindus indica*), and dawa dawa (*Parkia* sp.). Shea butter is a vegetable fat with many uses other than that of serving as food. It is especially useful in the excessively dry harmattan season, when it prevents the skin from cracking; it could also be used as a base for soap and mixed with earth for building. The leaves and fruits of the baobab were just as useful for food, while the fruits of the tamarind tree could, in addition, be used to make food preserves. There were diverse other wild plants that made significant contributions to the diet, and among these were plants from which salt could be extracted and others which became the mainstay of the population in times of famine.

There was also a variety of wild food plants in the forest. The two best known were the kola nut and oil palm (*Elaeis guineensis*) trees. The kola nut fruit, of which the commoner variety in the country was *Kola nitida*, was highly prized, particularly in Northern Ghana and the savanna areas of

West Africa as a whole; it was, besides, in great demand in the Sahara and the Maghreb. The fruit is a stimulant which sustains energetic effort and reduces thirst for water, hence the great demand for it in the drier areas of West Africa and the Sahara. Bosman, after commenting on the wide popularity of the fruit in Southern Ghana, added that its admirers 'pretend it helps to relish the palm wine'.[1]

The oil-palm tree, which is to be found in abundance in the forest as well as in the coastal bush, enjoyed an immense local popularity. Its fruit consists of a hard kernel clothed in a red fleshy pericarp from which palm oil, the basis of much of the local diet, is obtained. From the kernel too the equally popular palm kernel oil is derived which, like palm oil, can be put to many uses other than for cooking. Although the oil-palm tree was highly useful because of the oils derived from its fruit and because of the multifarious uses to which parts of the tree itself could be put, its popularity also undoubtedly depended, to a considerable extent, on the fact that palm wine could be drawn from it. Bosman devoted long passages to this aspect of the use of the oil-palm tree, and his description of the method by which the wine was drawn is remarkably modern:

> To obtain and draw off (palm wine), when the trees are old enough to be cut, they are bereft of all their branches, and rendered entirely bare; in which condition having remained a few days, a little hole is bored in the thickest part of the trunk, into which is inserted a small reeden pipe; and through that the palm wine drops into a pot set under to receive it, but it distils so slowly that in twenty-four hours scarce a bottle of wine issues from one tree. In this manner, proportionable to the goodness of the ground in which the tree is planted, it yields wine for twenty, thirty, or sometimes more days; and when it hath almost run its last, they kindle a fire at bottom, in order to draw more wine with the greater force...

Four types of palm wine were recognized. The first was the common sort produced everywhere and not commanding any special value. The second type was produced in Fantiland only, with Anomabu as the chief producer. It was called Quaker 'from its extraordinary exhilarating qualities, which are experienced by those who take large draughts of it; it is sold at double the price of the common sort, and so greedily bought up that there is seldom enough for the demand'. The third type, produced mostly in Axim and Ahanta districts, went by the name of 'Pardon'—'so that you may easily believe no villainy here can be committed so great, but that pardon is easily obtainable, if the person be in good braces of the god Bacchus!' The fourth and last type, manufactured mainly in Ahanta, Jabi, and Adom, was named 'Crissia'; its alcoholic content was the lowest. The immense popularity of palm wine of whatever kind must have resulted in

[1] Bosman, *Guinea*, Letter xv.

large-scale destruction of oil-palm trees, for which natural regeneration could not have compensated.

In addition to the kola nut and oil-palm trees were a host of other fruit trees that constituted important food resources. Among them was the coconut tree (*Cocos nucifera*) which, apart from the few that were cultivated in gardens attached to the castles, grew spontaneously from one end of the coast to the other. The tree itself could be put to a variety of uses, while its fruit was justly famous for the refreshing liquid and soft flesh it contains. Still more widespread were citrus fruit trees which grew in a wild or semi-wild state.

The list of useful wild plant resources given above is obviously incomplete. No mention has been made for example of edible herbs or of that important class of non-edible plants collected for other purposes: for example cotton (sometimes cultivated) for cloth weaving, and gourd (*Lagenaria siceraria*) which in various shapes served as domestic utensils.[1]

## Agriculture

It is true that agricultural products had no place in the country's overseas trade, except in so far as they were purchased for slave ships on their way to the New World; but their significance for the local economy was considerable. The bulk of internal trade appears to have been in agricultural products. Two systems of agriculture should be distinguished: European and local peasant agriculture. They differed in scale of operation and in the range of crops cultivated.

With the exception of the savannas of Northern Ghana and the south-east coastal plains which may have been more wooded, the physical environment in which agriculture was practised was in no way different from that of the present. The nature and distribution of temperature and rainfall in the coastal areas, for example, as described for the early eighteenth century were exactly the same as now.[2]

Almost every European castle on the coast owned a 'kitchen garden', not necessarily close to the castle, in which both local and temperate food crops were cultivated. Some of the gardens were fairly large and well laid out, including shaded avenues, as prints and drawings of the castles show.

[1] J. M. Dalziel, *The Useful Plants of West Tropical Africa* (London, 1955); T. F. Chipp, *The Forest Officers' Handbook of the Gold Coast, Ashanti and the Northern Territories* (London, 1922), pp. 55 ff.; F. R. Irvine, 'The Indigenous Food Plants of West African Peoples', *J. N. Y. Bot. Gdn.* XLIX, nos. 586–7 (1948). These works give fairly complete lists of the country's wild plant resources, with accounts of their uses.

[2] Bosman, op. cit. Letter VIII.

Although the epithet 'kitchen' was applied to the gardens or food farms, their importance transcended their primary function of supplying the castles with foodstuffs. They served also as experimental agricultural stations in which exotic and local crops were cultivated under careful management, and from which crops new to the country occasionally 'escaped' from the strict confines of the farms to the surrounding countryside. 'Kitchen gardens' may indeed have been the parent nurseries from which some of the crops of foreign origin that are now important in the country's economy eventually reached the countryside. It is not certain in all cases that the Europeans deliberately sought to introduce the new crops into the local agricultural economy, but the employment of slaves and free men drawn from the local population must in itself have ensured the diffusion of the new crops.

The Dutch owned many of the larger food farms on the coast, including probably the two largest at Elmina and Mouri. In these two places a greater range of crops was experimented with and on a larger scale than was done elsewhere, and the results of the experiments must no doubt have guided the selection of crops for cultivation in other castle food farms. It became apparent, for example, that pomegranates would not succeed on the coast, as a result of several trials at Elmina and Mouri where the crop always rotted on reaching maturity. Through similar trials it was discovered that 'Mourese vine', originally introduced by the Portuguese from Brazil, would apparently flourish in Mouri and nowhere else; and if the harvest from the crop at Mouri was poor, it was because of bad pruning by the unskilful hands of the slave in charge of the farm.[1]

Besides producing food for immediate consumption in the castles, the Dutch laid out plantations to produce for export. The introduction of plantation agriculture was not the work of interested individuals but rather the result of a deliberate Dutch government policy to broaden the range of their economic activities in the country. As far back as 1689 plans were formulated for the establishment of sugar cane, tobacco, indigo, and cotton plantations on the Pra river near Shama.[2] Of these it was the cotton plantations which apparently had the greatest success and more of which were established at Axim, Butri, Sekondi, and Elmina. Small quantities of cotton were being regularly exported to Holland by 1700; and to facilitate the process of separating the lint from the seeds, a certain negro from Curaçao, named Pieter, set up a cotton gin at Elmina in 1703.[3] Nevertheless the

[1] Bosman, op cit. Letter XVI.
[2] W.I.C. 54, letter from Elmina dated 15 November 1689.
[3] W.I.C. 484, letter from Elmina dated 10 October 1703.

possibility of raising crops other than cotton was not ignored, so that by 1700 the Dutch had successfully established at Mouri a lime plantation with a factory for extracting lime juice, two hundred ammen of which were exported annually to Holland.[1] A project suggested in 1703 by the English official William Cole to the Royal African Company to make a sugar cane, ginger, or cotton plantation behind Winneba did not materialize.[2]

Important as the European plantations and food farms were as forerunners of commercial agriculture in the country, their contribution to the country's total agricultural production in the time of Bosman was insignificant; neither did their products feature in the country's internal trade. Furthermore, their usefulness from the point of view of the subsequent development of commercial agriculture in the country was limited by the fact that they were not primarily intended to demonstrate to the local farmers the possibilities of that mode of farming.[3]

For the peasant agriculture, the land tenure system and farming practices were different. The Akan concept of land tenure in the time of Bosman was apparently different from what it was in the nineteenth and early twentieth centuries, the major difference being the tight control over land exercised by chiefs of the earlier period. In any political division the chief held all the land in his power, and no commoner could own land absolutely. Neither could farmers clear a piece of land and sow on it without the consent of the chief. All farmers were customarily obliged to cultivate, communally, the chief's land before they could work on their own, and part of the income from the sale of harvest from individual farms was compulsorily paid to the chief as farm rent. This system of land tenure was originally described for the coastal areas; but it probably also applied to Ashanti, though not necessarily to Northern Ghana where religious, rather than political, authorities exercised a more relaxed control over the land and made its acquisition by strangers comparatively easy.

Bush fallowing was the system of cultivation practised. This is a rotation of farm and bush whereby a piece of land is cultivated continuously for three or four years, depending on the inherent fertility of the soil, and then left in fallow for a length of time determined mainly by the pressure of population on the land, so that it would be recolonized by bush and eventually regain its lost fertility. A fresh plot of land is meanwhile chosen for cultivation. True shifting cultivation was practised in Northern Ghana mainly.

The usual implements for cultivation were the cutlass and the hoe. The

[1] Bosman, *Guinea*, Letter XVI. An aam was a liquid measure of from 37 to 41 gallons.
[2] T70/13, Letter from Winneba dated 27 July 1703 (Public Record Office, London).
[3] J. S. G. Gramberg, *Schetsen van Afrika's Westkust* (Amsterdam, 1861), pp. 31 ff.

plough was unknown; nor were animals used for farm work or integrated into the farming economy. All farm work was done communally and without any monetary reward, except that the host farmer was expected to provide food and drink for all during the period of work on his farm. Preparation of the land for sowing began with the burning of the bush, after which the charred bushes were slashed with cutlasses and thrown, together with tree trunks, into a broad heap about a foot or so high in the middle of the farm, and covered with earth. The heap was left on the farm for eight to ten days, during which the wood in it burned slowly to be converted to charcoal. It appears the land was not completely denuded of its vegetation cover, and mixed cropping was sometimes practised together with periodic monoculture, under which the type of crop grown depended on the season of the year. After the crop was sown, little else was done on the farm until the crop ripened; then a wooden platform was erected in the middle of the farm and children sat on it in the daytime to scare off birds.

Agricultural labour was not drawn from all sections of the community. The population was socially stratified according to a strict pattern, with paramount chiefs and others of like status belonging to the topmost rank, followed by *caboceros* or elders who advised the chief, guarded the community's welfare, and generally ensured peace in the community. Next were those who had 'acquired a great reputation by their riches, either devolved on them by their inheritance or gotten by trade'. The next rank lower down consisted of the common people who formed the bulk of the population. Slaves, at the bottom of the social ladder, were persons captured in war (*donko*), sold or mortgaged by their relations, or seized in payment for a debt (domestic slaves). It was the common people and the slaves who were engaged in cultivation and other forms of manual labour. Those higher up in the social hierarchy and some of the common people themselves owned slaves who did the farm work for them. Also forming a significant portion of the agricultural labour force were women, whatever their social status.[1]

Definite times were set aside for the various processes of agriculture, and these were determined by the seasonal distribution of rainfall and by religious beliefs. Farms were normally prepared for sowing in the dry season, while harvesting was staggered over a long period because of the different dates at which the different crops on the farms matured. There were, on the other hand, certain days on which neither farming nor any other economic activity was permitted. The days of the year were divided into major and minor lucky or unlucky days, according

[1] Bosman, op. cit. Letter IX.

to age-old religious beliefs. Work was permitted only on a lucky day, while an unlucky day was 'a sort of vacation to them, for then they do not travel, till their land or undertake anything of consequence, but remain altogether idle'. With some of the tribes the major lucky time extended over nineteen continuous days, while the minor lucky days numbered seven. Between these two periods were seven unlucky days. Even within the lucky period no agricultural work was permitted on days considered to be sacred to Mother Earth. Regional variations existed in the incidence and number of lucky or unlucky days, and at the limit were the coastal areas where all days were regarded alike and no distinction made between lucky or unlucky times.[1]

The agricultural landscape presented a rich variety of food crops and other valuable plants, some of which have now gone out of cultivation because of the introduction later of other varieties. The lists of cultivated plants given by Bosman and others, and discussed below, are clearly abbreviated, since the Europeans necessarily confined their excursions to the coastal areas and did not, therefore, know much about useful plants cultivated in Ashanti and beyond.

The term 'corn' is used here, as it was by Bosman, to include maize, millet (*Pannisetum cinerum*), and guinea corn (*Sorghum guineense*). Of the three, millet and guinea corn were the older and more popular, especially in the drier south-eastern coastal plains; maize appears to have been more important in the wetter western sections of the coast, except at Axim. The cereals were harvested twice a year with the first and major harvest generally in August and the second towards the end of the year. This regime applied to the coastal areas with their two rainfall maxima and not to Northern Ghana where the single rainfall maximum made for a single harvest. The quantity of corn sown or harvested depended, among other factors, on the political condition of the country.

Corn was cultivated along the whole coast but least of all at Axim where the ground was too wet on account of the regular heavy rainfall. In the forest country as a whole corn was hardly cultivated, except perhaps in Volta Region where immigrants from coastal lands further east may have brought with them the knowledge of its cultivation. In these inland areas it was guinea corn and not maize that was cultivated. Similarly in the savannas of Northern Ghana only millet and guinea corn, the traditional cereals, were cultivated.

One of the largest corn-producing areas on the coast was the stretch of land between Dixcove and about Komenda, and within this area the lands around Dixcove yielded exceptionally large harvests. The country around

[1] Bosman, *Guinea*, Letter x.

Elmina was, and had long been, a poor agricultural area, contrary to the boast of the Portuguese that it was the most fertile and most heavily cultivated of all the coastal areas. The Portuguese maintained the illusion by importing large quantities of foodstuffs from Axim and elsewhere and selling them to other European trading ships at Elmina.[1]

East of Elmina was the land of Fetu, given over to cultivation and another important producer of corn. But by about 1700 production was greatly diminished as a result of the partial depopulation of the land and destruction of farms which occurred during the wars with Komenda. Saboe or Asebu was likewise a well-cultivated country producing corn in abundance. Fantiland was probably the greatest producer of corn on the whole coast. not because of more favourable climatic or soil conditions, but probably owing to the fact that it possessed a relatively large population most of which was engaged in cultivation. A contributory factor was that its inland neighbours were apparently not so devoted to agriculture and consequently depended on Fantiland to some extent for food supplies. East of Fantiland, corn was generally produced in smaller quantities along the rest of the coast.

Rice was next to corn in importance as a food crop on the coast and in Northern Ghana. On the coast both the indigenous (*Oryza glaberrima*) and foreign (*O. sativa*) varieties were to be found, while only the indigenous variety, with perhaps acha or 'hungry rice' (*Digitaria exilis*), was cultivated in Northern Ghana. Axim and Ahanta, with their wet soils, heavy rainfall and high annual temperatures, were regarded as the sole producers of the cereal; but it is also likely that the land around the lower end of the Volta, periodically flooded by the river, was another important producer of the cereal.[2]

Two of the most important tubers were yam and sweet potato which were cultivated everywhere except in the grasslands of Northern Ghana. On the coast, except around Axim where neither climatic nor soil conditions were favourable for their cultivation, both yams and sweet potatoes were widely grown, with Mouri in the land of Saboe probably excelling in their production. The crops were also important in the agricultural economies of the Fanti and Ahanta areas. Cocoyam (*Colocasia esculentum*) was another important tuber. It was a traditional crop and was probably cultivated extensively in the forest.[3]

[1] Barbot, *North and South Guinea*, p. 159.

[2] It was certainly an established rice-growing area by the early 1780s. P. E. Isert, *Voyages en Guinée* (Paris, 1793), p. 105.

[3] Among the early references to the crop was that by Isert, who noticed its cultivation in Akwapim in 1783 and wrote that both the tuber and the leaves were regarded as food (op. cit. p. 263).

It is significant that Bosman did not mention one tuber crop that is now extremely popular along the coast and in the forest region—cassava. Neither did Barbot, who devoted long passages to the description and cultivation of other crops, write anything about it, although he printed a diagram which he labelled 'mangnoc', presumably manioc.[1] As evidence for the presence of cassava, the diagram by itself is unconvincing.[2] The tiger nut (*Cyperus esculenta*) was cultivated, as becomes evident from Bosman's careful description of the crop.

Plantains and bananas are forest crops and were widely cultivated behind the whole length of the coast. Plantain constituted a major item of diet in the forest, just as corn was the major food on the coast and in Northern Ghana. The distribution of plantains and bananas would have depended on the distribution of the rural population. Besides plantains and bananas there was a host of other fruits grown more or less extensively throughout the country. These included pineapples, 'Cormantyn apple' which was 'as big as a walnut, with its green hulk on; its rind is yellow, somewhat inclining to red: in the core are four large, flat, black kernels, which are surrounded by the pulp or the fruit itself; which is red and white, and of a sort of sharp, sweet taste, but most inclining to acid.'[3] Other fruits were pawpaws and water melons, some of which may have existed in a wild state.

Only a few vegetables and condiments were noted and described. In the pulse group, Angola beans, originally introduced by the Portuguese, were common. So were 'jojootjes' (unidentified) and 'gobbe-gobbes' which 'grow together in a cod under the earth, and shoot out a small leaf above the surface of the earth'. The crop referred to as 'gobbe-gobbes' was obviously the groundnut. There could have been other pulses like the Bambara bean, now cultivated mostly in Northern Ghana, and geocarpa bean, also a savanna crop.

Other vegetables must have included okro (*Hibiscus esculentus*), onion, and the garden egg plant, all of which now have a wide distribution in the forest and coastal areas. Okro is also known and cultivated in Northern Ghana. It would seem that the tomato, a crop of New World provenance, was absent, for there was no mention or description of it anywhere. Among the condiments and indulgents were red pepper, of which two varieties were known, and malaguetta pepper, also known as grain of paradise or guinea grain, which was by far the more popular from the point of view of

[1] Barbot, op. cit. p. 200.

[2] C. D. Adams does not prove his contention that cassava was generally cultivated on the Ghana coast as far back as the mid-seventeenth century. See his 'Activities of Danish Botanists in Guinea, 1783–1850', *Trans. Hist. Soc. Ghana*, II, 1 (1957).

[3] Bosman, op. cit. Letter XVI.

overseas trade. Its cultivation was widespread in the coastal areas. Sugar cane was also popular and seemed to flourish most at Axim and, from later evidence, in the flood plain of the Volta.[1] Tobacco, probably *Nicotina rustica*, was a highly popular indulgent or stimulant, and was consequently grown in large quantities almost throughout the whole country. Another type of tobacco, called tarragon, was also ubiquitous though not so highly prized as the former.

## Livestock rearing

This was in general a subsidiary occupation to farming, except possibly in parts of Northern Ghana where it may have existed as a separate occupation. In addition to poultry, the most important domesticated animals were cattle, sheep, goats, pigs, horses, asses, and dogs. Horses and asses, kept more as a means of transport than as beasts of burden, were confined to the tsetse-free areas of Northern Ghana, and attempts at keeping the animals on the coast failed as they did not survive for long. Such local horses as were seen by Europeans were described as poor specimens: 'They are very ill-shaped, their heads and necks, which they always carry downwards, are very like those of an ass; they go as if they were falling;...they are so very low, that a tall man, sitting upon their backs, may very near touch the ground with his feet'.[2] Surprisingly, asses were described as being taller and in much better physical shape than horses.

The remaining livestock, although ubiquitous, except pigs which were absent in the few Moslem areas in Northern Ghana, were found in greater concentrations in some parts of the country; they were apparently more numerous on the coast, from about Dixcove to the Togo border, than in the forest country. On the coast itself there were higher concentrations in Ahanta, Adom, around Elmina and in the Accra Plains. The cattle, generally diminutive in size and weighing not more than 250 lb when adult, probably belonged to the *Bos brachyceros* breed, although it is possible that some cattle of a different breed originally introduced by the Portuguese also existed. Leaving out Northern Ghana and some of the European castles where the animals were milked as well, cattle rearing was solely for the supply of beef. This is not to argue that Northern Ghana necessarily possessed a different breed of cattle, although this might have been the case with respect to the castles, for the cattle characteristically yielded so little milk that at Elmina it needed twenty or thirty of them to produce enough for

[1] Isert, op. cit. p. 60.

[2] Bosman, Letter XIV. It contains the rest of the account of livestock rearing.

the Director-General's table. *Bos brachyceros* cattle are notoriously poor yielders of milk.

Sheep, goats, and pigs were also poor specimens, excluding those kept on the European farms; earlier introductions of superior breeds by the Portuguese were too insignificant numerically to effect any improvements in the local breed. Typically the local pigs, for example, 'were worth nothing: the flesh is so floggy and the bacon so sorry; but those which we fatten ourselves may pass for tolerable ones...' Nevertheless the rearing of the animals was an important occupation. Far more popular than sheep, goats or pigs in the coastal areas and perhaps in other parts of the country as well was the dog, whose flesh was regarded as a delicacy and accordingly commanded a high price in the local markets.

Chickens were also bred throughout the country, not in special farms but in the homes where they were normally allowed to scrounge for food for themselves. Their numbers increased in times of peace but decreased sharply in wartime, since it was common practice for soldiers to seize chickens, wherever they found them, for food. It would appear that turkeys, now such important poultry animals in the country, were absent except the few that were kept in the castle farms, while ducks, introduced not long before Bosman's time, were poorly represented.

## Fishing

The major primary economic activity on the coast was sea fishing, but not in the Gã settlements where agriculture was the traditional occupation and was, until recently, given more attention than sea fishing.[1] On the coast between Kpone and the Volta sea fishing was also relatively unimportant, the reason apparently being that the beach was not easily accessible because of its steep seaward slope and the high ground backing it.[2] But there lagoon and river fishing abundantly compensated for the difficulties of sea fishing. There was also a great deal of fishing in lagoons and rivers elsewhere on the coast.

In the inland areas the rivers and Lake Busumtwe were traditional fishing grounds. Fishing in the Afram river, for example, was for centuries one of the major props of Guan occupation in the Afram Plains. Although there were no contemporary accounts of fishing methods employed inland, it would not be far wrong to suggest that methods employed in the twentieth century and generally regarded as being traditional did not differ sub-

[1] M. J. Field, *Religion and Medicine of the Gã people* (O.U.P., 1937), p. 88.

[2] Bosman, op. cit. Letter XVII.

stantially, except in degree of sophistication, from those of about 1700. In other words fishing may have been done in the inland rivers with canoes, harpoons, small cast nets, and hook and line. Also the fish may have been caught in basket traps or behind small temporary dams built across rivers. These methods were definitely employed in the coastal lagoons.[1]

In the coastal areas also inshore fishing, especially in the night, was common practice. It involved the use of a wooden torch, fuelled with palm oil, and a basket cage or trap with an open top. The torch was held in one hand with the fishing instrument in the other, and when the fish came close to where the fisherman stood the cage was quickly dropped over them. The fish were then picked up by hand and skewered on a sharp stick. Bream was generally caught in this way.

Of far greater importance was pelagic sea fishing in which a large percentage of the coastal population was employed. At Elmina, for example, fishing was almost the sole primary occupation, and it was not unusual for 500 to 600 fishing canoes, each typically seating not more than three men, to put out to sea in one morning.[2] The Elmina indeed continued their fishing operations outside their immediate territorial waters, and there was hardly a coastal settlement which did not accommodate a colony of Elmina fishermen. The colony at Anomabu appears to have been particularly large; consequently the Anomabu, who themselves were fishermen of repute, could boast of a daily fishing fleet of about 800 two- or three-seater canoes. Fishing was carried on throughout the week, except on a particular day set aside for religious reasons. This was normally a Tuesday, but sometimes a Friday, as in Ahanta.

In pelagic sea fishing various methods of catching fish were known and used singly or in combination at different times of the year. Between January and March, small fish were caught with hook and line which trailed through the sea as the canoe was paddled along. The cords to which the baited hooks were attached were often of local manufacture. In April and May surface-swimming fish like the ray were harpooned with a many-pronged spear. July and August were the herring months, and fishing was by means of hook and line with a lead sinker. The line, about 48 feet long and with one end of it wrapped round the shoulder, was not trailed through the water: rather its baited end was quickly dropped into the water where a shoal of fish had gathered and just as quickly pulled up again with fish attached to the hooks. September was the season for mackerel fishing, also

[1] Barbot, *North and South Guinea*, pp. 266 ff. From this is derived the rest of the account of fishing.

[2] Bosman, *Guinea*, Letter III.

done with hook and line. An additional feature was the use of floats consisting of strips of wood strung together and with cow bells attached to the ends. The ringing of the bells with the movement of the sea was believed to attract fish. In October and November large fishing nets, over 100 feet long and sometimes made from tree bast, were used together with the hook and line. The nets, left in the sea the previous evening with large stones attached to the corners to keep them in place, were visited in the morning and the fish that were entangled in the meshes removed. The nets were then brought back to dry on the beach. While the nets were in the sea their positions were marked by long sticks tied to the anchor stones and showing above the water. Large draw nets were also used in that season. December saw a variation of the hook-and-line method. The bait was a piece of sugar cane, and the other end of the long line was tied to the fisherman's head. The canoe was then rowed rapidly with the bait trailing through the water, and if a fish was hooked the tension in the line was felt on the forehead upon which the line was quickly pulled in.

From all accounts of the industry, the quantity and variety of fish caught throughout the year must have been enormous, particularly in the states of Fanti, Asebu, Fetu and Komenda. It was for this reason that the Dutch imposed the stiff irksome tax, amounting to one-fifth of the catch, in Mouri, Elmina, Shama, and Axim, where their power was very much felt. The Dutch believed that the fishing industry in those settlements was strong enough to withstand a tax of that magnitude. Everywhere also chiefs received often as much as one-third of the catch in the form of tax.[1]

## Hunting

The significance of hunting, to which must be added snail collecting in the forest, to local economies was as great as that of either agriculture or fishing. Even in the 1780s the only articles the Akwapim could sell at Accra were products of the chase.[2] Although all sections of the working population, except perhaps the coastal fishermen, practised a certain amount of hunting in addition to their regular occupations, there existed in almost every settlement a group of professionals solely dedicated to hunting. The occupation was widespread, for game abounded everywhere in the forest, the savannas of Northern Ghana, and in the coastal bush and grassland.

Where European goods freely circulated, as in Southern Ghana and

[1] Villault, *A Relation...*, p. 221.

[2] Isert, op. cit. pp. 259–60. The rest of the section on hunting is based on Bosman, op. cit. Letter XIV.

parts of Ashanti, the hunter used the long muzzle-loading gun; otherwise bows and iron-tipped arrows and spears constituted the principal weapons for the chase. Numerous devices for trapping animals were additionally used—cage traps, concealed holes, etc. The hunter's traditional companion was the dog which not only helped to spring game but also warned the hunter of impending danger. Tradition is full of accounts in which dogs were made to sample first strange food or waters of unknown rivers in order to test their safety for human consumption.

Animals regarded as game fell into three groups. Some were mainly for food; some were killed off principally because of their high nuisance value; and yet others, sometimes inedible, were hunted because of the high value placed on their products. The division was not hard and fast, for a single animal could at once belong to the three groups. The elephant, for example, was a pest which destroyed farms and often settlements, and therefore had to be destroyed; at the same time its ivory tusk was a highly prized object of trade, while its flesh was an abundant source of food. Elephants were ubiquitous, but tended to congregate in thinly populated areas. The coastal lands between Accra and Dixcove had relatively few elephants because of the long period of settlement there, the only temporary exception around 1700 being the land of Fetu which was laid waste and depopulated in the Komenda wars of the 1690s. Around 1700 the animals were not an uncommon sight in the European gardens at Elmina.

Animals such as deer, wild buffalo, wild hog, cutting grass, and the crocodile, most of them countrywide in their distribution, were considered to be great delicacies and were consequently hunted mainly for food. On the other hand wild cats, tigers, civet cats, wild dogs, etc. were destroyed because of the harm they did to man and property, although tiger skins also commanded a high scarcity value in the local markets. With the exception of elephants, the farm pests with the greatest economic significance were the ubiquitous wild apes and monkeys. 'Every stalk of millet they pluck is narrowly examined; and if they don't like it, they throw it away and pull another: so that this delicacy of theirs (the Africans) occasions more damage than their (own) thievery.'[1]

## Salt extraction

Salt was either mined or extracted from sea water. The major source of rock salt was Daboya, while the coastal areas were naturally responsible for producing the other type. At Daboya are a large number of saline 'soaks',

[1] Bosman, op. cit. Letter XIV.

and the method of extracting the salt may have been the same as that in use at the present. The salt-impregnated soil is scraped into containers, mixed with water and boiled till all the water evaporates and salt crystals are left. Ashanti and the forest country in general had no local sources of salt and accordingly purchased large quantities of the commodity from elsewhere.

On the coast practically every settlement had its salt works, but certain areas stood out as major centres of production, among which were Ada, Anomabu, Mouri and Elmina. The salt works at Ada were probably rather large and especially important since there were few profitable alternative occupations other than fishing in the Volta and neighbouring creeks.[1]

Salt was extracted from sea water in several ways:[2]

> Some boil the salt water so long in coppers till it come to salt; but as this is the most tedious, so it is not the most profitable way, and is practised only where the land is so high that the sea or salt rivers cannot probably flow over them: but at other places, where the sea or river water frequently overflows, they dig deep pits to receive the mentioned overflowing water; after which the freshest and finest part of the water is dried up by the scorching heat of the sun...
>
> In other places they have salt pans, where the sun dries up the water, so that the trouble of boiling is unnecessary; no pains being required except that only of gathering it out of the mentioned pans.
>
> Those who are either unable or unwilling to buy copper-boilers, or when the sea water requires such tedious boiling as would burn them; these, I say, use earthen pots, which they set ten to twelve next another; thus making two rows, being all cemented together with clay as if they had been done by a brick layer; and under the mentioned pots is something like a furnace of fire, which is continually supplied with wood. This is the most laborious way and produces neither so much salt, nor so much expedition as the other.

Examples of places where sea water was boiled for salt were Little Accra and, very likely, Sekondi and Takoradi, judging by the coastal topography as it was at the beginning of the eighteenth century. Ada's salt industry typified the process whereby sea water was exposed to evaporation in pits specially dug to contain it; while evaporation from salt pans was the normal method employed at such places as Elmina, Cape Coast, Winneba, and Osu. At the last place a great deal of salt was also made by the Danes. The dry season from January to March was the period for making salt through the evaporation process.[3]

The quality of the salt extracted from sea water was fairly high. Ada's

[1] Isert, *Voyages en Guinée*, p. 66. Isert's detailed account of the salt industry at Ada in 1784 echoed earlier but less detailed accounts. 'To each house at Ada', wrote Isert, 'were attached huts each of which could store at least fifty tons of pure salt.'

[2] Bosman, op. cit. Letter XVI.

[3] Villault, *A Relation*..., pp. 263–4.

salt was 'in no way inferior to that from Spain',[1] and on all parts of the coast, except at Accra, the salt was very white, but more so in Fantiland where, Bosman enthused, it almost excelled even snow.[2] Salt from Daboya was not as white as sea salt, but kept its properties much longer than the former which, under exposure to heat and damp, soon lost its freshness and savour.[3]

## Gold mining[4]

Gold occurs or is derived ultimately from Birimian rocks which cover about one-third of the land surface of Southern Ghana and Ashanti–Brong Ahafo. The rocks are also found in a few patches on the outer western and northern margins of the Volta Basin. From ancient times until about the 1870s gold was won, not directly from Birimian rocks since the necessary techniques for separating the metal from the hard ore were unknown, but from three geological formations all of which were closely related to the Birimian. These were alluvium from beds of rivers flowing on the Birimian; coastal sands, mostly between Apam and Axim, impregnated with particles of gold brought down, generally after rain, by running water from Birimian rocks; and, lastly, alluvial deposits, sometimes covered by a lateritic crust, occurring on the gentle slopes of old valleys of rivers flowing in Birimian terrain.

Panning, normally the work of women, was the principal means of winning gold from the loose alluvium and the coastal sands. The alluvium was worked throughout the year, in contrast to the coastal sands which were panned normally only after a heavy shower. The coastal sands besides yielded only small quantities of gold, a day's winnings often worth not more than sixpence,[5] while the recent river alluvium repaid efforts with more gold.

Most of the country's gold supplies came from mines sunk into the ancient alluvium. The first and major part of the mining operations was to break through the hard lateritic crust, after which the compacted alluvium underneath was easily dug out with simple hand tools. Baskets lowered into the mine brought to the surface the gold-impregnated earth, which was then crushed and panned. A mineshaft was narrow enough for a man to rest his back against one wall while his feet rested in niches cut into the opposite wall; and a number of shafts grouped together in an area were often inter-

[1] Isert, op. cit. p. 66.
[2] Bosman, op. cit. Letter XVI.
[3] Villault, op. cit. pp. 263–4.
[4] Bosman, op. cit. Letter VI.
[5] Sixpence as it was worth around 1702.

connected by subterranean tunnels. The depth of a mine depended on the height of the water table, as there was no means of pumping out water; and on the degree of consolidation of the alluvium. The gold won was of two types: pure gold dust and gold nuggets or rock gold. Gold dust commanded a high price in Europe; lumps of rock gold, some of which reportedly weighed as much as 200 'guineas', on the other hand fetched a comparatively low price because of the high proportion of their weight taken by useless rock.

Gold production was entirely in the hands of the local people who jealously guarded the secret of the locations of the mines. Attempts by Europeans to collect information on the mines failed, and where Europeans found gold-bearing deposits on the coast, the localities were invariably declared sacred by the indigenes in order to prevent mining by the Europeans. Failure on the part of the Europeans to observe the religious taboo always ended in serious trouble. In 1694, for example, the Dutch brought out geologists from Europe who began prospecting for gold in a hill regarded locally as sacred, about half a mile above Fort Vredenburgh in Komenda. This started a serious war between the Dutch and the people of Komenda. Again, an Englishman, Joseph Baggs, in the service of the African Company, imported mining equipment with which he planned to extract gold from Manku Hill about four miles west of Winneba. His plans came to a premature end with his death in 1700, but Joseph Baggs would have brought swift retribution upon himself from the people of Agona, had he been able to pursue the project.[1]

Gold mining was in many cases a state-controlled enterprise, and restrictions imposed on foreigners by chiefs and priests also applied to the common people whose deep sense of religion prevented them from mining in consecrated places. Frequent collapse of mines added substance to the warnings of priests against desecrating holy places. Only slaves and authorized free men worked in the mines. Where gold mines were not directly owned by the state, the owners were obliged to pay heavy taxes, often amounting to as much as half the total production, to the chiefs.[2] It is possible that in Ashanti the strict control traditionally exercised by the king on the production and sale of gold was already in operation. The king of Ashanti may also have controlled the industry in Denkera and other conquered territories, just as on his orders production in subject Akim was drastically reduced and practically brought to a standstill in the 1780s.[3]

Southern Ghana and Ashanti–Brong Ahafo produced the greatest part

[1] Bosman was certain of this, and recommended Mr Baggs' successor to bear that in mind.

[2] Barbot, op. cit. p. 230.

[3] Isert, op. cit. p. 217.

of the country's gold.[1] The important producers included Ashanti, Kwahu Tafo, Akim, Adansi (Bosman's Ananse), and Denkera which, before its destruction by the Ashanti, included the major gold area of Aowin, and the less important areas of Wasaw, Encasse, and Twifu. Other minor gold-producing states were Egwira, Adom, Abocroe, and Ankobra. The reputation of Asin (Accany) as a producer of gold stemmed from the fact that for a long time before the close of the seventeenth century gold from Ashanti and Akim reached the coast through Asin intermediaries. Asin itself did not produce much gold. After the battle of Feyiase gold from Ashanti reached the coast in ever larger quantities while Adansi, freed from the tyranny of Denkera domination, also recovered its position as a major producer of gold. The rich gold deposits at Obuasi were already being made to yield their treasures in the seventeenth century.[2] Indeed the old trade route from Begho to Elmina passed through Adansi, doubtless because of the latter's gold resources. The Akim also produced enormous quantities of gold almost all of which was exported through Accra.

## SECONDARY ECONOMIC ACTIVITIES

A relatively small percentage of the working population was engaged in the production of a number of craft industrial goods which supplied some essential needs of the agricultural, fishing, and hunting communities. Every village had its craft industries, while some villages were devoted to particular crafts by virtue of tradition, possession of special resources, and other factors. It is furthermore likely that in some villages it was craft industries, and not primary economic activities, that formed the basis of the economy. The degree of importance of the industries in some villages could have been a result of controls exercised by chiefs over distribution of economic activities in their domain. It will be recalled that chiefs were extremely powerful, directing in many cases not only political but also economic life; thus in the kingdom of Ashanti, under a strong and wealthy centralized government, certain villages were set aside mainly for craft industries,[3] just as other villages were invested with the function of supplying Kumasi, the capital, and other major centres with foodstuffs. Kumasi in addition became the chief centre of attraction for craftsmen in every part of Ashanti, and the pick of these were made to settle in or near the capital to work for the king of Ashanti. It is possible that other political units in the country

[1] It is possible that some of the alluvial gold deposits of the western portion of Northern Ghana were also being mined, perhaps under stimulus from Mande traders.

[2] W. E. F. Ward, *A History of Ghana* (London, 1958), p. 396.

[3] Rattray, *Religion and Art in Ashanti* (O.U.P., 1927), pp. 309–16.

similarly organized the distribution of economic activities. Such rational distribution must have been based on careful resource inventory.

The continued functioning of the craft industries as well as of other economic activities depended as much on demand for their products and the general political state of the country as on the fact that sons traditionally followed their fathers' occupations. The tradition, whatever its background, ensured that those essential occupations did not disappear from the community. Religion also had a part to play, in the sense that a craftsman's tool could be invested with supernatural powers and sacrifices made to it whenever it was used. Strict religious observances, for which the population was noted, thus meant regular employment of the tool.[1] There were several types of craft industry, the most important of which were metal working, pottery, wood working and cloth weaving. Leather working must also have been an important craft industry, but confined to Northern Ghana where saddles for horses, leather clothing and bags would be among the major products.

## Metal working

The most important metals on which craft industries were based were iron, brass, bronze, silver, and gold. Blacksmithing was apparently the most outstanding craft industry.[2] Indeed, it was so central to life in earlier times in West Africa as a whole that its practitioners formed a caste, like the Numu, occupying a special position in society; and no settlement was considered complete without a caste of blacksmiths. Iron was the metal that revolutionized politics and economy. Shaped into a spear, it had been a means of conquest; and converted to economic capital and as a factor of production, it gradually came to add a new dimension to many economic activities and particularly to agriculture, by making it possible to increase vastly the area under cultivation.

Almost every part of the country had its forges; but there were certain areas which appeared to have had a higher concentration of the industry. One such area, noted for its numerous slag heaps, was the stretch of coastal land belonging to Little Akron and Aguna, from about Tantum to roughly Fete.[3] It is not certain if Akpafu-Santrokofi, which was famous by the second half of the nineteenth century for its iron working, had already acquired that reputation by the beginning of the eighteenth century, although the industry had been important there 'generations before the

[1] Rattray, *Religion and Art in Ashanti*, pp. 309–16. [2] Bosman, op. cit. Letter IX.
[3] Marees, *Description...de Gunea*, p. 33.

German occupation' in 1884.[1] In Northern Ghana the Pudo and Navrongo areas may also have been important producers of ironware.

Iron was obtained from two sources: from European merchants and from local ore. Iron bars were always among the major trade articles demanded from European merchants, and the Dutch for example made considerable profit from selling the commodity.[2] Iron bars were indeed so precious that they were used at some of the ports by Europeans as currency with which to purchase local commodities.[3] Some of the iron bars obtained at the ports found their way into the interior.[4]

Equally important, and more so in those parts of the country outside the sphere of influence of European trade, were local sources of iron. Over extensive areas of the savanna and Derived Savanna regions of Northern Ghana, Brong Ahafo, and Buem in Volta Region is laterite, consisting of ferruginized concretions. The ferruginized nodules were collected from shallow pits sunk into the laterite and smelted in simple furnaces.[5] These local sources of iron became less important wherever, as in Ashanti and the coast generally, imported iron bars became abundant.[6]

The standard of workmanship in the iron as well as the other metal industries was high. It was readily acknowledged that 'with their sorry tools they [the blacksmiths] can make whatever is required in their agriculture and house keeping. They have no notion of steel, and yet they make their sables and all cutting instruments.'[7] It could also be that Ashanti craftsmen were already conversant with the *cire perdue* or lost wax technique and used it in the casting of their famous metal vessels, the *kuduo*.

With the exception of gold the remaining metals were scarce as they were imported in relatively small quantities. They were generally worked into ornaments. Gold on the other hand was available in large quantities for the smithies that abounded in most parts of the country, especially in Southern Ghana and Ashanti–Brong Ahafo. Gold smithing was a craft of long standing. It was concerned with the production of gold currency and gold ornaments for which there was insatiable demand from all sectors of the community. Indeed, one of the ways of storing wealth was to invest in gold ornaments which, while retaining their value as negotiable capital, could also serve as dress decoration. The Ashanti made, in addition to

[1] M. Darkoh, 'The Economic Life of Buem, 1884–1914', *Bull. Ghana Geog. Ass.* IX, I (January 1964).

[2] W.I.C. oc. II. Letter dated 3 February 1634 from Fort Nassau to Amsterdam.

[3] Marees, op. cit. p. 25.

[4] See below, p. 97.

[5] Rattray, R. S., *Religion and Art in Ashanti*, photograph opposite p. 314.

[6] Ibid. pp. 309–10.

[7] Bosman, op. cit. Letter IX. 'Sable' probably refers to the local sword or cutlass.

ornaments, their famous gold weights whose value transcended the purely utilitarian purpose they served, for they depicted and preserved scenes from all aspects of the daily life of the Ashanti. A collection of gold weights constitutes a precious solid picture from which a great deal could be learnt about Ashanti of the past.[1]

## Pottery

Every region had its pottery industry, but its detailed distribution was, in Ashanti at any rate, ruled by the court, whose decision must have been guided by a knowledge of the distribution of suitable clay. 'Under the old Ashanti regime' the villages of Tafo, Pankrono, Obuokrom, Sisirease, and Ekwea were wholly engaged in making pottery; they all possessed excellent clay for the purpose.[2]

It is possible that echoes of the changes that occurred in the pottery industry on the coast in the seventeenth century reached Ashanti as well. One possible evidence of change of technique in Ashanti could come from the traditional Ashanti name for a potter, *Kukunyonfo*, which means a weaver of pots. On the basis of this etymological evidence it might be suggested, but only tentatively, that pots were once made in Ashanti by plastering clay on a basket foundation, that is, a woven fabric, which later was burnt off in the process of firing.[3] Whatever the nature of change in pottery technique, there was certainly considerable regional variation in pottery design, as archaeological finds show, and this may be explained in terms of influences from the Western Sudan, the coastal ports, and of tradition, and the varied responses to these. Nevertheless products of the industry generally served the same variety of domestic purpose throughout the country, and included clay pipes for tobacco smoking.

Pot making was traditionally the work of women, although in Ashanti, for example, there was no taboo against men participating in the industry. The industry was hereditary, as with the others, but was handed down from mother to daughter; and in this way the craft survived. Religious observances and sanctions also safeguarded the survival of the craft, as well as ensuring high standards of production and the availability of ready markets.

[1] Sir Francis Fuller nevertheless wrote that the first Ashanti gold weights were made in the time of King Opoku Ware who reigned since the 1730s. *A Vanished Dynasty, Ashanti*, p. 28.

[2] Rattray, *Religion and Art in Ashanti*, p. 301.

[3] Ibid. p. 302.

## Wood working

The organization of the industry and the factors which ensured its survival were the same as those for the industries already mentioned. The industry was heavily encrusted with religious taboos, some of which were of economic significance; it was also an hereditary craft, passed down from father to son. The products of the industry showed a great variety, some of the major ones being religious works of art, drums and other musical instruments, chiefs' state umbrellas and stools (thrones), household furniture, building materials like doors, and canoes.

Manufacturing of some of the products was distributed in a special way. Royal stools and umbrellas, which in the Akan areas were specially carved by a selected group of craftsmen, were absent in Northern Ghana where chiefs traditionally sat on animal skins and not on stools under umbrellas. Similarly, wooden doors were generally unknown in Northern Ghana while in Southern Ghana and Ashanti–Brong Ahafo they were incorporated into the building architecture. Again, the distribution of canoe manufacture was a function mainly of the distribution of the fishing industry; so that canoe making was relatively unimportant in Northern Ghana compared with the coastal areas. On the coast itself the distribution of canoe manufacture depended on the availability of suitable trees, including the silk cotton, and the presence or otherwise of more remunerative alternative occupations. Takoradi and Axim excelled in the industry, producing fishing as well as large transport vessels, while Butri, Ekon, Komenda, Kormantin, and Winneba turned out vast numbers of smaller craft.[1] All the canoes built on the coast and elsewhere were dug-outs, except probably around Lake Bosumtwe where navigation on the lake has always been, according to tradition, by means of tiny rafts.

Products of wood carving evidenced a high degree of workmanship, the primary basis of which in Ashanti was probably religion:[2]

> I think it can be stated, with some certainty, that the art of wood-carving in Ashanti owed its origin largely to the demands made by religious factions, which were not compelled by an article in their animistic creed to abjure the representation of anthropomorphic or zoomorphic forms. On the contrary, a demand arose for shrines of varied shapes and forms to serve as dwelling-places for the various spirits. The souls of ancestors are supposed to have found an acceptable abode during life, and even more so after death, in the stools upon which the owners sat in their life-time. Hence arose the desire for seats of artistic form.

[1] Barbot, *North and South Guinea*, p. 266.
[2] Rattray, *Religion and Art in Ashanti*, p. 269.

## Cloth industry

The older branch of the industry, with antecedents going back to very remote times, was concerned with the production of bark cloth. The raw material was the bark of the tree (*Antiaris toxicaria*) called *Kyenkyen* by the Akan, which was removed in long narrow strips, softened in water and beaten with wooden mallets. A narrow strip of bark thus treated became a single piece of cloth, supple and several times the original width of the bark. The industry was found mainly in the forest areas, as the tree supplying the raw material is a forest species absent in other vegetation formations. The use of bark cloth continued down to the early years of the twentieth century, by some hunters and very poor families in Brong Ahafo and other remote forest areas of Ashanti and the Western Region of Southern Ghana. Evidence of the antiquity and former widespread use of the cloth in Ashanti is to be seen in the fact that part of the Odwira ceremony in Ashanti traditionally demands that the king should change into this crude fabric.

Cloth weaving was the younger branch of the industry. The loom was a simple one, essentially the same as that in use today, worked by both hands and feet.[1] The threads for the looms were originally spun from local cotton and later, in Ashanti–Brong Ahafo and Southern Ghana, from silk as well, unravelled from imported European cloth. In the coastal areas the industry, judging by the silence of European writers on the subject, was probably of lesser importance, perhaps owing to the fact that the locally made cloths had to compete in the local markets with the more easily available imported European cloths. The latter were immensely popular and always formed part of the cargo of merchant ships trading to the coast. Major presents to chiefs from Europeans on goodwill missions typically included imported cloth.

It appears on the other hand that the weaving industry was rather important in Northern Ghana and in Ashanti, where the village of Bonwire near Kumasi was the headquarters. Bonwire is reputed to have been the location of the first loom in Ashanti. The industry, as with the others, was hereditary, being handed down from father to son. It was also surrounded by economically significant religious taboos. Traditionally, the early stages of the industry, from picking the cotton lint to spinning it into thread, were in the hands of women, while the men engaged themselves solely in weaving and finishing processes. The looms produced long narrow strips of cloth, several of which were then sewn together to form a complete cloth. This

[1] Isert, *Voyages en Guinée*, pp. 124–5.

was dyed in several colours of which indigo was originally the most popular. Other coloured threads, particularly the red ones, were unpicked from imported cloths.[1]

Woven cloths, called *Kente* by the Akan, were expensive, in view of the slow and laborious processes involved in their production.[2] Only the wealthy and officials of state could afford them, while the common people wore the cheaper imported cottons or bark cloth. Kente was produced in various designs, most of which had cultural or historical significance. Traditionally, in Ashanti, all new designs came under the control of the king, who would either reserve them for himself or allocate them to great men or women in the kingdom as symbols of their status.[3]

[1] Ibid.
[2] T. E. Bowdich, *Mission from Cape Coast Castle to Ashantee* (London, 1819), p. 310.
[3] Rattray, *Religion and Art in Ashanti*, p. 235.

# 5. William Bosman's Gold Coast: trade and transport

Whatever coherence Ghana possessed in the time of Bosman, it owed, not to uniform political control, but to the intricate network of major and minor pathways along which men travelled to trade. Products from the different sectors of the economy were exchanged, with the volume and speed of exchange depending mainly on the political state of the country. Trade did more than merely bring the different parts of the country together; it also drew Ghana closer than before to far-off countries, from which it obtained products not available locally.

## INTERNAL TRADE[1]

Intra-state trade was conducted in a large number of markets scattered throughout a political unit or state. Markets were held daily or periodically, and were governed by a code of laws drawn up to protect trade and ensure orderly activity. The laws were strictly adhered to. Weapons, for example, were not allowed to be carried to markets, so that traders from distant parts who necessarily carried weapons to protect themselves against highwaymen were obliged to deposit them at the nearest village to the market before proceeding to the latter. The village chief make a regular income out of charging one shilling per head for looking after the weapons.[2]

Daily markets to which women traders mostly resorted were held in all the coastal settlements, and each settlement had an open space in the centre for the purpose. The commodities sold in the markets consisted mainly of foodstuffs whose composition varied with the locality, together with some European and Western Sudan goods the prices of which increased with distance from Western Sudan markets or the coastal ports. There were also a few products of craft industries, particularly those of gold and black smithing which were always in great demand. The Dutch at Elmina, for example, regularly purchased gold and silver hat bands made specially to

[1] The boundaries of the numerous political states were real enough to make it necessary to consider internal trade at two levels: intra-state and inter-state. See K. B. Dickson, 'Trade Patterns in Ghana at the Beginning of the Eighteenth Century', *Geogr. Rev.* LVI, 3 (July 1966).

[2] Barbot, *North and South Guinea*, pp. 274–5

suit their taste.[1] It was also from these markets that European factors often purchased provisions for slave ships on their way to the New World.

In addition to daily markets were those held weekly or at eight-day intervals; they were characterized by bulk purchases and exchange of commodities not normally sold in the daily markets. There were yet markets whose regularity lay somewhere between daily and weekly. The market at Abonee (Aburi) in Akwapim was typical; it functioned thrice a week, when Asin, Akwapim, Akwamu and other merchants met there to trade for European goods brought up from Accra.[2] Such periodic markets were traditionally held in large open spaces, not necessarily within a large settlement, and situated where they possessed ease of access from all parts of the region they served. Their sphere of influence was, as may be expected, wider than that of daily markets. The large open spaces for the periodic markets, if normally uninhabited, frequently became the sites of large settlements. An example is Agwasi, about six miles east of Cape Coast, whose very name indicates its origin as a market place.

Large fairs, held once or twice a year, were also common. They attracted merchants from still greater distances, and were important social occasions. The king of Fetu, for example, organized an annual eight-day fair and festival at Abrambo, which was attended by merchants and other subjects from all parts of this domain.[3] One of the famous annual fairs was held at Asin, and there Asin traders brought iron bars and other European goods purchased at the ports to sell to merchants from surrounding states.[4] In order to avoid overlap and competition, fairs in neighbouring regions were held at different times of the year.

The distinction between inter-state and intra-state trade was a matter of degree only. The range of goods and the volume of exchange in inter-state trade were far greater than in local trade, but distances involved in trading could often be as great in intra- as in inter-state trade.

Agricultural, fishing, and hunting products, salt, gold, slaves, European goods, and products of craft industries featured prominently in inter-state trade. The pattern of movements of agricultural products was a function of differences in physical environment and in regional specialization which in turn depended on physical as well as human factors. The movements followed several directions. There were first of all the normal major movements along east–west and west–east directions on the coast, which reflected mainly the uneven distribution of rainfall and soil fertility. Thus Axim sent rice to districts in drier parts of the coast in exchange for corn,

[1] Bosman, *Guinea*, Letter IX.
[2] Barbot, op. cit. p. 184.
[3] Ibid. p. 172.
[4] Ibid. p. 188.

sweet potatoes, yams and palm oil.[1] Elmina area, with poorer soils, depended heavily on neighbours on either side for agricultural products, unlike Asebu district which, with a long tradition of cultivation aided by better soils, produced yams and sweet potatoes on a scale large enough to have a surplus for sale to neighbouring states. Similarly, the vast quantities of corn produced in Fantiland attracted merchants from minor producing areas on the coast.

Livestock were also traded laterally on the coast, especially in an east–west direction. The principal source was the south-east coastal plains which were capable of supporting large herds of cattle on account of the low rainfall and extensive pastures there. Besides, cattle rearing was in comparison with other primary occupations accorded a greater importance in the plains than elsewhere. The neighbouring states of Labadi and Ningo occupied a special place in the cattle trade. The animals were bought at Lay, which was situated immediately to the east of Ningo, and fattened in the pasture grounds behind Labadi and Ningo before being transported to the markets at Accra and other places further west. Merchants from the recipient areas also came down to Accra to buy the animals, normally at the price of 'thirty crowns per bullock'.[2]

Agricultural products also moved in a south–north direction from the coast to the immediate interior. The causative factor in this case was not so much a matter of differences in physical environment as of preference for other forms of economic activity in the immediate interior. Immediately behind Axim, for example, gold mining and trade were far more profitable alternatives to agriculture, with the result that the latter occupation was given comparatively little attention. The gold-mining areas therefore depended on neighbouring Axim for foodstuffs. Similarly, the people of Asin, who were more interested in trade, did not apparently bring their land under adequate cultivation, but rather purchased quantities of provisions from the Asebu, their neighbours to the south.[3]

Within Ashanti it is possible that food crops did not move over long distances, in view of the policy of rational organization of economic activity within the kingdom which included the assignment of a number of agricultural villages to each major settlement in the member states. Nevertheless, products of restricted distribution like kola and palm oil must have crossed individual state boundaries in Ashanti and travelled long distances. The Ashanti did not trade on the coast for food crops; nor did they buy provisions from Northern Ghana, with the exception of shea butter which indeed penetrated to the coastal markets.

[1] Bosman, op. cit. Letter I.
[2] Barbot, op. cit. pp. 185–6.
[3] Bosman, op. cit. Letter IV.

There are no definite pointers to the patterns of agricultural commodity flow in Northern Ghana. There must naturally have been a basic pattern of movement from countryside to major centres of population; but the question of whether agricultural commodities travelled long distances must remain an unconfirmed possibility.

Prices of agricultural products were on the whole simply determined by the laws of supply and demand. A relatively scarce commodity like maize for which there was a large demand commanded a high price, while millet or sorghum, produced in much larger quantities, was usually cheap, costing only about 2*s.* 6*d.* per 1,000 stalks. In wartime the general price level rose because of the inevitable suspension of farm work; then 1,000 stalks of millet or sorghum sold for as much as an ounce of gold, which was then equivalent to about £4. The price of corn also rose in the lean period between harvests, but not as high as it did in wartime.[1]

The trade pattern for fish was straightforward since all the major surplus areas were on the coast while all the deficiency areas stretched inland from behind the coast. This predominant pattern of south–north movement was not significantly disturbed by the supply of fish from inland rivers. How far up country coastal fish, dried or smoked, was transported is not easily determined, but Ashanti was among the recipients. It is unlikely that the Ashanti in turn transmitted the commodity to Northern Ghana, and the possibility of northern trading caravans having come down to the sea to purchase fish is rather remote. If fish from the coast reached Northern Ghana, it could only have done so through Ada traders who transported it together with sea salt to Kete Krachi to meet northern traders.

Patterns of trade in products of the chase are not clear. Hunting was an occupation with a countrywide distribution; consequently its products would have travelled over limited distances to local markets mainly. The possibility of the existence of a wider and more embracing pattern of movements superimposed on the simple local patterns cannot be assumed with certainty. The only clue comes from the statement by Isert in 1786 that hunting, a major occupation in Akwapim, furnished the only products that the Akwapim could sell at Accra.

The directions of trade in salt depended on the source of supply. The primary pattern of movement of sea salt was south–north, in response to the insatiable demand from up country. Ashanti, with no salt resources of its own, was among the largest consumers, and received its supplies mostly through Asin and Fanti middlemen who made large profits out of selling salt to the Ashanti. Denkera, Aowin, and Wasaw traders, operating to the

[1] Bosman, op. cit. Letter XVI.

west of the Fanti and the Asin, may similarly have profited by the salt trade. Ada's salt travelled furthest inland, and its transport up country was a carefully organized business involving a fleet of canoes which carried the commodity to Kete Krachi at the northern limit of canoe navigation on the Volta, where it was sold to trading caravans from Northern Ghana. Ashanti was also an important market for salt from Ada, which was carried there along the great east–west routeway that linked Kumasi with the famous oracle Odente at Krachi.[1]

In Northern Ghana the principal source of salt was Daboya, and it served the whole region as well as places outside it. Caravans from Grunsi, Dagomba, Konkomba, Bassari, Kabre, etc. came to Daboya to buy salt. The Ashanti, on the other hand, preferring the variety from the coast, forbade the import of salt from Daboya and charged a crippling duty on the commodity whenever it crossed Ashanti's territorial boundaries.[2]

The salt trade rivalled that in gold in importance and profitability.

> It is not to be imagined what vast riches the Negroes get by boiling salt; and if they were always or for the most part in peace, those who follow that employment would in a short time amass unwieldy sums; for all the inland Negroes are obliged to fetch their salt from the shore; from where it is easy to infer that it must cost them very dear: wherefore the meaner sort are obliged to make use of a certain saltish herb instead of salt, which their purses will not reach.[3]

Bosman added for emphasis that in the inland areas of western Dahomey, and doubtless of Togo and Volta Region, a handful of salt was worth one or two slaves.

Like those of salt, the major movements of gold in the country were relatively straightforward, being determined by the relative pulls of the coastal markets at the ports and markets in the Western Sudan. The sphere of influence of the coastal ports extended inland as far as Ashanti, whence gold flowed southward through Asin and Mankesim middlemen. The role of Asin middlemen as agents for the sale of Ashanti, and of Akim, gold was largely destroyed by the imposition of Denkera overlordship, the establishment of Ashanti power, and the growth in strength of the Akim states in the early years of the eighteenth century. The merchants from those inland states then began to trade directly with the coast. Northern Ghana's gold by contrast fell under the attraction of the Western Sudan markets and accordingly flowed away from the coast.

Slaves, like gold, also normally entered directly into international trade

[1] Mahmoud El-Wakkad (translator), 'Qissatu Salga Tarikhu Gonja...', *Ghana Notes and Queries*, no. 3 (September–December 1961).

[2] Ibid.

[3] Bosman, op. cit. Letter XVI.

without being first collected through inter-state trade. This is not to deny the significance of slave marts where the victims (*ndonko*) were assembled to be purchased and sent south to the slave ships or north to the Western Sudan. Salaga, Mansu, and Aflao, traditional slave markets, must have been among the more famous ones.

The foregoing on the patterns of trade in gold and slaves applied equally to trade in European goods, except that the latter primarily flowed from the coast northwards. Not all European goods entered directly into intra- or inter-state trade. Guns and ammunition were for example generally transported directly from the ports to their final destination because of their crucial importance in power politics, and not traded for by the inland peoples through middlemen.

European goods were expensive because of their scarcity in relation to demand; so that a regular practice among the local merchants was to stock them against the rainy season when few ships were in the roads and prices rose even more steeply.[1] The demand for European goods, regarded in Southern Ghana and Ashanti as desirable ingredients for normal living, was unshakeable. The demand had become established through centuries of pressure by Europeans to inculcate a taste for European goods among the local people. Some of the goods may have reached Northern Ghana, but not more than a trickle. Northern Ghana itself, as well as Ashanti, received manufactured goods from the Western Sudan, and such goods would probably also have invaded the markets further south.

Finally there were the products of local craft industries. The patterns of trade in most of the products were complicated networks without any recognizable dominant trends, although certain articles like the Ashanti *kuduo*, produced on a restricted scale, were meant to supply particular markets. Trade in canoes was exceptionally uncomplicated, since it was conducted along simple linear directions along the coast. The fishing industry was the largest consumer of the commodity, and the manufacturing centres enjoyed a brisk trade with neighbours to the east and west of them on the coast. The vessels were also purchased by European merchants for the transfer of goods to and from their ships when trading on the difficult surf-beaten coast of Volta Region and beyond.[2] A large transport canoe fetched between £40 and £50.[3]

[1] Barbot, *North and South Guinea*, p. 259 [2] Ibid. p. 266. [3] Ibid. p. 152.

## INTERNATIONAL TRADE

The directions of the country's foreign trade around the beginning of the eighteenth century were adumbrated in chapter 2.[1] With regard to the coastwise trade with countries lying to the east, it was claimed that the people of Elmina, who were particularly skilled in canoe navigation, often sailed in large canoes as far as Angola; but this assertion could not be given much credence. What is certain and may probably explain the assertion is that skilled sailors from Elmina, and indeed from other coastal settlements as well, were regularly hired and taken, together with their dug-outs, aboard merchant ships trading to the slave coast and beyond. The purpose was for the hired sailors to transfer, across the violent surf, goods from the ships to shore and slaves in the opposite direction. Some sailors may have returned home with easily misinterpreted stories of how they navigated their canoes to distant foreign shores. Nevertheless coastwise voyages covering a hundred or more miles were regular occurrences;[2] these were necessary in view of the greater dangers of land travel.[3] The observant Bosman was aware of the relatively short coastwise voyages, but did not know of the more ambitious ones to Angola.

### Export trade

Table 1, listing the items of cargo carried by two Dutch ships returning from the coast to Holland at roughly the same times annually between the years 1702 and 1704, gives some idea of the relative quantities in which exports were sent overseas.

It will be noticed that the major item of slaves does not appear on the list. This is because the bulk export of slaves required specially adapted ships and not general cargo vessels such as the two Dutch ships referred to above. Thus the major and most regular overseas exports consisted of slaves, ivory, and gold. The quantity of ivory exports was not commensurate with the actual quantity produced, for the reason that a great deal of it was carved locally into musical instruments (trumpets) and ornaments. The same was true of wax, much of which was used in the country for purpose of lighting.[4]

[1] See pp. 41–6.

[2] See for example Christiansborg Diary in the Danish Administration Records (Furley Collection), entry dated 10 February 1702: 'Today it was learnt from some of the Negroes who had come up by canoe from Popo...' This is but one of many such references in the Danish Administration Records.

[3] See p. 109.

[4] Barbot, op. cit. p. 261.

TABLE I. *Cargo carried by two Dutch ships between 1702 and 1704*

| Export | 1702 | 1703 | 1704 |
|---|---|---|---|
| Gold | 506 mk. 7 oz. 13⅝ engel | 903 mk. 4 oz. 11½ engel | 500 mk. |
| Ivory | 17,497 lb. | 33,422 lb. | 13, 972½ lb. |
| Rice | 51,755 lb. | — | — |
| Guinea grain | 50,000 lb. | 36,094 lb. | — |
| Lime juice | 'some amen' | 42 amen | 80 amen |
| Crewel* | 5,164 lb. | 5,316 lb. | 2,370 lb. |
| Wax | — | 6,971 lb. | 4,000 lb. |

*Sources* W.I.C. 98, letters from Elmina dated 25 September 1702, 10 October 1703, 31 August 1704.

* This may have referred to spun cotton; it may not necessarily have been purchased on the Gold Coast.

Another major item of export not listed in the table was the kola nut which, in the absence of demand for it in Europe, was not sent down to the ports. Its principal destinations were the markets of the Western Sudan, to which it was taken by well-organized caravans from the forests of Ashanti and Brong Ahafo. The exact quantities involved are not ascertainable, but all the evidence—the long, regular kola nut caravans to Northern Ghana, the centuries-old popularity of the nuts throughout the Western Sudan and the Sahara—points to the fact that exports of the nuts must have been very large.

The export item on which the greatest amount of information is available is gold. Bosman estimated that as much as 7,000 marks worth of gold was exported annually but only if the country was at peace and all the trade paths open. Otherwise less than half that quantity was exported. A detailed analysis of the trade in a normal year was as follows:[1]

| | Marks |
|---|---|
| Dutch West India Company | 1,500 |
| English African Company | 1,200 |
| Dutch interlopers | 1,500 |
| English interlopers | 1,000 |
| Brandenburghers and Danes | 1,000 |
| Portuguese and French | 800 |
| Total gold export | 7,000 Marks |

[1] Bosman, op. cit. Letter VII.

Trade at several of the ports was somewhat impaired by the high proportion of adulterated gold offered to the European merchants. Instances of unwary merchants transporting to Europe whole cargoes of false gold were so common that the Dutch in 1702 offered to pay the chiefs of Komenda, Fetu, Sabou, Twifo, Mankesim, Abrambo and Adom one *benda* or an ounce of gold for each dishonest local gold merchant brought to Elmina dead or alive.[1] The upsurge of this dishonest practice was due in a large measure to the encouragement given the local merchants in earlier centuries by Europeans to sell adulterated gold to trade rivals, and it was not long before the instigators themselves began to suffer by it.

The usual devices adopted for falsifying gold were to fill hollow gold casts with copper or iron; to mix gold with silver and copper and give the resultant alloy a sophisticated finish with a gold colour; and to grind a species of coral or copper filings into fine powder and give it a golden tinge. Denkera merchants, when they controlled much of the trade in the Western Region, regularly brought down to the ports considerable quantities of adulterated gold, some of which the European traders were forced to accept since the Denkera agreed to sell pure gold only if the adulterated variety was accepted with it.[2] Thus Bosman wryly remarked that the Dutch fort at Butri, christened Batenstein, because of the brisk gold trade there, should be renamed Schadenstein (Bate signifies profit and Schade loss); he also strongly condemned the Ghanaian traders at Dixcove whom he described as 'intractable, fraudulent, villainous and obstinate'.[3] Fanti merchants were similarly powerful enough to force quantities of adulterated gold on European merchants. The gloomy situation was relieved by Asin and Akim merchants who sold pure gold; and so high was the quality of gold from Asin merchants that everywhere on the coast the best gold came to be known as 'Accany sica' or Asin gold.

The export trade in slaves was as profitable as it was uncomplicated. The supply of slaves, drawn from all parts of the country, depended mainly on the country's political climate: if peace prevailed the supply was meagre, while the opposite was true under a prolonged state of inter-tribal warfare. For example, some time in 1682 a slave ship stopped for days at the port of Lay without collecting a single slave, and yet only two months before, when an Akwamu war was raging, a French man-of-war collected 300 slaves in a very short time at the same port.[4] Nevertheless the interludes of peace were not as a rule long enough to discourage the flow of slaves to the coastal

[1] W.I.C. 98, letter dated 25 September 1702 from Elmina to Amsterdam.

[2] Bosman, *Guinea*, Letter VI.

[3] Bosman, op. cit. Letter VI.

[4] Barbot, op. cit. p. 186.

ports. Wars between the Akwamu and the Akim and some neighbouring states were alone regular enough to promote a steady march of slaves to the slave ships at Accra, while in Ada-Keta districts (referred to by Bosman as Coto (Ketu)) and forming part of the slave coast, a regular occupation for the inhabitants was to travel inland and abduct men for sale to the slave ships.[1]

## Import trade

In exchange for overseas exports were offered a wide range of goods which typically included the following basic items: linens, silks, and brocades, guns and ammunition, iron and silver bars, cowries, aggrey beads, copper and brass ware, and alcoholic drinks. From the Western Sudan also came fabrics of all kinds, brass ware, leather goods, possibly books, etc. Aggrey beads, whose origin and true nature are not known for certain,[2] were possibly imported from Benin in Nigeria until roughly after the close of the seventeenth century when references to them in European texts became less frequent. The beads were priceless in Ghana inasmuch as they were regarded as status symbols, and perhaps their less frequent occurrence in the list of imports after the seventeenth century may have been partly due to the flooding of the market with cheap glass substitutes.

A number of factors determined the prices of overseas imports, not least among which was the usual state of imbalance between supply and demand. European goods were never plentiful enough to satisfy the avid demand for them on the coast, and consequently the prices charged for them were several times higher than those ruling in Europe. As far back as the end of the fifteenth century, the Portuguese made profits of 500 per cent or more on the goods they sold at Elmina;[3] but the profits slowly decreased in succeeding centuries with the build-up of pressure of competition from European trade rivals, until at the close of the seventeenth century profits, although still substantial, were far below 500 per cent. It would be an oversimplification to assume a general decrease in prices of European goods and explain it simply in terms of growing competition among European traders; because those Europeans who, aided by superior firing power from their forts, succeeded in inculcating a dread among the local denizens for trading with ships other than their own, maintained a high profit on the sale

[1] Bosman, op. cit. Letter XVIII.

[2] J. D. Fage, 'Some Remarks on Beads and Trade in Lower Guinea in the Sixteenth and Seventeenth Centuries', *J. Afr. Hist.* III, 2 (1962).

[3] G. H. T. Kimble (translator and editor), *Esmeraldo de Situ Orbis by Duarte Pacheco Pereira* (London, 1937), Hakluyt Society, Second Series, LXXIX, 121.

of their goods. Such was the case with the Dutch settlements where Dutch merchants sold goods at prices fixed by the director-general.[1] Elsewhere the Dutch as well as other established Europeans also deliberately undercut trade rivals by selling almost at cost price. An added complication to the nature of price determinants resulted from the operations of interlopers who, wherever possible, undercut everyone and disturbed established patterns of trade. Ships of interlopers were given the name 'ten percent ships' since they disposed of their goods at a heavy discount and bought slaves at inflated prices especially at Winneba and places further east that were not efficiently patrolled by Dutch West Indian and African Company ships.

## MIDDLEMEN AND TRADE

No account of trade in Ghana in the period under consideration will be complete without special mention of middlemen whose jealously guarded functions were vital to trade at all levels. The main source of the importance and power of middlemen was their position with respect to the European trading posts on the coast, to which the complicated cross-currents of trade in Southern Ghana and Ashanti eventually drained. As trade with the coast increased, so did the importance of middlemen near the coast.

Not all the citizens of such states were engaged in the large-scale operations of inter-state and international trade. In all the states of Southern Ghana and Ashanti–Brong Ahafo and possibly in Northern Ghana too, trading was the prerogative of royalty, nobles and rich men. The reason for this may have been mainly economic and not necessarily a result of state policy, for trading at distant places in those times of general insecurity required a great deal of organization which involved a heavy outlay such as only wealthy persons could afford. A train of carriers had to be engaged to headload the goods, and armed men hired to protect them; taxes also had to be paid to the numerous chiefs through whose territories the caravans passed. Even a state caravan, led by a 'linguist's staff' and supposed to be accorded respect and given a safe conduct, was sometimes plundered.[2] The poorer sections of the population were thus effectively excluded from large-scale long-distance trade although there was no law expressly forbidding their participation in it. The possibility of common people and even slaves becoming wealthy merchants through their own

[1] Barbot, op. cit. p. 274.

[2] The Twifo were particularly guilty of this offence. See W.I.C. 97, letter dated 16 November 1701 from Elmina to Amsterdam.

trading efforts nevertheless existed and sometimes became a reality. Society fully recognized such a possibility and prescribed elaborate ceremonies to be performed as a means of notifying the public of the change of status.[1]

The great trading nations that acted as middlemen at one time or another in the late seventeenth century were Asin, Denkera, Fanti, Akwamu, and Ashanti. Much of the politics of Southern Ghana and Ashanti in the time of Bosman could be understood in terms of struggle for position with the greatest advantage for middleman trade. The Asin, who throughout most of the seventeenth century were renowned as traders, achieved that eminence after subjugating the Etsi (the Atis of Pacheco Pereira) who then traded extensively with the Europeans. Colonies of Asin traders, ruled by governors appointed by the paramount chief of Asin, were already established in all the major trading centres on the coast by the 1630s,[2] and it was not long before they monopolized much of the middleman trade between the Ashanti and all the European trading stations from about Elmina to Winneba.[3] The Asin were itinerant merchants who penetrated to most parts of Southern Ghana and Ashanti, and beyond to Begho in Brong Ahafo where they purchased hand-woven cloths for retail in the southern markets.[4] It is not certain if their far-flung trading activities extended to Northern Ghana.

In 1698 Denkera, whose power had been growing over a number of years, inflicted a crushing defeat on the Asin and forever removed them from the eminence they had occupied for over a century in the country's trade. The revival of the Asin nation under the wings of Ashanti power in the early years of the eighteenth century did not restore their former pre-eminence in trade, although the Dutch also helped by allowing them trade credits and generally encouraging them in every way. The Denkera meanwhile carved out a great empire for themselves and mediated in the trade between nearly the whole of the Western Region coast and the interior. They came to possess vast riches, and European traders, aware of the grip the Denkera held of the inland trade, willingly submitted to the sharp practices of their merchants. Denkera's supremacy in trade came to an end with their total defeat by the Ashanti in 1701; thereafter Denkera merchants conducted what trade was left them with the nearby ports of Shama, Komenda, Elmina, and Cape Coast.

The destruction of Asin by Denkera conferred the position of principal

[1] W. Bosman, op. cit. Letter IX.
[2] W.I.C. oc. 11, letter dated 12 June 1645 from Elmina to Amsterdam.
[3] Bosman, op. cit. Letter VI. [4] Barbot, op. cit. pp. 190–1.

middlemen in the Central Region on Fanti traders. The Fanti, who had centuries of trading experience behind them, were quick to exploit the advantage of their position between Ashanti and the Central Region coast, and by about 1700 they were powerful enough to close the trade routes to the Central Region ports and suspend trade if they so wished.[1] The Fanti were to maintain this position for over another century and to bring the fierce wrath of the Ashanti upon themselves by unscrupulously exploiting that position.

In Eastern Region were the Akwamu who in 1702 controlled the whole of the coastline from about Apam to Whydah in Dahomey, together with an extensive inland territory behind it. They maintained an exclusive hold on trade along the major pathways that ran through their territory, especially those ending at Accra and neighbouring ports. The Akwamu did not allow other inland merchants to trade directly with the ports, but caused European goods to be carried to the thrice-weekly market at Abonee where they were sold at over 100 per cent profit. At the market was an overseer, appointed by the king of Akwamu, who was empowered to fix prices for goods.[2] The Akwamu retained their trade monopoly in the Eastern Region until their empire collapsed in 1730.

Ashanti became a powerful commercial nation within the first decade of the eighteenth century, and was fully aware of the strong advantages of its situation between Northern Ghana and the Western Sudan as a whole on the one hand, and the rest of Ghana on the other. The importance of trade to the Ashanti was reflected in the extent to which they brought their organizing genius to bear on it. Careful regulations were drawn up which ensured the superiority of state trading interests and strengthened the position of the Ashanti as middlemen.[3] Ashanti became a vast clearing house for European and Western Sudan, including Northern Ghana, goods.

It may be added, finally, that individual middlemen derived their income both from trading with inland merchants and from charging European merchants duties on their imports and exports. All exports were dutiable except slaves, although it was not uncommon for powerful brokers to insist on duty being paid on them too. There was furthermore a convention, originally instituted by the Dutch when they were trying to undermine Portuguese trade, according to which European merchants were obliged to give presents, called 'Dassy' (Akan word for thanks), to brokers who agreed to sell their goods. European merchants found the custom irksome but still had to follow it for fear of losing their trade.[4]

[1] Bosman, *Guinea*, Letter IV.
[2] Barbot, *North and South Guinea*, p. 184.
[3] Rattray, *Ashanti Law and Constitution*, p. 111.
[4] Barbot, op. cit. p. 260.

## COMMUNICATIONS AND PORTS

Coastwise sea traffic was the least important: the volume of trade involved was only a small fraction of the country's total volume of trade. The principal trade items carried were agricultural commodities, including livestock, and the limiting factors on the quantities carried were the size of vessel and the risk of goods being damaged by sea water. In spite of these limitations, coastwise sea traffic was regular and more trouble-free than land routes which were liable to be interrupted by swollen rivers and other obstacles, or closed altogether for political reasons. Moreover tolls had to be paid on land routes.

As commercial highways, rivers were of comparatively little importance. The White Volta and other rivers in Northern Ghana could not be utilized as commercial arteries because of their seasonality of flow; in Ashanti and Southern Ghana most of the rivers, though with a regular flow, were similarly ineffective as arteries for regional trade owing to rapids and other natural obstructions, and the fact that they were not numerous enough to provide an adequate network of waterways reaching all parts of the country.

The four major rivers in Southern Ghana and Ashanti are, from west to east, the Tano, Ankobra, Pra and Volta. As far as the coastal ports were concerned, the Tano flowed in the wrong direction, debouching into the sea, as it does, in Ivory Coast. The Ankobra had a limited usefulness as a commercial waterway down which mainly gold was transported to Axim. Its current is swift, and it was navigable upstream for canoes for about 35 miles to Botoboi, a few miles south of the Dutch establishment of Fort Ruyghaver. The Pra suffered from many interruptions in its course and was therefore useless for large-scale commercial traffic. The Volta was the one river which vied in importance with nearby land routes as a highway for trade. It was navigable for canoes as far up as Krachi, from where the route was continued by land to Salaga. In the wet season navigation was possible to Daboya and other places upstream from Kete Krachi.

Land routes carried by far the greatest share of the country's trade. It is possible to distinguish certain major routeways which overshadowed all others in importance (fig. 8).

Begho–Pamu–Elmina is one of the oldest trade routes in the country.[1] It went south-west from Begho through Pamu and Dormaa and then swung south-eastward to Twifo and finally south to Elmina. It may have been part of this trade route which directed the coastward expansion of the Akwamu. The importance of this commercial highway may have been

[1] I. Wilks, *The Northern Factor in Ashanti History* (Ghana, 1961), p. 12.

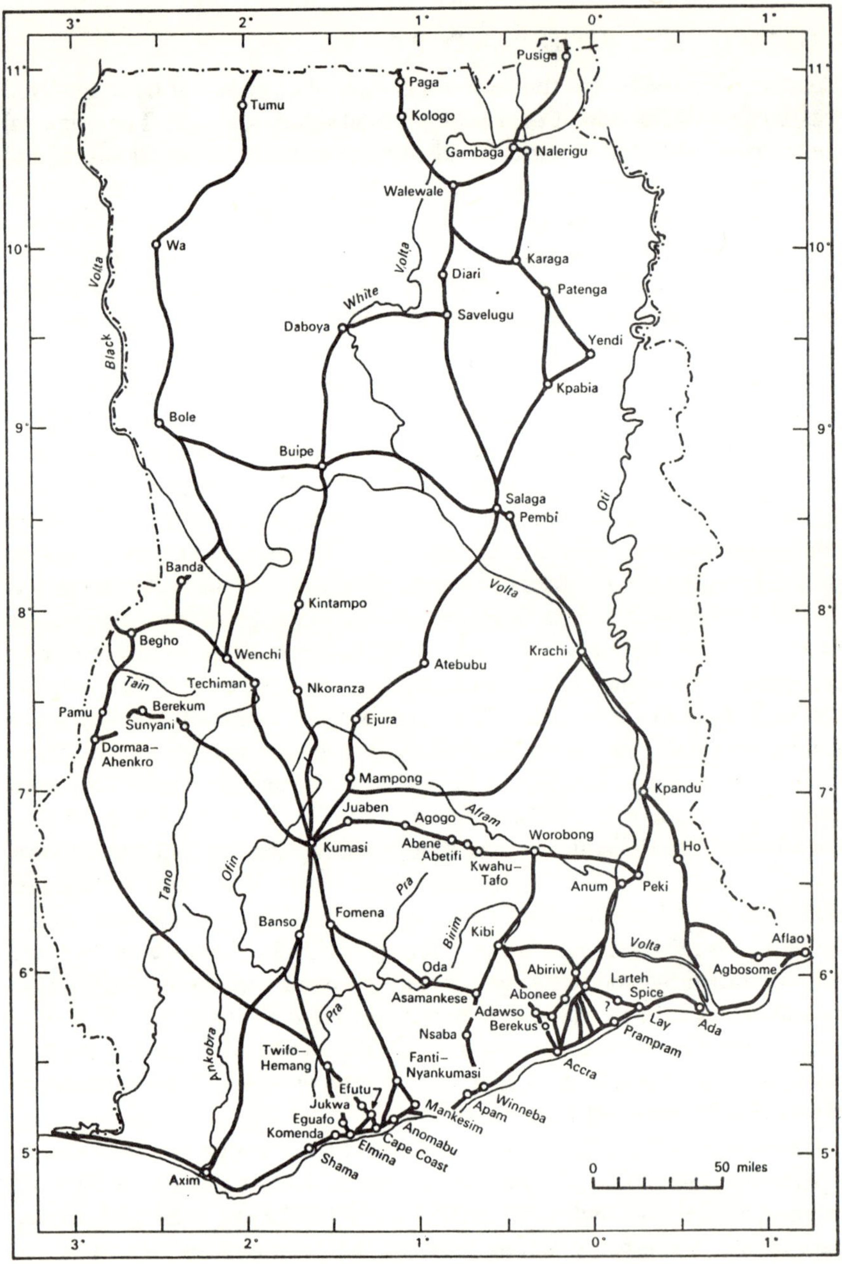


8 Major trade routes, *c.* 1702

somewhat diminished with the emergence of Kumasi as the capital of the powerful kingdom of Ashanti and the focus of many routeways from north of Kumasi.

Begho–Wenchi–Kumasi–Elmina is another ancient route whose northern terminus may originally have been Bono-Manso near Techiman.[1] From Kumasi southward it passed through Bankesieso, the old Denkera capital, which was sited not far from the rich auriferous beds of Obuasi. The early prosperity of Adansi was due to its position on this route; the same applied to the capital of Twifo, Twifo-Hemang, which was sited at the point of intersection of the route with the one from Elmina to Begho through Pamu. The section of the route from Kumasi through Denkera to Elmina was in constant use by the turn of the eighteenth century, and may probably have been the one on which van Nyendaal travelled on his trade and peace mission to the king of Ashanti in 1701.[2] It will be noticed that a branch route led off from Denkera to the Dutch port of Axim, but it served mainly to transport the gold from Denkera, although Ashanti traders may also have used it occasionally.

Kumasi–Cape Coast route, with a northward extension from Kumasi to Begho through Techiman and Wenchi, may also be called the Asin route because of its course through Asin and its regular use by Asin traders. There was probably a branch to Mankesim, another major centre for the transit trade between the coast and the immediate interior. Like the neighbouring one terminating at Elmina from Kumasi, the route provided one of the shortest and most direct links between Ashanti and the coast, and was therefore much used by Ashanti traders after 1701. It is likely that a branch route led off from Fomena, the capital of Adansi built after the destruction of Denkera in 1701, to Akim Oda (Nsuaem), the capital of the newly constituted Akim Kotoku state; from there the branch route may have continued through the old Akwamu capital of Asamankese to Nyanoase, near Nsawam, and finally to Accra. It is nevertheless unlikely that this subsidiary route in any way diverted trade from the Asin route, since it was much longer than the latter. The subsidiary route may not have been of much consequence, except its coastal end which carried a great deal of trade between Accra and Akwamu.

The original sixteenth-century or earlier route, to which the Kumasi–Kwahu–Accra route was a successor, initially led in a strict north-west–south-east direction from Begho through the Guan villages on the Afram River without touching Kumasi but probably passing through Kumawu.

[1] Meyerowitz, *The Akan Traditions of Origin* (London, 1950), p. 89.
[2] See below, p. 114.

Its later deflection through Kumasi resulted from the centripetal force exerted by the latter in its capacity as the capital of Ashanti. After crossing the Volta twice, perhaps in order to pass through the rich agricultural lands of Krepi and to avoid most of the Volta gorge where an ambush was easily laid, the route may have entered the Accra Plains along the foothills of the Akwapim Mountains or passed along the top of the mountains through Nsaki to Accra. The coastal end of the road from Nsaki to Accra must have been the one used by the Dutch emissaries van den Brouke, Nicolaas Dubois, and Pieter Pasop who set out from Fort Crevecoeur to the Akwamu capital in 1703. Their description of the journey shows that they went, not to Nyanoase, but to Nsaki through Berekuso (Fetu Bereku) and Asemeni (called Ouma and ruled by the Akwamu Chief Asemani).[1] The main route, although long, was an easy one because of the lowlands that marked practically the whole of its course, and persisted right through the nineteenth century.

The importance of the Aflao–Half Assini route which connected one end of the coast to the other, derived from the links it established between the coastal termini of the great routes of commerce from the interior. Wherever possible this coastwise route followed the sandy beach which was clear and open, unlike the tangled land vegetation, and formed the shortest link between any two seaside settlements. As a through route it may have suffered from competition with the coastwise sea route, but the different sections of it were vital to local trade.

Although there is no direct contemporary evidence for it, there could hardly be any doubt of the existence of the Krachi–coast axis which linked the principal Ewe settlements from the coast up to Kpandu with the transhipment centre of Kete Krachi. Its southern termini were Aflao, the ancient slave market, Ada, and Accra through Peki and Anum and the Accra Plains. As a commercial highway its importance may have been considerably reduced through nearness to the Volta waterway. Sections of the route must naturally have been important for local trade but, as a major trade route of more than local importance, it probably functioned mainly as a line of march for slaves on their way to the coast.

The Paga–Salaga route was one of the two most important and most ancient trade routes in Northern Ghana. It was followed and accurately described by Binger in 1888.[2] In addition to being vital to trade, the route was also significant politically since, with all its branches, it linked the three sister kingdoms of Mossi, Mamprusi, and Dagomba. It was a composite route with several alternatives, all of which ended at Salaga.

[1] W.I.C. 484, Letter dated 10 October 1703 to Amsterdam.

[2] L. Binger, *Du Niger au Golfe de Guinée* (Paris, 1892), II, 19–91.

From Paga, which is at the terminus of the shortest route from the Mossi capital of Wagadugu to Northern Ghana, the route led to Walewale from where a branch route connected to the Mamprusi capitals of Gambaga and Nalerigu. From Walewale the main route split into two, one branch going directly south through Savelugu to Salaga, and the other through Karaga to Yendi from where it led southward to Salaga. Yendi was itself connected directly to the Mamprusi capitals. The most westerly branch of the main route from Walewale via Savelugu was originally the sole major route from Paga south, and led via Daboya to Buipe on the Black Volta, before the transfer of the market from Buipe to Kpembe's zongo, Salaga, in the second half of the seventeenth century. From Salaga the route connected with Kete Krachi, on the one hand, and Kumasi, on the other, through Atebubu and Ejura. The route from Kumasi to Salaga was in the nineteenth century sometimes called the 'old road', 'from its antiquity and pre-eminence'.[1]

The Bole–Wa–Tumu route, linking the old town of Bole, through the Mossi- and Mande-dominated western portion of Northern Ghana, with Leo, Sati and eventually with Wagadugu in Upper Volta, was the second of the two ancient major trade axes in Northern Ghana.[2] There may have been alternative outlets for the route north of Wa and west of Tumu. The trajectory of the route was simple as it connected in the most direct way the two largest settlements in that part of Northern Ghana, Bole and Wa, with the nearest centres of population in Upper Volta. The Bole end of the route continued to the prosperous commercial centre of Bondoukou in Ivory Coast, to Bouna also in Ivory Coast, and to the ancient settlement of Techiman in Brong Ahafo which had longstanding relations with western Gonja. These southward connections from Bole contributed significantly to the commercial importance of the Bole–Tumu route by providing an effective link between Mossi traders from Upper Volta and Mande traders from Ivory Coast and elsewhere.

These were the great routes of commerce linking one end of Ghana to the other and Ghana itself to neighbouring countries; but they were not the only routes that were of importance to Ghana's internal trade. Weaving through the major routes to form a complicated network, which increased accessibility to the major routes themselves and to all parts of the country, were a large number of minor routes without which much of the country's internal trade would have been impossible. The Akim Abuakwa capital of Kibi for example, which was on none of the major trade routes, was effectively linked to Accra and neighbouring ports, to Winneba, and to the Kumasi–

[1] Joseph Dupuis, *Journal of a Residence in Ashantee* (London, 1824), II, p. xxviii.
[2] Binger, op. cit. (see folded map at end of vol. II).

Kwahu–Accra route. Other capitals in Southern Ghana were similarly connected to one or more of the coastal ports. In Ashanti and Brong Ahafo, one of the oldest and vital route connections was that between Krachi and the Kumasi–Mampong route; it was vital because of its function as a passageway for the essential item of salt from Kete Krachi to Kumasi.

In Northern Ghana the two major routeways were aligned north–south without important lateral connections except in the south in Gonja where a route linked Salaga, Buipe, and Bole (fig. 8). There may also have been another important lateral connection further north between Wa and Gambaga, in view of the traditional links between the two settlements. Be that as it may, the commercial importance of that lateral route was a certainty in the late nineteenth century. The two lateral connections on the one hand, and the Bole–Tumu and the north–south White Volta on the other, enclosed a large area in which there were probably no important trade routes. The area was referred to as Grunsi, an area where the aboriginal population with its Tindana, undisturbed by foreign invaders, lived with a medley of refugees from elsewhere in Northern Ghana; and the constant frictions among the different tribes stopped lines of communication from developing. Thus throughout Grunsi only wild paths, which were little frequented, connected the settlements.[1]

As a rule the routes did not keep to fixed trajectories but changed their alignments in various degrees with the seasons. A dry-weather route near a river would be diverted in the rainy season, when the river might be in flood, through a drier area away from the river. The necessity for finding alternative routes also arose frequently through the near chronic state of political instability in some parts of the country. It was for this reason that the coastal European merchants made it their central aim always to seek to placate powerful chiefs of middlemen states through which important trade routes passed. Thus instructions from the Royal African Company to their representatives on the coast always insisted on measures being taken to ensure the goodwill and co-operation of the chiefs. Thus, too, the Dutch sent van Nyendaal in 1701 to Osei Tutu, king of Ashanti, with instructions to plead for Ashanti traders to be allowed to come to the coast, and to assure the king that his traders would be guaranteed a free and safe passage through the notorious bandit-infested states of Adom and Twifo.[2] The Dutch again signed, in 1702, a 'treaty of general alliance and peace' with nearly all the chiefs in the Central Region, and a similar one with the king of Akwamu in 1703, under which the king agreed to ensure 'that none

[1] Binger, op. cit. pp. 34–5.

[2] Minutes of Council at Elmina, 5 June 1702 in W.I.C. 97 (Guinea 1), 1702.

of the Caboceers or Headchiefs under him shall close any of the paths to traders'.[1]

The trade routes were pathways trampled into being by the feet of countless thousands of traders, who not unnaturally must have avoided physical impediments wherever they occurred and thus created circuitous and serpentine routes which rarely led directly from one settlement to the other. The winding nature of the routes was a never-ending source of complaints from European travellers.

> They (the Africans) are full as indifferent and negligent in the making of their roads, they being generally as rough and perverse as the people themselves: a road which need not be above two miles in length, frequently becomes three by its crookedness and unevenness; and though they have been often made sensible of this inconvenience by us, and a very little trouble would mend them, yet they will not alter them; the way once made must still remain, though it leads them twice as far out of the way.[2]

No vehicular form of transport was used. Head porterage, undertaken mostly by slaves, was used by trading caravans throughout the country, while in Northern Ghana the ass was additionally used as a beast of burden. Only a few pack animals may have been used in the Derived Savanna of northern Brong Ahafo south of the Black Volta, for reasons first given in the nineteenth century, namely, the general absence of millet for the asses, the frequent marshes near the Black Volta, and the tall grass which the animals could not feed on. Pack animals were used only for a few months of the year, when the burnt-over land was covered with new succulent grass shoots.[3]

## Ports

From the time of the earliest European contact with the coast in the fifteenth century to the time of William Bosman, and indeed right down to the beginning of the nineteenth century, a port was chosen not necessarily for any advantages of site or shelter it may have possessed. The primary concern of the Europeans was to acquire a piece of dry ground, normally very close to the sea, on which to erect a warehouse or a castle, and such a place naturally functioned as a port, regardless of its suitability or otherwise for such a purpose. Thus neither the pounding surf nor the rocky coast stopped the Dutch from making Little Accra a port. Bitter jealousies among the Europeans also made them use different landing beaches at the same settle-

[1] See footnote 1 on p. 112.

[2] Bosman, op. cit. Letter IX.

[3] Binger, op. cit. p. 144.

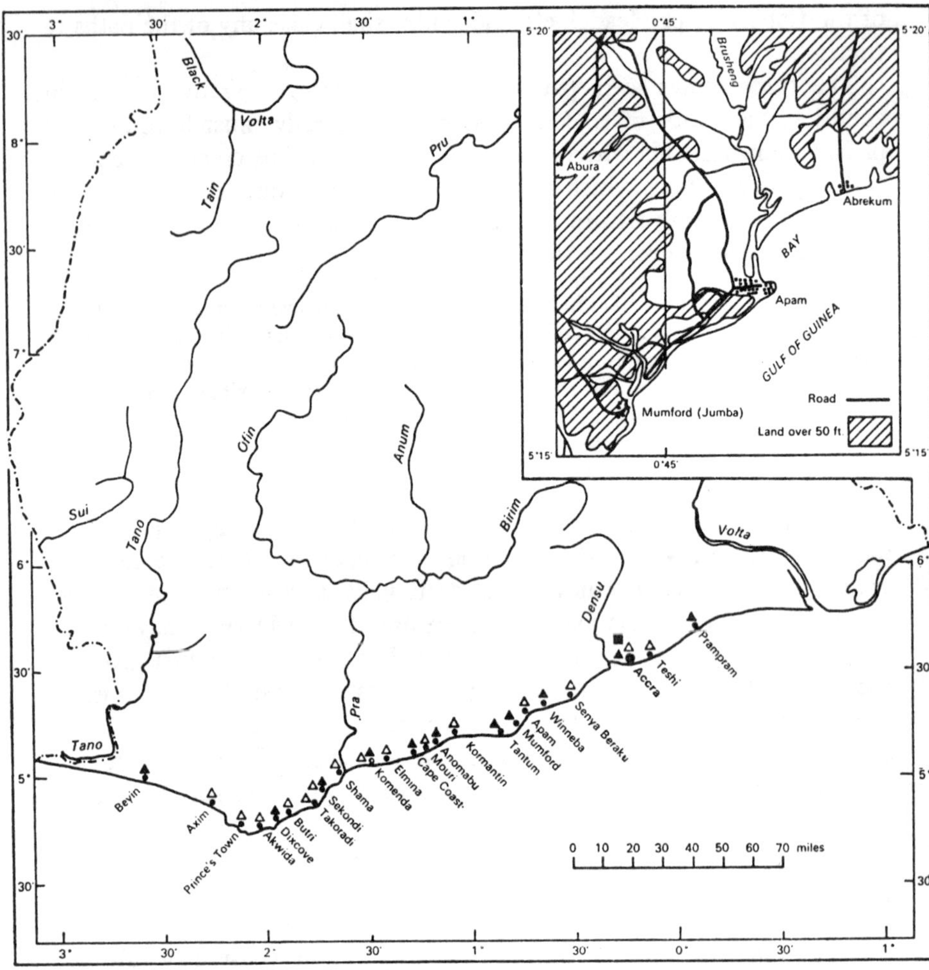


9 Port ownership, 1702. ● Port, ▲ British, △ Dutch, ■ Danish

ment, as at Accra, although not all the landings were safe. At all the ports, with the exception of Elmina where there was relatively deep water close to land, the little sailing ships stood some distance out at sea while canoes battled their way through heavy breakers to reach them.

Figure 9 shows the location of the principal ports and their ownership in about 1702. Many of the ports were situated on broad shallow bays which are a characteristic feature of the coast; but a few of the ports, like Winneba, Apam, Shama, Elmina, and Mouri, were on more pronounced bays with calm water in which the sailing ships could get much nearer to land (fig. 9

inset). The importance of a port was affected not so much by advantages of site, which were incidental in the choice of the port, as by a complex of political and other factors. Ports at places like Elmina, Cape Coast, and Christiansborg automatically became more important than their neighbours since they were the seats of European merchant companies. The importance of other ports depended on the size and wealth of the states which owned them; examples of such ports were Anomabu and Great Kormantin. Finally, some of the important ports were the termini of the great trade routes which brought the wealth of the interior to the coast. Axim, Elmina, Cape Coast and Accra were the major examples.

# 6. Ashanti power and economic geography

From the beginning of the eighteenth century to about 1850 the Ashanti, through a series of wars, became masters of practically the whole country. The significance of this event was not just political. The expansion of Ashanti power also had considerable influence on the country's economic geography, particularly in the areas of agriculture and trade.

## THE AGRICULTURAL LANDSCAPE[1]

Although agricultural production in the country did not come under the direct control of the Ashanti court, the agricultural landscape was nevertheless affected by the expansion of Ashanti power. The effect of the numerous wars on the agricultural landscape was one of stagnation or decay. The countryside was unsettled as the rural population was at one time or another forced to migrate. There was the remarkable instance of the forest of northern Sefwi, from the Tano to the Bia River near Krokosua which, after the Sefwi were defeated by the Ashanti in the 1730s, became the game preserve of Ashanti kings.[2] Consequently that area was little cultivated or settled for about a century. But the details of the picture of ruin are not so remarkable as the improvements, however minor, that did occur in the agricultural landscape in spite of the distinctly unfavourable social or political conditions.

### Peasant agriculture 1702–1806

The agricultural landscape of about 1806 was not appreciably different from what it was a century or more earlier.[3] There were nevertheless certain notable changes in Southern Ghana and Ashanti–Brong Ahafo,

[1] K. B. Dickson, 'The Agricultural Landscape of Southern Ghana and Ashanti-Brong Ahafo, 1800 to 1850', *Bull. Ghana Geog. Ass.* IX, 1 (January 1964).

[2] Fuller, *A Vanished Dynasty*, pp. 26–7. Also Holtsbaum, F. P., 'Sefwi and Its People', *Gold Coast Rev.* 1 (1925), p. 81.

[3] Compare the relevant sections of the works by Bosman and Barbot, for example, with the Reports of two Commissions of Inquiry appointed to look into the affairs of the country in the first decade of the nineteenth century. The earlier of the two Commissions, appointed by the Dutch Government, sat in 1801 (C.O.267/22, P.R.O.), and the second, which was British, sat in 1810 (C.O.267/29, P.R.O.).

particularly in the relative importance of food crops, which may have been reflected in the acreages devoted to their cultivation. These changes occurred following the spread of the two crops, cassava and maize.

It appears that the latest arrival in the agricultural landscape in Southern Ghana and Ashanti–Brong Ahafo up to about 1806 was cassava (*Manihot utilissima*) which by 1785 was extensively cultivated in the coastal areas, especially around Accra.[1] The two main types of cassava cultivated in Ghana today are either 'bitter' or 'sweet', and it is generally believed that both varieties are of New World provenance. The date of arrival of the crop in Ghana is not certain. It is unlikely to have been important in the country around 1700.[2] On the other hand it would be justifiable to regard as a generalization, not applicable to Ghana, the suggestion that the true importance of cassava in West Africa dated from its reintroduction by freed slaves migrating from Brazil to the Lagos–Dahomey coast from about 1780, and that nowhere on the mainland of West Africa, except Owerri in Nigeria, was it a crop of more than casual importance prior to the nineteenth century.[3] The spread of cassava in Southern Ghana may therefore have taken place between about 1700, the time of Bosman, and 1785 when Isert noted how widespread it was. Cassava is a crop that can spread quickly, considering its many superior advantages: it is one of the highest yielding plants of the vegetable kingdom, and its ability to yield a good harvest on very poor soils must have helped it to compete successfully on the coast with a crop like yam. Moreover, cassava requires little cultivation and can be grown without any difficulty from stem cuttings; its tubers could be left in the ground until required without deteriorating to any extent.

Maize, which had gained a firm foothold on the coast in the time of Bosman, began to spread into the inland areas of Southern Ghana where there are suitable physical conditions for its growth, and by 1800 it was well established in Akwapim[4] and Krepi[5] and doubtless in many other areas. The crop may also have been present in Ashanti and Brong Ahafo, but probably not over wide areas, for the cultivation of maize had been 'lately more extensively introduced into the interior of Ashantee; both from its importance in feeding their stock, and being portable for the supply of their armies'.[6] There is no indication of when the Ashanti first began to

[1] Isert, *Voyages en Guinée*, pp. 183–4. [2] See above, p. 80.
[3] W. O. Jones, *Manioc in Africa* (Stanford University Press, 1959), p. 73.
[4] Isert, op. cit. p. 260. [5] G. A. Robertson, *Notes on Africa* (London, 1819), p. 234.
[6] Ibid. p. 201. According to Bowdich, 'corn' was abundant in Ashanti; but he may have been referring to guinea corn and not maize, since he added that *pito*, a local beer, was brewed from the corn. See his *Mission from Cape Coast Castle to Ashantee* (London, 1819), p. 319.

appreciate the superior advantages of maize as a military ration. This could have been when they fought the Fanti at the coast for the first time in 1806, or it could have been earlier still. The crop itself may have reached Ashanti not many years before 1800.

The subsequent rise to fame of maize in Ashanti must have been rapid, for the Ashanti were a warrior nation engaged in wars most of the time, and the need for durable, compact, and easily portable rations must have been keenly felt. Plantains and yams, on which the Ashanti formerly relied almost exclusively, were heavy, clumsy, and perishable, requiring the employment of large numbers of noncombatants to headload them. Besides, maize is an annual, yielding two harvests a year, and its cultivation requires much less labour than that of the traditional Ashanti food crops.

## 1807–*c*. 1850

The year 1807 marked a turning point in the development of commercial agriculture in Ghana. It was from that time that the present agricultural landscape of Southern Ghana and Ashanti–Brong Ahafo truly began to be sketched. The changes hardly affected Northern Ghana.

The British Government declared the export slave trade illegal, and in so doing considerably weakened one of the major forces that had for centuries militated against agricultural improvement. The Danish Government had already abolished the export slave trade in 1802, but for its subjects only; the British Government on the other hand barred not only its subjects but also other nationals from continuing with the trade. Thus slave ships belonging to other nations were seized wherever possible and the slaves released. The vigour with which the British Government enforced its anti-slavery measures dealt a heavy blow to Ghana's economic life by removing its very foundation, for the centuries-old export slave trade had called into being a vast organization of wholesale dealers, brokers, slave collection centres, and other complementary occupations in which the majority of the country's population was engaged. The export slave trade was an economic activity in which the small businessman could share, and on which the purchasing power of the population probably mainly depended.

By abolishing the export slave trade, therefore, Britain made it imperative to find an alternative occupation and basis of the country's economic life. The solution came to lie in the development of export agriculture. It is true that a good deal of slave trading was still carried on surreptitiously, but the effect on the agricultural landscape of the vigorous measures against slavery became noticeable not long after abolition. The king of Ashanti, unable to sell all the slaves he had accumulated, settled some of them in several villages in Ashanti to farm the land. About 3 miles to the north-west of Bekwai was one such village, Amoafo, a large proportion of whose population, estimated at about 7,000, consisted of slaves taken prisoner in the Gyaman war of 1818. Similarly, in the settlements around Lake Bosumtwe were at the same time detained large numbers of Fanti, Asin, and also Gyaman prisoners of war, all supposedly numbering about 25,000.[1] There may also have been slave farmers in the numerous 'plantation villages' that surrounded major settlements throughout the country, as there were in those around Adumpore in the little Ashanti–Akim district of Yomoho, which supplied many markets, including those at Juaben, Bekwai, and Dompoase with foodstuffs.[2] Slaves may likewise have been settled in farming villages around the mouth of the Volta, where the Danish authorities were busily prosecuting slave dealers. Again, lands around major fetish centres like Prampram, Mlefi, Asentema in Akwapim, and Krachi were extensively cultivated by slaves liberated according to the age-old custom whereby a slave automatically became free once he took refuge in a fetish temple.[3]

Under the changed economic conditions where emphasis was placed on cultivation, the two crops maize and cassava continued to spread fast, the former replacing millet and guinea corn at the coast and the latter competing for supremacy in the forest with yam, which is better suited to the climatic conditions and the light sandy soils of the interior savanna zone.[4] Nevertheless it was neither maize nor cassava whose cultivation provided the new basis for the country's economic life. It was rather palm oil which eventually replaced slaves in the country's overseas trade. It began to flow in increasing quantities to the ports after the second decade of the nineteenth century, thanks to the large demand for it in Britain.[5] In 1818, for example, not more than sixty puncheons of palm oil were exported from Anomabu; a year later it was over one hundred puncheons, and in 1821

[1] Dupuis, *Journal*..., p. 61. [2] Ibid. pt. II, p. xxxi.

[3] Among early works that describe this ancient custom is P. E. Isert's *Voyages en Guinée*, p. 106 and pp. 250–1.

[4] J. B. Wills (ed.), *Agriculture and Land Use in Ghana* (O.U.P., 1962), p. 377.

[5] Gold production suffered a rapid decline after 1807 (although gold continued to be the most valuable export) since slaves could no longer be found for the hard task of mining. The reduced amounts of gold exported up to about 1850 came from Ashanti and Gyaman traders who still possessed slaves. It could also be that the known gold deposits were in any case becoming exhausted. Palm oil on the other hand was cheaper to produce and transport since the major producing areas were near the ports. See H. J. Bell, *History, Trade, Resources and Present Condition of the Gold Coast Settlement* (Liverpool, 1893), p. 37.

the number of puncheons of palm oil exported from Anomabu rose to 1,300.[1]

Already by the early 1820s there were areas in Southern Ghana which excelled others in palm oil production. The country behind Dixcove, it was estimated, exported not less than 40,000 gallons of palm oil annually; and that was when the palm oil trade was at a low ebb because of the poor price the oil fetched in England. At Sekondi apparently a considerable quantity of palm oil could be obtained if the farmers could be encouraged to bring it down. Production of palm oil decreased from about Sekondi to Cape Coast, east of which it increased once more, until it culminated in the large exports from Accra. In 1820 and 1821 two Accra merchants, Messrs Hansen and Bannerman, together exported 4,736 gallons and 38,684 gallons of palm oil.[2]

Exports were not confined to palm oil. In the time of Governor Hope Smith considerable quantities of maize were exported to Madeira and the West Indies, but the unprofitable result of some of these speculations, combined with the frequent tribal wars on the coast, compelled them to limit its cultivation to quantities required for local consumption.[3] There were also sporadic exports of coconuts and cotton from both peasant and European farms. Exports of coconuts from British ports apparently began in 1832, while those of cotton began earlier. Cotton was grown at Ada and in Krepi where the possibility of a more extensive cultivation of the crop was great.[4] Other export crops from the peasant farms were red pepper, malaguetta pepper or guinea grains, and rice (table 2).

Although the export figures are admittedly imperfect and constitute an inadequate statement of the country's export trade in agricultural commodities, they nevertheless demonstrate clearly the new awareness of cultivation as a source of wealth, and point to palm oil, guinea grains and coffee as the chief products of the agricultural export economy. The generally increasing volume of agricultural production for export was in the main due to the encouragement given to peasant agriculture by the Danish Administration, the Basel Mission, the British Administration, and the Wesleyan Mission.

The Danes seemed to have lost none of their zeal for the great work of agricultural education which they began towards the close of the eighteenth

[1] Letter from Mr James Swanzy to Sir Charles MacCarthy, dated 22 April 1822, Anomabu. See C.O.267/56, P.R.O. Organized export of palm oil was probably established by 1810.

[2] Sir Charles MacCarthy, 'Report on the Forts and Settlements on the Gold Coast', 1822, C.O.267/56, P.R.O.

[3] C.O.267/93, P.R.O. Also known as the Rowan Report (1827).

[4] Rowan Report, C.O.267/93, P.R.O., appendix no. 30.

TABLE 2. *Exports from British settlements in Southern Ghana, 1822–41**

| Year | Rice† (cwt) | Palm oil (tons) | Coffee (lb.) | Pepper (lb.) | Guinea grain (lb.) | Gum copal (cwt) |
|---|---|---|---|---|---|---|
| 1822 | — | 480 | — | — | — | — |
| 1823 | — | 38 | — | — | — | — |
| 1824 | — | 255 | — | — | — | — |
| 1825 | — | 260 | — | — | — | — |
| 1826‡ | — | 217 | — | — | — | — |
| 1827 | — | 248 | 15,581 | 85 | 12,306 | 36 |
| 1828 | 264 | 368 | 14,017 | 4 | 1,603 | 2 |
| 1829 | — | 350 | — | 1,001 | 5,302 | 5 |
| 1830 | — | 678 | — | 29,071 | 15,283 | 2 |
| 1831 | 952 | 838 | 12,265 | 3,914 | 6,415 | 17 |
| 1832 | — | 827 | — | 568 | 39,896 | 11 |
| 1833 | 135 | 1,230 | 42,814 | 64 | 84,403 | 105 |
| 1834 | — | 1,074 | 68,797 | 174 | 31,408 | 62 |
| 1835 | — | 950 | 33,317 | 2,432 | 31,592 | 163 |
| 1836 | 23 | 1,102 | 25,856 | 8,231 | 32,574 | 360 |
| 1837 | — | 1,099 | 130,949 | 5 | 6,241 | 2 |
| 1838 | — | 1,784 | 64,696 | — | — | 9 |
| 1839 | — | 2,017 | 2,994 | 5 | 16,635 | 7 |
| 1840 | — | 2,339 | 58 | 6 | 13,351 | 34 |
| 1841 | — | 2,137 | — | — | 6,482 | 81 |

* Table compiled from the Rowan Report, C.O.267/93, P.R.O., appendix no. 21 and from appendix no. 36 of Minutes of Evidence taken before the Select Committee on West Coast of Africa, 1842. Export figures, other than those for palm oil, are unavailable for all the British settlements in Southern Ghana for years between 1822 and 1826. The other commodities were nevertheless exported within those years, as may be seen from the few figures supplied by individual merchants at Accra and Anomabu, but not included in the table.

† This refers to polished rice. Rice in the husk was also exported but not frequently. 1,546 bushels and 1,298 bushels of husk rice were exported in 1825 and 1826 respectively.

‡ 1826, from 1 January to 30 June.

century.[1] They made several more plantations after 1807 and succeeded in stimulating commercial agriculture in the areas in which the plantations were located. But after the 1830s the Danes, who were already caught up in the whirlwind of local politics and whose every activity was regarded with suspicion in many of the areas they worked in, appeared to have lost interest in their agricultural extension programmes. The work of teaching improved agriculture to the local farmers then fell to the Basel Mission which pursued its activities under the aegis of the Danish Government.

The story of the struggle of the Basel Mission for survival in Ghana in the

[1] See below, p. 128.

late 1820s and early 1830s is an heroic one.[1] After several heartbreaking reverses, the Rev. Riis eventually managed to open a mission station at Akropong in 1835, and from this base he and other missionaries who came later to join him toured Akim, Akwapim, Krobo, and the Krepi plains on the left bank of the Volta. The Rev. Riis also visited Kumasi in 1839. The missionaries were from the beginning keen on fostering commercial agriculture in Akwapim, and towards that end laid out demonstration vegetable gardens at Akropong (from which they also obtained the much-needed vegetables for their diet) which the local farmers reportedly looked on with idle interest.[2]

In 1841 the Basel Mission took the first significant step for the material welfare of the flock: the Rev. Riis and two others went to a missionary conference in Antigua to recruit craftsmen, farmers, and teachers from among the Negro converts for Ghana. Towards the end of 1842 twenty-four West Indians left for Ghana and landed at Cape Coast in April 1843; by July of the same year they were all settled at Akropong. They were supplied with cutlasses and hoes with which they cleared the ground for food farms and plantations, but the coffee seeds and sugar cane cuttings they were promised for their plantations took more than two years to arrive. In 1846 the mission felt able to declare, without any misgiving, that the West Indians were industrious, taking good care of their food farms, and that they were a good example to the local farmers whose curiosity about commercial agriculture the West Indians had succeeded in arousing. The mission changed its mind about the West Indians the following year. The latter were understandably frustrated and resentful; their crops had failed owing to unsuitable soils and depredations of termites in which the area abounded.[3]

In 1847 arrived Mr Mohr who, aided by some of the West Indian immigrants, made fresh plantations or demonstration farms on which he planted coffee and other tropical crops brought by the West Indians. Of the crops introduced by the West Indians, those that came to acquire the greatest importance in the country were a variety of cocoyam (*Xanthosoma sagittifolium*) which did not previously exist in the country,[4] and mango, varieties of which may have been already present locally. Arrowroot, a rich source of starch, was also introduced but has now practically gone out of cultiva-

[1] A brief but comprehensive summary of the extension work in agriculture undertaken by the Basel missionaries will be found in George Macdonald, *The Gold Coast, Past and Present* (London, 1898), pp. 319–28.

[2] *Digest of Basel Mission Archives on Ghana (Manuscripts), 1828–1851*, I, EC.1/33, National Archives of Ghana (NAG).

[3] Ibid.

[4] F. R. Irvine, *Plants of the Gold Coast* (O.U.P., 1930), p. 400.

tion. Groundnuts were also prominent on the mission farms and indeed on most farms in Southern Ghana.[1] It was from the time of Mr Mohr that the Basel Mission began to make real progress in the teaching of agriculture to the local people. In 1850 the numerous young coffee plantations in Akropong and the surrounding areas were in a flourishing state, and the older mission plantations yielded a harvest of 200 lb. of excellent coffee beans. The success of the coffee and other farms and of the mission's policy of agricultural education did not unfortunately neutralize the resentful attitude of the West Indian immigrants, most of whom were repatriated in 1850.

The Basel Mission was not alone in working for agricultural improvement in the country: the British Government was also keen on promoting commercial agriculture, but its policy towards that end, which had been promulgated for over two decades, only acquired definite shape and strength from 1830 onwards. The architect of the British Government's success in promoting commercial agriculture was Governor George Maclean, who took up the reins of government in the early part of 1830. The chaos of the years before his arrival had made it impossible to improve agriculture, which it was hoped would take the place of the slave trade. Within the first ten years of Maclean's governorship palm oil exports from Southern Ghana more than trebled (table 2, p. 123).

In 1841 Governor Maclean received letters from estate proprietors and managers in the West Indies asking about the possibility of recruiting from Ghana a number of free men for labour on their estates, and offering fairly generous terms of employment. Governor Maclean was enthusiastic and was of the opinion that such a scheme, if the Colonial Office would allow it, would ultimately benefit Ghana. The Ghanaian farmers, he argued, would return home with a full practical knowledge of tropical agriculture and with sufficient capital to start their own plantations, and their farming would be a salutary example to the local peasants. The scheme was nevertheless shelved until 1848, a year after Governor Maclean's death, when it was finally approved by the Colonial Office. Governor Maclean's sanguine hopes remained unfulfilled, because no one was willing to emigrate from Ghana to the West Indies.[2]

The achievements of the Wesleyan Mission in its role as promoter of commercial agriculture were modest, and whatever success blessed the efforts of the mission was due in the main to the enthusiastic work done

[1] Robertson, *Notes on Africa*, p. 202.

[2] (NAG), ADM 1/448, despatch from Cape Coast Castle, dated 31 August 1841 to Lord John Russell; ADM 1/450, despatch dated 29 November 1848 from W. Winniett to Earl Grey.

by the Rev. Thomas B. Freeman. A great desire for improved agriculture manifested itself among his converts in Fantiland. The converts, especially those at Dominase on the Cape Coast–Prasu road, for example asked him to bring back with him from England a supply of seeds, agricultural implements, 'and anything that would be useful to them in cultivating their native soil'.[1] The request was put before the English Society for the Extinction of the Slave Trade, which generously made funds available for purchasing the necessary materials.[2] Mr Freeman established two model farms at Dominase and Mansu, the former slave market. Missionaries were stationed at each place, and one of their primary objectives was that of 'instructing in the practical science of agriculture all those natives, whether christians or heathens, who may feel disposed to turn their attention to it'.[3] The model farms were by all accounts successful, but they appear to have been the only farms of their kind established by the Wesleyan Mission up to about 1850.

## Plantation agriculture 1702–1806

Areally, plantations were not significant in the agricultural landscape, but their very insignificance needs underlining since it emphasized the stupendous obstacles that lay in the way of agricultural improvement. Until about the close of the eighteenth century almost all the major attempts at establishing plantation agriculture in the country were made by the Dutch. Their early cotton plantations on the coast[4] were extended and improved in the succeeding years. Plantations for crops other than cotton were also laid out in a few settlements on the coast, as at Butri where the Dutch in 1708 prepared the ground for a large sugar cane plantation as well as setting up a rum factory near by to absorb the sugar cane from the plantation. Two hundred slaves were imported from Dahomey to work on the plantation, as well as materials from Holland needed for the factory. The Butri plantation was conceived on such a generous scale that the British governor, Sir Dalby Thomas, expressed the fear that if it was successful the Dutch would in a few years be able to sell sugar cheaply and seriously threaten the British sugar plantations in the Caribbean.[5]

Nevertheless the Dutch plantations were not entirely successful, and many of them were indeed neglected and allowed to run wild. The cotton

[1] Rev. John Beecham, Evidence before Select Committee on West Coast of Africa, 1842, *Minutes*, paragraph 3648.
[2] Idem, *Ashantee and the Gold Coast* (London, 1841), p. 307.
[3] See footnote 1.
[4] See above, pp. 75–6.
[5] Barbot, *North and South Guinea*, p. 443.

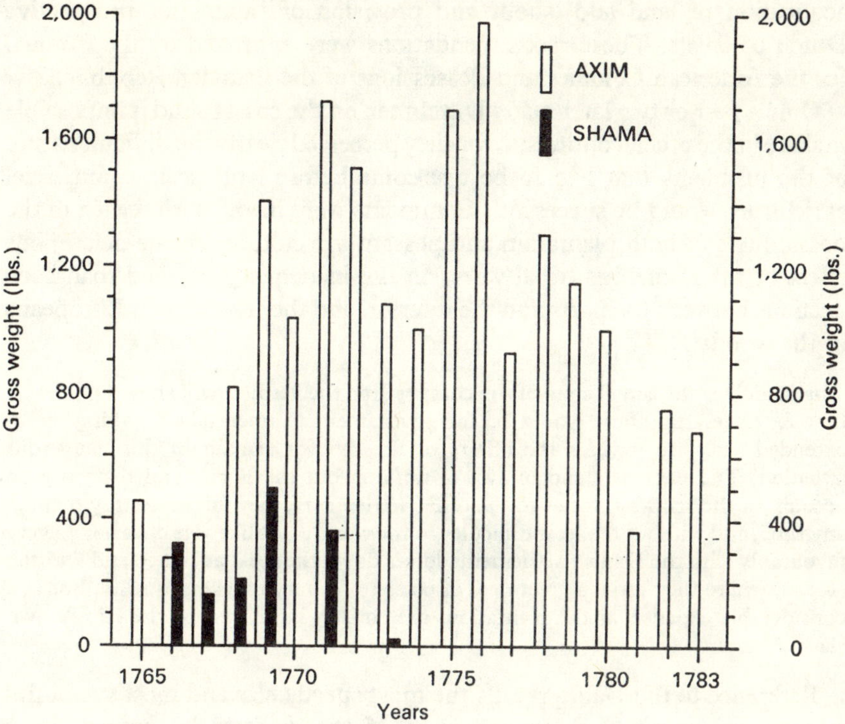


10 Dutch exports of cotton

plantations persisted longest, but even they were eventually forced into decay by the country's political, economic, and social conditions which were distinctly against ready progress in agriculture. Figure 10 shows how the Dutch cotton plantations at Axim, the most flourishing in the country, were gradually dragged towards ruin between 1775 and 1783 in spite of bold efforts to revive them, until they eventually stopped yielding and were practically abandoned in 1800. The plantations at Shama, which had also survived many vicissitudes, were abandoned in 1772 at a time when they could yield only 13 lb. (gross weight) of raw cotton as compared with 363 lb. gross weight in the previous year.

In spite of these failures the Dutch still believed in the possibility of making plantations on the coast. The Commissioners for Civil Affairs recommended in 1801 that no time ought to be lost in promoting the cultivation of 'such articles as this coast has been found to produce with but little trouble and labour'. Then followed detailed proposals on the acquisition of land and labour and provision of capital for prospective Dutch colonists. These recommendations were approved by the Council for the American Colonies and Possessions of the Batavian Republic.[1]

Only a year or two later many Dutchmen on the coast found it impossible to share in the official optimism, for they perceived clearly the difficult nature of the problems that had to be overcome before large-scale commercial agriculture would be successful. Comments were made, with regard to the possibilities of both plantation and peasant agriculture, on the deleterious effect of the numerous tribal wars, on the inadequacy of good road connections between the ports and the interior, and the 'unsafety of Europeans in the woods'.

This sketch of the actual state of the country [ran the verdict] will show sufficiently how extremely unsafe it would be for government to undertake anything on an extended scale, as long as the affairs of the interior remain in this dangerous situation. The negroes stand in awe of nothing but the Forts; and that only on account of the artillery: for as to the other settlements, they might destroy them at any time, and without the least difficulty in the world... It likewise does not go very favourably with the Danish settlements lower down the coast at Ningo and Quittah (Keta), where they grow a great deal of cotton of a very excellent quality, but at a considerable expense, as the plantations are entirely cultivated by the King's own slaves.[2]

Reference to the Danes recalls the most spectacular and most successful attempt made, since about the close of the eighteenth century, by a Colonial Power to introduce commercial agriculture in the country mainly for the edification of the local peasant farmers. In 1788 the Danish Government planned to introduce plantation agriculture in its settlements in Ghana as a preparatory measure to dropping its share in the export slave trade fourteen years from that date, and P. E. Isert was entrusted with the work of setting up plantations near the Danish forts to demonstrate the cultivation of coffee, cocoa, cotton, etc. After initial reverses at Big Ada, where he planned to establish the first plantation, Isert finally obtained land for the purpose at a place near Akropong in Akwapim, on which he planted cotton and tobacco among other crops. Isert's work came to an abrupt end with his death in 1789, but three years later his work was once more taken up and vigorously pursued by men like Lieut.-Col. Roer, whose sister also taught the girls at Akwapim to spin cotton; J. N. Flindt, who was commander of the fort at Ada; J. P. D. Wriesberg, Governor-General of the Danish settlements; and Peter Thonning, a botanist. New plantations were made in Akwapim, Ada, Keta, and near Christiansborg. Cotton thrived on

[1] C.O. 267/22, P.R.O. [2] Ibid.

all the plantations, while those at Akwapim additionally carried coffee. The plough was also introduced in Akwapim by the Danes in the 1790s.[1]

The British, who with the Dutch and the Danes constituted the major Colonial Powers in the country, were not behind in planning and expressing the need to develop both plantation and peasant agriculture, but they achieved little. Colonel Torrane, the British Governor, made a coffee plantation near the Kakum River about four miles north of Cape Coast Castle, and that was about all. For the rest, cultivation was not carried on beyond the 'kitchen gardens' near the castle.

## 1807–*c.* 1850

After 1806 plantation agriculture began to recover from its drooping state but only to a limited extent, for the operative political, social, and economic factors in the country still made it difficult for large plantations to enjoy the expected economies of scale. Tribal wars were still frequent. Neither was it possible, for many reasons, to expect a steady supply of labour drawn from free men, while the productivity of slave labour, which was still plentiful, was generally admitted to be low. The constant mobility of free labour could only be stopped if high enough wages could be offered on the plantations, but the requisite capital was not forthcoming from Europe. In sum, the success of plantations on the scale envisaged by the Europeans could not in any way be guaranteed. Large plantations were extremely expensive to run.

In spite of these formidable limitations, the Dutch achieved a certain measure of success in plantation agriculture. For example a Dutch mulatto, Mr Neiser, made a large plantation about two miles behind Elmina between 1810 and 1815, on which he planted 35,000 cotton plants, and towards the end of the decade he employed eighty men to prepare another piece of ground for a coffee plantation. A well-kept road, at least 30 feet broad, led from the castle to the cotton plantation.[2]

Danish efforts in the direction of plantation agriculture received a fresh stimulus in 1807 when Christian Schionning was appointed governor of the Danish settlements. Schionning, an enthusiastic agriculturist, not only improved the plantations left by his predecessor but also made a large one for coffee at Dahkubi in the Akwapim Mountains. In 1810 there were no fewer than 36,500 coffee bushes on the plantation, but the Ashanti invasion

[1] Dickson, op. cit. Also H. Jeppesen, 'Danske Plantageanlaeg på Guldkysten, 1788–1850', *Geog. Tidsskr.* LXV (1966).

[2] William Hutton, *A Voyage to Africa in the Year 1820* (London, 1820), pp. 53–4.

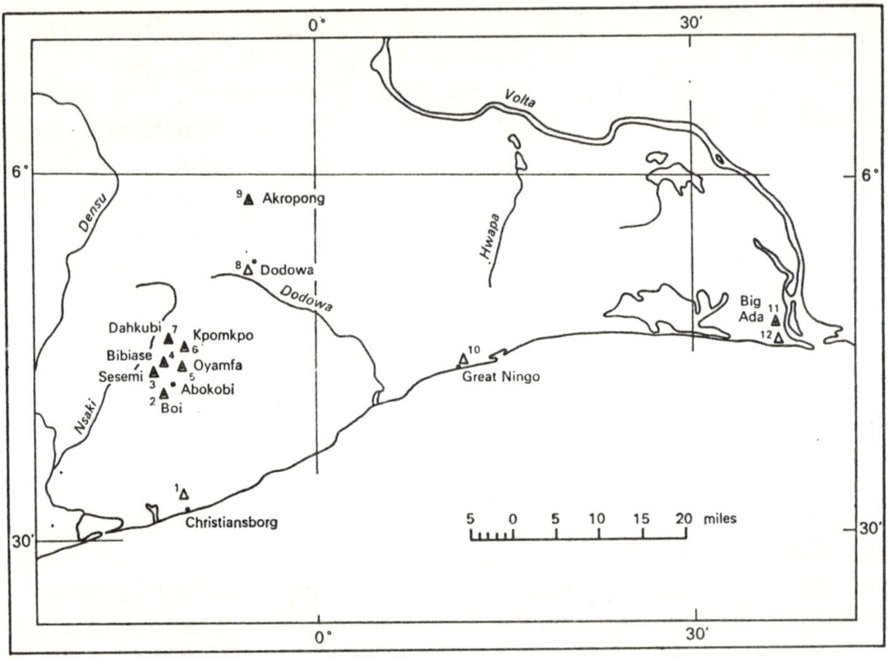


11 Danish plantations: ¹△ Frederiksberg; ²△ De Forenede Broedre; ³△ Frederiksgave; ⁴△ Bibiase Plantation; ⁵△ Oyamfa Plantation; ⁶△ The Kpomkpo Establishment; ⁷△ Dahkubi Plantation; ⁸△ Frederiksted; ⁹△ Frederiksnopel; ¹⁰△ Fredensborg Fort; ¹¹△ Jaegerlyst; ¹²△ Ejebo

of Akwapim in 1811 which resulted in partial ruin of the plantation discouraged Schionning. Thereafter little was done by the Danes about plantation agriculture until 1835 when another governor, F. S. Moerc, made a plantation, called Frederiksgave, at the foot of the Akwapim Mountains. By 1838 there were several Danish plantations in Akwapim and in the south-east coastal plains (fig. 11).[1] The Danes once more found it impossible to continue with plantation agriculture or with imparting agricultural knowledge to the local peasants, and they remained inactive, after delegating their programmes for agricultural improvement in the country to the Basel Mission, until they sold their possessions to the British and left the coast in 1850.

The British also made a move in the direction of commercial agriculture soon after 1807, but their efforts were not so sustained and so successful as

[1] The information for this map is taken from the files of the Ghana National Museum.

those of the Danes or the Dutch. Coffee was already cultivated at Cape Coast—there were over 4,000 coffee bushes on the plantation—as well as cotton in the time of Governor Torrane; and samples of cotton were repeatedly sent to England. The plantations were ignored after the time of Torrane, in spite of the earnest hopes and good intentions of several individuals. Edward William White, Torrane's successor, admitted in 1810 that the British had achieved little in commercial or plantation agriculture in Southern Ghana, but went on to declare that the British were making great efforts to improve the farms they had made and that there was no doubt of eventual success in the cultivation of coffee and cotton.[1] To what extent these hopes were fulfilled after several years may be judged from the following description of the British plantation at Cape Coast:[2]

> The (African) Committee have, it is true, sent out cotton seed; and they have, also, made a profession of encouraging agriculture: they have succeeded so far, by this assiduity, that one acre of land is cleared, about six miles from Cape Coast, where some esculent plants, and leguminous vegetables, are cultivated to a sufficient extent to deck, sometimes, the Governor's table; there may be, also, fifty or an hundred cotton plants on the same spot of ground.

Apparently the vegetables were produced in quantities that were not even large enough to satisfy the needs of the residents in Cape Coast Castle, who therefore had to go to the Dutch farms at Elmina for further supplies.

The period of George Maclean's governorship saw a resurgence of British interest in plantation agriculture, and in 1837 Mr Swanzy, one of the principal merchants in Southern Ghana, endeavoured to revive the derelict plantation originally made by Torrane at Cape Coast. He employed a hundred men to work on the plantation, which was christened 'Napoleon', under the supervision of H. C. Wilson, an expert on tropical agriculture. The enterprise was successful and the first harvest of cotton from the plantation was exported to England; but exception was taken in the English market to the shortness of the staple, and the price offered was consequently low. Cotton cultivation at Napoleon thus proved to be unprofitable, and the cotton plants were neglected and allowed to grow wild.[3] In about 1839 Mr Swanzy once more had part of Napoleon plantation cleared, this time for coffee imported from Principe Island. Two years later the plantation covered an area of 60 to 70 acres and carried 3,393 coffee bushes, 800 of which were in bearing. Again this enterprise was doomed to

[1] C.O. 267/29, P.R.O.
[2] Robertson, op. cit. p. 137.
[3] C.O. 267/71, P.R.O., Report of Commission of Inquiry on the Western Coast of Africa, 1841 (Madden Report).

failure so long as a duty of 1*s*. 3*d*. per lb. was paid on African coffee in England, as compared with the 6*d*. per lb. on West Indian coffee.[1]

Yet another attempt was made in 1850, this time by the British Administration itself, to revive cotton cultivation at Napoleon, and 25,000 cotton plants were sown on the plantation under the supervision of an American agriculturist specially sent out for the purpose.[2] This renewed activity probably resulted from the encouraging report given by J. A. Turner, a cotton cloth manufacturer in Manchester, on samples of cotton from 'a small plantation' sent to England in the late 1840s. The samples were returned from England in the form of cloth, 'not a little to the delight of the native labourers employed on the plantation'.[3] Nevertheless the new cotton plantation also failed through the difficulty of obtaining a regular supply of labour. Governor Winniett's desperate proposal that pawns, jailed criminals, and idle domestic slaves, 'some of them roguish and irresponsible', should be employed compulsorily on the plantation was not implemented.[4]

The repeated failure of large-scale agricultural enterprises and indeed of many of the grand schemes for improving peasant agriculture in the country up to about 1850 underlines the fact that the requisite conditions under which agriculture would be successful were not yet fully present. The problems were many, but dominating the rest was that of political insecurity and social instability[5] created by the numerous wars with nearly all of which the Ashanti were either directly or indirectly connected.

## TRADE AND TRADE ROUTES

The changes that occurred in the country's trade were heralded in the late seventeenth century and they centred mainly on Ashanti's geographical position in the middle of the country. It was customary for the Ashanti court not to allow traders from subject states in the interior to proceed directly to the European trading posts on the coast except with special permission which, if granted, insisted that the traders passed through Kumasi.[6] Similarly, merchants from Southern Ghana could only trade beyond Ashanti through Kumasi.

[1] Ibid.

[2] Evidence of A. Swanzy before the Select Committee on West Africa, 1865. See paragraph 4827 of *Minutes*.

[3] (NAG), ADM 1/451, despatch 22 May 1850.

[4] Dickson, 'The Agricultural Landscape...1800 to 1850'.

[5] Rowan Report.

[6] African no. 268, *Further Correspondence Regarding Affairs of the Gold Coast* (Colonial Office, February 1884), enclosure in Paper no. 2 is a letter from the governor, Sir Samuel Rowe, dated Christiansborg Castle, 29 March 1883, containing confidential instructions to Captain Barrow on his mission to Ashanti.

One road along which traders from Salaga and eastern Brong Ahafo could have travelled to the coast without passing anywhere near Kumasi was that from Salaga through Kete and Krachi to Ada or Accra; but two factors limited its usefulness in that respect. The first of these was the great fetish god Dente at Krachi which, perhaps to preserve the natural value of that place as a transhipment point, strictly forbade traders from the interior or the coast from passing beyond there. A later illustration of this was the case of the Accra merchant R. Bannerman and the Frenchman J. Bonnat who in 1875 travelled up the Volta with the object of opening up trading relations between the coast and Salaga and other northern markets. They encountered considerable difficulty in passing through Kete and Krachi, and it was not until after a delay of three days, during which they lavished gifts on the fetish Dente, that they were allowed to proceed from there to Salaga; but all the Krepi attendants with them were turned back.[1] The second factor involved the Ashanti who established on the Krachi–Ada route a check point, which later grew into the settlement of Ahinkro, where officials enforced the embargo on the passage of European goods, especially firearms and ammunition, directly from the coast into the interior.[2]

Ashanti thus became the great heart that pumped life along the major commercial arteries that led southward to the coastal ports or northward to and beyond Northern Ghana. To regularize trade in the Ashanti provinces in Southern Ghana, Brong Ahafo, and Northern Ghana, and to ensure a steady flow of revenue therefrom to the court treasury, the king of Ashanti stationed trade officials, toll gatherers, and administrators in several major settlements, including those at important crossroads. Elmina, Cape Coast, and Accra on the coast were the most important seats of Ashanti traders and diplomatic officials; in the interior the Akwapim town of Mamfe, situated at the junction of major trade routes from Ashanti and Akim to the coast, was one of many such settlements in Southern Ghana with Ashanti officials.[3] Many important trade-route settlements in Brong Ahafo likewise had Ashanti officials stationed in them, especially since the early nineteenth century. The settlements included Atebubu, Nsawkaw, and Nsuta (near Techiman). In subject Northern Ghana, Salaga, Daboya, and Yendi were some of the seats of Ashanti officials.[4]

[1] African no. 95, *Dr. Gouldsbury's Report of His Journey into the Interior of the Gold Coast* (Colonial Office, May 1876). It will subsequently be referred to as Gouldsbury Report.

[2] BPP, Cmd. 3386, *Further Correspondence Regarding Affairs of the Gold Coast* (Colonial Office, August 1882). Enclosure 2 in Paper no. 42 is 'Report by Captain Rupert La Trobe Lonsdale of his Mission to Coomassie, Salagha, Yendi, etc.' henceforth referred to as Lonsdale Report.

[3] Isert, *Voyages en Guinée*, p. 250.

[4] I. Wilks, *Ashanti Government in the Nineteenth Century* (Institute of African Studies, University of Ghana, 1964), Draft paper no. 3, Unpublished and Restricted, pp. 39–45.

Regularization of trade in Ashanti kingdom affected the role and importance of established trade routes, some of which became the major venues for Ashanti trade to the coast or to Northern Ghana. All major commercial arteries radiated from Kumasi, and the volume of trade along them depended, apart from purely political considerations which occasionally diverted trade elsewhere, on the extent and importance of European trade at the port termini. In this way the direct routes from Kumasi to Accra, Cape Coast and Elmina came to acquire additional importance, judging by their frequent use throughout the eighteenth and nineteenth centuries by Ashanti traders. In Northern Ghana the route from Kumasi through Atebubu, Salaga to Yendi and across to Hausaland through Sansanne Mango became the most important commercial artery after the Ashanti deliberately transferred to it in the early nineteenth century their trade on the ancient Kumasi–Begho route.[1]

The growing influence of Ashanti on patterns of trade did not extend to improvement of the condition of the trade routes, many of which had their courses marked at several points by swamps, fallen trees, and 'barriers of matted vegetation'.[2] Perhaps there was no pressing need for radical improvement of the routes since carriages and other forms of vehicular transport were generally absent, and the usual mode of travel by foot allowed greater flexibility and ease of by-passing obstacles. Nevertheless serious blockages were always removed on the orders of the chiefs in whose territory they occurred. This was traditional practice.

It is in connection with improvement of land transport that may be seen clear evidence of the germination of ideas with the British that were to lead to their complete involvement in the political and economic affairs of the country. Already, by the early nineteenth century, the British were showing interest in the physical condition of the trade routes in limited areas in Southern Ghana, and whenever reports reached them of impassable routes in those areas they employed men to remove the obstructions or cut alternative routes.[3] Yet political considerations did not always allow the British to pursue their laudable policy of improving land transport; so that the Administration, for a brief period in the 1820s, deliberately but paradoxically kept the routes in a poor condition in order to prevent easy communication between the British forts and Kumasi.[4] Nevertheless the British made some efforts, though disjointed, at building roads to link some of their forts. A good carriage road was built under the direction of

[1] Bowdich, *Mission...*, p. 181.
[2] Dupuis, *Journal*, pt. II, p. xxix.
[3] Ibid.
[4] *Ibid.* p. xxx.

Sir Charles MacCarthy in 1822 from Cape Coast to Anomabu but was allowed to deteriorate after Sir Charles's death in 1823.[1] Later attempts at road construction were by Governor Winniett who, in 1847, appointed John de Graft of Cape Coast an Overseer of Public Roads and requisitioned tools to be used for 'improving the streets and roads in the neighbourhood of Cape Coast for the use of the Civil Government on the Gold Coast'.[2] The effects of these measures were also temporary.

## PORTS[3]

As in the case of trade routes, the changing fortunes of ports mirrored the changing nature of the country's economic geography. The numerous ports that served the country at the beginning of the eighteenth century were gradually reduced in number in succeeding years as patterns of trade and production in the country changed. In the same way the status and function of certain ports were confirmed or reduced.

As long as exports were confined mainly to gold, slaves, and ivory, changes in port status were often temporary and not of a significant magnitude; and this was true for the period up to 1806. To these exports must be added timber which began to appear more frequently on the export lists in the course of the eighteenth century. Timber was exported mainly from Axim and neighbouring ports; but by 1800 the immediate vicinity of the port at Axim and of the other ports had been denuded of exportable timber. Exports then practically ceased, since it had become necessary to transport timber over long distances from the forest to the ports, a task that proved too formidable in the absence of wagons or machines and tools for working the wood.[4]

After 1806 agricultural commodities, especially palm oil, began to feature more prominently in the country's overseas trade, and changes in port status correspondingly became more rapid and more significant. It was about this time too that the European Powers on the coast began to look more closely at port location with respect to the physical features of the site, and to discourage trade at those ports where navigation and landing were difficult. For example, attention was drawn in 1822 to the dangers of navigating the narrow and difficult channel between the rocks in the little

[1] ADM 1/451 (NAG), letter dated 22 May 1850 from Governor Winniett.
[2] ADM 1/449 (NAG), letter dated 31 July 1847 from Governor Winniett.
[3] Dickson, 'Evolution of Seaports in Ghana: 1800–1928', *Ann. Ass. Am. Geogr.* LV, 1 (March 1965). Unless otherwise stated, the details in this section on ports are to be found in the article.
[4] C.O. 267/22, P.R.O.

bay at whose head the town of Dixcove stood, and the implication drawn that there was no reason why ships should stop there.[1]

### Western region

Between 1822 and 1827 the busier ports in the Western Region were Axim, Dutch Sekondi, and Dixcove, although Dixcove had gradually been losing its trade over the previous ten years or so. The remaining ports were in a state of rapid decline, for reasons exemplified by the case of the port of Beyin. First, there was the violent surf which rendered the process of landing goods or loading them on to ships at Beyin dangerous. Secondly, the port's trade was interfered with by the local chief, who did not scruple to rob merchants or maltreat European officials residing in his town. Lastly, the flow of the principal exports of Beyin, gold and ivory from Denkera and Wasaw, was repeatedly interrupted through dissensions among the tribes in the hinterland on the one hand, and between the chief of Beyin and the chiefs controlling the trade routes linking Beyin with its hinterland on the other. It is thus not surprising that Fort Appollonia at Beyin was abandoned as early as 1820, and that Beyin in 1827 exported not more than 2,000 oz. of gold and about 4 tons of ivory. Butri and Shama were, in addition to reasons similar to those outlined for the loss of trade at Beyin, too close to Sekondi to exist and flourish independently.

Dixcove lost much of its trade for slightly different reasons. On considerations of physical geography alone the port of Dixcove, in spite of what Sir Robert Mends wrote about it,[2] was no worse than most ports on the surf-bound coast. The reasons for the loss of trade at Dixcove were threefold. In the first place, as in the case of Beyin, interminable quarrels between the chief of Dixcove and the chief of Wasaw reduced the port's trade in gold and ivory—particularly in gold—to insignificant proportions. In the second place, taxes levied on the inhabitants of Dixcove by the king of Ashanti, who had political control over them, were so heavy and extortionate as to stifle economic activity and encourage emigration from the town. The third reason, of temporary validity, was the low price offered at the time in England for palm oil, one of the principal exports of Dixcove. In 1827,

[1] C.O. 267/56, P.R.O., despatch dated 22 May 1822. Also C.O. 267/93, P.R.O., *Report of the Commissioners of Inquiry into the State of the Colony of Sierra Leone and Its Dependencies* (1827), by Major James Rowan (Rowan Report). This and Sir Charles McCarthy's general report on the British 'Forts and Settlements on the Gold Coast' (1822) constitute the best earliest material since 1800 on the country's ports and their trade. Although the two documents were written five years apart, they supplement each other in a most satisfactory manner.

[2] C.O. 267/56, P.R.O.

therefore, Dixcove exported little more than 100 oz. of gold (700 to 1,200 oz. in former times) and about 40,000 gallons of palm oil—which was still considerable, compared with what most other ports handled, but apparently much smaller than what used to pass through Dixcove itself. There was only one European merchant at Dixcove in 1827, and 'his house remained unfinished and neglected'.[1]

Axim, situated near the mouth of the Ankobra river, was the busiest of the three outstanding ports in the Western Region. Apart from having a safe landing beach, the town was also the seat of the vice-president of the Dutch Administration. Moreover, Axim was easily accessible to the gold-producing interior both by means of the established trade route leading to it from Ashanti through Wasaw country, and by means of the Ankobra river which was navigable for a considerable distance upstream by small vessels.

The success of Dutch Sekondi as a port rested on the fact that it possessed a good landing beach fairly well sheltered from strong winds, and on its nearness to Wasaw, a rich source of gold and ivory. Takoradi, another Dutch settlement near Sekondi but as a port of lesser significance than the latter, was considered to hold great promise as a future port because of its sheltered site, and the protection afforded it by the guns of the fort at Dutch Sekondi. It is true there were dangerous reefs at Takoradi but these were rather thought to be of great value in forming a safe harbour for vessels, although it was conceded that the reefs were dangerous to pass in the night by sailors unacquainted with the coast. It was further suggested that it would be wise for the British to take possession of Takoradi and Dutch Sekondi, so that they could own 'one of the strongest and most desirable situations on the coast, particularly as there is also a sheltered harbour for vessels immediately under the Dutch fort at Succondee (Sekondi)'.[2]

## Central Region

In the Central Region the best port, from the point of view of shelter for ships and of facilities for loading or unloading them, was easily Elmina, the seat of the Dutch Administration. The great castle stood, and still stands, near the mouth of the River Benya, on a calm bay which was deep enough for the shallow-draught ships of the period to come very close to land. In addition the Dutch had built, within the first half of the eighteenth century, a wooden wharf on which stood a crane for landing goods which could then

[1] Rowan Report. [2] Hutton, *A Voyage to Africa*, p. 43.

be taken into the castle through a gate opening directly on to the wharf.[1] The port dealt extensively in slaves, gold and ivory, mostly from Ashanti, and in small quantities of agricultural produce. The uniqueness of the port is explained not only by its possession of a wharf but also by the fact that the town's welfare was the special concern of the king of Ashanti who had the right to collect ground rent from the Dutch. Elmina was consequently a favourite rendezvous for Ashanti traders.

Eight miles to the east of Elmina was the port of Cape Coast, the seat of the British Administration. Its trade was apparently as important as that of Elmina, but unlike the latter it had no port facilities for handling cargo. The landing was bad and several observers lamented the fact that the British Administration had thought neither of building a quay, for which the reef projecting into the sea from near the castle would have provided a natural foundation, nor of developing and using the little bay with relatively calm water about two miles east of the town.[2]

Nevertheless merchant ships called regularly and conducted brisk trade at the port, in spite of the heavy surf, the treacherous reefs, and the constant risk of shipwreck. The principal exports were gold, mainly from Akim and Ashanti, and ivory from the forest country behind the port, including Ashanti. Small quantities of palm oil from the immediate interior and, occasionally, maize were also exported. The port's trade was virtually at the mercy of the Ashanti who could always bring it to a standstill by re-routing their goods to Elmina and other Dutch ports. Thus the main anxiety of the British in their relations with the Ashanti was to keep the Cape Coast–Kumasi trade route open at all times.

Cape Coast was an important trading centre: almost every contemporary work on the country bore witness to it. The prosperity was reflected in the stone houses in the town, among other things, for, outside Elmina where the normal building material was the local sandstone, there was hardly any other town in the country in which the inhabitants undertook the expensive and difficult task of building in stone. The major exceptions were Accra and Cape Coast, and the latter boasted of fourteen stone houses in 1827, each worth anything up to £2,500 at the time.[3] The proliferation of warehouses in the town was also a good indication of the extent of trading activities at Cape Coast.

A few miles east of Cape Coast was the Dutch port of Mouri which used to be an important slave port but had lost practically all its trade by the end of the first decade of the nineteenth century. The port did not survive the

[1] G. Sale et al. (ed.), *The Modern Part of an Universal History* (London, 1760), XVII, 54–5.

[2] Robertson, *Notes on Africa*, p. 130.

[3] Rowan Report.

first Ashanti invasion of the coast in 1806. Next to Mouri was the port of Anomabu which was said in 1803 to be 'the centre of commerce for the Gold Coast', with fifteen to twenty ships daily anchored in the roads to load on merchandise. Some of the merchants at Anomabu even came from as far as Dahomey.[1] The situation was different fifteen years later: its trade had been diverted to other ports, and many of the inhabitants who sought refuge in the neighbouring towns during the Ashanti war of 1806 had not returned.[2] There was a certain amount of recovery in the early 1820s, and about 137,000 oz. of gold, 8 tons of ivory, and 1,300 puncheons, equivalent to about 500 tons, of palm oil were exported annually. Also, the town itself, with an estimated population of about 3,000, was being steadily rebuilt. The persistence of the port could be explained by its central position on the country's coastline, and by its having a tolerably good landing beach.

The ports of Amoku, Kormatin, Tantum and, to some extent, Saltpond were of no consequence, having lost practically all their trade to Anomabu; similarly the port of Apam had been forced into obscurity by the wider influence of Winneba, which itself was not as important as it used to be in about 1800, although it still exported considerable quantities of gold from Akim and palm oil from Agona country. The port of Winneba possessed a number of advantages with respect to site and location. The bay on which the port stood was calm and safe for navigation, and the port was the terminus of a short route to the rich gold country of Akim. Also, Winneba was regarded as one of the healthiest spots on the coast. The loss of trade at Winneba after 1810 was due, not to a change in physical or economic factors, but to the unpopularity of the town's inhabitants with the British after the murder of the governor of the British fort there in 1812. The fort was destroyed by the British, and for many years thereafter any British warship that passed by the town fired a broadside into it. The bombardment may have destroyed the town but not its geographical advantages of site and location, for it was not long before the African Company thought it would be desirable to build a large fort at Winneba in order to safeguard its trade there.[3] East of Winneba was Senya Beraku which never achieved eminence as a port; its trade in gold and ivory never amounted to more than £500 annually.

[1] P. Labarthe, *Voyage à la Côte de Guinée* (Paris, 1803), p. 71.

[2] Robertson, op. cit. p. 147.

[3] Ibid. p. 156.

## Eastern Region

The Eastern Region began roughly with the port of Accra. The port of Accra was a busy one: gold dust, ivory, palm oil, maize, cattle, and other miscellaneous products arrived in a steady stream. Gold came from Akim and Ashanti; palm oil from the Akwapim Mountains and their foothills and from Krobo. Maize was cultivated in the Accra Plains, where herds of cattle were also reared. The cattle were shipped from the port, not to Europe, but to other European forts on the coast. Also, small quantities of coffee and cotton were apparently exported now and then. Outside Cape Coast and Elmina, the greatest number of European merchants resided at Accra, not to mention the large number of African merchants who also lived there. Some of these merchants had invested large sums of money in huge stone houses, of which there were no fewer than eight in the town. For these reasons, to which must be added the fact that Accra was the terminus of one of the principal trade routes between the coast and Ashanti, Accra ranked as a major port, although the landings at Dutch and Danish sections of the town could be dangerous.

Of the remaining ports east of Accra only three—Prampram, Ada, and Keta—deserve notice. Prampram was a small palm-oil port serving, like Accra, Krobo and the Akwapim Mountains, and it maintained this function throughout the greater part of the nineteenth century. Ada, a Danish port at the mouth of the Volta River, was not of much consequence, although it used to be a major slave port. It exported, in the 1820s, small quantities of palm oil; it was mainly used as 'a port of communication between Christiansborg and Keta'.[1] The same was true of Keta which exported little else besides palm oil and, like Ada, was a watering station for ships.

Thus was the state of trade at the seaports in the 1820s and indeed throughout the next thirty years or so. The few changes that occurred after the 1820s were minor and temporary.

[1] Robertson, p. 226.

# PART III

## *From about 1850 to 1936*

# 7. Agriculture, fishing, and the timber industry

By about the middle of the nineteenth century Ashanti was no longer the sole unchallenged economic and political power in the country. The British had become a serious rival, and their growing influence was to make for a significant change in the country's economic geography since that time. It was as a direct result of their intervention in the country's economic life that, despite their slow progress since the early years of the nineteenth century, the primary economic activities, more specifically export agriculture, emerged around mid-century as the basis of existence for a significant portion of the population in Southern Ghana. For the next eighty years or so, in much of Southern Ghana, all else was subordinate to the theme of the widening agricultural landscape. During this period another primary economic activity, timber logging, came to buttress the economy in parts of Southern Ghana, especially in the Western Region.

## AGRICULTURE IN SOUTHERN GHANA AND ASHANTI–BRONG AHAFO

Two major factors, in addition to the fundamental one of the abolition of the export slave trade and the general encouragement given afterwards to agriculture by the Europeans, aided the emergence of export agriculture as the dominant economic activity in much of Southern Ghana. The middle of the century marked the culmination of about two decades of some measure of internal peace during which agriculture received a great deal of attention. About this time too the supply of the cowrie shell, the medium of exchange in Fanti country, was increased so much that a great stimulus was given to all branches of trade, but particularly to trade in palm oil.[1] In 1853 palm oil, for the first time, displaced gold as the country's principal export. It lost this premier position in 1856 only to regain it soon afterwards. Export agriculture had come to stay.

[1] Brodie Cruickshank, *Eighteen Years on the Gold Coast of Africa* (London, 1853), II, 31. Also, A. Swanzy's evidence before the Select Committee on West Africa in 1865, paragraphs 4689 and 4690 of the *Minutes*.

The *Blue Book* for 1853 gives the following agricultural exports from Southern Ghana in that year:[1]

| *Product* | *Quantity* | *Value* |
|---|---|---|
| Palm oil | 1,750 tons | £70,000 |
| Gum copal | 80 tons | £3,000 |

This list is obviously incomplete and should be extended to include kola nuts, cotton, and coffee principally. Kola nuts had never ceased to occupy a distinguished position in the country's export list, while cotton and coffee had been exported more or less regularly since the early years of the nineteenth century.

From about the middle of the century the agricultural landscape began to expand areally and its content became more diversified. During the last two decades of the century, cultivation for export became important in Ashanti–Brong Ahafo, and to the five export crops were added many new ones, the latest and most important of which was cocoa.

## The oil palm

Around the middle of the nineteenth century the most important areas for the cultivation or caring of the oil-palm tree were Krobo and Shai districts in Eastern Region. The oil palms there grew on plantations made by the farmers themselves.[2] Next in importance were Winneba and Saltpond districts; the inhabitants of Winneba especially were said to be great agriculturists.[3] Both districts owed their importance in agriculture in general to the fact that they were surrounded by friendly tribes and were therefore generally free from those war panics that from time to time convulsed various districts in Southern Ghana. After Winneba and Saltpond districts came Akwapim and Volta Region.[4]

The areas in Southern Ghana and Ashanti–Brong Ahafo where the oil-palm tree was not regarded as a major source of income were preoccupied

[1] See appendix 2.

[2] Rev. E. Schrenk of the Basel Mission said in his evidence before the Select Committee on West Africa in 1865: 'There is a large plain near the Volta which once had no trees on it about one hundred years ago, and the whole of that plain is now a palm forest.' The trees had been planted by the local farmers, and palm oil manufacture was 'a kind of industry which suited the African, and one of the first industries they had'. See paragraphs 3302–5 of the *Minutes*. The Krobo oil-palm plantations are also mentioned in J. A. B. Horton, *West African Countries and Peoples* (London, 1868), pp. 141–2.

[3] John Duncan, *Travels in West Africa: 1845–6* (London, 1847), p. 75. Also Horton, op. cit. p. 139.

[4] The order of importance of the major palm-oil areas is suggested by the figures of regional production in despatch of 11 September 1861, in C.O. 96/55, P.R.O.

with something else. In Western Region gold mining was, as before, the principal occupation, especially in Wasaw. Similarly, in Akim Abuakwa, the inhabitants ignored the oil-palm tree and devoted their energies to gold mining. Asin and western Akim were also covered with thick forest abounding in oil palms, but they produced very little palm oil. Asin was said to be very sparsely populated with the inhabitants generally poor and 'in utter barbarism'; western Akim was just as poorly developed.[1]

For some years from about 1850 the importance of the oil-palm tree in the rural economy increased mainly because of the increasing value of palm oil in the country's overseas trade. There were occasions, nevertheless, when the crop lost some of its importance, for the export trade in palm oil was subject to the effects of the unstable political conditions in the country, especially up to the 1880s, and to the changes in world market conditions (fig. 12). Between 1853 and 1860 the drops in exports were directly attributable to the disturbances, particularly serious in the Eastern Region, caused by the implementation of the Poll Tax Ordinance of 1853. In 1863 the Ashanti invaded Saltpond district, an event which threw the whole of Southern Ghana into a state of deep confusion and severely dislocated all economic activities. Yet another war, this time between the Awuna on one side and the Gã, Ada, Krobo, and Akwapim on the other, served to depress the export trade in palm oil. The war ended in 1869. It was a year before this date that exports of palm kernels, the nut cores of oil-palm fruits, began in response to the greater demands for vegetable oils in industrial Europe.

Again, all exports ceased with the onset of the Anglo-Ashanti war of 1873–4.[2] Between 1875 and 1885 the fluctuations in the exports of oil-palm products were generally a result of changes in the price offered for the commodities in Europe. The exceptions were the years 1878 and 1885 when Awuna insurgence made the Volta River, a major commercial highway for Eastern and Volta Regions, unsafe for navigation and thus caused significant drops in exports of palm kernels, most of which came from those areas.

In 1885 also occurred a marked drop in the price for palm oil in the European markets. This crippled Ghana's export trade in the commodity for many years and exposed the weakness of the foundations on which the palm-oil industry rested. The methods of preparation were rudimentary and resulted in palm oil of inferior quality with a high free-fatty-acid content; besides, the middlemen at several ports deliberately adulterated

[1] Horton, op. cit. p. 130.

[2] Palm-kernel production was not resumed in Krobo for some months after the war, for contact with the shells was regarded as a cause of smallpox.

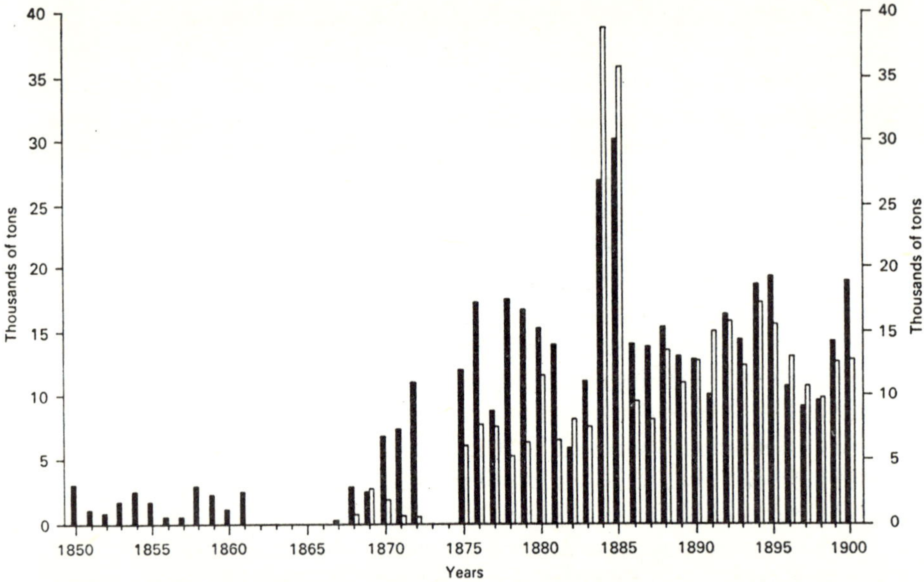


12*a* Palm oil and palm kernel exports from British Southern Ghana, 1850–1900

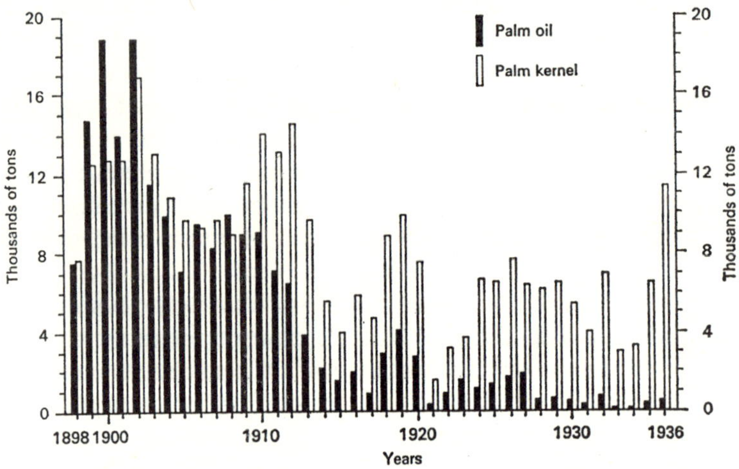


12*b* Palm oil and palm kernel exports from British Southern Ghana, 1900–36

the palm oil by mixing it with other substances. It was only at the Eastern Region ports that the palm oil offered for sale was of reasonably high quality. Yet the generally poor sort of palm oil that reached the overseas markets was expensively produced owing to the high cost of transport: of the total cost of production, transport alone accounted for about fifty per cent.[1] The process of cracking the palm nuts to obtain the kernels was wasteful and involved an enormous amount of labour. Nut cracking machines could not be used efficiently since the poor road transport system made it impossible to supply the machines with large regular amounts of palm nuts. It was estimated that vast quantities of palm nuts, worth about £1,000,000, were allowed to rot every year because of transport difficulties.[2]

The expense involved in producing palm oil and palm kernels compared rather unfavourably with that for cocoa whose production was indeed extraordinarily cheap. Consequently, farmers began to turn their attention from the oil palm to cocoa which was spreading very fast throughout the countryside of Southern Ghana and Ashanti–Brong Ahafo. In 1906 palm oil, which for over three-quarters of a century was the most valuable agricultural export, yielded pride of place to cocoa and stood third, in value, in the list of agricultural exports. By 1910 farmers in some areas, for example Abura district in Central Region, were not merely ignoring the oil-palm tree but felling them to make room for cocoa.[3] The outstanding exception was Krobo where the oil-palm tree continued to be carefully cultivated in spite of the fact that the cocoa had spread into the area. Probably the basic factor that explained the situation in Krobo was that palm oil from the area was of high quality and therefore always found a ready market. In Krobo the oil-palm tree was basic to agricultural existence, and it is not therefore surprising that by-laws prohibiting the felling of oil-palm trees were passed for the first time in the country by the Konor of Yilo Krobo.[4]

The foregoing on the erratic nature of exports of oil-palm products did not refer to the German colony of Togoland (of which Volta Region formed part) where production was carefully maintained on an even keel. The broad aim of the German Administration was to make Togoland as prosperous as possible by thoroughly developing such natural resources as it possessed.[5] This was part of the great plan for the industrial expansion

[1] *Report on Economic Agriculture on the Gold Coast (1889)*, Cmd. 5894-40.
[2] Ibid. [3] Department of Agriculture, *Annual Report*, 1910.
[4] *Gold Coast Government Gazette*, 5 July 1913.
[5] For the work of the Germans in Togoland, see R. Cornevin, *Histoire du Togo*, chapter 7; Albert F. Calvert, *Togoland* (London, 1918), *passim*; and *Colonial Report—Togoland*, 1920–1.

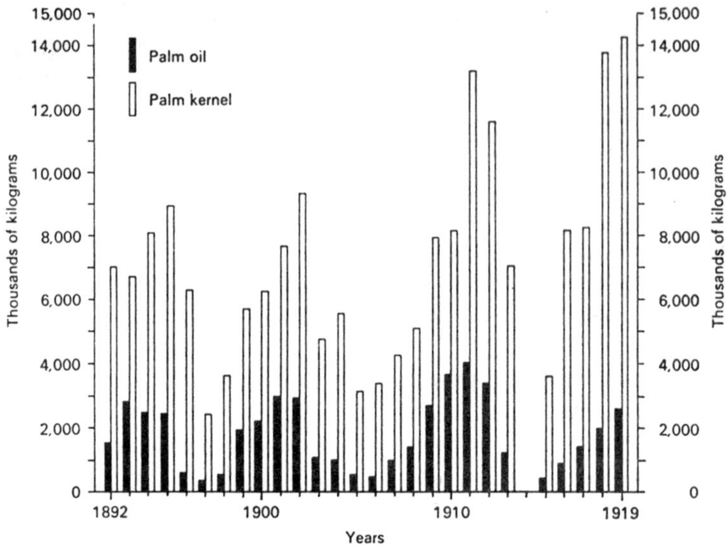


13 Palm oil and palm kernel exports from German Togoland, 1892–1919

of Germany: Togoland would supply Germany with raw materials and in return become a market for Germany's industrial products. Therefore agricultural production in Togoland was not left to chance. The Germans opened an Agricultural Training College at Tove and experimental stations at a number of places where farmers received instruction in methods of cultivation and were supplied with superior varieties of seeds or seedlings for planting on their farms.

Also, the Germans established oil-palm plantations in addition to those of the peasant farmers, and inspected the palm oil at the ports to ensure high quality. With equal seriousness they tackled the problem of shelling palm nuts effectively for the kernels and set up several experimental nut-cracking machines. With the exception of the two well-defined periods of 1896–8 and 1905–8 when world markets were affected by a general depression, the trend of production of oil-palm products in Volta Region was normally one of increase (fig. 13).

After 1910 a major effort was made to stabilize the production of palm oil and palm kernels in Southern Ghana, excluding the Volta Region. Numerous oil-palm plantations were made (fig. 14) following the passing of the Palm Oil Ordinance of 1913, but the only plantations which eventually showed profit were those in Western Region. The main difficulty

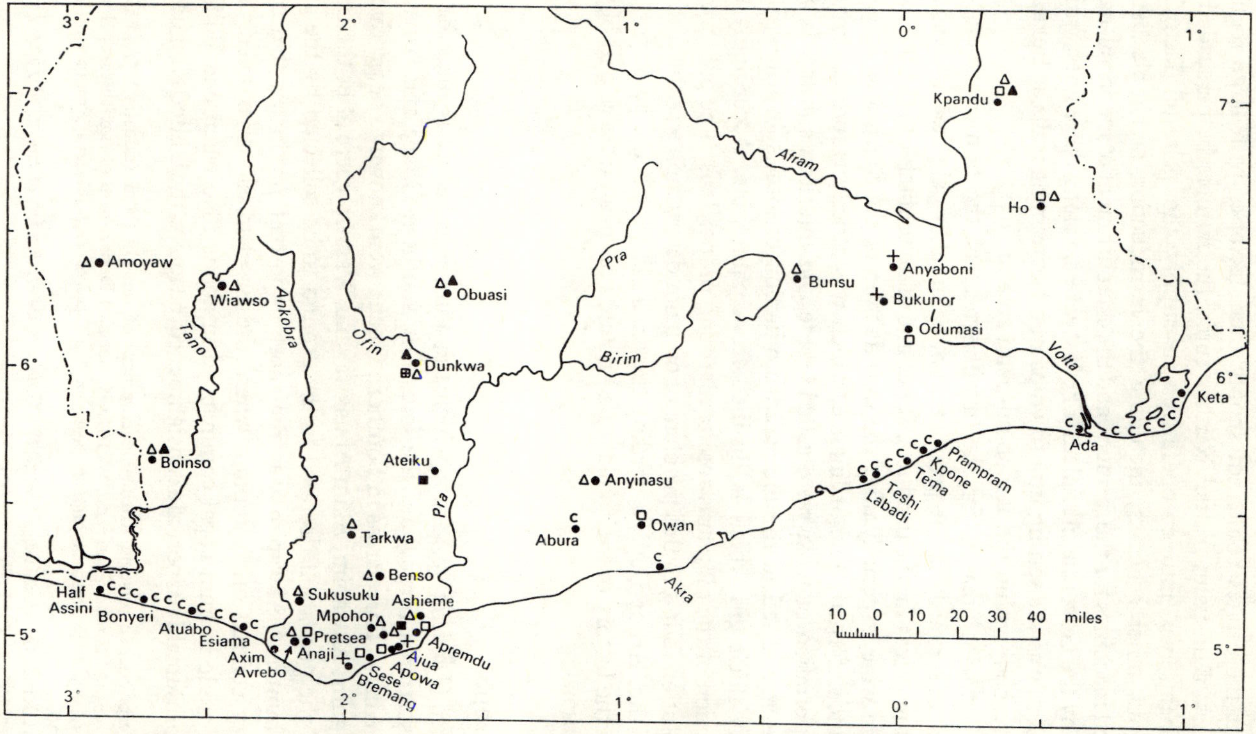


14 Plantations, 1900–36. ■ Bananas, C coconut, □ oil palm, △ rubber, ▲ cocoa, ⊞ coffee, + palm oil factory

was that the estates could not supply their factories with large regular quantities of oil-palm fruits.[1] Neither could the farmers be persuaded to form themselves into co-operatives to supply the palm-oil factories. Numerous other schemes, including the introduction of simple hand-operated machines for the farmers, and the establishment of model oil-palm estates by the Government failed. The last scheme along these lines, which also failed, was the setting up of two palm oil-extracting mills at Bukunor and Anyaboni within the Krobo oil-palm area in 1931.

The principal reason for the unwillingness of the farmers to engage themselves seriously in the production of palm oil or palm kernels was the ruling low prices for the products. It became more profitable to tap the trees for palm wine, especially after the introduction of the Spirituous Liquors Ordinance of 1920. The ordinance, which was strictly enforced, forbade the importation of what were called 'trade and injurious spirits'. It was unpopular and led to the increased production of local substitutes, particularly illicit gin which is distilled from palm wine. Accordingly the destruction of the oil palms rose to alarming proportions. The only workable solution found to this problem of oil palm destruction was the institution of the 'Arbor Day', according to which villagers chose an important date in the history of their village and planted oil-palm trees as part of the celebrations.[2]

## Gum copal

The tree (*Daniella* sp.) from which this gum is collected is, like the oil palm, scattered throughout the forests of Southern Ghana and Ashanti–Brong Ahafo. Three areas in Southern Ghana were known to be producers of the gum: Akwapim, Akim Abuakwa[3] and Wasaw, where after the rainy season the gum itself dropped to the ground to be collected by the gum copal hunters.[4] Akwapim was the most important producer; there the industry centred on Akropong where the Basel missionaries lived. The export trade in gum copal commenced in about 1850 when one William Addo presumably exported a consignment of 64 tons to the United Kingdom.[5]

1 'Correspondence relating to the Development of the Oil Palm Industry', *Gold Coast Government Sessional Paper*, no. IV, 1924–5. See also Department of Agriculture, *Annual Reports*, 1911–36, and *Annual Reports on the Central and Western Provinces*, 1912–1929/30.

2 Sir Frederick Gordon Guggisberg, *The Gold Coast—A Review of Events of 1924–25 and the Prospects of 1925–26* (Accra, 1925).

3 Divisional Court Records, S.C.T.2, I, 28 January 1861, NAG.

4 Thomas J. Hutchinson, *Impressions of West Africa* (London, 1858), p. 62.

5 Horton, op. cit. p. 146.

As in the case of the oil-palm products, the export of gum copal fluctuated a great deal in response to political upheavals within the country and fluctuations in the price offered for it in Europe (fig. 15). Ghana's gum copal on the whole fetched a low price because of its poor quality and could not compete with the superior variety from East Africa. Up to the 1880s the gum tree steadily lost its importance and was ignored in preference for coffee whose cultivation in the forest areas was steadily increasing.

In the late 1880s and subsequently for a few years, the production of gum copal increased owing to the greater demand for the product in the United States and, to a lesser extent, in Europe. Also, Ashanti with its vast resource of gum copal trees began to produce for export in the same period, and soon it became the largest exporter of the product in the country. This was because cocoa was yet a minor crop in Ashanti, so that when cocoa cultivation began to spread rapidly throughout Ashanti after 1906–7, the centre of gum copal production shifted to the forest of western Brong Ahafo where cocoa cultivation remained unimportant. A similar process of displacement or total elimination of gum copal production occurred in Southern Ghana with the continuing spread of cocoa cultivation. By 1907 gum copal exports stood at about 398,000 lb., but three years later the figure had dropped to about 54,000 lb. Persistent efforts by District Commissioners and agricultural officers in Ashanti to revive interest in the production of gum copal were unsuccessful. By 1936 gum copal production had completely ceased.

### The kola tree

Kola trees still grew wild in the forest areas (fig. 16); nevertheless they continued to be of exceptional importance in the agricultural landscape because of the long-established demand for the nuts in the drier areas of Africa north of the equator. The interior markets for the kola nut were stable, and for that reason whatever fluctuations occurred in the exports of the product throughout the period under review were related to local political factors and not to frequent price changes in the foreign markets.

The kola nut trade was further strengthened when the kola resources of Southern Ghana, which had hitherto contributed little to the overland trade, began to be sent overseas through the coastal ports. The overseas trade made a modest beginning with the experimental export of two packages (weight unknown) to the United Kingdom in 1867. As with other cash crops, exports were interrupted during the political turmoils of the

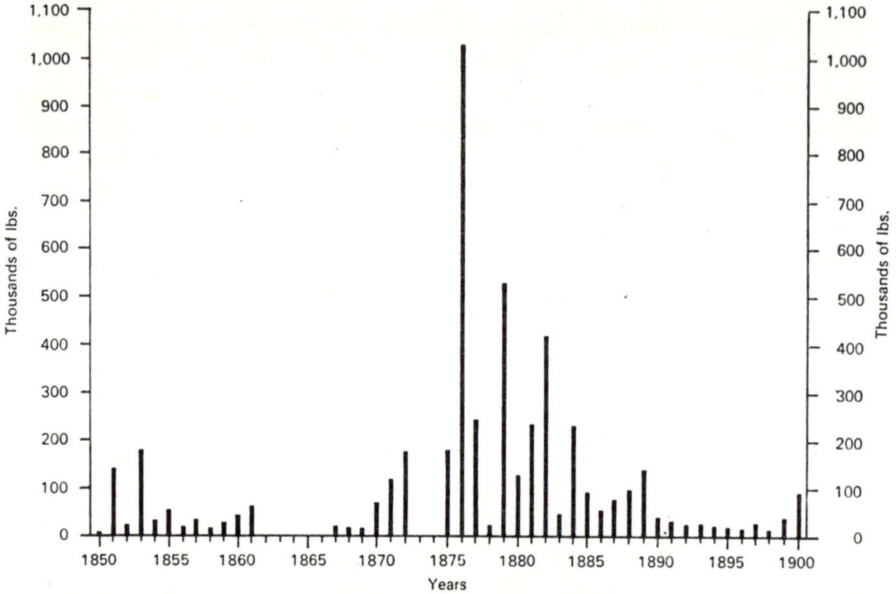


15*a* Gum copal exports, 1850–1900

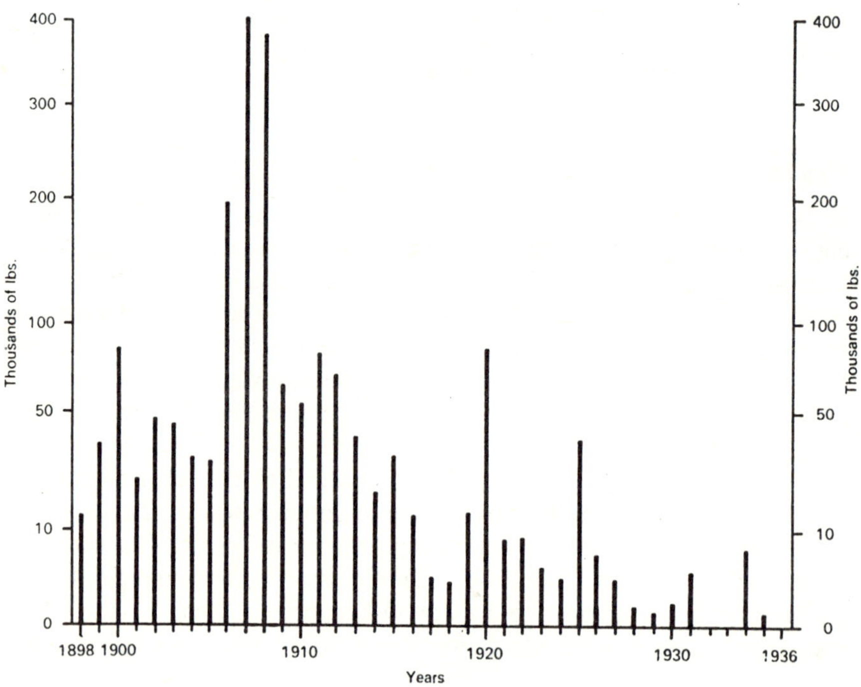


15*b* Gum copal exports, 1900–36

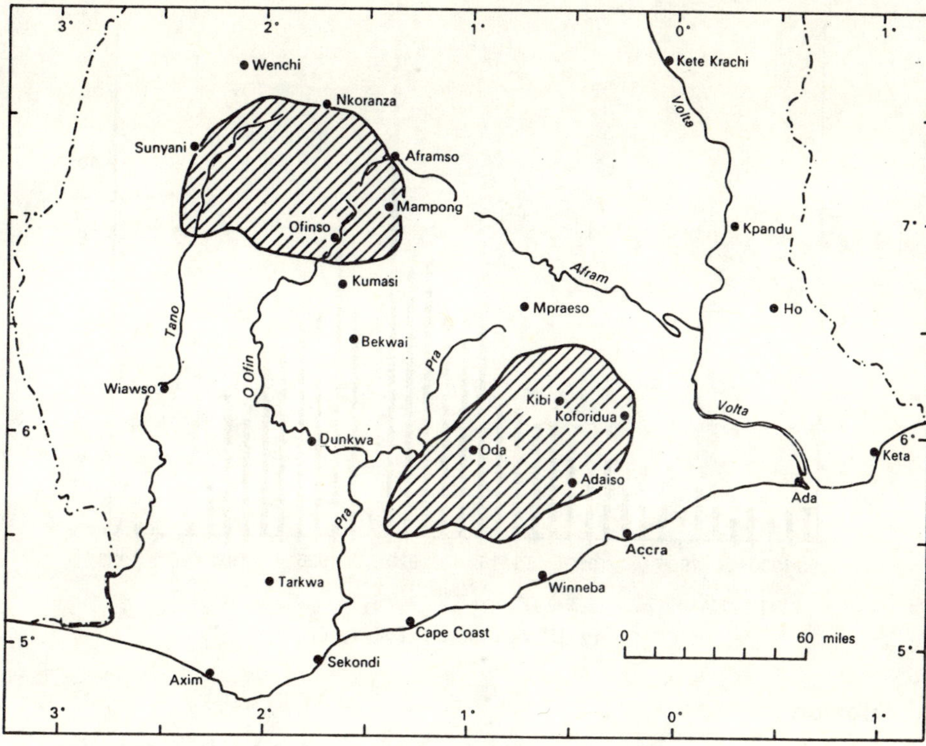


16 Main kola-producing areas, 1932

early 1870s, but they increased again and attained the unprecedented level of about 400 packages, worth just over £2,000, in 1884 and 1885.

An event that was to strengthen the overseas trade in kola nuts was the emergence, after the 1870s, of Lagos as the principal market, for this market was far more stable than those in Europe and the United States and was large enough to absorb as much kola as could be sent in. The supply side was also stabilized to some extent in Volta Region where the Germans established kola plantations at Ho and Kpandu, while in the rest of Southern Ghana the stabilizing factor was the increasing southward flow of the nuts from Ashanti, particularly after about 1893 (fig. 17).

The total trade in kola nuts continued to increase right up to 1936. The drop in overseas exports after 1921 simply meant an increase in the quantities exported to the interior markets of West Africa by the overland routes. The kola nut tree was the only cash crop that could face the challenge posed by the rapid spread of cocoa cultivation.

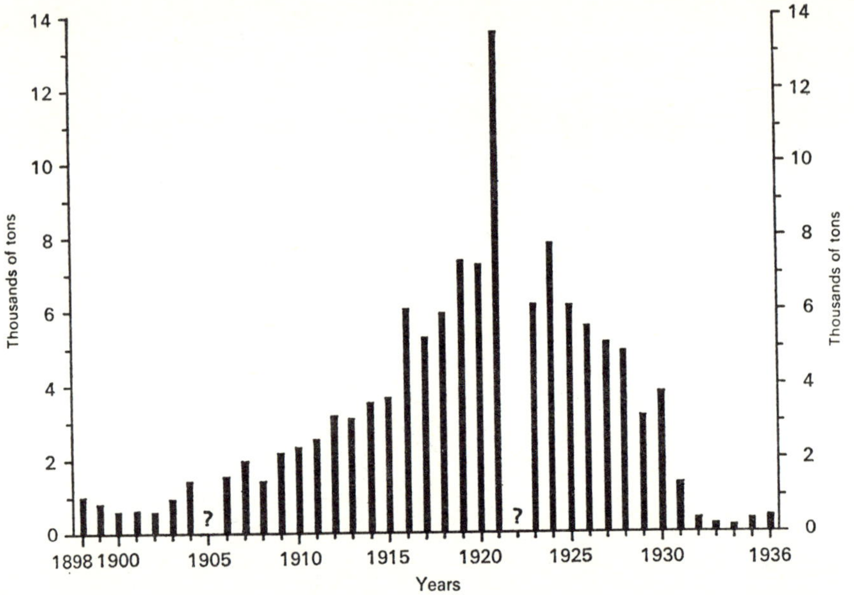


17 Kola exports, 1898–1936

## Cotton

Of the cash crops cotton was the one with a countrywide distribution; accordingly the history of its cultivation was complex. Also, it was one of the few crops whose cultivation was regarded by the resident Europeans as holding great possibilities.

The earlier attempts by the British and the Dutch to cultivate the crop continued after 1850, though without success. The British formed an Agricultural Society at Cape Coast in 1857, and one of its objectives was to encourage Fanti farmers to grow cotton for export. A few bales of cotton were exported from Fantiland to England in 1859, and that was all: there were no more exports after that date. The British could not demonstrate to the farmers that cotton cultivation was a profitable occupation, and not unnaturally the farmers lost interest. If the farmers unpicked the threads of imported Manchester cottons to use for weaving cloth, it was not because they were too lazy to grow cotton for yarn, an accusation that was frequently voiced,[1] but because the farmers merely wanted threads with red and yellow colours which they could not easily produce themselves.[2]

[1] For example, C. A. Gordon, *Life on the Gold Coast* (London, 1874), p. 43.

[2] See above, p. 95. Also, despatch of 4 January 1832 in C.O. 267/117, P.R.O.

The Dutch were no more successful with their cotton plantations near Elmina.[1] Mr da Rocha Vieira, a Brazilian who had contracted with the Dutch Administration to develop the plantations, found the conditions of work too trying. He 'was so teased and harassed that he was glad to embark secretly on a ship for Bahia without even claiming any of the money which was still owing to him'.[2] Other efforts by private Dutch individuals similarly failed.

All the cotton exports came from Krepi in the Eastern Region, but the quantities were limited by the size of the market.[3] The suspension of cotton supplies to England during the American Civil War provided the opportunity for a wider market, and the response to this was the extension of the acreage under the crop in Krobo and Akwapim and also in Krepi where some European merchants additionally established cotton gins. The enthusiasm for cotton cultivation was brought to a close by the end of the American Civil War which enabled England to return to its former source of supply. From that point onwards cotton progressively became scarce in the agricultural landscape. The situation was considerably worsened by the Ashanti–Akwamu invasion of Krepi in 1868–9 which resulted in a total devastation of the countryside, the destruction of the major cotton markets including Kpong, and the emigration of large numbers of Krepi farmers to Akwapim.[4] The Volta waterway, which served Krepi, was closed to traffic, while the surrounding countryside was infested with bandits who severely discouraged settlement on the land.[5] The Anglo-Ashanti war of 1873–4 prolonged the period of decay in Krepi. By 1885 the situation had reverted to normal: the Krepi farmers had returned from exile; the merchant firm of F. and A. Swanzy had established a plantation of Egyptian cotton at Krepi and were actively engaged in helping the farmers to re-establish themselves.

In 1903 and 1906 European experts on cotton cultivation visited Krepi and other parts of British Southern Ghana, holding meetings with the cotton farmers and encouraging them to grow more of the crop by distributing improved varieties of cotton seeds supplied by the British Cotton Growing Association. The results of their endeavour were meagre, for the basic problem of an inadequate local market was not solved. The cotton-

1 Governor Schomerus, 'Annual Report', 1853, despatches dated 30 September and October 1854 in *Nederlandsche Bezeittingen ter Kuste van Guinea* (KVG) 394, Furley Collection (F.C.) in Balme Library, University of Ghana, Legon.

2 J. S. G. Gramberg, *Schetsen van Afrika's Westkust* (Amsterdam, 1861), p. 31, etc.

3 Despatch 5 August 1858 in C.O. 96/43, P.R.O.

4 Despatch 10 May 1882 in C.O. 96/139, P.R.O.

5 Despatch 13 October 1871 in C.O. 96/89, P.R.O.

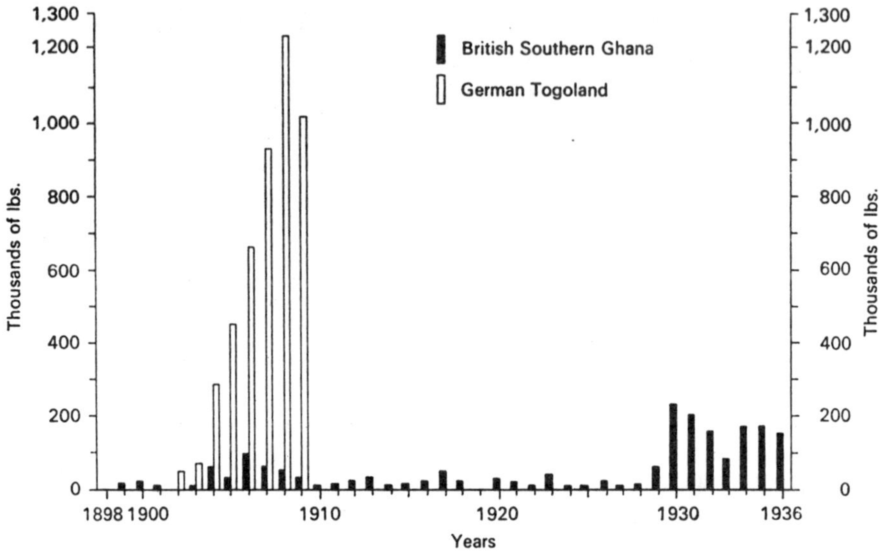


18 Cotton exports, 1898–1936

buying and experimental stations opened at Anum and Labolabo in Krepi in 1904 did not function satisfactorily; in particular they could not purchase all the cotton brought in by the farmers. Throughout British Southern Ghana and Ashanti–Brong Ahafo cotton farmers turned to cocoa cultivation.

In neighbouring German Togoland, on the other hand, cotton cultivation was more successful. The Administration itself was deeply involved in it; the cotton farmers were taught how to cultivate cotton and were supplied with superior varieties of cotton seeds; a number of carefully distributed buying stations purchased all the cotton produced by the farmers. German Togoland exported 44,000 lb. of cotton lint in 1902 and slightly over a million pounds (weight) in 1910. Not once between the two dates did the export graph take a serious downward dip (fig. 18).

Cotton production in the Volta Region and indeed in the rest of the country suffered seriously during and after the First World War, in spite of transitory revivals in some parts of the Volta Region, including Ada district. Cotton diseases were partly responsible for the drop in production but it was the low prices for cotton, coinciding with the increasing prices for cocoa after 1925, which constituted the main problem. By 1936 cotton was of no importance in the agricultural landscape.

## Coffee

Coffee cultivation spread throughout much of the Eastern Region after the Basel missionaries began it in Akwapim in the 1840s. By the late 1850s the Basel Mission had turned over its coffee farms to the local people at low rentals.[1] Within the Eastern Region were also a number of large coffee plantations belonging to certain individuals, including the Rev. Thomas B. Freeman whose plantation, with over 30,000 coffee plants, was located near the River Densu behind Weija.[2] Outside the Eastern Region the only coffee plantation of note was that at Half Assini, belonging to a Frenchman, M. Ondier.[3] The plantations generally carried *Coffea arabica* while *C. robusta* was widely cultivated on the peasant farms from which the bulk of the exports came.

The systematic export of coffee from peasant farms in British Southern Ghana began in the late 1860s with a small consignment of five packages, weighing about 650 lb. Exports increased quickly although they fluctuated a great deal and, as in the case of other crops, the fluctuations were largely accounted for by the incidence of local political disturbances and by the variations in the price offered for the crop in Europe (fig. 19). The quality of Ghana's coffee was rather low.

After the 1880s prices for coffee became more favourable and several Europeans established plantations for the crop. A few plantations were also made in German Togoland but the German Administration did not pay as much attention to them as they did to plantations of cocoa, cotton, or the oil-palm tree which they regarded as being more important. Coffee from the plantations was of high quality but it formed an insignificant proportion of the total coffee exports.

The rise in the price for coffee also stimulated production by the peasant farmers particularly in Krobo and Akwapim, and there was a large demand for coffee seeds from Aburi Gardens.[4] The British Administration helped production by setting up at Begoro in 1895 a machine for pulping and curing coffee berries. This process was normally undertaken by hand and was slow and inefficient.[5] But this machine was the only one of its kind set up in the country, and so the bulk of the coffee exports continued to be of low quality. The price paid for coffee soon fell by about fifty per cent between 1897 and 1899, at a time when cocoa cultivation was steadily gaining ground. Cocoa and coffee were cultivated in the same physical

[1] Alfred Moloney, *Sketch of the Forestry of West Africa* (London, 1878), p. 108.
[2] Horton, *West African Countries and Peoples*, p. 147.
[3] Moloney, op. cit. p. 111. [4] *Kew Bulletin*, no. 61 (1892), p. 15.
[5] *Colonial Report—Gold Coast Colony*, 1895.

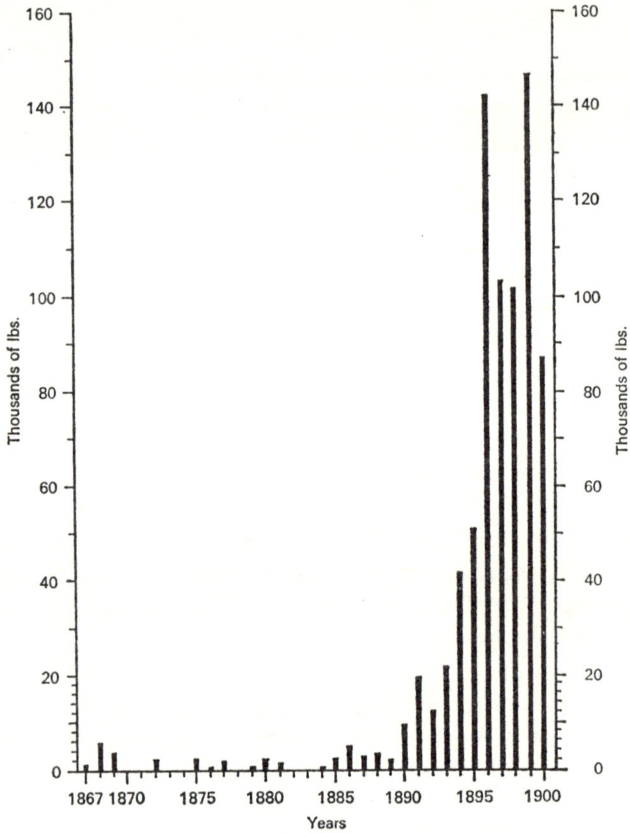


19*a* Coffee exports, 1867–1900

environment, and it was not long before the farmers began to convert coffee farms to cocoa. Coffee exports practically ceased between 1904 and 1923.

The revival of coffee cultivation after 1923 followed the introduction of cash inducement to farmers who successfully developed coffee farms in selected areas throughout Southern Ghana and Ashanti–Brong Ahafo.[1] The success of the scheme was made possible by the higher prices for coffee after 1925 and, in Kumasi region of Ashanti, also by the installation of a power-driven huller at Kumasi between 1934 and 1935. Nevertheless coffee remained a minor crop on the farms in view of the greater interest in cocoa cultivation. Besides, the local market for coffee was poorly

[1] Department of Agriculture, *Annual Reports*, 1912 to 1935/36.

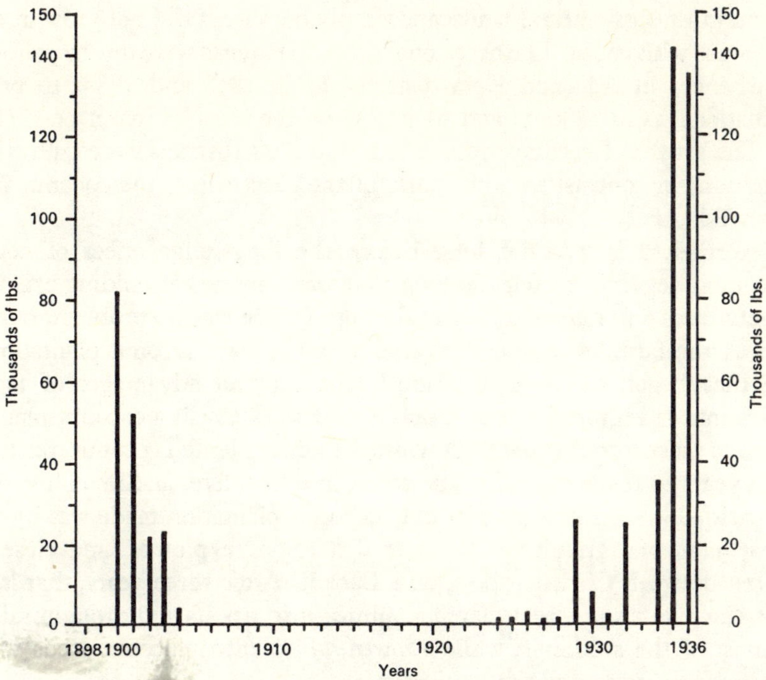


19*b* Coffee exports, 1900–36

organized: for the whole of Southern Ghana and Ashanti–Brong Ahafo there were not more than four towns—Accra, Kumasi, Sekondi and Koforidua—where farmers could sell their coffee.

## The coconut tree[1]

The coconut tree which had long fringed the whole length of Ghana's coastline only came to be recognized as an economic resource from about 1875, although copra (the dried kernel of coconut) had been exported, but sporadically, from about 1832. From the start Ada and Keta districts stood out as the major source areas. It was not until later that Ahanta district also became noted for the cultivation of the coconut tree and export of copra. The early pre-eminence of Ada and Keta districts in the copra export trade may be accounted for by the absence of profitable alternative occupations. Up to the close of the nineteenth century the coconut tree held

[1] The section on the coconut tree is derived from Dickson, 'Development of the Copra Industry in Ghana', *J. Trop. Geogr.* XIX (December 1964).

its own in the agricultural landscape simply because it did not grow in the same areas with cocoa. The occasional drops in exports were due to political disturbances in Ada and Keta districts, as in 1878 and 1885; to price fluctuations, as in 1880–1; and to attacks on the trees by insect pests (fig. 20). The groves of coconut trees in Ada and Keta districts were cultivated plantations in contrast to other parts of the coast where the coconut tree grew wild.

Nevertheless it was not long before the long-range effect of cocoa cultivation began to be felt. So long as it was a matter of tending existing coconut trees and harvesting them for copra there was no problem, but as soon as the farmers were urged (after 1900) to start coconut plantations, then they began to consider seriously the superior advantages of cocoa cultivation. It required just as much labour to establish a coconut plantation as to make a cocoa farm; but while the newly planted coconut tree took seven years to reach maturity, the cocoa tree took five, and its cultivation also yielded greater profits. The only coconut plantation made was by the Department of Agriculture. It covered a 223-acre plot of land close to the sea between Christiansborg and Labadi. After three years, that is in 1904, the plantation was declared a failure: insect pests and drought killed off most of the seedlings, while a few newly planted coconut seeds were reportedly exhumed by the local people.

The discovery that coconut oil could be used in place of animal fat for the manufacture of margarine greatly widened the market for copra in Britain and France, especially after 1904. The increase in the price for copra led to the planting of more coconut trees, especially between Atitete and Denu in Keta district.

During the First World War the output of copra increased a great deal since the export of copra to Britain was given priority. A cash bonus was awarded every farmer who successfully raised over a hundred coconut palms within a year. A few European-owned plantations were also established within this period. After the war years there was a drive to encourage farmers all along the coast to make coconut plantations, but the response was poor. Outside the Western Region the main problem was the superior attraction of cocoa cultivation a few miles inland from the coast, while in the Western Region the problem consisted of the difficulty of renting land from rich absentee landlords for coconut farms, and the poverty and sparseness of the population.

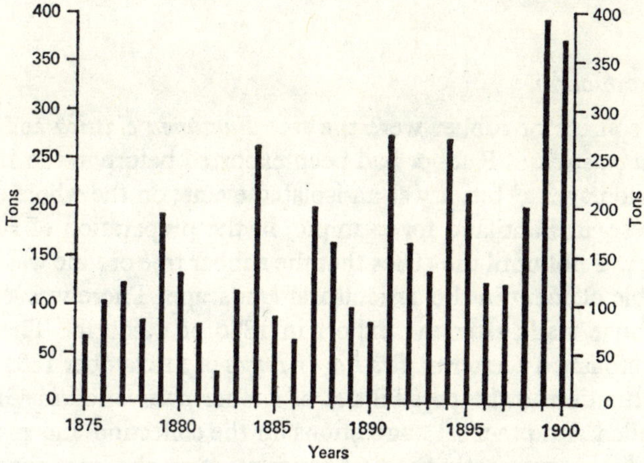


20*a* Copra exports, 1875–1900

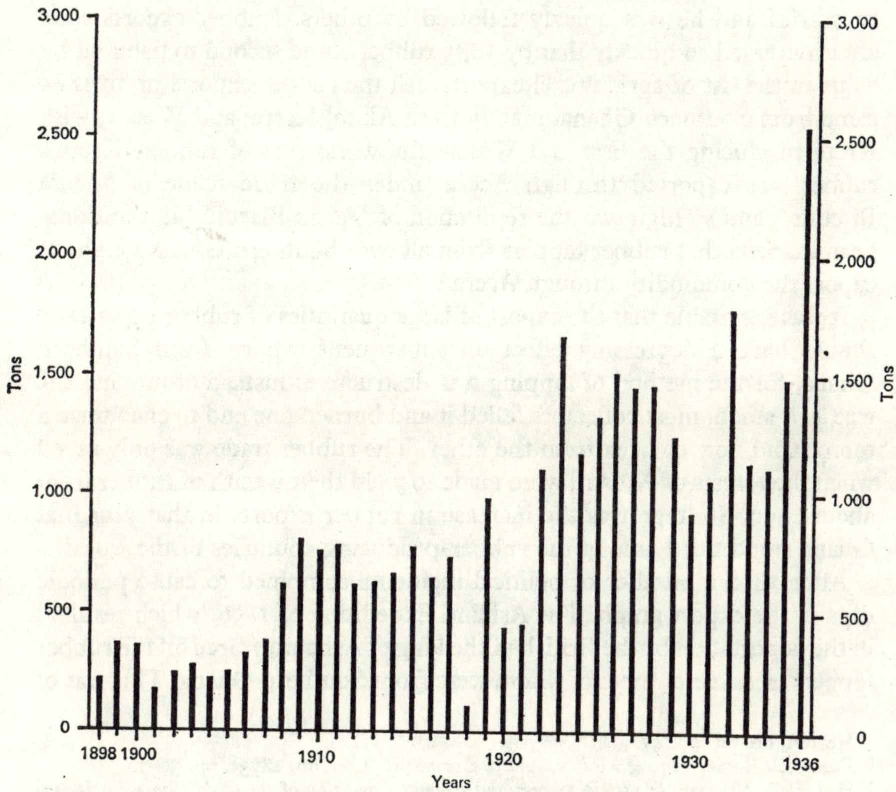


20*b* Copra exports, 1900–36

## Rubber

### *Peasant production*

The local sources of rubber were the tree *Funtumia elastica* and the vine *Landolphia owariensis*. Rubber had been exported before in the 1860s by a Basel Mission agent,[1] but it was an isolated event; on the whole there was little interest, in Fantiland for example, in the preparation of rubber for export.[2] It was not until the 1880s that the rubber tree or vine was regarded as a valuable element in the agricultural landscape. There was a brief lull in the rubber trade after the export in 1880 of 1,200 lb. Then Alfred Moloney published a letter in *The Lagos Times* of 11 October 1882 in which he drew attention to the possibilities of rubber cultivation in Ghana and made detailed and practical suggestions on the collection and preparation of the product. Apparently the first experiment on the lines suggested by Moloney was conducted at Cape Coast by T. C. Grant; it proved to be successful and he was quickly followed by others. Rubber exports soon after increased so quickly that by 1885 rubber stood second to palm oil by value in the list of agricultural exports. All the rubber exports up to 1885 came from Southern Ghana, mainly from Akim, Krepi, and Wasaw, with Krepi producing the best and Wasaw the worst sort of rubber. Krepi's rubber was exported through Accra under the trade name of 'Accra Biscuits', and so high was the reputation of 'Accra Biscuits' in the European markets that rubber tappers from all over Southern Ghana sought to export the commodity through Accra.[3]

It was inevitable that the export of large quantities of rubber up to 1885 should have a depressing effect on subsequent exports from Southern Ghana, for the method of tapping was destructive: instead of tapping the tree as it stood, most collectors felled it and burned one end to encourage a more rapid flow of latex from the other. The rubber trade was only saved when the forests of Ashanti were made to yield their wealth of rubber from about 1890. So huge was the increase in rubber exports in that year that Ghana stood third among the rubber-producing countries of the world.

After 1890 a number of political incidents combined to cause periodic dips in the export graph. The Ashanti Expedition of 1896, which resulted in the deportation by the British of the king of Ashanti, scared off the rubber tappers in Ashanti, most of whom were from Southern Ghana. This was of

[1] Horton, op. cit. p. 147.

[2] Frederick Boyle, *Through Fanteeland to Coomassie* (London, 1873), pp. 36–7.

[3] H. J. Bell, *History, Trade, Resources and Present Condition of the Gold Coast Settlement* (Liverpool, 1893), p. 29.

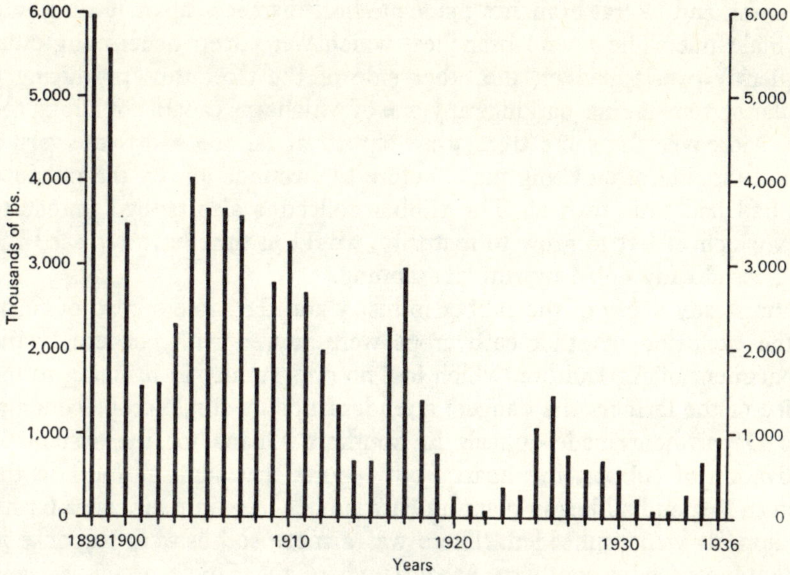


21 Rubber exports, 1898–1936

temporary duration, for the rubber tappers soon returned to Ashanti and produced large quantities of the commodity in response to the increased demand in England where rubber was needed for the manufacture of solid tyres for motor vehicles and carriages and of pneumatic tyres for bicycles. Production decreased again with the onset of the Anglo-Ashanti war of 1900–1; besides, it was becoming increasingly difficult to get the labour required to headload the commodity down to the ports.[1] Rubber exports fell steadily between 1904 and 1908 (fig. 21).

Up to 1908 the continued fall in the trade was also explained by two factors: the inferior quality of the product and consequently the low price paid for it, and the destructive method of tapping. The low quality of the rubber was mainly the result of deliberate adulteration of the latex with indefinite proportions of latices from other trees.

The problem of preserving the rubber trees was tackled early[2] and a few farmers began to tap the standing trees. But this new method itself was often just as disastrous. A main longitudinal channel was cut down the length of

[1] *Colonial Report—Gold Coast Colony*, 1901.

[2] In 1891 Chief Enemil of Eastern Wasaw published by-laws severely punishing anyone who wilfully destroyed or damaged a rubber tree in his district. See *Gold Coast Government Gazette*, 31 March 1891.

the trunk and lateral branches made at short distances apart leading into the main one. The lateral branches, which were deep penetrating cuts, frequently overlapped on the other side of the tree, thus producing a regular system of ring-barkings any one of which was capable of killing the tree. Moreover the same trees were tapped at far too short intervals, a second tapping often being made before the wounds left by the previous one had had time to heal. The rubber collectors also tapped immature trees which, if left to grow to maturity, would in time have replaced the old trees already killed by ruthless tapping.[1]

The steady decay of the rubber industry and the rapid spread of cocoa to the exclusion of other cash crops were viewed with concern by the Department of Agriculture, which lost no opportunity in bringing to the notice of the farmers the dangers attendant upon a single-crop economy. The Department made appeals in Southern Ghana for the systematic cultivation of rubber, but apart from reports that some farmers in the Eastern Region had begun planting Para rubber trees in their cocoa farms, the appeals went unheeded. There was a more enthusiastic response in Ashanti, especially southern Ashanti, where the Chiefs of Obuasi and Bekwai were supplied with about 15,000 Funtumia seedlings between 1907 and 1909. The Department of Agriculture also established at Sunyani and Kintampo in 1907 two small experimental rubber plantations whose primary object was to distribute seedlings to the local farmers. Efforts were also made to induce the rubber collectors to convert the latex into 'biscuits' instead of lumps, since the former were more acceptable to the merchants, but they were not successful. The rubber collectors knew how to convert the latex into 'biscuits', but they explained that they made more profit on the lumps, the greater weight extracted from the same quantity of latex more than compensating for the lower price.[2] Nevertheless total exports from the country increased from about 1·7 million lb. in 1908 to about 3·2 million lb. in 1910.

Between 1910 and 1914 rubber production fell as a result of low prices. The increased demand in Britain during the war years once more stimulated production, but only temporarily, for it became difficult to sell the country's low grade peasant-produced rubber once the war was over and Britain had re-established its trade relations with the plantation-rubber-producing countries of the Far East. The export of rubber from peasant farms practically ceased after 1926.

[1] See the section on Ghana (Gold Coast) in 'Reports on Rubber in the Gold Coast and Sierra Leone', *Colonial Reports*, Miscellaneous, no. 28, 1904.

[2] *Colonial Reports—Ashanti*, 1907–11. Also Department of Agriculture, *Annual Report*, 1909.

### *Plantation rubber*

A small proportion of the rubber exports came from European-owned plantations which began to appear in increasing numbers after 1906. Before that date the only plantations were that at Bunsu, belonging to the African Product Developing Company, and that at Tarkwa.[1] The situation changed after 1906 when European capitalists, following the favourable reports by the Department of Agriculture on the experimental planting of Para rubber in the country, began to be interested in the possibility of making rubber plantations in Ghana. Of the numerous companies floated, only three became a reality before the First World War, with plantations at Etukrom near Bunsu, at Pretsea and Mpohor, and near Axim (fig. 14, p. 149).[2] All the plantations, with a few others made after the war, continued to produce varying quantities for export right up to 1936.

## Cocoa

Cocoa first appeared on the export list of 1885, and about fifteen years later it had completely overshadowed all other crops in the country's export trade. Cocoa cultivation was confined to the Closed Forest zone which covers an area of about 31,000 square miles. Within this zone the physical conditions favour cocoa cultivation: suitable ochrosols cover the greater part of the area, and the climate, with its equatorial rainfall regime, is appropriately moist.[3]

The earliest attempts at cocoa cultivation in the country were by the Basel missionaries at Akropong in Akwapim. In 1859 they experimented unsuccessfully with cocoa seedlings imported from Surinam. They nevertheless persisted with their experiments, and in 1866 the single cocoa tree that remained on the experimental farm yielded a harvest of some fifteen healthy cocoa pods. A few of the seeds from the pods were sown on the mission farm and the rest distributed to the mission stations at Aburi, Mampong, and Krobo Odumase.[4] But whatever interest was aroused among the local farmers in cocoa cultivation disappeared after the Ashanti invasions of Akwapim and Krobo between 1868 and 1873.

1 *Colonial Reports—Gold Coast Colony*, 1903–5.

2 The Germans in the Volta Region were not interested in plantation rubber.

3 S. N. Adams and A. D. McKelvie, 'Environmental Requirements of Cocoa in the Gold Coast', *Report of Cocoa Conference* (London, 1955), pp. 22–7. Also J. Wills (ed.), *Agriculture and Land Use in Ghana* (O.U.P., 1962), pp. 92–104.

4 Gustaf Adolf Wanner, *The First Cocoa Trees in Ghana, 1858–1868* (Basel Trading Company Ltd., Basel, 1962), *passim*.

The next and successful introduction of cocoa cultivation was by Tetteh Quashie, a Ghanaian, who returned with a few cocoa pods from Fernando Po in 1878. He made his experimental farm at Mampong in Akwapim. His first harvest in 1883 was eagerly purchased by the local farmers at phenomenally high prices, and after a cautious entry into the export market in 1885 where he was paid only £6. 1*s.* for 121 lb. of cocoa beans, he settled down to exploit the unusually favourable local market.[1] The next export of cocoa was in 1891 when 80 lb. of cocoa beans were sold for £4. It is probable that Tetteh Quashie and his colleagues would have continued to ignore the export trade if the Aburi Botanical Gardens had not flooded the local market after 1890 with cocoa seedlings which were sold very cheaply.

Part of the credit for the establishment of the cocoa-growing industry on a firm basis must go to the governor, Sir William B. Griffith, who in 1886 imported cocoa pods from San Thomé and started off the nursery at Aburi from which seedlings were supplied to the farmers. Under his direction was also published scientific information on the cultivation of cocoa for the guidance of farmers interested in 'that remunerative industry'.[2]

The speed with which cocoa cultivation spread in Southern Ghana was spectacular: by about 1895 the cocoa tree was to be seen in almost every part of Southern Ghana. The role of the Aburi Botanical Gardens, to which farmers came from every part of Southern Ghana for cocoa seedlings and for information on farming methods, was crucial. Private-owned plantations like that of the Glasgow firm of Messrs Miller Brothers and Co. at Jukwa in the Central Region also served as centres of dispersal for the crop.

The fall in the price of coffee in 1898 diverted more attention to cocoa cultivation; in the same year a further impetus came from a scheme initiated by the governor, Sir F. M. Hodgson, which partially removed the necessity for farmers to borrow money from the extortionate moneylenders. Half the estimated full value of cocoa brought to the Aburi Botanical Gardens was immediately paid to the farmer and the rest paid after the crop had been sold overseas.[3] This scheme was for the benefit of farmers in British Southern Ghana, but the Germans were equally serious about promoting cocoa cultivation in the forest lands of the Volta Region where cultivation began in about 1890. The Germans were as thorough with cocoa as they were with cotton cultivation. A factor in the spread of cocoa cultivation common to both the Volta Region and the rest of Southern Ghana was

[1] 'Cocoa on the Gold Coast, Was Tetteh Quashie the first to plant it?' in *West India Committee Circular*, 19 March 1931.

[2] *Gold Coast Government Gazette*, 31 October 1888.

[3] *Colonial Report—Gold Coast Colony*, 1898.

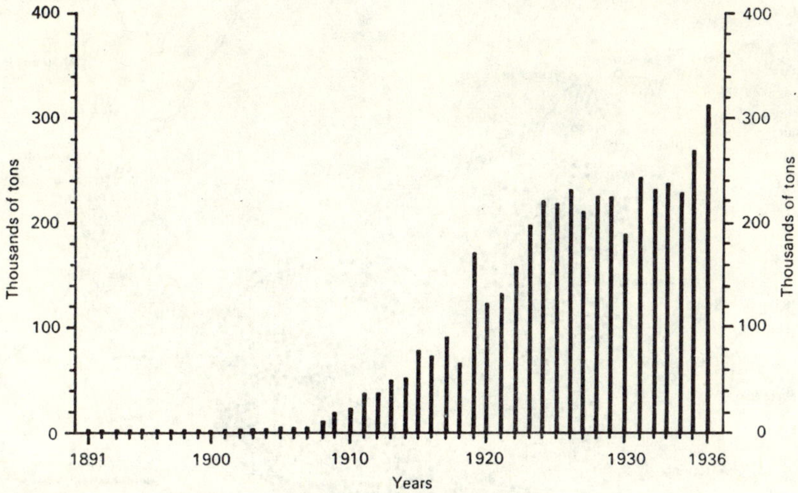


22 Cocoa exports, 1891–1936

the migration from Akwapim of bands of energetic farmers who purchased land elsewhere for cocoa farming.[1]

In Ashanti–Brong Ahafo, the cultivation of cocoa did not really gain ground until after pacification in 1902. Then cocoa trees began to displace the forest to the east of Kumasi. The fall in the price of rubber in 1902 and the extension of the Sekondi–Obuasi railway to Kumasi in 1903 were the main factors that accounted for the success of cocoa cultivation in its initial stages in Ashanti. The spread of the crop was westward from Kumasi and by 1905 it had travelled along the ancient Kumasi–Berekum road and had become established in the Pamu–Sunyani–Goaso triangle. The year 1906 was significant in the history of cocoa cultivation in Ashanti–Brong Ahafo. Following a petition from the chiefs of Ashanti, the first of a number of agricultural stations that soon after appeared in many parts of the Region was opened in southern Ashanti, and from there cocoa seedlings were readily distributed to Ashanti farmers.

If the speed with which cocoa cultivation spread throughout Southern Ghana and Ashanti–Brong Ahafo was phenomenal, equally so was the speed with which Ghana climbed up the scale of the world's chief exporters of cocoa. In 1906 the firm of William Cadbury began to purchase Ghana's cocoa on a large scale; in 1910 Ghana was the world's second largest exporter of cocoa, and the crop was the most valuable export from Ghana:

[1] Polly Hill, *Migrant Cocoa Farmers of Southern Ghana* (C.U.P., 1963), pp. 219–38.

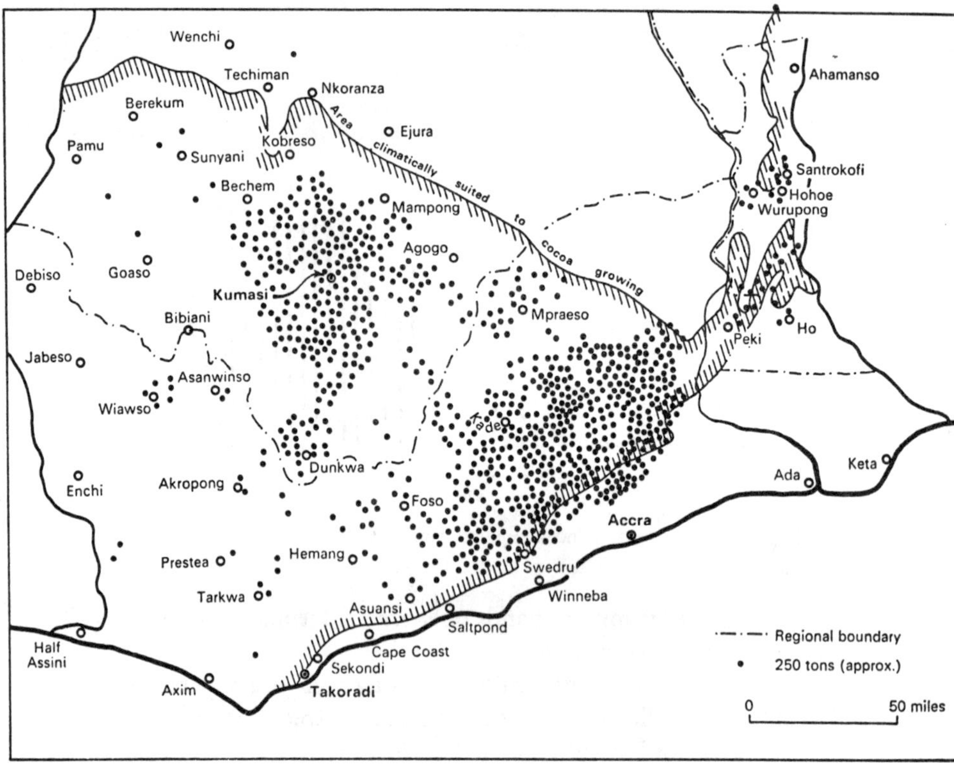


23*a* Cocoa purchases, 1927

it was worth more than gold. In 1911 Ghana became the world's largest exporter of cocoa (fig. 22).

The period between 1912 and 1936 saw the maximum expansion of cocoa cultivation in Ghana in spite of the numerous adverse conditions of the world market which led to reductions in the output of many other crops (fig. 23). It is true that the shortage of shipping to carry the crop to Britain and the United States during the First World War shook the confidence of the cocoa farmers, but the release of shipping after the war led to a resurgence of enthusiasm for cocoa cultivation which was in no way affected by the world depression and other economic crises, including a cocoa 'hold up', that occurred in the 1920s and the early 1930s. It did not matter if the prices offered for the cocoa were low, for the peasant farmer with his low overhead costs could still make a profit, however small.

The large exports of cocoa were at the expense of quality, and the product

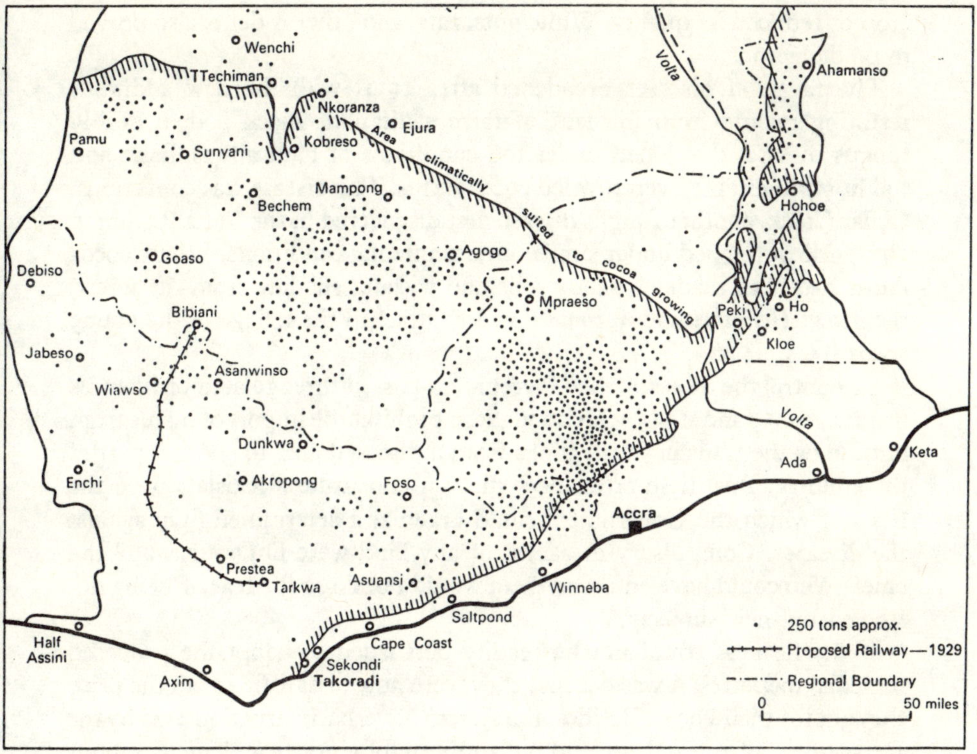


23*b* Cocoa purchases, 1936–7

was acquiring a bad name in the European markets. The reputable firm of William Cadbury even took the precaution of not letting the world know that it was buying cocoa from Ghana.[1]

Cocoa diseases were among the many factors responsible for the low quality.[2] The earliest disease to be noticed was *sankonuabe* (the Akan phrase for 'go back to your oil palms'). It was caused by an insect (*Sahlbergella* sp.) which attacked the cocoa tree by puncturing the bark and sucking the sap. The affected trees either produced inferior cocoa or died. By the time the disease was first noticed in 1909 it had done a great deal of damage in the older cocoa areas.[3] There were many other diseases about the same time, like die-back, brown rot, and leaf curl which took a heavy toll of the cocoa

[1] Evidence of William Cadbury in *Minutes of West African Lands Committee 1912–1917*, Q. 10,660.

[2] Among the causes of low quality was the transport problem, the subject of chapter 10.

[3] Department of Agriculture, *Annual Reports*, 1909–36. The account of cocoa diseases is from these reports.

crop or reduced its quality. White ants, rats, and other rodents also proved to be dangerous.

The range of diseases broadened after 1911, with the new additions resulting mainly from the lack of farm sanitation. Black pod, a deadly fungus disease, developed under the conditions of high atmospheric and soil humidity in the overcrowded cocoa farms. The disease was contagious. Collar Crack, another fungus disease first discovered in the Volta Region in 1922, also developed under similar environmental conditions. Where cocoa farms had been made on sandy soils and without shading from the forest, the insect *Heliothrips rubrocinctus* readily attacked the foliage of the young cocoa trees.

To control the diseases, the Government passed three related ordinances in 1912, 1923, and 1935 which sought to prohibit the import of plants from outside or the transfer of seedlings from a diseased area to another part of the country. But these ordinances did not constitute a legislation on the basis of which the Government could organize a determined fight against the diseases. Compulsory measures of any kind were unpopular, and the chiefs who could have enforced them would not do so for fear of being destooled by their subjects.

If the farmers could not be readily persuaded to adopt the proposed remedial measures, it was because they were now dissatisfied with the price they got for their cocoa. Besides, the system of verbal instruction used by the Department of Agriculture and not supported by practical demonstrations in the field failed to convince the farmers of the validity of the proposed control measures. Yet the farmers were in great need of organized instruction, for cocoa cultivation with its attendant problems was a completely new experience for them.

The methods used in preparing the cocoa beans for export were also responsible for the low quality. Before 1900 the cocoa beans were simply washed and then dried in the sun without being fermented. After 1900 the beans were allowed to ferment before being dried, but they were unwashed. Experiments conducted at the Aburi Botanical Gardens were differently assessed by brokers in Europe to whom samples of cocoa beans prepared by different methods were sent. The method of preparing the beans had nevertheless improved by the beginning of the First World War, although it still suffered from two deficiencies: some farmers broke their fermenting heap too soon in response to a favourable market, while others failed to mix or turn over the beans during the drying process in the sun. The result was the production of discoloured and improperly dried beans. A system of compulsory inspection at the ports, introduced in 1934, did not solve the problem, for the Department of Agriculture, which operated the system, did not have the necessary legal backing to refuse the export of low-grade cocoa. Also, the certificate of purity issued by the department was not recognized internationally.[1]

The low quality of the cocoa beans was also inherent in the species of cocoa grown. The amelonado variety typically yields cocoa beans of inferior grade. Four new superior varieties were introduced after 1900, but they proved unsuitable: either they did not yield as much as the amelonado variety or could not survive the crude and elementary methods of cultivation.

Finally, the local market conditions themselves were not such as would encourage the preparation of high-quality cocoa beans. The same price was offered for all grades of cocoa until about 1908 when a few merchants began offering differential prices based on grade. The argument against grading the cocoa was that high-quality cocoa was not absolutely essential in the manufacture of chocolate. At a later stage when grading became common practice, the operations of middlemen discouraged the production of high-grade cocoa. By paying for the cocoa in advance and cheating the farmers with the aid of faulty weighing machines, they effectively created a market for nothing but low-grade cocoa.

It was to help the farmers avoid the middlemen that the co-operative movement was inaugurated in 1929. There were both producer and marketing societies. After a number of initial difficulties, the co-operative movement gathered momentum, and the total number of societies reached 400 by the end of 1936.[2]

## AGRICULTURE IN NORTHERN GHANA

In Northern Ghana the agricultural landscape at the end of the nineteenth century apparently differed little from what it was before. The impulses that made for changes in agriculture in Southern Ghana and Ashanti–Brong Ahafo were not felt in Northern Ghana. Trade, including slave trade, was the principal source of income in Northern Ghana, and the possibility of developing export agriculture was ignored.

By the beginning of the twentieth century Northern Ghana's trade was very much reduced. The British had stopped slave trading; the Western Sudan was impoverished; and Ashanti looked more to the coastal ports for trade. It then became necessary to develop export agriculture, as

[1] C. Y. Shephard, 'Report on the Economics of Peasant Agriculture in the Gold Coast', *Gold Coast Government Sessional Paper*, no. 1 (1936).

[2] Dickson, *Cocoa in Ghana* (Microfilm Methods Ltd., London, 1965), pp. 221–4.

was done earlier in the south, to be the support for Northern Ghana's economy.

A resource inventory showed that cotton and tobacco were the only crops that could be cultivated on a large enough scale for export. The choice eventually fell on cotton, which would be produced in southern Gonja near the Volta. There land was available, labour was cheap, and transport would be provided at low cost by the large canoes which returned practically empty to the coast after disposing of their cargoes of salt at Yeji, Longoro, and Daboya.[1]

A pilot scheme to investigate the feasibility of cotton cultivation on a commercial scale was immediately launched at Salaga and pronounced successful in 1903. Interest may have quickened in the cultivation of the crop in Gonja and Dagomba, as was reported, but none of the harvest from the newly made farms was exported. In 1906 experimental plots of American Black Rattler and Volta River cotton were laid out, at the request of the British Cotton Growing Association, at Yeji and Salaga in an attempt to introduce a higher yielding variety. At both Yeji and Salaga the American cotton failed while the Volta River variety succeeded at Yeji; but the experiments were apparently discontinued. The British Cotton Growing Association next sent out in 1909 a cotton expert who toured Northern Ghana with the object of arousing greater enthusiasm for cotton cultivation. He made a demonstration farm at Tamale where he also publicly demonstrated a cotton gin and press which reportedly caused a sensation. He also announced to the cotton growers that the British Cotton Growing Association was prepared to buy all the cotton brought to the market.

The response was disappointing and the quantities of cotton brought to the market fell far short of expectation. The root cause lay, not in the total acreage under cultivation which was by all accounts large enough, but in a combination of two circumstances. Transport costs were high for the good producing areas which lay at considerable distances from the Volta, and the numbers of able-bodied men in the rural population were reduced at an alarming rate through emigration to the gold mines in Ashanti and Southern Ghana. The emigration, paradoxically, was deliberatedly encouraged by the British who in 1906 selected men from all parts of the region and sent them, under appropriate supervision, on an extensive tour of the gold mines of Ashanti. There they were impressed by the size of the wages and the comparative decency of general living conditions. This touched off a flood of young men from Northern Ghana to Ashanti and Southern Ghana.

[1] African (West) no. 585, *Gold Coast: Further Correspondence Relating to the Northern Territories* (Colonial Office, 1899), Paper no. 96, and *Annual Reports on the Northern Territories*, 1901–1936/37.

Nevertheless the hope persisted that Northern Ghana might become a major exporter of cotton, and in 1912 alone over a ton of cotton seeds was distributed, under the auspices of the British Cotton Growing Association, among the farmers throughout the region, but more so in Dagomba. Only the American Black Rattler variety was distributed since it proved to yield 9 per cent more lint than the local variety. Also in 1914, cotton gins were installed at Wa and Gambaga—there was already one at Tamale—to serve farmers in the respective districts, and apparently the saving thus effected in the cost of transporting to Tamale, formerly the only collecting centre, resulted in increased production throughout Northern Ghana. Of the total quantity of 24,263 lb. of cotton lint exported from Northern Ghana in 1914, 13,307 lb. were purchased at Tamale, 6,431 lb. at Gambaga, 3,970 lb. at Wa, and 555 lb. outside those buying stations. In 1915 Northern Ghana exported a total of 27,882 lb. of cotton.

While exports increased every year, they were far from being commensurate with the quantities of cotton seed distributed. And so in 1916 the British Cotton Growing Association, which had been showing some uneasiness the previous year or two about the wisdom of investing in Northern Ghana, ended its operations and handed over its buildings at Tamale to the Government.[1] After 1916 no more was said about developing an export economy in Northern Ghana based on agricultural products.

The reasons for the failure of export agriculture were not new. Above all was the difficulty which faced farmers in several areas of satisfying their basic food requirements. There was little awareness of the fundamental importance of this problem, for the only step taken towards providing a solution was to distribute, in 1911, sweet potatoes, cassava, ginger and red pepper to farmers for planting. Sweet potatoes and cassava were already present but unimportant. Of the plants distributed, only the sweet potato achieved immediate popularity. Cassava, a bulky food that could have helped to stave off famine, was unpopular because of the traditional attitude which regarded it more as a plant for marking farm boundaries than as food.[2]

A few years before the idea of developing cotton plantations was dropped, the Government began to pay a great deal of attention to the cattle-rearing industry, which promised to be a suitable mainstay for Northern Ghana's economy. But the cattle-rearing industry as it existed was beset with many

[1] *Annual Report on the Northern Territories*, 1916.

[2] African (West) no. 549, *Gold Coast: Correspondence Relating to the Northern Territories* (Colonial Office, January–June 1898), enclosure in Paper no. 172, 'Report on Gonja Country' (January 1898), by Assistant Inspector C. H. Armitage.

serious problems whose solution was essential before any improvement could be hoped for. The basic problem, parent to the rest, was the social concept of cattle, not as economic capital capable of yielding a steady income, but as a status symbol and index of wealth. The problem was common to tropical Africa. Stemming from this was the problem of inadequate care of the cattle. The responsibility for looking after the animals was often delegated to inexperienced young boys and, in places like Builsa and Kusasi, to professional Fulani herdsmen whose reward did not necessarily depend on the state of health in which the animals were kept. Consequently the animals were an easy prey to anthrax and pleuro-pneumonia.[1]

The problem of how to improve the breed of the cattle was the first to be tackled. In 1912 the Department of Agriculture started a stock farm at its station at Tamale with 23 head of Mossi cattle which were imported for purposes of cross-breeding experiments with the local straight-backed West African Shorthorn. After the interruption of the war years, the experiments with cattle breeds were resumed on a larger scale and the headquarters of the Veterinary Department moved from Kumasi to Tamale in 1922. In the same year a veterinary school was opened at Tamale. In order to have more room for experiments, the veterinary laboratories and school were moved in the early 1930s to Pong-Tamale. Then investigations were extended to the possibility of producing improved breeds of sheep and goats as well.

In the 1930s the Veterinary Department began its extension work in Northern Ghana. It immediately came up against the problems outlined earlier, including another social custom which prescribed the slaughter of the best young bulls, needed for breeding purposes, at religious festivals. The only solution to this particular problem adopted by the Veterinary Department was to issue bulls bred at Pong-Tamale only to those chiefs who were certain not to sacrifice them. Between 1933 and 1936 about 200 bulls were issued, mainly in Kusasi and Builsa districts. Within that period there was noticeable improvement in the local breed.

Earlier, in 1931, a scheme was launched to facilitate the process of breeding and distributing high-grade bulls. It involved the establishment of Native Authority stock farms which the chiefs were to stock with local cows-in-calf for subsequent service by improved bulls supplied by the Veterinary Department. The first calf born as a result of crossing with an

[1] *Annual Reports on the Northern Territories*, 1901–1936/37, and the *Annual Reports* of the Veterinary Department of the Department of Animal Health covering the same period.

improved bull became available for eventual distribution to the community by the Native Administration, while the parent cows were restored to their owners only when they were in calf again. The scheme failed for this reason, that the owners of the cows did not exactly understand it; since they never expected to see their cows again, they supplied the worst in the herd for the stock farms. Many of the stock farms were closed down in 1935.

Thus the breed of cattle in Northern Ghana remained largely unimproved. The problem was not only sociological but also economic: the cattle herders had not yet appreciated the need to improve the breed of their cattle. Although the traditional attitude was strong, it could have given way to a more rational attitude if there had been suitable market incentives. But as far as the cattle herders were concerned, it was not altogether desirable to put all their cattle on the road to the markets of Ashanti and Southern Ghana. The memory of an event in 1908 still lingered, though not as strongly as before.

In 1908 the Government abolished caravan tolls on cattle. This it did in order to encourage the cattle herders from both Upper Volta and Northern Ghana to bring more of the animals to the markets in the south, where the Public Health Department had mounted a massive 'eat-more-meat' campaign. The result of the abolition of the tax was contrary to what was expected. The cattle traders, who had hitherto regarded the payment of caravan tolls as entitling them to Government protection, feared that they would no longer be safe on the highway from Northern Ghana to Ashanti since 'protection money' was no longer demanded from them.[1] This attitude did not completely disappear until the beginning of the Second World War.

Meanwhile there were other problems which were susceptible to purely scientific treatment. The most outstanding of these were cattle diseases. Poor specimens of cattle were better than dead ones, and for this reason the cattle owners co-operated fully with the Veterinary Department's fight against the diseases. An added incentive to co-operation came from the launching of an insurance scheme under which a cattle owner paid the sum of one shilling for each animal he brought to an immunization camp and received £1 for each death.[2] It was not long before rinderpest was completely eliminated, not only in Northern Ghana but also in the south-east coastal plains where the cattle-rearing industry was otherwise ignored by the Veterinary Department.

[1] *Annual Report of the Northern Territories*, 1919.
[2] *Annual Report on the Gold Coast*, 1938/39, p. 42.

## FISHING[1]

From about 1890 onwards occurred a series of changes in fishing gear and methods which resulted in the expansion and greater stability of the sea-fishing industry. It appears that most of the innovations were first seen in Fanti country, the traditional seat of the fishing industry, before they spread to other parts of the coast. Primarily the innovations were in the nets used.

One of the earliest innovations was a fine-meshed bottom net called *tengirafo* by the Fanti because of the resemblance to telegraph lines when the net was stretched out in the sea. The story of the introduction of this net is not known. Perhaps the net may have been brought directly from Europe, for this was the time when the cry everywhere among educated Africans was for the adoption from Europe of those ideas and techniques that would speed up the country's economic development.

Next came the *ali* drift net, apparently from Nigeria in about 1900, to Nungua and Teshi from where it spread westward along the coast. Soon after appeared the seine net and newer varieties of the bottom and drift nets, perhaps introduced from Europe or, as in the case of the large-mesh variety of the *ali* net, evolved locally. Further modifications were made locally in the seine and other nets after about the 1920s. Apparently the latest net to be introduced was the turtle net which was first brought to Keta in the 1930s. All these nets were bigger than the traditional ones and therefore called for bigger canoes with suitable structural modifications.

## THE TIMBER INDUSTRY[2]

After 1800, when the timber industry behind Axim disappeared as a result of technological difficulties related to extraction and transport, the product did not feature in the export trade until 1887 when 240 superficial feet of wood were exported on an experimental basis.[3] Timber logging had begun once more because, with Britain controlling much of Southern Ghana, there were no longer any political barriers to the use of the rivers as a means of transporting the logs to the coast. Exports increased so dramatically that by 1894 they had reached the astonishing volume of about 450,000 cubic feet. The timber industry was fully established. Numerous timber concessions were taken by foreign capitalists, labour was readily attracted from

[1] The available information on changes in fishing gear is extremely sketchy, and what there is may be gathered from F. R. Irvine's *The Fishes and Fisheries of the Gold Coast* (London, 1947), pp. 24–38.

[2] The main sources of information are the *Colonial Reports on the Gold Coast Colony*, 1888–1920, and *Trade Reports*, 1899–1936.

[3] There was always the internal market for timber.

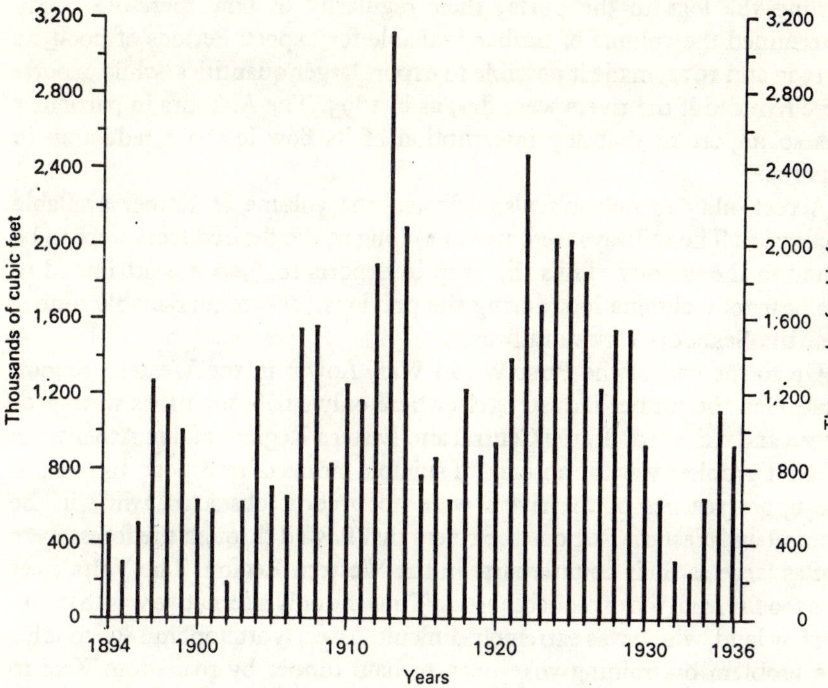


24 Timber exports, 1894–1936

both inside and outside the country, and the Government, through the Timber Protection Ordinance of 1907, wisely forbade the cutting of timber below a certain girth.

After the 1890s the volume of exports depended primarily on the state of demand in the consuming countries of Western Europe and the United States of America. Thus exports, after reaching the remarkably high level of about 3 million cubic feet in 1913, dropped to less than half that volume during the First World War. Apart from the fact that it was difficult to obtain shipping for the logs, the demand had dropped off with the virtual closing down of the cabinet-making trade in Europe. Another drop in demand both in Europe and the United States of America during the depression years of the early 1930s severely reduced exports to an average of about 500,000 cubic feet per annum (fig. 24).

The Tano,[1] Ankobra, and Pra rivers were the principal means of trans-

[1] The Sutre Falls at Tanoso were by-passed by a light narrow-gauge railway completed in 1927–8 by Messrs Miller Brothers and Co. See *Report on the Western Province, 1927–28*, p. 15.

porting the logs to the ports; their regularity of flow therefore partly determined the volume of timber available for export. Periods of flood, as in 1907 and 1912, made it possible to export larger quantities, while exports were reduced if the rivers were dry, as in 1895. The Ankobra in particular was so important that any interruption of its flow led to a reduction in exports.

Accessibility to railways also affected the volume of timber available for export. The railways were useful as long as the desired trees were to be found in the vicinity. Thus the drop in exports in 1906 was attributed to the near total elimination, during the previous year, of marketable timber near the Sekondi–Tarkwa railway.

Up to the end of the First World War, Aowin in the Western Region controlled the timber industry; elsewhere only small quantities were produced and exported. In the Central and Eastern Regions and in Ashanti the greatest problem was the absence of suitable means of transport. In Ashanti the upper reaches of the rivers were not free of obstacles, while in the Central and Eastern Regions the rivers that flowed through the forest were not as large as their counterparts in the Western Region. The Volta river was too far from the exploitable areas. Thus the only alternative was to transport by land, which was extremely difficult. An early attempt in 1896 to solve the problem by training yoke oxen to haul timber by road from Kibi to Accra failed. It was not until the opening of the Accra–Kumasi railway in 1923 and the Huni Valley–Kade railway in 1927 that it became possible to develop the timber industry in the Eastern and Central Regions.

Of the numerous species of forest trees probably only one, African mahogany or *Khaya ivorensis*, was in popular demand overseas. It replaced *K. senegalensis* which occurs in savanna woodland and was the first of the African mahoganies to appear on the world market from the Gambia.[1] In addition to *K. ivorensis* may have been exported small quantities of sapele or *Entandrophragma cylindricum*.[2] Both belong to the same family and are very similar in appearance and quality. They provide much larger and better quality of logs than *K. senegalensis*, and are easier to work.

[1] Wills, *Agriculture and Land Use in Ghana*, pp. 238–9.

[2] Ibid. The range of timber species exploited broadened a little after the Second World War, but it did not alter the distribution of production.

# 8. Mining

## GOLD

### African gold mining

Up to the 1870s gold production continued to be in the hands of Ghanaian miners who worked within a general technical and organizational framework that showed close similarity to that of the time of William Bosman. The only major exception was in connection with the employment of slaves which became increasingly difficult, mainly in Southern Ghana, from about the first decade of the nineteenth century. The greatest portion of the gold produced was still from detrital sources; a smaller quantity was won from the disintegrated portions of reef outcrops, especially the banket of the Tarkwa hills, while insignificant amounts were extracted through rudimentary methods involving the crushing and 'calabashing' of tough auriferous quartz or banket. Centuries-old techniques of mining persisted, with all their limitations.

A clearer picture of the spatial distribution of gold mining or of the shallow pits dug by Ghanaian miners in Northern Ghana and Brong Ahafo in the nineteenth and earlier centuries did not emerge until the 1930s when the Geological Survey Department reported on the subject after a country-wide survey.[1] In Northern Ghana the majority of the pits were observed around Bole, Dokuripe, Kwe, Wasipe, and near Fumbo in weathered Birimian greenstone, and were supposedly worked originally by Banda miners (fig. 25). Nowhere else in Northern Ghana did the pits occur in significant numbers. South of the Black Volta, in Brong Ahafo, nearly all the pits were congregated in the Banda area and a few miles to the south, close to the Ivory Coast border. At Yoyo on the highest terrace of the Black Volta, 7 miles north-west of Kasa and 2½ miles due west of the Black Volta, were discovered numerous old abandoned shafts believed to have been worked originally by Gyaman miners since the 1870s; similar old workings were found strung along the Fanko river about 2 miles south-west of Yoyo. A few miles south of the Black Volta below Ntereso occurred extensive old gold workings in a clearly marked belt of Birimian greenstone, and at Abanko to the north-west of Wenchi was similarly found an extensive area

[1] Geological Survey Department, *Annual Reports*, 1935–6 and 1936–7. Also the Department's Memoir no. 4, *Gold in the Gold Coast*.

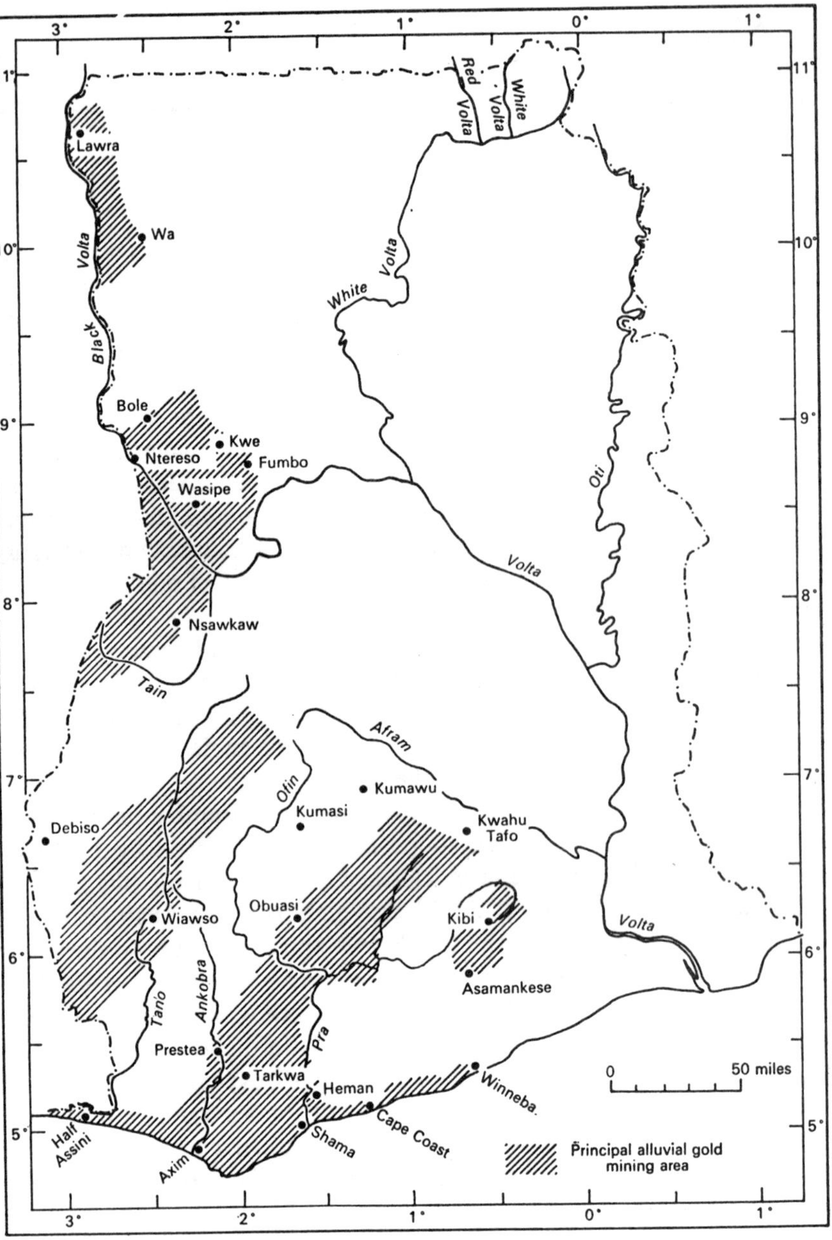


25 Principal alluvial gold mining areas: eighteenth and nineteenth centuries

of old shafts sited in eluvial quartz gravel which had been derived from the quartz reefs and lenses lying near the Black Volta. Outside Northern Ghana and Brong Ahafo the distribution of abandoned gold workings was as described earlier in chapter 4.

An important development in the gold-mining industry in the late nineteenth century, which reflected the gradual easing of political tension among some of the tribes south of the Black Volta, was the acquisition of mining concessions in the interior by educated people from the coast. The migration of Fanti and other tribal peoples from the coast to seek their fortune in the interior was not new, and had indeed been significant to many economic activities in the interior, especially to the organization of the retail trade in parts of Ashanti. The difference lay in the educational background of the migrants. Many of those who went into the interior within the second half of the nineteenth century not only transmitted the large demand for gold by the Europeans on the coast and acted as middlemen between them and the miners, but also attempted to organize the industry along fairly modern lines of large-scale production. The influx of educated coastal peoples into the mining areas was part of the gold rush of the second half of the nineteenth century in which overseas capitalists shared.

Prominent among the African concessionaires at Tarkwa in the early 1880s were Mr Dawson of Cape Coast, who had an extensive background experience in commerce, and Dr Horton, a medical officer, who acquired a large number of land concessions in the mining areas of Wasaw before the main rush that followed the activities of J. Bonnat in Tarkwa district. Some of the concessions were later sold to private companies, and it was even believed in some quarters that Dr Horton backed the Dixcove–Tarkwa railway scheme in order to increase the sale value of his concessions.[1] Elsewhere, at Obuasi, were three Fanti concessionaires, J. E. Ellis, J. E. Biney, and J. P. Brown, from whom Cade acquired the Obuasi mines and who, before Cade, had already organized production at Obuasi on a generous scale.[2] Brandon Kirby observed in 1884 that gold mining had attracted large numbers of 'educated natives from the Protectorate' to Atobiase and Nkwanta in Ashanti, and that the success of the industry there was in some measure to be attributed to the immigrants.[3] The

[1] See monthly reports of the civil Commissioner at Tarkwa, 1881–2 in African no. 249, *Further Correspondence Regarding Affairs of the Gold Coast* (Colonial Office, June 1883).

[2] African (West) no. 513, *Correspondence Relating to Land Grants and Concessions in the Gold Coast Protectorate* (Colonial Office, April 1897), enclosure in Paper no. 34.

[3] BPP, Cmd. 4477, *Further Correspondence Regarding the Affairs of the Gold Coast* (Colonial Office, July 1885), enclosure in Paper no. 41.

educated local concessionaires played a further useful role in the gold-mining industry in addition to stimulating production: they mediated between the local chiefs and the newly arrived foreign European companies in the capacity of political agents, and in this way helped to smooth the transition to modern mining.

### The beginnings of modern mining up to 1900

The late nineteenth century saw the reorganization, by foreign capitalists, of the gold-mining industry which hitherto had been exclusively in African hands. The significance of the introduction of modern mining lay in its use of a more sophisticated technology to release the enormous quantities of gold that had for centuries remained locked up, through the inadequacy of local mining methods, in quartz reefs and unweathered Birimian rocks. Already by 1875 four Europeans were actively engaged in gold mining without the aid of machinery, at Etapa in eastern Wasaw amidst thousands of private Ghanaian miners. This early European enterprise collapsed within a few months of its inception through the operation of many factors, among which the lack of adequate financial backing loomed large. Three of the men left the country and the fourth, after further unsuccessful essays in eastern Akim, became an employee of the Public Works Department at Accra.[1]

Initially, the introduction of large-scale gold mining by European capitalists was the work of J. Bonnat, the French trader and adventurer who, after several forays into the field of commerce, turned his attention to prospecting for gold in Tarkwa district.[2] The enthusiastic report he gave in France of his prospecting led to the formation of the African Gold Coast Company; and agents of the company, including Bonnat, arrived in the country in 1877. A year later they acquired a land concession at Tarkwa, the first of a large number of mining concessions that in later years became associated with the company. Three new companies quickly followed in the order named: Messrs Swanzy and Co., the Effuenta Gold Mining Co., and the Gold Coast Mining Company. By 1881, the year in which formal administrative reports on Tarkwa district began to be written, extensive preparations for mining, including the erection of several kinds of machines, had been made by the four mining companies; and at the beginning of the

[1] BPP, Cmd. 1343, *Papers Relating to H.M. Possessions in West Africa* (Colonial Office, 1875), Paper no. 47, and BPP, Cmd. 1402, *Papers Relating to H.M. Possessions in West Africa* (Colonial Office, 1876), Paper no. 65.

[2] W. F. Holmes, 'Notes on the Early History of Tarkwa as a Gold Mining District', *Gold Coast Rev.* II, 1 (January–June 1926), 78–117.

following year the stamping or crushing of ores was commenced at the Effuenta mines.

The success of the mining companies, especially that of the Effuenta Gold Mining Company, started off a gold rush with all its well-known associations of fraudulent and genuine mining companies and hasty misinformed individuals coming into the country and expecting to be rich within a short period. So wild were newspaper reports in Britain, for example, that two Englishmen arrived at Axim with two donkeys and little else, with the intention of journeying 'far up country' to buy concessions. One died while going up the Tano river and the other returned to the coast and left the country. There was also the case of the clerk and the baker from England who came out together to the country in 1882 with the idea of picking up 'some of the gold to be seen on the streets of the towns after rains'.[1]

Just as numerous individual prospectors were overtaken by misfortune, so did the majority of the new mining companies succumb in the face of the harsh realities that gold mining in the country involved, and by the end of 1882 not more than six companies showed any signs of permanence. Their estates were all congregated on the Tarkwa hills which run in a north-east–south-west direction from the village of Aboso to Tamso. At Aboso were the 'Swanzy mines' of Messrs F. and A. Swanzy and Co., and the estate of the Aboso Gold Mining Co.(French); about two miles north of Tarkwa at Abontiakoon were the mines of the Gold Coast (Abontiakoon) Mining Co.; the hill above Tarkwa itself was the scene of operations of the earliest of the companies, the African Gold Coast Co.; about two miles south of Tarkwa were situated the mines of the Effuenta Gold Mining Co.; and at Tamso were those of the Tarkwa Gold Mines Co. (fig. 26).

By the end of 1882 the mines worked by the six companies showed uneven stages of development as a result of differences in capital backing, quality of personnel, and the date at which mining commenced. The Effuenta Gold Mining Company, under the management of an experienced mining engineer, was the most advanced and possessed a 20-stamp battery for crushing ores. Next in order of development were the 'Swanzy mines', whose ownership had been transferred to the newly constituted Wasaw (Gold Coast) Gold Mining Company. The degree of success attained by this company was in a large measure due to the efficient management of Mr Crocker after whom the village of Crockerville, built around the mines, was named. The first shaft, near Crockerville, was abandoned because of the ineffectiveness of the machines used to pump out water which lay at no

[1] African no. 249, enclosure in Paper no. 33.

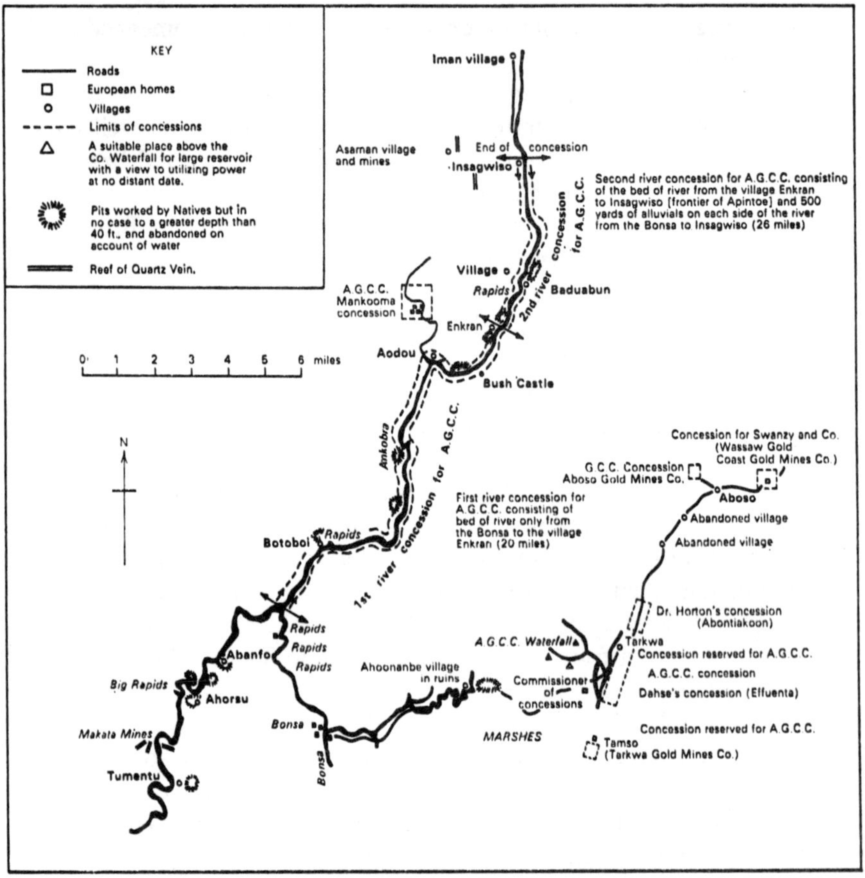


26 Gold-mining concessions in 1879 (after J. Bonnat)

great depth below the land surface. A second series of shafts at Adja Bippo was more successful and became the main source of gold for the company. Instead of paying a fixed daily wage, as was done everywhere else, the company leased the shafts to its workmen who received one-third of the output as their payment. This was done as an incentive to the workmen whose labour was all the more necessary because of the primitiveness of the mining gear installed by the company. The mining concession worked by the Gold Coast Mining Company was one of those originally owned by Dr Horton, and it was reportedly undergoing rapid development. The Aboso Mining Company was formed in 1880 but made little progress within the first two years of its existence, owing to the scare of a threatened Ashanti invasion which resulted in all the employees deserting the mine. The same stage of development marked the remaining two companies but for different reasons: the Tamso concession was acquired by the Tarkwa Gold Mines Company in early 1882, and therefore development had not gone, by the end of the year, beyond the preliminary stages of clearing the site and sinking shallow shafts. On the other hand, the mines belonging to the African Gold Coast Company were partially neglected because of the company's weak financial position; indeed, the company's estate was taken over by the newly formed Tarkwa and Aboso Gold Mining Company towards the end of the 1880s.

Two major problems substantially reduced the prospects of success of the gold-mining industry as a whole. They were the seasonality of the labour supply and the utter inadequacy of the existing means of transport connecting the mines to the coastal ports. The problems persisted to the end of the nineteenth century and, in the case of the labour problem, into the twentieth century. The seasonality of the labour force was attributable to a complex of factors, such as the desire of the employees to rejoin their families in the home areas; the limited wants of the employees, which were easily satisfied by the wages collected after a few months' work; and the absence in the mining areas of stabilizing factors like satisfactory housing and the firm rule of civil law. The problem was also complicated by the fact that all the mining companies, except the Wasaw (Gold Coast) Gold Mining Company, preferred Kroo labour to local Ghanaian labour on the assumption that the former was more efficient than the latter. Consequently the regular departure of labourers created a vacuum which was only filled by importing, at considerable expense, a further supply of labourers from Liberia or elsewhere on the West African coast.

The transport problem centred on the poorness of the routeways and on the absence of a satisfactory means for bulk transport, which necessitated the employment of human carriers who not infrequently disappeared into the surrounding bush with their loads. Thus machine parts had to be imported in duplicate to ensure that some would eventually reach their destination. Besides, the employment of head porterage severely limited the size and weight, and therefore the productive capacity, of mining machinery that could be imported; hence the heaviest piece of machinery in use at Tarkwa did not weigh more than 3 cwt. Each mining company in turn cleared a temporary road from its concession to the coast, but they would not, supposedly out of mutual jealousy, come together to share the expense of building a good and serviceable road to the coast. In the face of such difficulties the progress of the mining industry was slow, and well-informed foreign capitalists were reluctant to invest in it.

Thus the prospects of the industry remained until the British Administration firmly took over, in the late 1880s, the responsibility of directing the country's economic life, and in subsequent years built several good roads from the coast to the mining district as well as a railway from Sekondi to Tarkwa, which was opened to traffic in 1898. The intention of the Administration to solve the transport problem signalled another period of rapid inflow of overseas capital, and from about 1895 onwards the taking up of concessions became more frequent. To regularize the acquisition of concessions generally and to define the Administration's attitude towards the question of ownership of land in the country, a concessions ordinance was passed in 1897 which unleased a torrent of protest from the chiefs and peoples of Southern Ghana. The ordinance was later modified, but not substantially enough to negate the right assumed by the Administration to award concessions of traditional tribal land. In spite of these measures adopted to help the gold-mining industry, gold exports actually decreased in the 1890s through the scare created by the potentially explosive situation that followed the deportation of the king of Ashanti by the British.

Meanwhile the British Administration itself shared in the resurgence of enthusiasm for gold mining, and sent out officers, not necessarily trained for the purpose, to prospect for gold in Southern Ghana. One of the areas that received a great deal of attention was Mankwadi, about 4 miles west of Winneba, where in 1883 one European prospector, Mr Vesenmayer, was extracting gold from both alluvium and quartz.[1] The refusal of the Administration to grant Mr Vesenmayer a Certificate of Validity, which would have given him exclusive rights to gold mining at Mankwadi, indicated the Administration's belief in the possible existence of rich and extensive auriferous sources in the area, and its interest in organizing and controlling mining in parts of Southern Ghana. Thus Mr Eyre went, on behalf of the Administration, on a prospecting mission to certain areas in Southern Ghana in 1888 and wrote a lengthy and optimistic report on 'the auriferous properties of the Winneba District'.[2] Nevertheless the Administration was not financially in a position to undertake the organization of mining enterprises; the Mankwadi alluvial and rock gold sources were never worked, and private companies were awarded Certificates of Validity over areas in Southern Ghana with gold prospects. One such area was Akim Abuakwa where the Goldfields of Eastern Akim Ltd. began to work the auriferous beds in the 1890s.

The eagerness of overseas companies to invest in mines in the country

[1] Despatch of 11 August 1883, in C.O. 96/150, P.R.O.

[2] BPP, Cmd. 5620–4, *Gold Coast: Reports on Gold Mines* (August 1889).

induced many local miners to sell or concede their estates at handsome profits. It was with the sole intention of making a thorough inspection of one such property, a gold mine at Obuasi in Ashanti, that Mr Cade arrived in the country in 1895 on behalf of his firm, Smith and Cade. The concession Mr Cade was interested in had already been made over by the chief of Adansi to three Fanti businessmen who in turn wanted to sell it to him.[1] Mr Cade soon confirmed the unparalleled richness of the ore body in the mine which the Fanti businessmen had been working since 1890 with the help of 200 labourers. He lost no time in accepting the concession and having the transaction confirmed by the chiefs of Bekwai and Adansi; but the Colonial Office was not, for political reasons, prepared to endorse any transaction which included land in Ashanti. The concession was eventually ratified by the Colonial Office in 1897 and, not long after, the Obuasi gold mines, under the management of the Ashanti Goldfields Corporation, began to pour out their fabulous wealth.

The preparations for mining at Obuasi were undertaken on an unprecedented scale. The latest types of mining gear were installed; permanent houses were built for the engineers and other personnel officers; large reservoirs were constructed to supply water for mining purposes as well as for the rapidly growing population of Obuasi; the ore-crushing mills were connected to the shafts and tunnels by tramways, etc. So immediate was the success of the mining enterprise at Obuasi that the corporation offered in August 1898—an offer which was rejected by the Colonial Office —to pay the sum of £5,000 to the Administration towards the cost of a survey which would lead to an extension of the Sekondi–Tarkwa railway to Kumasi, through the corporation's Obuasi concession.[2] The widespread fame of the Obuasi mine induced a great deal of European capital into the development of gold mining in many other areas in Ashanti and Ashanti-Akim.

## 1900–1912

The pace of development of modern mining quickened appreciably after 1900, the year in which occurred a temporary cessation of gold production in South Africa. Britain then turned to the gold mines of Ghana, among others, for relief and in this way sent interest in the industry among foreign companies soaring to great heights. An additional source of stimulus for

[1] For the identity of the Fanti businessmen, see above, p. 181.

[2] African (West) no. 531, *Further Correspondence Relating to Land Concessions and Railways on the Gold Coast* (Colonial Office, April 1899), Paper no. 338.

overseas investors was the steady stream of reports of the extraordinary richness of the gold reefs in the country. The result of the operation of these two powerful stimuli was a second gold rush which lasted two years only, from 1900 to 1901 inclusive, but led to the opening of new mines in Ashanti and also in Southern Ghana. Brong Ahafo and Northern Ghana were generally outside the operational sphere of the mining companies, for the only forays into those regions were by the Wa, Banda, and Felicia Syndicates which, around 1902, became interested in the possibility of working the gold deposits in the neighbourhood of Banda, Bole, and Wa. The activities of the syndicates never went beyond the prospecting stage.

In Southern Ghana and Ashanti a large number of concessions were taken within a matter of months. The sole criterion for choosing a concession was its possession of old and abandoned gold workings, and within the brief peak period of 1900–1 the total number of concessions taken rose to 3,500. Of this number many were abandoned within a year or two, leaving the small total of 114 concessions with Certificates of Validity by 1904; and of this residual number not more than 40 were truly successful and showing profit balances. Seven of these were in Ashanti (with 4 of the companies at Obuasi) and the remaining 33 in Southern Ghana, where 18 of them were grouped on the Tarkwa banket reef. All the companies were able to erect batteries of heavy stamps and generally undertake expensive capital developments on their estates. The Ashanti Goldfields Corporation, perhaps the largest producer, had respectively at Obuasi and Ayeim 91 and 40 heavy stamps, together capable of crushing 10,000 tons of ore a month. Also at Obuasi and Ayeim were complete cyanide plants which could respectively treat 5,000 and 2,000 tons of tailings a month. The Corporation, which commenced crushing ores in March 1898, had by 1904 produced about 126,000 oz. of bullion. In Southern Ghana the company with the largest number of heavy stamps was Abontiakoon Block 1 Company at Tarkwa, followed by the companies with mines at Prestea and Brumase. The size of mining operations was reflected in the extent to which the surrounding forest cover was cut down for fuel and pit props. The problem of fuel supply was especially acute at Obuasi where the extent of deforestation was greatest.

Included among the numerous concessions taken since the beginning of the century were a few consisting of stretches of river, on which dredges operated. In Southern Ghana, in about 1904, the Ankobra (Tarkwa and Aboso) Dredging Company and the West African Mining and Dredging Company respectively operated dredges on the middle and lower reaches of the Ankobra, while dredging in the Birim was in the hands of the

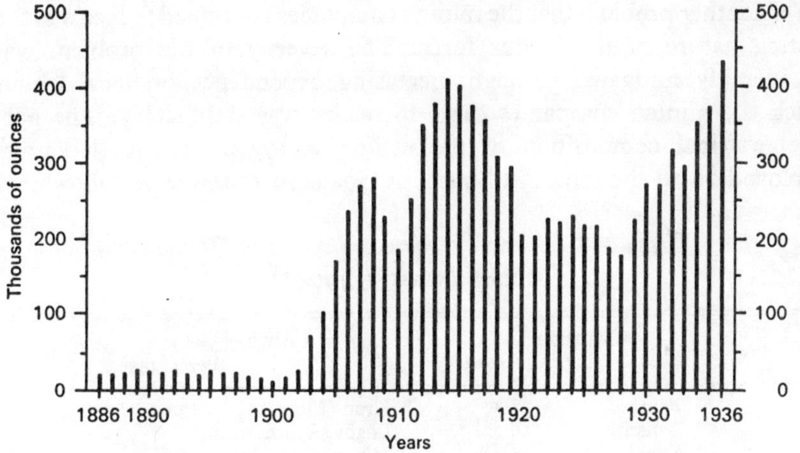


27 Gold exports, 1886–1936

Pritchards Dredging Company and the Birim Valley Gold Mining and Dredging Company. In Ashanti two companies, the Ashanti Goldfields Auxiliary Ltd and the Ofin River Gold Estates Ltd, owned dredges on the Ofin River near Dunkwa.

The heightened interest in gold mining since the beginning of the twentieth century showed not only in the multiplication of mining companies but also in the tremendous leaps of gold exports from about 6,000 oz. in 1901 to over four times as much in 1902, to about 71,000 oz. in 1903, and to about 104,000 oz. in 1904. After that date, when the number of mining companies was much reduced compared with what it was two years previously, the rate of increase of gold exports slowed down a little; yet the export figure reached over 281,000 oz. in 1908 (fig. 27).

The early neglect of many of the concessions was largely attributable to the very way in which they were acquired. The over-eagerness of competing companies to acquire them resulted, in many cases, in the chiefs, to whom alone applications for concessions in recognized tribal lands could be made, granting overlapping concessions; for the chiefs had no more than vague notions of the boundaries of the concessions they granted. Such occurrences involved many companies in expensive litigation. Also, the concessions were often so large that it was difficult to prospect effectively and locate reefs. This resulted in the temporary neglect of a large number of concessions, while the concessionaires hopefully waited for the results of detailed geological investigations in small contiguous estates to give them an indication of the mineral wealth potential of their own concessions.

Yet another problem that the mining companies continued to face was the floating nature of the labour force. The severity of the problem was considerably mitigated through increasing dependence on local labour which the mining companies came to realize was satisfactory. The percentage tribal composition of the estimated 17,044 African labourers employed on all the mines in Southern Ghana in 1904 was as follows:

TABLE 3. *Sources of African Labour in Ghana's Mining Industry, 1904**

| Ghanaian | Percentage | Alien | Percentage |
|---|---|---|---|
| Fanti | 38·40 | Kroo (Liberian) | 13·97 |
| Ashanti | 16·22 | Lagos (Southern Nigerian) | 6·97 |
| Krepi | 11·35 | Bassa | 4·97 |
| Apollonian | 1·42 | Mendi | 4·36 |
| | | Hausa | 2·34 |
| Total | 67·39 | Total | 32·61 |

* From Department of Mines, *Annual Report*, 1904.

The influx of labour from Northern Ghana, which was to assume much significance in the operation of the mining industry in both Southern Ghana and Ashanti, truly began after 1906.

## 1913–1936

It was within the period 1912 to 1936 that a clearer and more definite direction was given to the course of events that later produced the salient characteristics of the mining economy before Independence in 1957. In 1913 was formed the first Geological Survey Department under the directorship of A. E. Kitson. The new department lost no time in organizing a series of extended tours of the country, and within a few years it was able to investigate and report fully on the variety of mineral wealth in the country. The emphasis on economic geology was deliberate: the Administration wanted a resource inventory of the whole country after it assumed full political control over it at the beginning of the twentieth century.

The gold-mining industry attracted the greatest attention. Nevertheless the intensity of exploitation was not even throughout the period under study. The industry was severely affected by the First World War and the depression years that followed, and exports decreased from over 400,000 oz.

in 1914 to less than half that quantity in 1928. The industry recovered soon after, with exports soaring to the unprecedented figure of over 600,000 oz. in 1938.

Within this period the Geological Survey Department completed a countrywide reconnaissance survey and produced the first geological map of the whole of Ghana, described as provisional, in 1928. In 1934 followed a more detailed geological map of the area south of the Black Volta, and on this map were located the producing gold mines as well as prospects. Several new auriferous areas were discovered and quickly taken over by mining companies. For example, the Marlu Gold Mining Areas Ltd came to operate near the old Bogosu mine, about ten miles north-west of Prestea, and was the only company to mine by opencast as well as underground methods. The Bibiani Gold Mines Ltd was formed in 1927 to work the quartz reefs at Bibiani; and the Ashanti-Adowsena (Banket) Goldfields Ltd began mining in 1935 in the conglomerate beds at Ntronang, about 50 miles south-east of Kumasi. Perhaps the most exciting discovery of gold was that at Nangodi in the Upper Region in 1933 by Messrs McGuinness and Reid. The ore body, occurring in a fault zone in Upper Birimian basaltic greenstone, was a lens of quartz, about 200 feet long and 3–4 feet wide, with an average dip to the north-west of 60–80°. Within a year of its discovery mining gear was installed and production begun. Between May 1934 and March 1935 the quantity of gold produced totalled 2,671 crude oz.

## OIL

For practically the whole of the nineteenth century the only mineral that received attention was gold; but towards the very end of the century the possibility of mining oil began to be looked into, as a result of the discovery of oil seepages in the Sekondian carboniferous rocks that disappear under the sea west of Sekondi in the Western Region. The West African Mahogany and Petroleum Company Ltd was soon formed in about 1895, and its prospectus announced that Mr Haig of the company collected crude oil from seepages about 40 miles west of Axim and forwarded two large sample barrels to Liverpool where the oil sold at 70*s*. per ton.

The news of oil discovery excited much interest in Britain, and the West African Oil Syndicate, formed as an offshoot of the West African Mahogany and Petroleum Company Ltd, acquired two concessions in Apollonia, called the Epou-Tachinta and Alaganzuli concessions. A geologist sent out to investigate the oil potential reported that in the dry season oil covered large portions of the surface of the lagoons that abounded on the concessions;

and in numerous other places, especially on the sides of shallow pools of water near the sea, he discovered oil percolating through a black bituminous deposit. 'The indications', he concluded, 'are unquestionably of such a character as to afford ample ground for the most favourable anticipations respecting the results to be obtained by drilling.'[1] By the beginning of 1896 the company had two European representatives stationed on the concessions, and later in the year three experienced American mining engineers arrived with a complete set of drilling machinery capable of boring to a depth of 1,000 feet. The company intended, if prospecting was successful, to build a light pier to a point beyond the surf, where tankers could come near enough to load on the oil through pipes. The site of the pier would be near Epou at Stoopville, named after Mr Stoop, chairman of the company. These plans never materialized, for the company was disappointed at the negative results of the boring tests and lost interest in the concessions.

## MANGANESE[2]

In 1914 the Geological Survey also discovered economic quantities of high-grade (50–55 per cent purity) manganese deposits near Nsuta. The ores were found in Upper Birimian rocks which generally have a well-defined horizon of low-grade manganese-bearing formation (7–30 per cent purity). Soon after the discovery, the Wasaw Exploring Syndicate, later known as the African Manganese Company, acquired the Dagwin Extension concession which covered the Dagwin–Nsuta deposits, and the first shipment of ore from the concession was made in September 1916. Numerous other deposits of manganese were discovered in subsequent years in every administrative region in the country, but either they were too small to warrant the expense of working them or the grade was too low for export. The only worthwhile exceptions were the deposits around Dixcove which occur in two main lines of beds: in the hills from about half a mile north-west of Kwesikrom to the hill west of Asani, and from Jimra Bepo to near Hotopo. They were later mined, mainly at Himakrom and Hotopo.

The Dagwin–Nsuta manganese deposits are found on two parallel ridges extending for just over 2 miles in a roughly north-east direction and with the same general alignment as the Tarkwa Banket Series. A characteristic feature of the deposits which makes their working relatively inexpensive is

[1] African (West) no. 513, Papers no. 18 and no. 88.

[2] *Annual Reports* of the Mines and Geological Survey Departments, 1914–39. See also Geological *Memoir* no. 5.

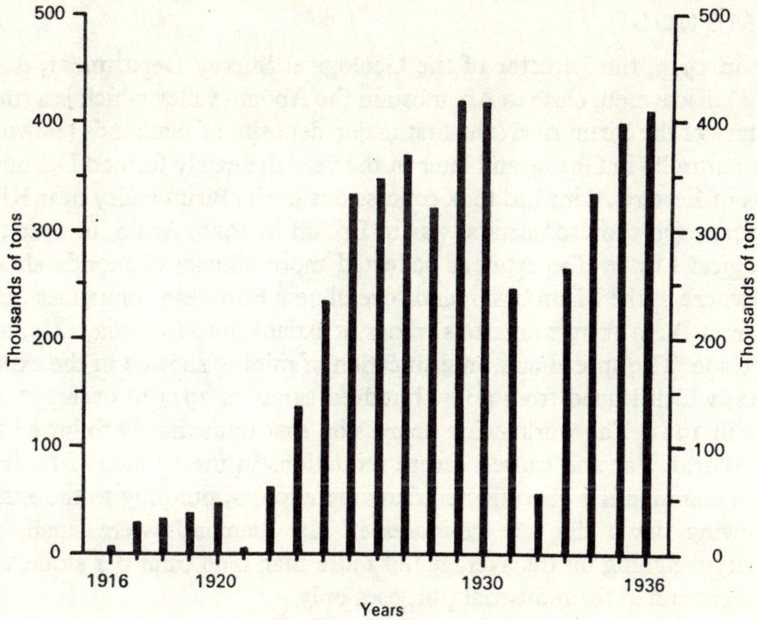


28 Manganese exports, 1916–36

that the main ore occurrences form five prominent hills, named *A* to *E* from south to north, and consist of lenticular bodies with an overburden averaging about 30 feet thick and containing about 40 per cent manganese. Mining was consequently the opencast type, and the ore, excavated mainly by steam and diesel shovels, was transported to the washing plant by railway.

Manganese is an essential element in the manufacture of tough steel; thus exports, supported by a steady demand from industrial Europe, increased very rapidly, from about 30,000 tons in 1918 to about fourteen times as much in 1930. Exports were briefly, though severely, affected by the world economic depression of the early 1930s, tumbling down to the extremely low figure of about 51,000 tons in 1932; but they soon recovered, owing to the importance of the ore to industry, and rose by an average annual increase of 100,000 tons to the pre Second World War record of 527,036 tons in 1937 (fig. 28).

## DIAMONDS[1]

Early in 1919, the Director of the Geological Survey Department, A. E. Kitson, discovered, close to Abomosu in the Abomo valley which is a small tributary of the Birim river, the first major deposits of diamonds known to occur naturally in Ghana, and later in the year the newly formed Diamond Fields of Eastern Akim Ltd took concessions in the Birim valley near Kibi. The first export, of 102 carats, was to Britain in 1920. Again, in 1920 the Geological Survey Department collected more alluvial diamonds almost everywhere in the Birim basin, and several new European companies came to extract them from numerous mines at Atiankama, Akwatia, Oda, and near Kade. The spread and intensification of mining showed in the export figures, which leaped from a few hundred carats in 1923 to over 750,000 carats in 1933. The world-wide depression that immediately followed the First World War and caused severe reductions in the volume of trade in several commodities also affected diamond exports, but only to the extent of slowing down the rate of increase. The diamonds were small, the majority weighing on the average not more than 0·06 carat per stone, and they were suited for industrial purposes only.

In the Birim diamond field all the deposits worked profitably by European companies were included within the area bounded by a line through Kade, Prankese, Osenasi, Manso, Oda, and the Pra–Birim confluence, with most of the producing mines situated not less than 4 miles from the Birim river. The payable sources of diamonds were the shallow gravels, derived from Birimian rocks, that lay with an average thickness of 2–3 feet in the beds and flats of the smaller streams; and mining consisted simply of removing the thin overburden of sandy clay and silt (2 feet thick on the average) and scooping out the diamantiferous gravels. Terraces of the larger streams rarely contained economic quantities of diamonds, except where the terrace gravel had been reworked by small streams cutting through them. These areas, with the richest concentrations of the mineral and accounting for over 80 per cent of production in the Birim basin, were situated in parallel strike zones, each less than a mile and a half wide and underlain by metamorphosed Birimian rocks.

A second diamond field, the Bonsa diamond field, was discovered in 1922. The first diamond samples, also alluvial, were collected by the Geological Survey Department, and subsequent searches by European mining companies and individual Ghanaian prospectors revealed the

[1] See Geological Survey Department *Annual Reports*, 1935–6 and 1936–7, and Geological *Bulletin* no. 12.

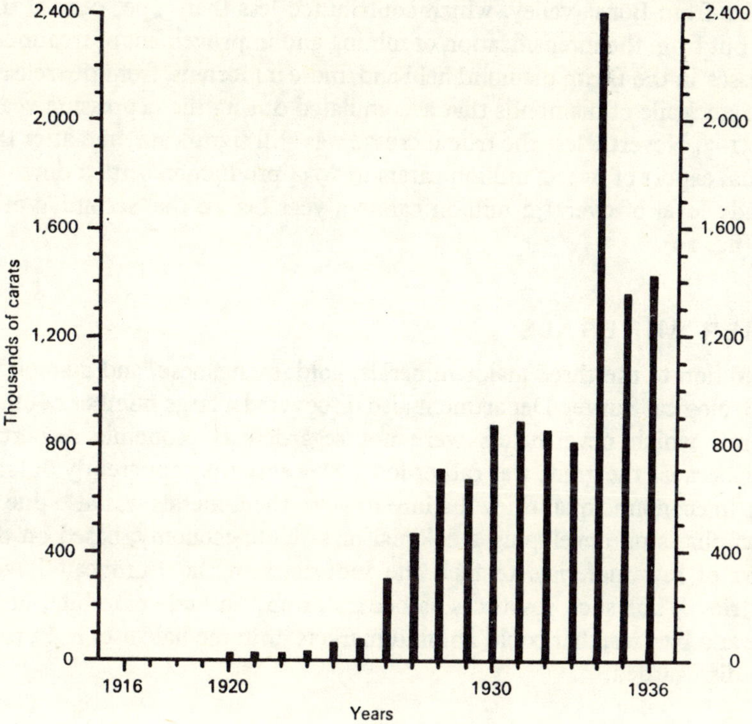


29 Diamond exports, 1916–36

concentration of the mineral in an area about fourteen miles wide, stretching from near Tarkwa to Simpa. The deposits were not large enough to justify the erection of mining and treatment plants by the mining companies; on the other hand the deposits were large enough to promote a big influx of Ghanaian miners. From 1933 they began extracting the diamonds by digging and panning the gravels of several small streams on the north and south sides of the Bonsa, near Simpa and Dompim. The gravels, like those of the Birim diamond field, averaged about 2 feet in thickness with an overburden of 2–3 feet; but they appear to have been derived from the Kawere conglomerate of the Tarkwaian, which in the Bonsa diamond field consists largely of rocks of the Upper Birimian. The diamonds were similar to those from the Birim basin in quality and size.

The two diamond fields together accounted for all the exports of the mineral from Ghana. The increase in export between 1933 and 1934 was phenomenal; it was over 1·5 million carats. It resulted, not from the new supplies from Bonsa valley, which contributed less than 3 per cent of the total, but from the intensification of mining and improvement of treatment processes in the Birim diamond field and, more important, from the release of the stockpile of diamonds that accumulated during the depression years of 1931–3. Nevertheless the true increase was still significant, and after the unusual export of over 2 million carats in 1934 production settled down to a steady level of over 1·2 million carats a year before the Second World War (fig. 29).

## OTHER MINERALS

In addition to the three major minerals, gold, manganese, and diamonds, the Geological Survey Department also discovered a large number of other minerals which nevertheless were not regarded as economic resources either because the grade was rather low or because they apparently did not occur in economic quantities. Failure to work the minerals was also due to the emphasis on developing a colonial or satellite economy, based on the export of raw materials to feed the industries in the European Power countries. Thus such resources as bauxite, iron, tin and columbite, limestone and barytes, that could not find markets or immediate uses in Europe were disregarded.

### Bauxite[1]

The land surface of Ashanti and Southern Ghana consists for the most part of highly dissected plateau surfaces and remnants of peneplains and ranges of hills separated by wide flat-bottomed valleys. General elevation, well below 1,000 feet, decreases steadily to the south, but occasionally higher hills dominate the countryside, rising to 1,500–2,500 feet. Rocks in this hot, humid and forested region are deeply weathered and fresh rock is rarely seen at the surface except on steep slopes and in river or stream valley beds. Laterization has developed to a maximum degree in the region, which thus has all the major bauxite deposits in Ghana.

Bauxite was first discovered by the Geological Survey Department at Mpraeso in 1914, and a visit to the area two years later revealed the existence of large high-grade (about 61 per cent alumina and about 9 per cent ferrous oxide) deposits of the mineral on top of Mt Ejuanema which is about 2,600 feet high. The deposits, underlain by flat-bedded Voltaian shales, form a capping with an average thickness of 20–25 feet on the crest

[1] See Geological Survey Department's *Annual Reports*, 1935–6 and 1936–7, *Bulletin* no. 7.

and upper slopes of Mt Ejuanema, and A. E. Kitson estimated the reserves to be about 4 million tons. Many other deposits were subsequently discovered elsewhere, but from the economic standpoint the largest and most promising deposits were those at Yenahin, discovered in 1920 and situated 40 miles west of Kumasi in the hills near Chichiwere and Mpesaso; in the group of hills from 4 to 6 miles N.N.E. of Sefwi Bekwai, where the deposits were discovered in 1921; in the hills east of the Bia river near Asempanaiye (1922); and on the Atewa–Atwiredu Range near Kibi, discovered piecemeal between about 1919 and 1928. All the deposits were derived from underlying Birimian rocks.

The bauxite caps near Yenahin occur on the flat tops of the Chichiwere–Tinte Hills, at altitudes of 2,200 feet to 2,400 feet, and are scattered over a distance of some twenty miles. The thickness of the deposit varies from 20 feet to 50 feet, and detailed tests conducted in 1930 indicated that the quality of the bauxite was at least as high as that of the Mt Ejuanema deposits. The ore reserves were estimated to be about 168 million tons, assuming an overall average minimum thickness of 20 feet and excluding low-grade ore.

Near Sefwi Bekwai, the major deposits occur on the tops of three hills, Supirri, Ichiniso, and Kaneiyeribo, with altitudes ranging from 1,500 feet to 1,800 feet. The cappings range in thickness from a few feet to more than 20 feet, and analysis of the ore showed that the average percentage alumina and ferric oxide contents were respectively 55 and 11. The total quantity of ore in the deposits was believed to be not less than 30 million tons.

The Bia or Asempanaiye deposits, which are not extensive, are found on a range of hills between Asempanaiye and Pomakrom and have a variable thickness. The ore, which also varies a great deal in composition, averages approximately 48 per cent alumina and 22 per cent ferric oxide. As in the Bia deposits, the grade of the ore in the extensive bauxite cappings on the flat tops of the hills within the Atewa–Atwiredu Range varies a great deal, and the thickness of the deposits also varies from about 6 feet upwards.

## Iron

The most significant iron-ore deposits were those in Shiene–Tweleba area on the Togo frontier in eastern Gonja, first reported on by the Geological Survey Department in 1928. Later the department conducted an intensive prospecting of the deposits by trenching and drilling, and estimated that approximately 100 million tons of siliceous ore, embedded in quartzitic rocks, were available for opencast mining. The average percentage iron content of the ore was 45; it was also demonstrated that beneficiated ore containing an average of 56·7 per cent could be produced. The sole hindrance to the exploitation of the deposits was the factor of accessibility, for only poor and difficult roads linked the area with the south. The cheapest means of bulk transport to serve the Shiene–Tweleba area would have been the railway, but the possibility of building one in that direction was never considered. The factor of inaccessibility also partly explained why the possibility of working the lodes of titaniferous magnetite at Pudo, near Navrongo in the Upper Region, was not seriously considered.

Outside the Shiene–Tweleba and Pudo reserves were observed many areas throughout the country with huge quantities of superficial limonite embedded in laterite, with the quality of the ore varying from high-grade haematite to poor siliceous ore. Some of this was worked and smelted locally, but the deposits were of no real significance in the overall national economy.

## Tin and columbite

Before the Geological Survey Department was formed and systematic prospecting began, District Commissioners throughout the country were instructed to prospect, if possible, on their own and report on any mineral deposits they came across. Among the minerals that should be especially looked for was tin, and the Chief Commissioner of Northern Ghana, assuming for some reason that cassiterite was more likely to occur in the north, showed everywhere in the region samples of tin from Nigeria and offered a reward of £10 to anyone who brought in samples. The reward was never claimed.

The first report on cassiterite was made by the Geological Survey Department which found the ore in pegmatite and aplites at Mankwadi and Abrem on the coast, and with columbite in beach and stream gravels in the same localities. Prospecting began in earnest after the First World War, and between 1923 and 1927 small deposits of cassiterite of no economic value were discovered in the debris from a pegmatite dyke between Kwamsang and Suko in Kumasi district. None of these interested mining companies, except the small deposit at Mankwadi which was worked and exhausted in the 1930s by a European company.

### Limestone and barytes

After about 1915 several deposits of limestone (mostly magnesian), suitable for agricultural and building purposes as well as for the manufacture of cement, were discovered and mapped in Southern Ghana and Ashanti-Brong Ahafo; but most of them could not be worked to any extent because of their situation away from the existing main roads and railways. The largest and most promising deposits south of the Black Volta were those near Bonyere and Half Assini in the Western Region; near Mankrong on the Afram river; near Anyaboni to the north-east of Koforidua; and at Labadi, Accra. In Northern Ghana ample reserves of limestone were found in the Baka–Kabalipe–Buipe area in western Gonja.

Barytes, the heavy, inert, and stable mineral used as a raw material for the barium chemical industry and in the manufacture of a wide range of goods such as plastics, ink, face powder and enamels, occurred in association with the limestones in the bed of the White Volta, 3 miles north of Daboya in Northern Ghana. Deposits were also found to occur in the limestone beds immediately to the west of Du near the old Walewale–Navrongo motor road. Outside Northern Ghana the only deposit of the mineral was a solitary lump between Abodom and Agona Swedru, discovered in 1918. The barytes remained unexploited.

### Waterpower

The possibility of utilizing rivers for producing hydro-electric power was among the items listed early for consideration; but it was not until 1925 that the Geological Survey Department commenced its investigations. Interest was quickened after A. E. Kitson made a waterpower survey of the Asuboni river on the Kwahu plateau, of the middle and lower Afram, and of the Volta from the Akosombo gorge to the Afram–Volta confluence, and reported that a 50-foot-high dam built across the Volta at Akosombo would produce 50,000 h.p. of hydro-electricity. Other rivers were subsequently surveyed, including the Pra which was regarded as a possible supplier of electricity to the nearby mines and to the Accra–Kumasi railway. None of the schemes for building power dams was implemented, for it was considered that the economy, based as it was on the application of masses of cheap and generally unskilled labour to the production of export commodities, did not require so much inanimate energy.

# 9. Economic and social conditions

One of the chief interests in this period lies in why the agricultural and general economic development of the country up to about 1900 was so painfully slow. For over half a century palm oil was the most important agricultural export from the country, but the palm-oil industry was insignificant compared with that in the neighbouring country of Nigeria, and exports of the product from Ghana could have stopped without creating the slightest impression upon the world market. With the exception of gold, exports of non-agricultural products were similarly unimportant in quantity or value. There were many causes, in addition to political unrest, for the backward state of economic development, and of agriculture in particular, in the country, and the principal ones among them were, according to nineteenth-century writers: (i) the policy of the Colonial Powers towards Ghana; (ii) domestic slavery, polygamy, and social slavery; (iii) laziness of the farmers; (iv) poverty of the farmer; (v) small and unstable rural population; (vi) the transport problem (see chapter 10).

## POLICY OF THE COLONIAL POWERS TOWARDS GHANA

Around the middle of the nineteenth century the major Colonial Powers in the country were Britain and Holland. They were joined in the 1880s by Germany which took over political control in the Volta Region. While the Germans exercised a more positive control over Volta Region, the attitude of the British towards assuming responsibility for the economic or social welfare of their territory was, for some time, one of indecision. The Dutch, since the 1850s, were even less interested than the British in the internal affairs of the country.[1]

Several factors hindered the effective administration and development of the country by the British, whose sphere of influence was widest.[2] The

[1] Despatch of 23 March 1870, no. 32 in C.O. 96/84, P.R.O. Their attitude of non-interference was given a clear expression in a letter by Colonel Natglas, Governor of Dutch possessions in the country, to Sir A. E. Kennedy, Governor-in-Chief of British West Africa. An extract from this letter is quoted in appendix 3.

[2] Despatch of 7 July 1862 in C.O. 96/58, P.R.O. Among all the despatches to the Colonial Office since about 1850, this, by Mr Ross, Acting Governor, was the only one that openly criticized the policy of the British Government towards its West African colonies. Parts of the Report are quoted in appendix 4.

British made too many changes in the administrative organization and in the delegation of authority to be able to adopt and follow a consistent development policy for any length of time. The governors were changed far too often, and each governor adopted policies which were contradictory to those of his predecessor. Also, very little was known about the country, and this ignorance gave birth to rumours which in the early stages were dangerous enough to scare off foreign investors interested in the country. This was no exaggeration:[1]

The Gold Coast is one of the most noxious and worthless of our African Settlements. I remember seeing it stated in a letter of a Commissary that most of the meat had to be imported, because the very cattle could not live there. The mortality of officers on the spot is not very large. They sicken, and come home disabled, and die in England.

Another hindrance to rapid progress was the refusal of the Dutch to co-operate with the British in adopting common economic policies. For example, the British Administration wanted to increase the revenue of the country by imposing customs duties, but the Dutch, who also controlled several of the ports, flatly refused to adopt similar measures, with the result that ships for a time stopped calling at the ports controlled by the British Administration. From the point of view of the British, the only solution was for the Dutch to hand over their possessions to them, but the Dutch would not agree to that because they still drove a brisk trade with Ashanti for slaves whom they exported to Java, dressed up as soldiers. The Dutch eventually left the country in 1872.

Yet another factor of prime importance was the attitude towards the country's physical environment as one in which a European could not live for any length of time. A senior European Government official stationed in the country admitted in later years that until about the turn of the century West Africa as a whole was one of those places to which most Englishmen went as a last resource.[2] This fearsome attitude towards the physical environment engendered a whole series of ludicrous adaptations in the mode of living which only served to make the Europeans more uncomfortable. The attitude was not altogether unjustified for, until quinine was placed on the market in the nineteenth century, malaria and other diseases for which Europeans had no efficacious remedies took a heavy toll of

[1] Minute attached to Despatch of 4 November 1868 in C.O. 96/77, P.R.O. In fairness to the author, Mr Elliot, it should be said that he derived his opinion from despatches from Ghana. Ross himself wrote a description of the country's climate and its effect on health which was gruesome enough. See appendix 5.

[2] Decima Moore Guggisberg and Major F. G. Guggisberg, *We Two in West Africa* (London, 1909), p. 10.

European life in West Africa. But quinine itself, as it was later discovered, was not always the perfect answer to pernicious fevers, for excessive use of the drug could produce unpleasant side-effects. The term 'Coast', by which Englishmen associated with West Africa referred to the country, consequently had unpleasant connotations which bred instinctive fear.[1]

Running through all the explanations offered by nineteenth-century writers for Britain's hesitation to participate fully and constructively in the country's life was this theme of the 'murderous' physical environment. By contrast the Germans apparently had no such qualms about staying in that same environment.

Perhaps the most important factor accounting for the slow pace of economic development in much of Ghana for the greater part of the nineteenth century was the nature of British interference in the country's internal politics. The arrival of Sir Charles MacCarthy in the country in 1822 marked the commencement of the British policy of open hostility towards the Ashanti which continued throughout the rest of the nineteenth century.[2] Current nineteenth-century European opinion regarded the Ashanti as a savage, war-loving people, yet in most cases it was the British who provoked Ashanti wrath by breaking faith with the Ashanti and displaying a total disregard for the treaties they had executed. The Ashanti were on the whole honest in their political relations with the British and on many occasions made overtures of friendship which were stultified by the unreliable conduct of some local British Government officials.

Finally, in 1873–4, the British mounted a massive offensive, in which the famous Black Watch Regiment took part, and defeated the Ashanti. The objective of the British was the total dissolution of the Ashanti Confederacy, and this they achieved by instituting measures which encouraged rebellion of the member states of the Confederacy against the king of Ashanti at Kumasi, and which sought to break the economic power of Ashanti.[3] In 1902 Ashanti was annexed to the British Crown.

By interfering with the power of Ashanti from the early nineteenth century, the British disrupted an orderly economic and political organization embracing the whole country, with Ashanti as the nerve centre. This they did without providing an effective substitute for several decades. The criticism by Ross of Britain's hesitation to institute the necessary frame-

[1] The Guggisbergs saw an example of this dread of the 'Coast' in 1905 when they were travelling by ship from Liverpool to Ghana (op. cit. pp. 1–2). On 'sniffing the Coast' soon after leaving Grand Canary, two nervous European passengers immediately went into their cabins to take quinine!

[2] R. A. Freeman, *Travels and Life in Ashanti and Jaman* (London, 1898), pp. 471–2.

[3] See below, p. 214.

work within which to pursue policies of economic development was one among many—from merchants and private organizations. The Manchester Chamber of Commerce for example presented to the Colonial Office in 1883 a memorandum in which it complained that exports of Lancashire cotton goods to Ghana had diminished during the previous five years, and that although the revenue of the country had increased, very little was being done for its material benefit or for the benefit of the trade which produced the revenue. The Chamber recommended, among other things, the building of railways under the guarantee of the the Colonial Treasury.[1]

Nevertheless, glimpses of greater interest were already discernible in the early 1880s in the attitude of the British Administration towards the country's economic development. Roads were being cleared to facilitate trade, the country was being systematically explored and detailed reports made. The real turning point came in about 1890, or a little before, when the indecisive and lukewarm attitude of the British Administration was replaced by a positive desire to develop and exploit the economic resources of the country. Roads and railways were planned, the country was explored more intensively, and investigations made into ways of improving agriculture, which was recognized as the foundation of the country's prosperity.[2]

Perhaps the greatest achievement in the sphere of agricultural development was the opening at Aburi of an agricultural station in 1890. This was the work of Sir William Brandford Griffith, who may rightly be regarded as the father of improved agriculture in Ghana. His aim in establishing the Aburi Botanical Gardens, as the station was called, was to teach the people to cultivate economic plants in a systematic manner for export and to introduce new cash crops that could be cultivated with advantage. This emphasis upon exploiting the country's economic resources as well as improving the material welfare of the people was in direct contrast with the policy of the Germans, whose magnificent achievements in the Volta Region were made with forced labour and with the proceeds of heavy taxation.

[1] BPP, Cmd. 4052, *Further Correspondence respecting the Affairs of the Gold Coast* (Colonial Office, June 1884), Papers nos. 44 and 45.

[2] *Report on Economic Agriculture on the Gold Coast* (1889 and 1891), Cmd. 5894-40 and Cmd. 6270.

## DOMESTIC SLAVERY, POLYGAMY, AND SOCIAL SLAVERY

In Ghana the bulk of the population was, according to most nineteenth-century writers, of slave origin and their actions were (at least before 1874) said to be circumscribed by the wishes of their masters, while much of the free male population was rendered inactive by the custom of polygamy or impoverished by a system of social slavery.

It was sometimes argued that the system of domestic slavery had no harmful effect on the country's economic progress. The slave was to all intents and purposes part of his master's family and was treated as such, and there were instances of domestic slaves having inherited the property of their dead masters. The slave could sometimes marry his master's daughter or, if the slave was female, be married by the master himself. The slave therefore had every incentive to be industrious, and the fact that he did not often apply himself to any occupation with zeal was due to his inherent laziness.[1] There were many arguments of this nature, but counter-arguments were equally numerous. If a domestic slave was considered to be part of his master's family, he was not necessarily regarded as equal in social status with the rest of the family; the members of a household were divided into classes, each with a different set of privileges, and the son or nephew, for example, was higher in the social scale than the pawned slave, who in turn despised the *donko*.[2] A domestic slave who succeeded his master was probably the issue of marriage between the master and a female slave. If a domestic slave married a free woman, he was more often in the position of a privileged inferior, and if the head of a household married a female slave, the latter only became one of the numerous wives who had to work to feed their master. The domestic slave was therefore no more than an ordinary slave who was sometimes treated gently.

While the plantation slave was forced to produce the raw materials needed in industrial Europe, the domestic slave in Ghana was comparatively useless, it was argued, because his energies were left almost wholly unproductive. Besides, as long as there were domestic slaves the bulk of the free population would not work, with the result that the country as a whole had no tradition of serious agriculture. The Rev. Schrenck of the Basel Mission, who had been in the country for several years, observed in 1875 that the pupils passing through his school objected to farm work because

[1] For critical comments on some contrasting views on the subject of domestic slavery, see Thomas J. Hutchinson, 'The Social and Domestic Slavery on Western Africa, and Its Evil Influence on Commercial Progress' in *Jl. R. Soc. Arts* (26 February 1875), pp. 312 ff.

[2] The *donko*, usually from an alien tribe, was acquired through outright purchase.

it was associated with slaves.[1] Another observer concluded, after reviewing labour conditions in West Africa as a whole, that the idea of a 'bold peasantry, its country's pride' was completely unknown there. The husband traded and fought battles, and left sowing and reaping to his wives and slaves; even a slave would rather buy himself a slave than buy his own liberty.[2]

The relationship that nineteenth-century writers sought to establish between the institution of domestic slavery and the slow progress of serious commercial agriculture was not justifiable. The choice in Ghana lay between export agriculture, which was new and not always rewarding, and the far more profitable alternatives of gold mining and trading, in which slave labour also played a major role. The problem associated with the practice of employing slaves was not so much the inefficiency of slave labour as the psychological barrier that, for a brief period after the abolition of domestic slavery, prevented the free population from readily engaging in occupations formerly relegated to slaves.

Britain's attitude towards domestic slavery was one of uncertainty until 1874, when the system was officially abolished.[3] In 1855 the British Administration accepted domestic slavery as an established local institution, and slaves were not given protection in the forts unless they could prove acts of cruelty on the part of their masters.[4] In 1866 the Administration was apparently against domestic slavery, for Mr Dawson, a Ghanaian merchant, was indicted for importing five persons from Whydah to Cape Coast to be his domestic slaves. These were set free by the Chief Justice, William Hackett.[5] But in 1868 it was asserted that domestic slavery existed in all its various forms, and that men, women, and children were being sold 'within a few yards of the Governor's residence'.[6] Even after 1874 domestic slavery continued, but with children only as the victims.[7]

Nevertheless domestic slavery, in all its forms, died a natural death with the creation of new economic conditions which did not admit of the comparatively inefficient slave labour. The cultivation of crops for export needed the personal attention of the landlord or that of paid, and therefore

[1] The Rev. Schrenck made this observation during the discussion that followed a paper on the country's economy read at a meeting of the Royal Society of Arts in London in 1875. See *Jl. R. Soc. Arts* (2 April 1875), p. 424.

[2] R. F. Burton and V. L. Cameron, *To the Gold Coast for Gold* (London, 1883), II, 328. Also Horton, *West African Countries and Peoples*, p. 118.

[3] In German Togoland, domestic slavery was abolished in 1902.

[4] Despatch, 7 April 1855 (Judicial) in C.O. 96/41, P.R.O.

[5] Despatch of 17 September 1866 in C.O. 96/72, P.R.O.

[6] Horton, op. cit. p. 131.

[7] *Aborigines Protection Society*, new series, 1890–1896, IV.

generally more conscientious, labour. Moreover, the courts became more alert and severely punished offenders.

Polygamy, it was argued, was just another form of domestic slavery, for a man's several wives were by customary law bound to submit to his absolute control. The social status of women in Ashanti, except that of the wives of princes, war captains, linguists, etc., was even lower than it was in Southern Ghana, for the Ashanti husband could exercise the power of death over his wives. One observer went so far as to say that all women in West Africa were slaves, be they mothers, wives, daughters, or sisters even of kings; they were not only bought and sold but were completely at the mercy of their owners.

The institution of polygamy was deeply woven into the social fabric of nineteenth-century Ghana, and it frequently happened that a man's property almost wholly consisted in the wives left him by his predecessor. A married man no doubt helped with farm work, but he could hardly exert himself fully when the attractions of an easier life were so tempting.[1]

The view of polygamy as a hindrance to economic progress showed a lack of appreciation of the true nature of the existing economic conditions. The provision of food, through purchase or cultivation, was normally regarded as part of a wife's household duties. The male population was in its turn engaged in occupations that were considered to be far more profitable financially and, understandably, export agriculture was at first graded much lower as a source of income than trading or working in gold mines.

The advance of Christianity with its insistence on monogamy, and the spread of Western education, very slowly made for the rise of women in social status. Moreover, the practice of leaving farm work to housewives was incompatible with cash crop farming, which demanded more efficient paid labour.

Social slavery, said to be akin to domestic slavery, apparently worked in a more subtle way but with effects no less harmful. The rulers of society, the chiefs, elders, fetish priests, etc., were said to keep the populace in subjection and maintained their power by passing a number of apparently harmless but really oppressive laws; and although there were courts and magistrates in most parts of the country, the traditional authority of the rulers still carried weight. Moreover, the laws were not always of such a nature as could be appealed against, for they might be connected with religious observances which a law court could not interfere with. As an example of social slavery was cited the despotic power of a fetish priest in Akim Abuakwa who had the right, on the death of a person, to order the

[1] Hutchinson, op. cit. Also Horton, op. cit. pp. 107–18.

body to be placed in an upright position inside the dead man's house.[1] If the corpse remained upright, all the property of the dead man was allowed to his family; but if it fell—which the fetish priest knew was bound to happen—the whole estate and effects of the dead person were handed over to the fetish. Another illustration of social slavery was the tribunals of elders who lived on fees derived from suits tried before them. The tribunals were regarded as agencies of extortion, and a prosperous farmer might suddenly find himself stripped of his possessions on one pretext or another.

A fetish priest was a very important person in the society of nineteenth-century Ghana, and his power penetrated all layers of society, from the *donko* to the chief. Wars would be waged or marshes drained only with the approval and blessing of the fetish priest, since in the first instance it was considered wise to have the support of the gods, and in the second instance the stagnant waters might be the abode of some spirits. There are legends of how bridges over rivers collapsed and how European road engineers died because the river gods and the spirits of the forests through which the roads passed were not appeased.

This custom of consulting fetish priests before embarking on any project could sometimes be inimical to economic progress, it was argued, because the fetish priest, either deliberately or through ignorance, often forecast failure for an economic venture that would probably have been successful and of great benefit to the community. It will be recalled that towards the end of 1874 palm nuts were allowed to rot on the ground in Krobo because the cracking of the nuts was regarded by the fetish priests as the cause of smallpox.[2] In 1907 an Acting Commissioner of Ashanti related how a fetish priest, through a fantastic prophecy, brought the production of rubber in western Brong Ahafo to a temporary standstill.[3] This fetish priest, at Techiman, announced the arrival of a new god who was to bring riches to the poor and reduce the rich to abject poverty; at his coming the black man was to become white and the white man black. Anyone found tapping rubber trees, farming, or hunting in the forest, the fetish priest warned, would on the god's arrival be turned into an antelope.

The use of the term social slavery was in itself an indication of the misconceptions harboured in the nineteenth century about social organization and practices in the country. The majority of the instances of social slavery cited in the literature formed part of a body of religious or social taboos which at least must once have had economic or even political

[1] Hutchinson, op. cit.

[2] See above, p. 145.

[3] *Colonial Report—Ashanti*, 1907.

relevance. It was inevitable that these taboos and customs should conflict with ideas held by the Europeans who in any case regarded the African as a less civilized person and who at that time reacted differently to the situations with which the taboos were connected. This is not to deny that insistence on some taboos out of sheer ignorance and conservatism could sometimes be a real hindrance to improvement; but happily instances of taboos frustrating the execution of major economic policies, when they were eventually forthcoming from the British, were very few.

## LAZINESS OF THE FARMERS

It was another grave misconception that the Ghanaian was the supremely lazy person that many nineteenth-century writers imagined him to be. Here are four short but typical excerpts from the wealth of variations on the popular theme of the 'native's inherent laziness':[1]

> (*a*) In the neighbourhood of Begoro...are innumerable gum trees and india-rubbers; and both might prove a fertile source of wealth, had the natives enough human intelligence and industry to avail themselves of the treasures which Nature showers upon them with so lavish a hand.
>
> (*b*) With the exception of the few who are engaged in hunting, and who stay out for a week or more in the forests on the bare chance of shooting a leopard or deer, the large bulk of the male population follow no regular occupation, but dawdle or sleep about the towns and villages, while the women are at work.
>
> (*c*) Your African Christian is meticulous upon the subject of the 'sabbath'; he will do as little work as possible for six days, and scrupulously repose upon the seventh.
>
> (*d*) I repeat: their beau ideal of life is to do nothing for six days in the week and to rest on the seventh. They are quite prepared to keep, after their fashion, 365 sabbaths per annum.

The first quotation was typical of the many statements which took no account of the occupations the Ghanaian was really interested in and, in this particular instance, no account was taken of the fact that in Akim Abuakwa gold mining was a far more profitable occupation than the collection of rubber or gum copal. The second quotation represented an exaggerated misunderstanding of the existing social institutions. There was occupational differentiation according to sex, and if the male population was seen around the houses while the women were at work on the farms, it was because food farming was by custom left to women. The last two quotations are examples of the popular but empty witticisms that are only

[1] The first two quotations are from Captain J. S. Hay's 'On the District of Akem in West Africa' in *J. Roy. Geogr. Soc.* XLVI (1876), 302, 304. The last two quotations are from Burton and Cameron, op. cit. II, 93, 328–9.

too common in nineteenth-century literature on Ghana. The Ghanaian, contrary to popular belief, was not entirely unaware of the need to improve agriculture in the country. This awareness was expressed emphatically in the Constitution of the Fanti Confederation.[1] For several reasons, mainly political, the Fanti Confederation was unable to implement its vast schemes of economic development.

The Rev. Schrenk of the Basel Mission knew the Ghanaian better. When asked if the Ghanaian's laziness would 'not permit them to be steady labourers in any occupation whatever', he told the simple truth that the Ghanaian, like any other person, was willing to work for profit and did not care to be engaged in any occupation that was to be its own reward.[2] The greatest monument to the Ghanaian's willingness to work for profit was the cocoa industry, whose rapid spread throughout Southern Ghana and Ashanti was the subject of many admiring comments and loud praises by Government officials among others.[3]

## POVERTY OF THE FARMER

This was a serious problem.[4] As far as his personal wants were concerned the farmer could live with little money. But if he was so unfortunate as to lose his wife, his child, his father or, most important of all, his uncle, then 'custom' must be made, regardless of expense. Guns must be fired, rum must be provided, and every comer must be entertained for at least one week after death. The custom must be repeated after an interval of six weeks, and finally, after an interval of one year. Goats and sheep must be sacrificed at the funeral and at other times as directed by the fetish priest, and perhaps more sacrifices made to placate the ghost of the deceased. The farmer could not by himself pay for all this, and so he pawned his estate or borrowed from a moneylender. Interest at the rate of fifty, seventy-five, or a hundred per cent was added to the principal, and until the loan was repaid the debtor must work for his creditor two days in the week, nothing being allowed for his labour. This might, and frequently did, go on for years, until the debtor was fortunate enough to find the means of paying both the principal and interest. The observance of the customs was enforced

[1] BPP, 'Fanti Confederation' (Colonial Office, London, 1873). See, for example, sections 3 and 5 under article 8.

[2] *Minutes of Select Committee on West Africa* (1865), paragraph 3440.

[3] An example is E. D. Morel's article, 'Free grown Cocoa' in *Daily Chronicle*, 25 February 1909.

[4] The problem of indebtedness of the farmer was frankly discussed in the *Report on Economic Agriculture on the Gold Coast (1889)*, Cmd. 5894–40.

by superstition and submitted to from fear; fear of the anger of the dead, fear of the wrath of the fetish, and fear of public opinion which applauded the man who made a big 'custom' and stigmatized as stingy the man who spared on such an occasion.

Another source of poverty was the practice of engaging in expensive and protracted lawsuits about ownership of land. The disputes became more frequent with the growing importance of cash-crop farming, and huge debts were incurred by the litigants. One dispute of long standing was that between the inhabitants of British and Dutch Sekondi about the right to an oil-palm plantation, a short distance from Sekondi on the Wasaw road, and the disputants not infrequently resorted to arms in support of their claims. Generally, the debts arising from these land disputes could only be paid off with borrowed money, for which village lands were often mortgaged.

## SMALL AND UNSTABLE RURAL POPULATION

The effects of the factor of poverty were aggravated by the fact that the population was too small in relation to the area of the country to allow the soils to be fully utilized. From the Poll Tax returns of 1853, the population of the British Protectorate in Southern Ghana appeared to be about 151,346, although current opinion at the time put the figure at about 450,000. After 1853 there were no more serious attempts to estimate the size of the population until 1874, when the figure of 540,000 was arrived at by adding up the number of fighting men every district in Southern Ghana and Ashanti possessed, and multiplying the total by the factor four.[1] The first true population census in 1891 gave the figure of 764,508 for Southern Ghana, excluding Kwahu and Krepi, and the second census in 1901 gave the figure 1,241,887 for both Southern Ghana and Ashanti.[2] These figures are generally recognized to be too low, but even a population of 2 million for both Southern Ghana and Ashanti would only give a density of about 35 persons to the square mile, far too small for effective utilization of the land by a people whose principal agricultural implements were the hoe and the cutlass.

Numerous factors accounted for the small size of the population. A medical officer in 1859 mentioned three of them: the high death rate among children, polygamy—'because the habits which it engenders materially diminish the number of births', and the easy access to cheap trade spirits

[1] Despatch of 21 December 1883 in C.O. 96/153, P.R.O.
[2] The population figures did not cover the Volta Region.

whose consumption was rather prejudicial to life.[1] Also within this small population emerged a new class of people—scholars. Almost every person, especially along the coast, who could read and write preferred trading to farming, and for this reason the Fanti were called a 'nation of peddlers'.[2] The opinion was consequently expressed officially that unless competitive foreign labour was introduced, the Fanti, whose *moral* induced him to prefer trade to commerce, would never be a tiller of the soil.[3]

The most important factor that limited the size and agricultural productivity of the population derived from the internecine tribal wars. From about 1860 wars erupted on several occasions with devastating force between Ashanti and Southern Ghana, or within each of the two regions, causing major population movements and severely curtailing agricultural or general economic enterprise. One of the most significant shifts of population in the second half of the nineteenth century was that of the Juaben who, after their defeat by the king of Ashanti, moved in a large mass to Southern Ghana in 1876 to seek protection under the British. They were settled in a thinly populated part of the Eastern Region where they founded the state of New Juaben with Koforidua as the capital. This was a loss to Ashanti, for while much of old Juaben lay uncultivated, the empty lands of New Juaben were rapidly colonized, and became the scene of feverish agricultural activity.

Ashanti incurred further losses of population through emigration during the civil wars of the 1880s. In 1886 the Bekwai routed the Adansi, burnt their capital Fomena and so completely destroyed the countryside of Adansi that scarcely a house was left standing. This was confirmed in 1888 by a traveller who passed through the area on foot on his way to Kumasi. During the five days it took him to reach Bekwai from the village of Atase Nkwanta, close to the north bank of the Pra, he travelled through the 'Adansi wilderness' where he did not come across a single inhabited settlement.[4] Over 12,000 Adansi refugees crossed the Pra and the Ofin rivers into Southern Ghana: about 7,000 were settled in Denkera villages, about 4,000 in Asin villages, and the rest in western Akim villages.[5] Thousands of people from Nkwanta and Deniase fled with the Adansi and settled in Denkera and Wasaw, from where some were removed and resettled near Butri on the coast. A few thousands of the Adansi were also later resettled,

[1] Despatch of 11 July 1859 in C.O. 96/45, P.R.O.
[2] Brodie Cruickshank, *Eighteen Years on the Gold Coast of Africa* (London, 1853), II, 36.
[3] Enclosure in despatch of 2 November 1870 in C.O. 96/85, P.R.O.
[4] R. A. Freeman, *Travels and Life in Ashanti and Jaman* (London, 1898), pp. 37–55.
[5] BPP, Cmd. 4906, *Further Correspondence Respecting the Affairs of the Gold Coast* (Colonial Office, September 1886), Paper no. 28.

in 1887, near Nsaba in Agona country.[1] In 1888 the paramount chief of Kokofu, with about 15,000 men, women, and children was similarly driven across the Pra by the combined armies of Bekwai and Kumasi; the refugees first settled in the villages around Kotoko near the Pra, and between Asikuma and Nsuaem (Akim Oda), but were later removed to the sparsely populated area near Akroso, about 30 miles south-east of Nsuaem on the borders of Agona and western Akim.[2]

Population movements resulting from wars were also frequent in Northern Ghana throughout the closing decades of the nineteenth century. Slave raids, particularly those conducted by Samori and Babatu, in many cases forced the rural population to abandon rich cultivable lands to flee to safer but less hospitable or fertile areas. The north-western portion of Northern Ghana was particularly affected. Nevertheless there existed a compensating factor that mitigated the unwholesome economic consequences of the drain of population from Northern Ghana, for wars and other unsettling disturbances in neighbouring countries also promoted an inflow, though of modest proportions, of population into Northern Ghana. In about the middle of the 1880s, for example, some sparsely populated areas of western Gonja became the recipients of Ligbi tribesmen who had fled, on account of wars, from Bondoukou. They built characteristically well-planned settlements, and quickly converted the existing wilderness to rich farms. Takla, Soso, and Tasalima or Soukowra (which means 'new village') were already large prosperous agricultural and trading villages by 1888.[3]

In spite of the tribal wars the rural population, from about the 1860s, became progressively less restricted in its distribution than it was in the early 1850s. With the establishment of commercial agriculture, the population began to move into the countryside on a significant scale.[4] The Krobo moved down from their dry, hilltop settlements in the Accra Plains to colonize neighbouring forest lands extending northward towards the Afram river; and the equally energetic Akwapim similarly founded new settlements all around the foot of the Akwapim Mountains and farther afield. Towards the end of the nineteenth century, in 1892, occurred another major population movement involving the Shai who were evicted, by

[1] BPP, Cmd. 5357, *Further Correspondence Respecting the Affairs of the Gold Coast* (Colonial Office, April 1888), Papers nos. 24, 25, and 31 with all their enclosures.

[2] BPP, Cmd. 5615, *Further Correspondence Respecting the Affairs of the Gold Coast* (Colonial Office, December 1888), Papers nos. 39, 41, and 45 with their enclosures.

[3] Binger, *Du Niger au Golfe de Guinée*, II, 145–52.

[4] Brodie Cruickshank (op. cit. II, 285–8) exaggerated when he claimed that by about 1850 the split-up of large nucleated villages following the movement to the countryside had begun. The current official as well as private opinion was contrary to this often-quoted view of Cruickshank's. See, for example, the *Blue Book* for 1854.

Government order, from their easily defended settlements on the tops of the Shai Hills in the Accra Plains. The Shai penetrated deep into the neighbouring forest country of New Juaben and Akim, buying up land both for settlement and cocoa cultivation. Nankese, one of the early cocoa villages in Akim, for example owed its cocoa boom in the early years of the twentieth century as much to the zeal of local farmers as to that of immigrant Shai farmers.

# 10. The transport problem

## TRADE ROUTE NETWORK

For many years after about 1850 no significant change occurred in the existing loose network of important trade routes. Trade routes and politics were so closely interwoven that as long as Ashanti remained the economic and political heart of the country all major routes led from Kumasi to selected ports on the coast and to certain major settlements in the north (fig. 30).[1]

With the dissolution of the Ashanti empire after 1874 there was general confusion and political unrest in all the subject states, which resulted in the closing of many trade routes to Ashanti and in serious dislocation of trade. This prompted the British Administration to attempt to reorganize both trade and the trade route network. To this end numerous missions, charged with the task of opening new as well as old trade routes, were sent from the coast into the interior.

The central aim that guided the British Administration in the fashioning of the trade route network was to re-route trade away from Kumasi and to encourage trade with the seaboard by the most direct routes.[2] The economic power of Kumasi, and therefore of Ashanti, would be broken while Southern Ghana's trading economy would be strengthened.[3] Also, with Kumasi out of the way, the British would be able to consolidate their trade with the northern markets.

Dr Gouldsbury's mission into the interior was the first of a series. He journeyed from Accra through Kumasi and Atebubu to Salaga and Yendi in 1876.[4] At the eastern Gonja capital of Kpembe Dr Gouldsbury drew attention to Akim as an alternative source of kola nuts, which the Ashanti could no longer send to Salaga, and promised to secure a safe and through passage in the Volta Region for northern traders desiring direct contact with the coast-based European traders. His return journey took him through Kete and Krachi, Kpandu and Battor where he crossed the Volta for the

[1] Dickson, 'The Development of Road Transport in Southern Ghana and Ashanti since about 1850', *Trans. Hist. Soc. Ghana*, v, 1 (1961).

[2] African no. 268, *Further Correspondence Regarding affairs of the Gold Coast* (Colonial Office, February 1884), enclosure in Paper no. 2.

[3] BPP, Cmd. 4477, *Further Correspondence Respecting the Affairs of the Gold Coast* (Colonial Office, July 1885), Paper no. 37.

[4] Gouldsbury Report (Africa no. 95).

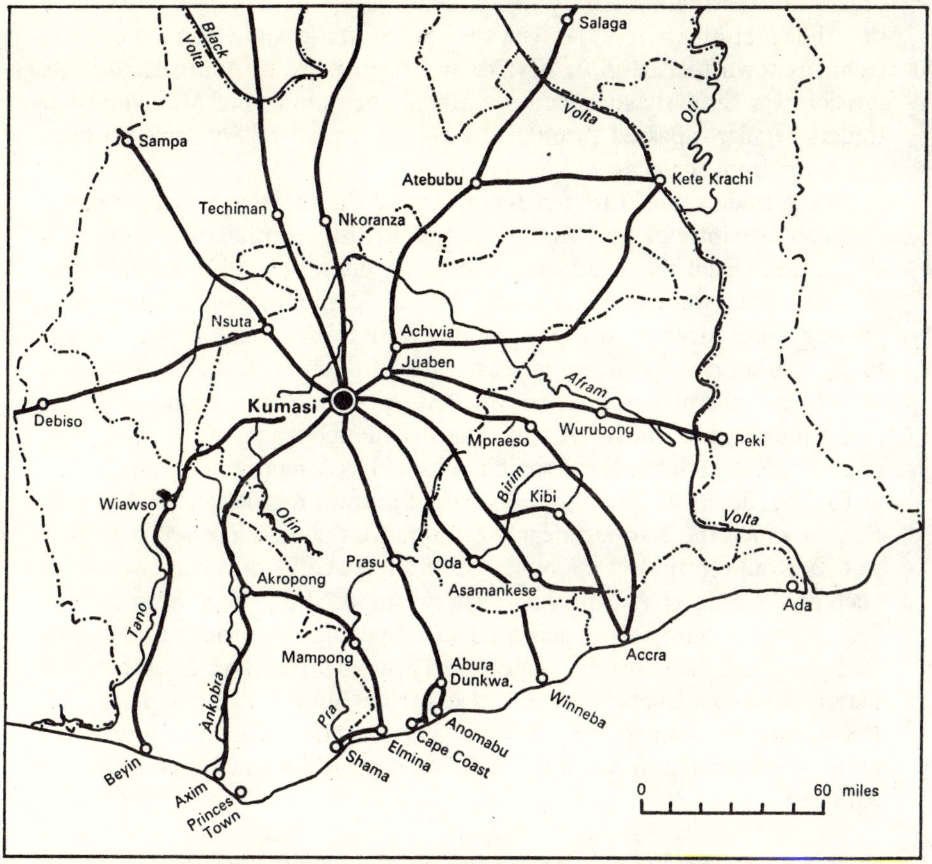


30 Kumasi: the focus of major trade routes, *c.* 1850

last phase of the journey to Accra. Dr Gouldsbury's mission was successful: at Krachi he was assured that traders from Salaga or the coast would no longer be stopped from proceeding beyond that point, a piece of news that was received at Salaga 'with a general expression of satisfaction and congratulation'. The Buem promised to keep their part of the route open, while the Krepi additionally agreed to discontinue the practice of panyarring—abducting men to be sold into slavery.

Next the British Administration sent Captain Lonsdale in 1881–2 on a mission similar to that of Dr Gouldsbury.[1] Captain Lonsdale followed

[1] Lonsdale Report in BPP, Cmd. 3386, *Further Correspondence Regarding Affairs of the Gold Coast* (Colonial Office, August 1882). The instructions to Captain Lonsdale are contained in Paper no. 7.

practically the same itinerary as Dr Gouldsbury. It was at his insistence that the chief of Atebubu revived the ancient trade route that led directly from his town to Abetifi in Kwahu and from there to Akim. Lonsdale's mission was similarly successful: in 1882 large numbers of Mohammedan traders regularly passed through the Krobo market of Somanya on their way to or from the coast.[1]

Where trade routes through Kumasi were the shortest and most direct between the interior and the coast, the British Administration did not divert trade from them to longer alternative ones, but rather ensured that Kumasi could not assume its former role as clearing house for trade goods passing along those routes. The shortest route from Accra or Cape Coast to the market of Kintampo was that through Kumasi and Nkoranza, and one of the major achievements of the British police officer, Brandon Kirby, on his journey into the interior in 1884 was the reopening of the upper end of the route, which the Nkoranza had blocked to Ashanti traders since 1881 at Kofiase, about two days journey from the town of Nkoranza.[2] A condition on which the Nkoranza agreed to remove the blockade was that their traders would in no way be molested or subjected to heavy fines or taxes such as the king of Ashanti had hitherto imposed on them. South of the Pra, Brandon Kirby also succeeded in reopening an ancient trade route that provided the shortest connection between Prasu and Accra; it had deteriorated to a hunter's track and led from Atawase, a ferry point near Prasu, through Asin country to Akim Swedru where it linked up with the better-known route to Accra through Nsuaem, Akim Mansu, Akroso, and Adipong.

The exploration of trade routes in Northern Ghana was undertaken since the late 1880s mainly by the British, the French, and the Germans.[3] Volta Region on the other hand was since the 1880s the domain of German explorers only.[4] The journeys of exploration organized by these Colonial

[1] African no. 249, *Further Correspondence Regarding Affairs of the Gold Coast* (Colonial Office, June 1883). Enclosure 1 in Paper no. 11 is Commander Rumsey's 'General Report on the River Volta District'. Also, enclosure in Paper no. 14 is 'Report of Assistant Inspector Thompson, Gold Coast Constabulary, on His Journey from Accra to Prahsue and thence to Elmina' (June 1882). Inspector Thompson confirmed the presence of northern merchants in the kola areas of Akim; so did Commander Rumsey.

[2] BPP, Cmd. 4477, enclosure in Paper no. 41: 'Report by Brandon Kirby, Special Commissioner, of his Mission to Coomassie and the Interior Provinces of the Ashanti Kingdom,' from 3 January to 2 April 1884.

[3] Excellent reports on the region were written by G. E. Ferguson and many District Commissioners. The Frenchman Captain L. Binger's *Du Niger au Golfe de Guinée*, II, is the most informative.

[4] For a useful abbreviated list of German explorers and their published works on the Volta Region, see M. Darkoh, 'The Economic Life of Buem 1884–1914', *Bull. Ghana Geogr. Ass.* IX, 1 (January 1964)

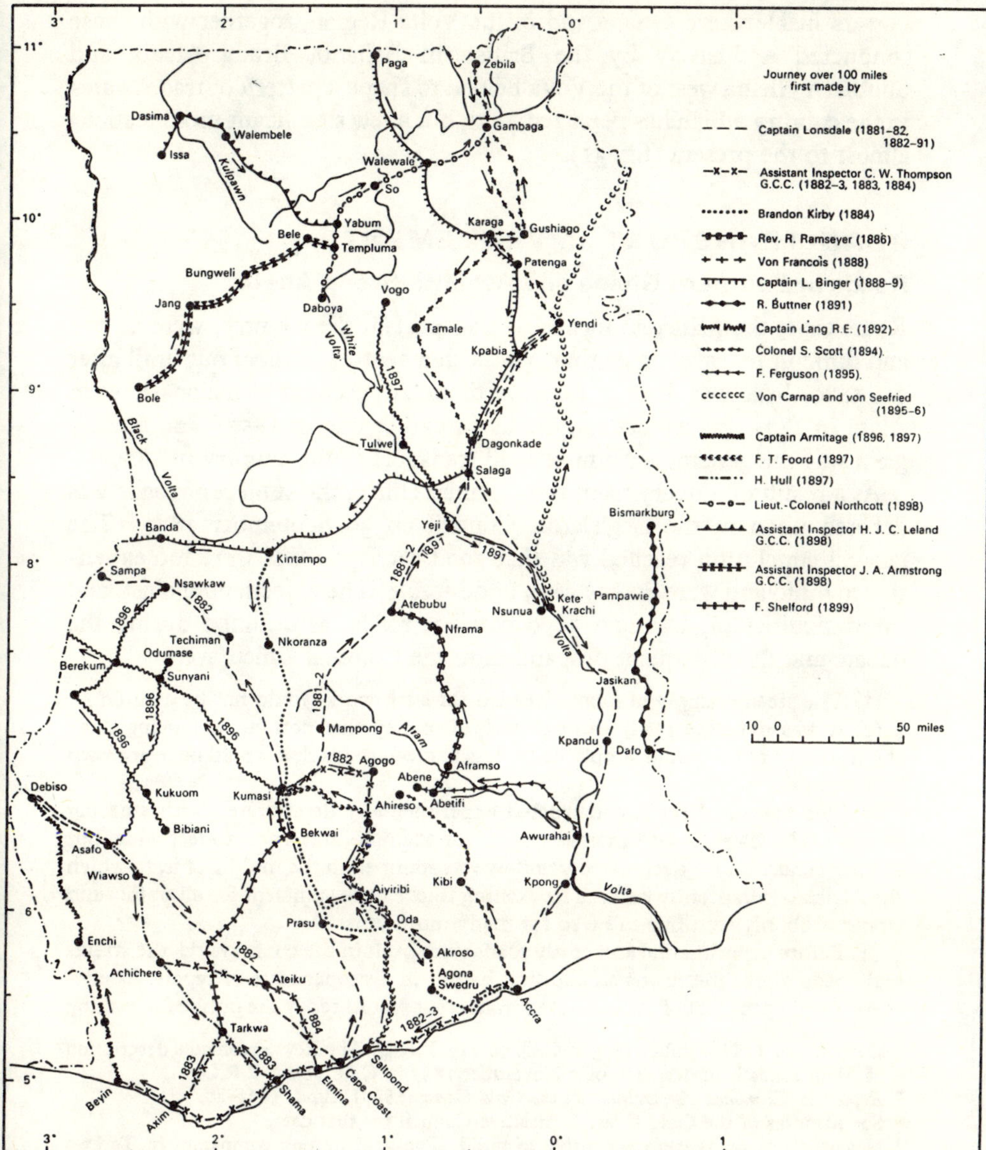


31 Major journeys of exploration, 1880–99

Powers in Northern Ghana and in the Volta Region, together with those conducted exclusively by the British in Ashanti, Brong Ahafo, and Southern Ghana west of the Volta helped to shape a pattern of trade routes in the country which has persisted, with but a few significant modifications almost to the present (fig. 31).

## ROAD TRANSPORT IMPROVEMENT

### Roads in Southern Ghana and Ashanti–Brong Ahafo

Routeways, the principal means of transport in the country, were as bad and difficult to travel on as they had been a century earlier; but until after the 1880s little was done to improve them. An account of major routes in Akim in 1875 was almost as grim as an earlier one in 1857,[1] and equally grim was the general account of land transport in the country in 1889.[2]

As a result of a query from the Colonial Office, the subject of roads was debated upon in the Legislative Council on 30 September 1870.[3] The general conclusion reached was that good carriage roads were too expensive to build and were, in any case, undesirable. The objections against, and the difficulties of, building good carriage roads, as outlined during the debate and in subsequent despatches to the Colonial Office, were:

(1) The steady supply of labour needed for such work would not be assured.

(2) It was not necessarily through lack of money that nothing was being done about roads,[4] but it would simply be useless to clean roads that would be overgrown in a year.

(3) The few good roads constructed experimentally deteriorated with amazing rapidity. The Cape Coast–Anomabu road, for example, was 15 to 20 feet wide, but in a very short time a deep narrow hollow was stamped in the middle of it, to which the Africans persistently kept.[5] The existing tracks were sufficient for all traffic, and would probably continue to be so for many more years.

(4) Before experimental and costly roads were built in the countryside, the streets and roads about the towns should first be put in a proper state of repair. Besides there was no prospect of concentrated traffic that would repay the public for making

1 Despatch of 13 November 1875 in C.O. 96/116, P.R.O. The Rev. Freeman's description of Akim roads is in despatch of 7 November 1857 in C.O. 96/41, P.R.O.

2 *Report on Economic Agriculture on the Gold Coast* (1889), Cmd. 5894–40.

3 See Minutes of the Gold Coast Legislative Council for that date.

4 Nevertheless, roads were expensive to build. The gold-mining companies in Tarkwa district suggested, in 1881, that the Government should build a road from Axim to Tarkwa; but the Administration pointed out that a mile-long road constructed by the Tarkwa and Aboso Gold Mining Company in the neighbourhood of their mines cost over £500, and the country was not rich enough to undertake such expensive schemes. See BPP, Cmd. 4477.

5 Ghanaian travellers had the habit of walking in Indian file, initially determined by the narrowness of the routes.

good roads, except in Krobo (palm oil) which already had access to the Volta. Good cart roads were not worth constructing west of Accra or, indeed, in any part of the country, except a short stretch of road from Accra to Abokobi to facilitate travel to the sanatorium at Aburi. It would suffice, for all practical purposes, to improve the existing pathways, that is, convert them into good hammock roads 6 feet wide.

(5) Even if good roads were built, there would be no vehicles to travel on them. There were no beasts of burden; the cattle, besides being rather scarce, weighed 'little more than an English prize sheep', and it would require a dozen of them to draw the load of an ordinary carthorse—at a much slower pace than a man travelled on foot in the country.

(6) The Africans preferred headloading to wheeled transport. The governor had failed to introduce wheelbarrows and carts for public works for, if left to their own devices, the Africans put into the barrows half of what they could carry and placed *both* upon their heads. 'Nature has endowed them with a power of neck and dorsal muscles, such as no other men possess, and they use this power in preference to any other.'

(7) The Administration had no power locally to enable it to carry out a scheme such as that proposed by the Colonial Office. In the existing political state of the country, any such proceeding by the Administration would be received with extreme distrust by the Africans, whose most distinguishing characteristic was to suspect any innovation, even if it was obviously to their own advantage.

(8) The Africans themselves did not want good roads, because an enemy might use them in time of war.

In spite of these arguments desultory attempts at road construction and at using wheeled transport or draught animals were made, even before 1870, by the British Administration itself, by some trading and mining companies, and the Basel Mission. In the late 1850s the Basel Mission attempted, through one of their laymen, Mr Hock, to establish a system of bullock carts and failed; the mission also tried to build a road from Christiansborg to Akropong in Akwapim, but gave up after a year or two.[1] In 1885, a mule belonging to the Administration was driven about fifteen miles from Accra towards Aburi; the mule could not stand up to the journey and was sent back to Accra where it soon died of sleeping sickness.[2] A British officer, Colonel White, in 1887 tried to use four oxen from Madeira as draught animals, but they died within the year.[3] After these failures the Administration contented itself with having the existing pathways kept clear of bush, and accordingly passed the drastic Public Labour Ordinance of 1882 to ensure that the pathways would always be kept clean. Thus, up to 1890, the only roads that could be so designated were the Accra–Kpong road, the military road from Cape Coast to Prasu, the coastal road from Elmina to Cape Coast, and the road from Shama to Tarkwa.

[1] Despatch of 2 November 1870 in C.O. 96/85, P.R.O.

[2] *Further Report on Economic Agriculture on the Gold Coast* (1891), Cmd. 6270.

[3] Ibid. These were only a few of the attempts to use draught animals.

The turning point in road construction came when the governor, Sir W. B. Griffith, appointed an Inspector of Trade Roads in 1890. The first task the inspector performed was to convert, in 1890–1, the 25 miles of bush track between Anyako behind Keta lagoon and Kpeve, and the much-frequented track between Cape Coast and Anomabu into good roads.[1] He also began the work of improving the tracks connecting the ports with the interior.

In 1895 the newly formed Roads Department was abolished and its staff placed under the Director of Public Works, whose duties already included the construction of roads. By that time a certain amount of progress had been made: the construction of the Saltpond–Oda road had been carried to a distance of 15 miles; 120 miles of the trade road along the right bank of the Volta between Kpong and Tinkranku, originally proposed by northern salt traders who wanted easier access to Kpong, had been surveyed; work on a road from Accra through Nsawam and Apedwa to Kibi had begun; and a wooden bridge had been thrown across the Sweet River between Elmina and Cape Coast.

The Public Works Department pressed on with their programme and built several new and vitally important trade roads between 1895 and the end of the century. One such road was that from Debisu to Wam through the Akonansa forest in western Brong Ahafo, which was opened to traffic in 1899. The opening of this road touched off the rapid growth of Wam as a market centre. Wam became the resort of rubber tappers and brokers from Debisu and nearby settlements, who before then had had to travel much longer distances—distances over two or three days' journey longer than that between Debisu and Wam—to the nearest rubber-collecting centre in the Ivory Coast.[2] Neither were the Germans behind in planning and executing major programmes of road construction in the Volta Region: they built many fine trunk roads with an average width of 16 feet, while in the rest of Southern Ghana the roads had an average width of 12 feet.

The programme of road construction came up against the old problem of how to make sure of a steady supply of labour, and the problem was dealt with in markedly different ways by the British and German Administrations. The British Administration passed two ordinances: the Roads

[1] Unless otherwise stated, the rest of the section on roads in Southern Ghana and Ashanti–Brong Ahafo is derived from *Colonial Reports* on the Gold Coast Colony and Ashanti, 1888–1910.

[2] African (West) no. 585, *Gold Coast: Further Correspondence Relating to Northern Territories* (Colonial Office, 1899). Enclosure 1 in Paper no. 151 is a letter dated Pamu, 26 June 1899 from H. J. C. Leland, Commissioner, Western Frontier, to the Colonial Secretary at Accra.

Ordinance of 1894 according to which the bush paths should be cleaned quarterly by the chiefs who would be paid ten shillings per mile per quarter; and the mild Compulsory Labour Ordinance of 1895 which replaced the harsh Public Labour Ordinance of 1882. The German Administration, on the other hand, characteristically disposed of the problem in a summary fashion: they compelled the people, with threats of heavy fines, to work on the public roads, and the labourers, sometimes forced to draw upon the labour of their families as well, had to provide for their own keep while employed on the roads. Results were more spectacular in the Volta Region where excellent roads converged on the administrative headquarters of Ho.

Another landmark was made in the history of road construction in British Southern Ghana when Governor Nathan, in his address to the Legislative Council in 1901, outlined a new policy for road construction which was remarkable for its far-sightedness. He advocated the building of roads good enough for motor-cars and traction engines. Such roads, he explained, would be easy to keep clear, and the use of motor vehicles would free, for other essential occupations, a large proportion of the country's labour force employed for the slow and uncertain work of carrying stores into the interior.[1] This emphasis on the possibility of motor traffic, at a time when commercial motor vehicles were not allowed on English roads, was a happy one, for it prepared the ground for the fresh outburst of road construction which followed the introduction into the country of commercial motor vehicles.

In 1902 the Goldfields of Eastern Akim Ltd began, with Government assistance, an 18-foot vehicle road from Accra to Kibi and completed it in 1905. Work was begun on a 12-foot vehicle road from Saltpond to Oda; the road from Accra to Ayimensa and Dodowa was converted into a 16-foot vehicle road and re-metalled over part of its length; and in 1908 the Winneba–Swedru road was reconstructed for use by motor lorries in view of the rising importance of cocoa cultivation in Winneba district. In Ada–Keta district three roads—the Anyako–Wute–Sesakpe road (36 miles), the Afieyingbe–Whenyi road (15 miles), and the Denu–Dokplata road (23 miles)—were built not only to open up the areas concerned but also to ensure that agricultural produce from the district was shipped from ports under the British Administration and not from the port of Lome in German Togoland. Several other short stretches of road were constructed throughout Southern Ghana, and by 1911 over 2,000 miles of bush roads were also being cleaned by the chiefs under the Roads Ordinance of 1894.

Road developments in Ashanti and Brong Ahafo began after 1910,

[1] *Minutes of the Gold Coast Legislative Council*, 16 January 1901.

although the existing bush tracks were cleared occasionally under the provisions of the Ashanti Administration Ordinance of 1902. It appears that only two serious attempts at motor road construction were made in Ashanti–Brong Ahafo before 1910. The earlier of the two attempts was in connection with the Yeji–Krachi road which was begun in 1906 to by-pass the stretch of the Black Volta between those two points. Next was the construction of the Kumasi–Yeji road, begun in 1909 and intended to connect Kumasi with the newly created administrative and trade centre of Tamale.

The years between 1912 and 1936 formed the critical period in the history of road transport development in Southern Ghana and Ashanti–Brong Ahafo. The Government initiated an extensive programme of road building which was scarcely interrupted by the First World War. Many chiefs also passed by-laws under the relevant ordinances to ensure that the roads under their supervision were satisfactorily maintained, and the people themselves, without Government aid, built many miles of feeder roads (fig. 32).

The primary reason for these developments was the expansion of cocoa farming, which needed better transport facilities. In the inaccessible areas, the cocoa beans were stored for long periods in warehouses to await the few occasions on which motor lorries bumped their way along the poor roads to collect them. The beans deteriorated in quality during the period of storage, and often reached the ports in a poor condition. In such areas too the farmers often sold the crop, as it stood, to itinerant middlemen who picked, cured, and transported it to the nearest port. This resulted in injury to the trees and in an indifferently prepared product. Consequently the enthusiasm for road building in Ashanti, for example, was so great that it was not unusual for villagers to give road engineers a free hand to demolish houses or cut their way through cocoa farms, provided the road passed through or near the village.[1]

In Southern Ghana, the total mileage of new roads constructed was small, as most of the important trade roads had been constructed by 1911.[2] Among the longest of the new roads built were those from Senchi to Ho, and from Adidome to Ho; their importance lay in the fact that they connected the Volta Region with the rest of Southern Ghana.[3] Within the Volta Region

[1] See sections on transport in *Colonial Report—Ashanti*, 1914 to 1924.

[2] See *Colonial Reports* on Gold Coast Colony and Ashanti, 1911–36, and on Togoland, 1920–36; Public Works Department's *Annual Reports*, 1911–36, and *Annual Reports* on Eastern, Central, and Western Provinces, 1912–1929/30.

[3] The partition of German Togoland after the First World War left the railways in the territory wholly in the French area, and interposed a boundary between British Togoland and its natural outlets. British Togoland was therefore left without any direct means of

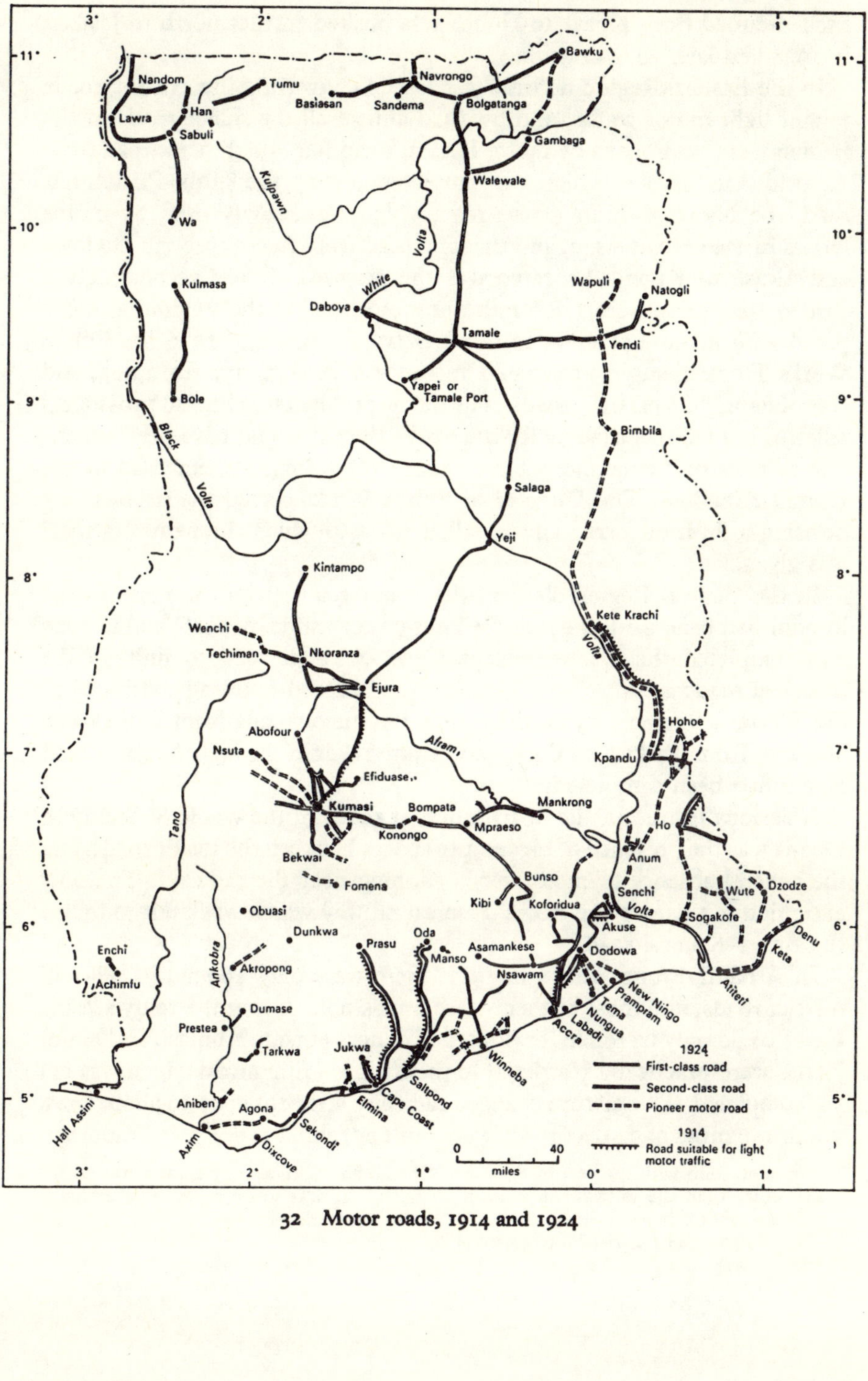


32 Motor roads, 1914 and 1924

itself the road from Kpeve to Hohoe was pushed further north to Jasikan in 1928 and later to Worawora.[1]

In the Eastern Region no time was lost in converting the existing roads to suit light motor traffic, and by 1916 almost all the major roads in the Region were being used by motor lorries, including the difficult road from Koforidua to Mpraeso which was completed in 1915, the Krobo Plantations road, the Nsawam–Asamankese road which was heavily used by motor lorries in the cocoa season, and the long road from Accra through Dodowa and Akuse to Kpong. So rapid was the progress of road reconstruction that by 1925 there were 1,306 miles of motor road in the Region, as compared with about 145 miles in 1911. Between 1925 and 1936 the Public Works Department concentrated mainly on re-aligning, regrading, and consolidating the existing roads. The major problem was how to provide an efficient but cheap surfacing for the roads, since it would have been expensive to construct concrete roads or adopt the tarmac system used in the United Kingdom. The Director of Public Works solved the problem by devising a form of *tar*red and *met*alled road, to which the name 'tarmet' was given.

In the Central Region also, all the major roads from the ports to the interior had been made suitable for light motor traffic by 1916, and in 1920 was completed the Nsawam–Cape Coast–Sekondi road to link up the principal roads running from north to south. Road building continued in the Western Region too, until by 1925 the major roads from Dunkwa to Wiawso, from Tarkwa to Enchi, and from Sekondi through Axim to Half Assini had been completed.

A curious feature of the distribution of roads in the whole of Southern Ghana was the presence of big, empty spaces between the major roads, and the general absence of motor roads running near the railways. The only exception to this was the Accra–Kumasi railway which was built to follow the Accra–Kumasi road.[2]

In Ashanti–Brong Ahafo, in 1911, there were only about 280 miles of district roads, and most of them were impassable during the rainy season. Casks could only be rolled for limited distances outside Kumasi, and motor lorries were practically restricted to the Kumasi–Ejura road which was not yet completed. The picture changed radically after 1911: up to about 1925, about 150 miles of district roads were built or rebuilt every year. Important

communication with the rest of Southern Ghana, and without any trade outlet to the sea, other than the railways in French Togoland. It was to overcome this difficulty that the two roads from Senchi and Adidome to Ho were built.

[1] *Annual Report on Eastern Province*, 1928–9.

[2] See below, p. 233.

among these were the Ntonsu–Efiduasi road, the roads from Kumasi to Bompata, Goaso, Wenchi, and Sunyani, and the roads from Bekwai to Manso Nkwanta and to Lake Bosumtwe, from Obuasi to the Pra through Banka, from Nkoranza to Kintampo, and from Sunyani to Wenchi.

The Ntonsu–Efiduasi road was only 17 miles long, but its effect on cocoa production in the surrounding area was dramatic. The area of which the village of Efiduasi was the centre was one of the largest producers of cocoa in Ashanti, and up to 1913 the only means of transporting cocoa from the area to the railhead at Kumasi was by rolling it in barrels to Agona on the Kumasi–Ejura road, and then by lorries, or again by cask-rolling, to Kumasi—a total distance of 35 miles. This circuitous route was adopted since it was impossible to roll barrels along the old road from Ntonsu to Kumasi. The Kumasi Chamber of Commerce then petitioned for a branch road from Ntonsu (mile 14 on the Kumasi–Ejura road) to Efiduasi, which would enable lorries to run directly from the latter village to Kumasi. When the road was opened in 1914, there were 400 tons of cocoa, the result of one month's purchases, waiting at Efiduasi to be transported to Kumasi. The area tapped by the new road extended as far as Agogo and Bompata.

Two other roads that deserve special mention were the Kumasi–Bompata and Kumasi–Sunyani roads. The former, in addition to being the only road along which cocoa from a large part of Ashanti–Akim was transported to Kumasi, also formed a valuable link between Kumasi and the main road from Accra, through Nkawkaw, to the south-eastern border of Ashanti. The opening of the latter, the Kumasi–Sunyani road, to motor traffic in the 1925–6 cocoa season brought immense prosperity to cocoa farmers in western Ashanti and Brong Ahafo. Formerly, all the cocoa from Sunyani area was either headloaded to the roadhead at Kunsu or hauled by motor lorries to Kumasi through Ejura, and in both cases the farmer was the loser. But in the 1925–6 cocoa season, it was estimated that the farmers' profits were between 100 and 300 per cent more than in the previous years.[1]

## Roads in Northern Ghana

Northern Ghana was not immediately included in the programme for road development, and yet the problem there in the second half of the nineteenth century was even more desperate than in Southern Ghana or Ashanti–Brong Ahafo. Not only were the majority of the routeways in Northern Ghana seasonal, but also the trade route network density was much lower than elsewhere in the country. Besides, the physical condition of the prin-

[1] *Colonial Report—Ashanti*, 1926.

cipal routeways was bad. The routeways consisted of the merest tracks, along which it was only possible to move in single file. Their narrowness was at all times inconvenient for carriers with bulky loads, and in the rains the long grass blocked them in many places to an extent that made progress along them both slow and difficult.[1]

The appointment of Colonel Northcott in 1897 as British Commissioner and Commandant of Northern Ghana, which was then not completely under British control, marked the beginning of change in road transport in the region. Colonel Northcott realized correctly that the first attack on the economic backwardness of Northern Ghana should be the improvement of road transport both to serve the region and to forge close economic ties between the region and the rest of Ghana. Consequently urgent orders were issued to District Commissioners to commence the rebuilding of the main trade routes, making them 14 feet wide, ditched on either side and raised above the general level of the surrounding countryside. The first few roads to be so built between 1898 and 1899 were those from Zoguiri and Walewale to Gambaga, and the 70-mile road from Wuyima on the White Volta to Daganga through Gambaga. The new roads increased the accessibility and hence the market status of Gambaga.

Colonel Northcott went further and planned a transport service based on the use of pack and draught animals, and for a beginning requested six ox-carts and a team of draught oxen for transporting Government stores from Wuyima to Gambaga. The oxen got as far as Kintampo where a number of them died; the rest were sold off to spare the Government any further expense. The carts did not fare any better: their component parts were taken to Kumasi where they were allowed to disintegrate. Colonel Northcott's plans were doomed to failure; his views were opposed to those of Governor Hodgson who informed the Colonial Office that the use of oxen or bullocks for draught purposes in Northern Ghana would be impracticable.

The impasse over Colonel Northcott's plans and recommendations persisted until the British, having established their rule throughout Northern Ghana and agreed on common frontiers with German Togoland in 1902 and with the northern Ivory Coast and Upper Volta in 1904, were seriously confronted with the problem of developing the economic resources of the region. Then a programme for road transport improvement was drawn up.[2] Among the earliest roads to be improved after 1902 was the one

[1] African (West) no. 585, Paper no. 96, 'Report on Administration of Northern Territories, 1898–99' by Lieut.-Col. H. P. Northcott.

[2] See *Annual Reports on the Northern Territories*, 1901–10.

linking Gambaga, then the British administrative headquarters, with the international market of Salaga, through Karaga, Patenga, and Yendi. Rest houses, for the convenience and comfort of European officials, were built at major stopping places on the laterite road, which was completed in 1903. New roads were also cleared between Wa and Gambaga, and between Yeji and Salaga in 1904. Everywhere the building of earth-surfaced roads proceeded at a rapid pace, but more so in Dagomba and Mamprusi.

A new policy on the laying out of roads came into being with the transfer in 1907 of the British administrative headquarters from Gambaga to Tamale. The first step in the creation of Tamale as a major distributing centre was the start in 1907 of a good tarred motor road from there to Yeji through Salaga; the road was intended to link up with the one to be constructed from Kumasi to Yeji.

The distribution of the existing transport facilities by 1912 left too many areas isolated to be an effective instrument in the economic development of Northern Ghana. The inadequacy of the road network was a vital problem, yet between 1912 and 1936 the road network pattern was practically the same as in 1912. The only changes were the building of a few more miles of laterite all-weather roads, the conversion in the 1920s of the Prang–Tamale–Gambaga road to one suitable for all-weather motor traffic, and the building of a new motor road from Tamale to Bole in the 1930s. These were roads on which existing commercial traffic was already considerable; nowhere else were roads built specially to open up undeveloped rural areas.

## Motor transport

To reduce the cost of transport, farms, especially cocoa farms, were generally made, in the early years of the present century, as near the roads as possible, except in the Volta Region where farmers often cleared land away from the highways with the object of evading German Administrative Officers and tax collectors. Nevertheless, the migration of farms to the roadsides only partially solved the problem of high transport costs, for headloading was still the commonest means of transport and was expensive. Although cask rolling, introduced towards the end of the nineteenth century, was cheaper, it was not the answer to the problem of high transport costs. The casks needed re-coopering several times before they arrived at their destination, and the nails that worked themselves loose and fell on the roads were a source of much discomfort to the naked feet of the 'rollers'. At a later date, when roads were metalled, cask rolling and headloading became increasingly difficult and more unsatisfactory as the 'rollers' and the carriers were incapacitated by sore feet from walking on the roads. The Government Transport Department, which employed large numbers of carriers, tried out a solution to this problem of sore feet, in 1908 only, by tarring the feet of the carriers, because coal tar 'fills the cracks and is a good antiseptic, besides affording some protection if applied thick'.

The use of some vehicular form of transport was clearly indicated. The earliest wheeled vehicles in the country were the hand carts and the horse-drawn carriages used by the Basel Mission and some of the merchants in the immediate vicinity of their factories in the 1860s; but they were usually for transporting persons and not merchandise. It was in the gold-mining district of Tarkwa that some of the earliest experiments with freight carts were made. The pressure for improved road transport there was overwhelming, and the first concrete response to it came from Mr Gowan, manager of the Abontiakoon mine, who in 1882 introduced two trucks to carry mining machinery from Bonsa to Abontiakoon. It took 57 men a fortnight to drag the trucks, carrying a total of 1½ tons of machinery, along the 17 miles of muddy track that separated Bonsa and Abontiakoon. Mr Gowan next made slight improvements in the track by putting down logs of timber over the swampy sections, and subsequently succeeded in having only 26 men drag his trucks half way to Bonsa from Abontiakoon and back within three days. The second operation, although far less expensive than the first, was still not cheap enough to be an adequate answer to the transport problem, for it was difficult to keep the track in a tolerable state of repair.[1]

Although the first mechanically operated vehicle seen in Ghana—an unwieldy and short-lived steam traction engine—was brought out during the Anglo-Ashanti war of 1873–4, the earliest serious suggestion for the use of motor vehicles came in 1898 from Colonel Northcott. He backed up his argument by reminding the Colonial Office that the French were already using motor vehicles in their West African colonies, a fact of no mean political and economic significance. The suggestion was nevertheless firmly opposed by Governor Hodgson who expressed his conviction that motor-cars would be absolutely useless without the investment of a large capital in the building of suitable roads, which the country could not afford.[2] He conceded that one or two motor-cars might be sent out for trial, 'and that the trial be on Colonel Northcott's road between Wuyima and Gambaga, which he states is available for motor-car traffic, if the cars

[1] African no. 249; enclosure in Paper no. 24 is 'Fourth Monthly Report on the Tarkwa Gold Mining District', dated 31 July 1882, by Henry Higgins.

[2] African (West) no. 585 (1899). See Papers nos. 96, 179, and enclosure 6 in Paper no. 180.

can be got up there'. The controversy over the introduction of motor vehicles raged until Joseph Chamberlain, the Secretary of State, put forward a compromise suggestion in 1900 to the effect that a single motor-car might be introduced experimentally on the roads near Accra or Cape Coast. Thus the first motor-car arrived in Ghana in 1902, for the use of Governor Nathan.[1] It was a Gardner-Serpollet, paraffin-fired and steam driven; it was a success and it ushered in the motor-car age.

Further supplies of motor vehicles were imported in subsequent years by private merchants and not by the Government which in 1906 owned only one motor lorry, but they did not come into general use until after the First World War. The use of the motor vehicles, most of which were in the Eastern Region, was itself a mixed blessing, for while the trucks undoubtedly reduced transport costs they also churned up the roads into quagmires or reduced them to powder far more quickly than it was possible to keep them in repair. The result was the passing, in 1907, of the Motor Traffic Ordinance (no. 17 of 1907) which stated, among other things, that no licence would be granted for any motor-car or carriage weighing more than 6 tons and fitted with ribbed tyres. The solution of the transport problem had to await the coming, after about 1914, of the light American Ford trucks which, with their high road clearance, were eminently suited to the irregularly surfaced roads. The use of these trucks effected a major revolution in road transport in the country.

## RAILWAYS

A fuller realization of the potential of the gold mines at Tarkwa and the urgent need to provide a means for quicker and cheaper evacuation of the metal to the coastal ports first led to the consideration of the possibilities of rail transport in the country. Motor vehicles, such as they were, could not by themselves cope with the rapidly rising demand of the mining industry for cheap bulk transport facilities.

Accordingly, the mining companies employed a civil engineer, Mr Barham, in 1882 to survey a railway route from the coast to Tarkwa. Mr Barham surveyed three possible routes to Tarkwa: from Dixcove and Axim, and a composite route consisting of a short railway from Axim to Enframadi on the Ankobra, then by steam launch to Tumentu, also on the Ankobra, and finally to Tarkwa from Tumentu by railway. Mr Barham eventually selected Axim as the coastal terminus on account of its good

[1] Sir Frederick G. Guggisberg, *The Gold Coast: A Review of the Events of 1920–26 and the Prospects of 1927–28* (Accra, 1927), pp. 79–80.

landing and warehouse installations, and proposed a rail route direct from there to Tarkwa (fig. 33). The project was put before the Government, which replied that it would be prepared to take over and run the line, provided its promoters could prove conclusively that there would be enough freight to justify the existence of the railway.[1] Apparently the economic survey asked for by the Government was never made, and the project fell through. In 1883 a group of merchants proposed another railway, this time from Cape Coast to Asin Denkera; but the Colonial Office itself did not consider the scheme a particularly brilliant one since the line traversed a difficult hilly country.[2] The Government's reply was the same as that to the promoters of the Axim–Tarkwa railway. The Government further suggested that the River Amisa, which ran into the heart of Asin country, might perhaps be used instead of a railway.[3]

In spite of these early setbacks, the question of intersecting the country with light railways was still very much under discussion, and by 1892 it had been agreed that a preliminary survey of the country should be made for the purpose.[4] The Government-sponsored survey, which included the selection of a harbour site, was commenced in February 1893 by Captain Lang, R.E., and Mr Foord, a civil engineer, who presented their report in 1894. The first route surveyed lay between Akim Oda and Kormantin on the coast, a distance of 65 miles; but it was recommended that in order to avoid the bit of difficult country around Oda the terminal station should be at Ewusa, a small village about 2½ miles south of Oda. Kormatin was selected as the starting point for the railway because its small bay, sheltered from the turbulent surf, would be the most suitable place on that part of the coast for a port and for landing rolling stock. Apam was later suggested as an alternative starting point for the railway, and a route from there to Afitri, a village on the Kormantin–Oda route, was surveyed.[5] The proposed route from Apam possessed two advantages over that from Kormantin: Apam, it was discovered, had a better landing stage; and the length of the railway from there would be 10½ miles shorter than that from Kormantin. The gauge suggested for the railway was 3 feet 6 inches.

[1] For details of the scheme, see BPP (1883), Cmd. 3687; and for the Government's reply, see BPP (1885), Cmd. 4477.

[2] See minutes attached to despatch of 19 May 1883, in C.O. 96/150, P.R.O.

[3] Reference for Government's reply as in footnote 1.

[4] Unless otherwise indicated, the remaining section on railways is based on *Colonial Reports* on Gold Coast and Ashanti, 1890–1927.

[5] There were some who thought that Accra, being the headquarters of the Government and possessing a large amount of fixed capital, should be the starting point of the first railway.

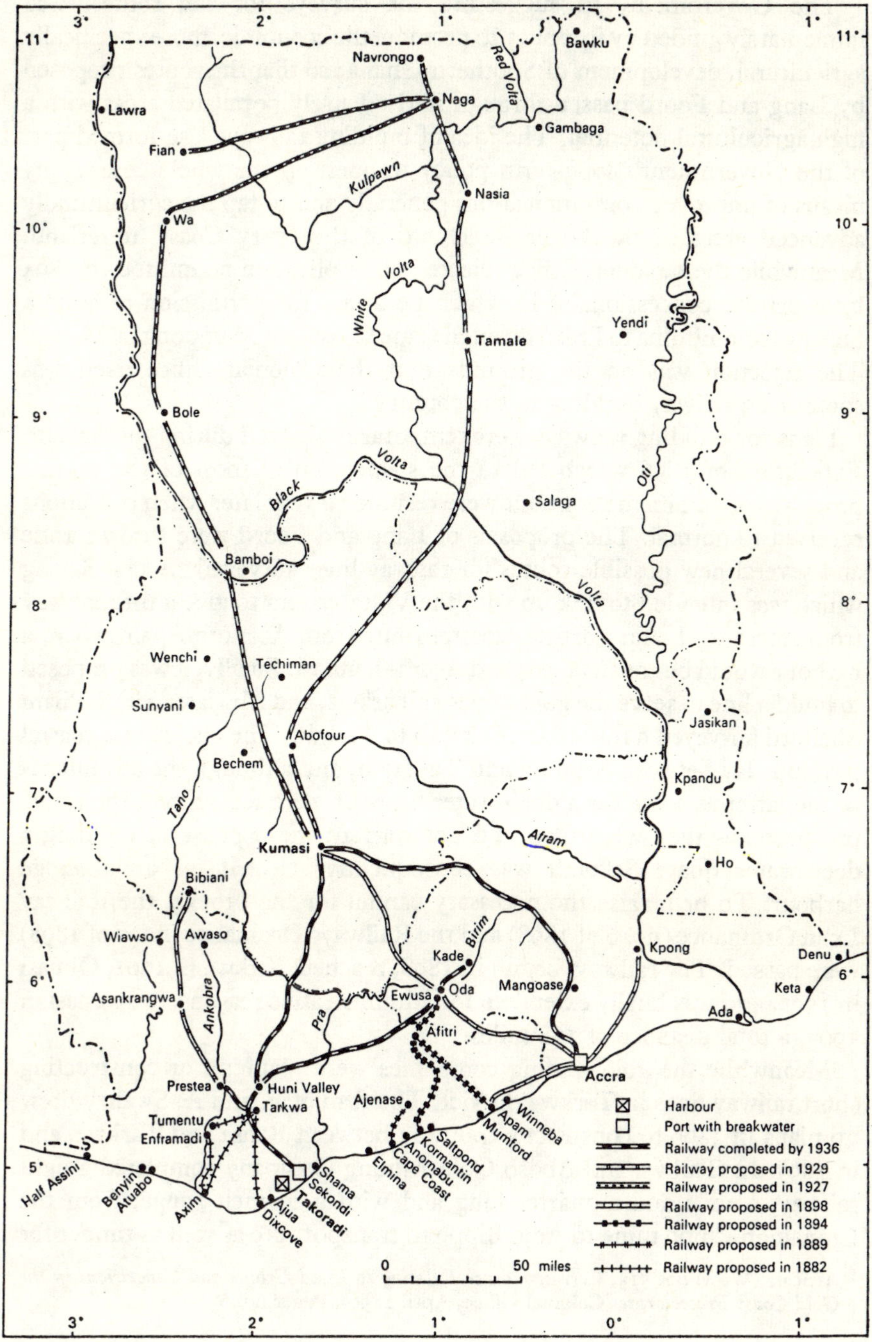


33 Port and railway development, 1850–1936

The Government, in suggesting the surveys for rail routes, was immediately guided by its policy to promote the economic, more specifically agricultural, development of Southern Ghana; so that the routes proposed by Lang and Foord passed through fairly densely populated areas with a high agricultural potential. The idea of building railways also formed part of the Government's long-term policy to open up the whole country by means of improved communications generally and to tap the agriculturally advanced areas of the Niger Bend and of the Ivory Coast hinterland. Meanwhile the Colonial Office rejected an application submitted in 1894 by a private concessionaire in which he asked for permission to build a railway from Elmina to Prasu through Cape Coast and Mampong or Mansu. The rejection was on the grounds that the Colonial Office itself was sponsoring railway building in the country.[1]

Plans for building railways were temporarily shelved during the Ashanti Expedition of 1896 which led to the suspension of most of the normal processes of administration, but were resumed a year later when conditions reverted to normal. The proposals of Lang and Foord were thrown aside and several new possible routes for railway lines surveyed: Accra–Kpong which was intended to link up with the Volta system to give a throughway from Accra to the far north; a coastal route from Accra to Apam where a harbour would be constructed; and Accra–Kumasi. Finally, it was proposed to build a line to serve the gold mines at Tarkwa, and Mr (later Sir) William Shelford surveyed a route from Sekondi to Tarkwa. The choice of a coastal terminus lay between Sekondi and Takoradi, and although the advantages of the latter as a site for a deep-water harbour were recognized, the traffic prospects, as they were then, did not warrant the expense of building a deep-water quay. Sekondi was consequently selected for a lighterage harbour. To help raise the necessary capital for the project, the Railway Loan Ordinance (no. 6 of 1898) and the Railways Ordinance (no. 7 of 1898) were passed. The railway, begun in 1898, reached Tarkwa in 1901, Obuasi in 1902, and was finally extended, for administrative reasons, to Kumasi in 1903, a total distance of 168 miles.

Meanwhile the gold-mining companies were planning or constructing short railway lines in Tarkwa district. The firm of F. and A. Swanzy drew up plans in 1896 to construct a tramway between Bonsa and Tarkwa, and in 1897 the Tarkwa and Aboso Gold Mining Company completed a light railway, a mile and a quarter long and with a 20 inch gauge, from the Cinnamon Bippo mine to Adja Bippo to transport ore as well as timber for

[1] African (West) no. 513, *Correspondence Relating to Land Grants and Concessions in the Gold Coast Protectorate* (Colonial Office, April 1897), Paper no. 6.

fuel and pit props.[1] The last important railway construction by a mining company was by the Prestea Mines Ltd, which in 1905 completed a 25-mile light railway from Brumase to Prestea to help bring up machinery for the installation of a battery of stamps at Prestea.[2]

The discovery of more gold veins at Tarkwa and the increasing profitability of the older mines sited at a distance from Tarkwa made the construction of a branch line from Tarkwa necessary. Begun from Tarkwa in 1908, the branch line reached Prestea in 1911. Sir William Shelford also surveyed another major line from Accra to Kumasi which was meant to serve the young and thriving cocoa-growing industry of the Eastern Region. The line was begun from Accra in 1909 and completed in 1923. In the same year work was begun on the Central Region railway from Huni Valley to Kade which was opened to traffic in December 1927. Plans were also made in 1927 for a railway from Kumasi to Northern Ghana—three separate routes were surveyed—which was meant to integrate the economy of Northern Ghana with that of Ashanti and Southern Ghana. It was also hoped the railway would stimulate cocoa production in northern Ashanti.[3] The project was not executed for lack of funds.

While new railway lines were being planned or built, much attention was also paid to the old Sekondi–Kumasi railway which was too light for heavy traffic, and whose numerous grades and curves were a constant source of trouble to the heavier engines that had been introduced. The section between Sekondi and Obuasi was therefore replaced with heavier rails and steel sleepers, and regraded and re-aligned between 1919 and 1926.[4]

Despite the improvement in rail transport, the volume of traffic conveyed was far less than expected, and in 1932 a committee was appointed to consider what steps should be taken 'in view of the serious losses suffered by the railway during recent years mainly owing to road competition'.[5] On the recommendations of the committee, the Carriage of Goods by Road Ordinance was passed in 1936, according to which the carriage of specified goods was prohibited over scheduled roads. Cocoa, for example, could not be conveyed over certain roads from the interior to the ports; neither were imported goods, especially beer, allowed to reach Ashanti from the coast by

[1] African (West) no. 513, Paper no. 202. Also African (West) no. 531, *Further Correspondence Relating to Land Concessions and Railways on the Gold Coast* (Colonial Office, April 1899), Papers nos. 190 (Appendix A), and 234.

[2] Department of Mines, *Annual Reports*, 1904 and 1905.

[3] See Gold Coast Legislative Council Debates, 1 March 1928 and 15 February 1929.

[4] Railway Administration's *Annual Reports*, 1911–26.

[5] 'Report of the Road–Rail Transport Committee', *Gold Coast Government Sessional Paper* no. VI (1945).

road. The restrictions applied to sixteen stretches of road, all of which were alongside the Takoradi–Kumasi and Accra–Kumasi railway lines or within the triangular piece of land two sides of which were formed by the two railway lines. The roads were equipped with barriers at which vehicles passing through were inspected and recorded by the police.

The bulk of the country's cocoa still reached the ports by road, in spite of the restrictions placed on road transport, for the latter possessed two major advantages over rail transport. The number of passengers carried by a motor vehicle was in practice governed, not by the licensed carrying capacity of the vehicle or by safety regulations, but simply by the physical limits of the space into which the passengers, together with the planks on which they sat accompanied by their goods and livestock, could be squeezed. It was thus possible for motor vehicle passengers to travel with their goods and personally supervise their disposal, which was something rail transport did not allow.

## PORTS

The development of railways was accompanied by that of ports (fig. 33). In 1903 two jetties—one wooden and the other iron—were completed at Sekondi, the rail terminal. The construction of another iron jetty was begun in 1906, and the near-by village called Low Town demolished and replaced by an extensive dockyard. By 1910 the existing breakwater had been extended by about 143 feet and rails laid on it; by 1914 it was practically completed.

The improvement of the landing stage at Accra had also been long contemplated. It was even seriously suggested in 1884 that the decrepit colonial steamer, *Ekuro*, should be sunk to fill the gap in the reef jutting into the sea behind James Fort, so as to make the reef a sort of natural quay.[1] In 1895 two engineers, appointed by Messrs Coode, Son and Matthews, arrived in the country to survey the reefs and to design a breakwater which would afford shelter to lighters and launches, as well as providing an area of smooth water where heavy goods could be landed or shipped. Nevertheless it was not until 1905 that work began on the breakwater, and although it was hoped to have it completed by 1909, the breakwater was still under construction in 1914.

It had long been evident that the safety of the large ships employed to handle the increased volume of trade could not be guaranteed at the surf ports. Between 1907 and 1910 seven ships were wrecked at Takoradi,

[1] Despatch of 24 October 1884 in C.O. 96/160, P.R.O.

Sekondi, Axim, and in the Ankobra River[1]—an eloquent argument for building a harbour. Moreover, the protection afforded by the breakwaters at Accra and Sekondi was largely neutralized by the silting up of the water by sand. At Accra the pumping of the sand was discontinued in 1918 because of the heavy expenditure involved. Dredging at Sekondi continued until 1927, the year before the artificial deep-water harbour at Takoradi was opened.

Takoradi harbour consisted of two breakwaters enclosing 220 acres of water.[2] Transit sheds, open storage accommodation for 40,000 tons of bagged cocoa, and cranes were built on the deep-water and lighter wharfs, along which ran both roads and railways. In 1934 the headquarters of the Railway Administration were removed from Sekondi to Takoradi, thus completing in every detail the unified scheme for rail and harbour development first envisaged in 1898.[3]

## RIVERS

The importance of the Volta, Ankobra, Tano and Pra rivers as commercial arteries increased after the 1850s. The same was true of a few of the smaller rivers which became important to trade at the ports located at or near their mouths. For example, when navigation ceased temporarily in the late 1880s or early 1890s on the River Ayensu, Winneba lost much of its trade in oil-palm products. The river, which enters the sea a few miles east of Winneba, was choked with driftwood.[4] Of the four largest rivers the Volta was the most important from the point of view of transport, as it had always been. Its development for steamship navigation was regarded as the surest way of elevating the palm-oil industry in the Eastern Region to a status comparable to that of the palm-oil industry in Nigeria, and of aiding generally the agricultural development of the eastern half of Northern Ghana.

The first serious survey of the Volta was conducted in 1861 by Governor Andrews and Lieutenant Dolben of H.M.S. *Bloodhound*. They crossed the bar at the mouth of the river in surf boats and proceeded upstream for a distance of about 120 miles, the furthest it was found practicable for the boats to go without coming to an effectual barrier.[5] A special survey of the bar was made in 1864 by Lieutenant Foot, but not without opposition from

[1] Dickson, 'Evolution of Seaports in Ghana: 1800–1928', *Ann. Ass. Am. Geogr.* LV, 1 (March 1965).
[2] Railway Administration's *Annual Report*, 1928.
[3] Railway Administration's *Annual Reports*, 1928–34.
[4] Freeman, *Travels and Life in Ashanti and Jaman*, p. 548.
[5] Despatch of 11 November 1861 in C.O. 96/55, P.R.O.

the local inhabitants, especially the chief of Ada, who protested that 'the river had been measured before, and that if the bar was crossed for trading purposes the profits derived from the present system of transhipping goods or palm oil by land (from Ada) to the beach at Addafoa etc. would be lost to the country'.[1]

During the Awuna wars of the 1860s and 1870s, it was repeatedly urged in despatches to the Colonial Office that a steamer should be stationed on the Volta to maintain peace in the area and ensure free and safe navigation on the river. Yet it was not until 1882 that another survey of the bar at the mouth of the river was made to examine the possibility of sending steamers up the river. This survey was conducted by Commander Rumsey, Civil Commandant of the districts bordering the river.[2] Subsequent surveys of the bar were made in 1883 and in 1884, but these did not benefit trade at Ada since the majority of the merchants trading at that port were not prepared to use a steamer to transfer their goods across the bar; neither were the steamboat companies trading to the coast ready to use small steamers at Ada, as they were doing at Lagos and in the Oil Rivers.[3] In the early 1880s only the Basel Mission, Messrs Miller Brothers Ltd and Messrs F. and A. Swanzy were operating steam launches between Amedica, the outport of Akuse on the Volta, and Ada. Another survey of the Volta bar in the late nineteenth century was carried out in 1895 by the two engineers appointed to survey the reefs at Accra.[4] Their report was not encouraging.

Towards the very end of the century a new factor increased the urgency for the development of the Volta waterway by the British. This was the presence in the Volta Region of the Germans and the markets they created there which threatened to capture most of the trade in the lands bordering the Volta. The British reaction to the threat was to establish equivalent markets at places like Nsunua, Awurahai and Yeji,[5] and strengthen the older ones at Atebubu, Kpong, etc. For greater accessibility to their markets the British planned once more to develop the Volta waterway. The most comprehensive plan for the fullest possible use of the Volta for transport purposes was drawn up by Colonel Northcott in 1899, and it envisaged a through waterway between Ada and Wuyima on the White Volta, which was meant to be the port for Gambaga. Short tramways would circumvent the rapids at Kpong and Kete, and stern-wheelers would operate on the navigable stretches up to Wuyima. Colonel Northcott suggested a preliminary survey of the river, including the bar at its mouth, and

[1] Despatch of 6 January 1864 in C.O. 96/64, P.R.O.

[2] Despatch of 13 September 1882 in C.O. 96/143, P.R.O.

[3] Despatch of 9 February 1884 in C.O. 96/155, P.R.O.

[4] See above, p. 234.

[5] African (West) no. 585, Papers nos. 112, 113, and 121.

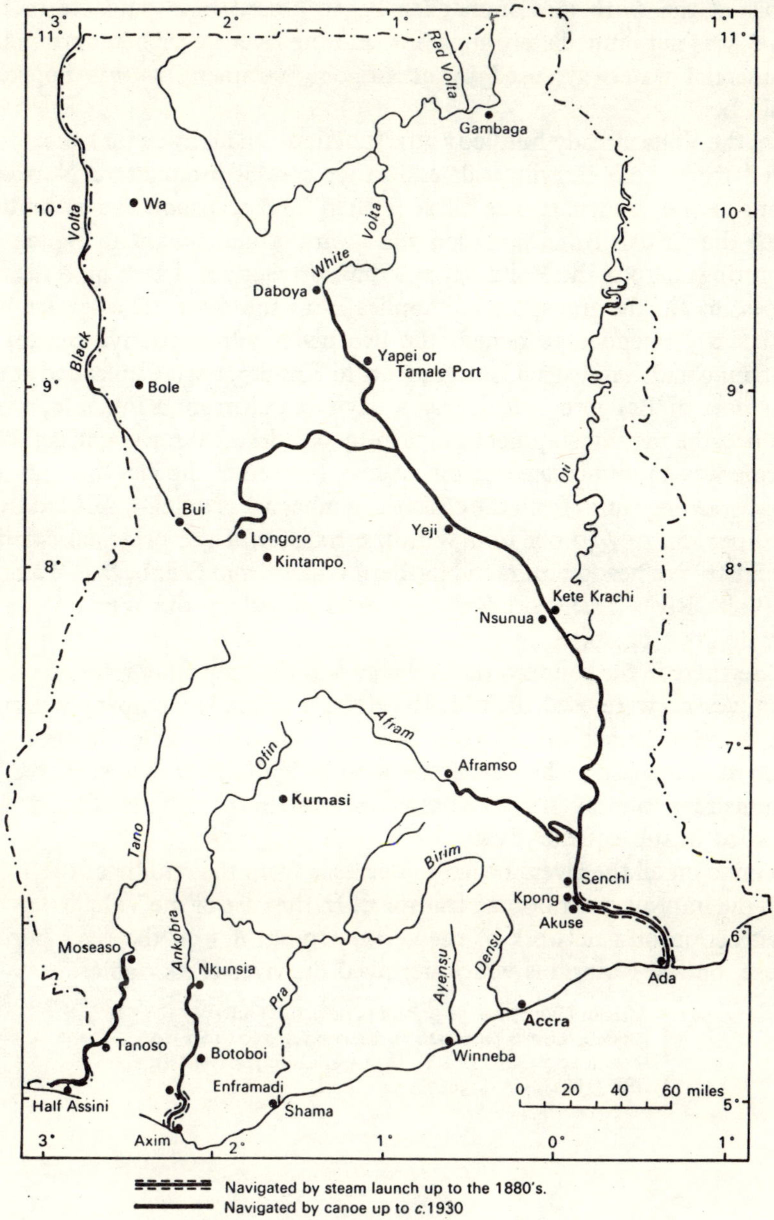


34 Important commercial river transport, *c.* 1850–*c.* 1930

entrusted the work to Commander Paget Jones.[1] The outcome of the survey was not immediately apparent, and the river never became a grand commercial waterway, used by ocean-going steamers, as was hoped it would be.

Yet the Volta already fulfilled a vital function as a highway for canoes that traded from Ada, carrying salt and other coastal products to Northern Ghana. River transport was cheaper than land transport, an advantage which the British Administration was aware of and sought to exploit by instituting in 1902 the Volta River Transport Service, based on a fleet of canoes, to aid the transport of supplies from the coast. The service was particularly intended to benefit the two major administrative centres of Kintampo and Gambaga. Consignments to Kintampo were unloaded at the river port of Longoro, which was a day's march from Kintampo, while Yeji became the transhipment point for goods destined for Gambaga. The scheme was an immediate success, as may be seen in the fact that the cost of transporting stores from the coast to Gambaga was quickly reduced from £100 per ton to £40 per ton. With the transfer of the principal colonial administrative headquarters in Northern Ghana from Gambaga to Tamale, the Volta River Transport Service was extended up the White Volta to Tamale Port (fig. 34).[2]

Elsewhere in the country, the Ankobra was the only other river on which steam vessels were used. In 1881 the Effuenta Mining Company was running a steam launch on the river between Enframadi in the interior and Axim at the coast.[3] The bar at the mouth of the river was surveyed by Commander Rumsey in 1882,[4] but no increase in the volume of traffic was recorded in subsequent years.

Traffic on all the rivers began to decrease from the middle of the 1920s with the improvement of road transport. In the case of the Volta it was the construction of a network of roads converging, not on the river port of Akuse, but on Koforidua which deprived the river of its traffic.

[1] African (West) no. 585, Papers nos. 146 and 179.
[2] *Annual Reports on Northern Territories*, 1901 to 1910.
[3] Burton and Cameron, *To the Gold Coast for Gold*, II, 199.
[4] BPP (1882), Cmd. 3687.

# 11. The determinants of urban growth[1]

A combination of some of the political and economic determinants which came into operation after the 1850s profoundly affected the growth and distribution of towns in the country. In the first place, Britain acquired sole control over much of Southern Ghana after it bought out the Danes in 1850 and the Dutch in 1872, and was thus able to formulate and execute uniform policies of economic and social development throughout the region. Secondly, Britain defeated the powerful kingdom of Ashanti in a decisive battle in 1874 and eventually annexed it to the Crown in 1902; in so doing Britain unleashed a flood of repercussions that did not always result in orderly economic activity and growth. Thirdly, the introduction of modern mining techniques and the blossoming of the gold-mining industry in Southern Ghana and Ashanti, as well as the improvement of transport, led to dramatic changes in the size and status of many settlements. Just as dramatic in its effect on settlements was, fourthly, the spread of cocoa cultivation with the associated programmes for further road and railway construction. Lastly, the Anglo-German political and economic rivalry in eastern Brong Ahafo and Northern Ghana also had outstanding consequences on the growth of some settlements in those regions.

## PARKLAND TOWNS IN SOUTHERN GHANA AND ASHANTI–BRONG AHAFO

In the parkland belt of Brong Ahafo and northern Volta Region the growth of towns depended on the interaction between trade and politics. Aiding the growth of towns were the extensive commercial activities of Hausa and Mande merchants who founded large *zongos* or foreigners' colonies attached to several of the towns, making the latter the foci of trade for large areas. But the amount of trade depended to a large extent on the political atmosphere in the savanna and forest regions on either side. The Anglo-German rivalry in Northern Ghana was reflected in the changing fortunes of towns in the parkland zone (the eastern end of the parkland zone itself was the scene of Anglo-German rivalry). Similarly, the civil wars in Ashanti in the 1880s altered the fate of many parkland towns, especially those that were directly involved in the wars.

[1] A town is here defined primarily on the basis of predominance of cultural, administrative, commercial and other non-rural functions, and not necessarily by population size.

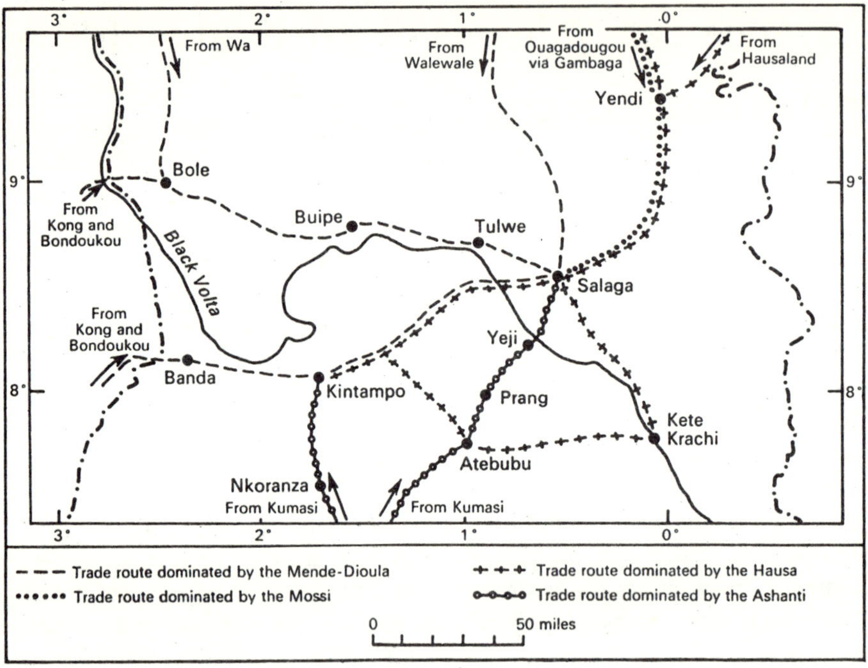


35 Trade route connections of Kintampo, Atebubu, Kete and Salaga, *c.* 1890

All the parkland towns were intimately connected by a web of commercial relations, so that loss of trade, from whatever causes, in any one town produced complex reactions in the others. The details of these interrelationships are illustrated by the changing fortunes of Kintampo, Kete Krachi, and Atebubu (fig. 35).

The early growth of Kintampo must in some way have been connected with its position on the Kumasi–Buipe–Daboya trade route which became important many years after the beginning of the eighteenth century. Kintampo could have been a convenient resting place for those who traded south to Kumasi. It is true that the Mande traders had long been established at Buipe and Salaga, but the extension of their activities through Kintampo in the direction of Kumasi became significant only after Kumasi itself emerged as the premier town of Ashanti and the focus of all major trade routes from the coast as well as the interior. Also, Kintampo may have become significant as one of the frontier or custom-house villages that dotted the margins of Ashanti mainly after the second half of the eighteenth century.

Whatever the circumstances surrounding the early growth of Kintampo, it was already known to Europeans in the early nineteenth century when it was mentioned as one of the trading settlements on the Kumasi–Buipe trade route.[1] But then it was apparently no more than a small village where Ligbi or Mande traders came to buy kola nuts.[2] It remained in this lowly status until after 1874 when it suddenly became one of the major commercial centres in the country.

Ashanti, after its defeat in 1874, lost political control over many subject states, including eastern Gonja where Salaga functioned as the major clearing house for kola nuts from Ashanti and for livestock, cloth, etc. from Northern Ghana or outside. After several ineffectual attempts at restoring the link between Kumasi and Salaga, the Ashanti court deliberately established a large market at Kintampo, making it the headquarters of the kola nut trade.[3] This had the effect of drawing the Hausa and other caravans away from Salaga to Kintampo where they could trade for the prize commodity, kola nuts; and the importance of Kintampo rose as rapidly as that of Salaga declined. Kintampo also became a major distributor of European goods from the coast, which further enhanced its importance.

Just as Salaga began to decay after the flow of Ashanti kola nuts there was interrupted, so did Kintampo start on the downward path of decline when the Nkoranza, rebelling against the Ashanti court, closed the road from Kumasi to Kintampo in 1881.[4] Although the Nkoranza themselves continued to supply kola nuts, the immense quantities that poured out from the Ashanti forest were no longer available to Kintampo. Also, the principal European goods, whose easy import from the coast added to Kintampo's status as a market, practically disappeared from there as a result of the blocking of the Nkoranza–Kumasi and other coastward trade routes. The small quantities that found their way to Kintampo were imported from French warehouses between Axim and Liberia, through Bondoukou.

Kintampo's decline was nevertheless not so dramatic and sudden as that of Salaga. Kintampo was described in 1884 as 'the largest market in this part of Africa', with a fixed Ashanti population of between 3,000 and 4,000 and a floating population, from as far away as Sierra Leone, Timbuktu and Northern Nigeria, numbering between 30,000 and 40,000 (fig. 36).[5] For a brief period after 1884 Kintampo's trade revived with the reopening of the Nkoranza–Kumasi road, but this was no more than an uneasy truce. By

[1] Dupuis, *Journal of a Residence in Ashantee*, pt. II, p. xxxvi. He referred to Kintampo as Kantano.

[2] Binger, *Du Niger au Golfe de Guinée*, II, 136–44. This is the reference for the rest of the section on Kintampo.

[3] Lonsdale Report.

[4] BPP, Cmd. 4477, *Further Correspondence Respecting the Affairs of the Gold Coast* (Colonial Office, July 1885), enclosure in paper no. 41.

[5] Ibid.

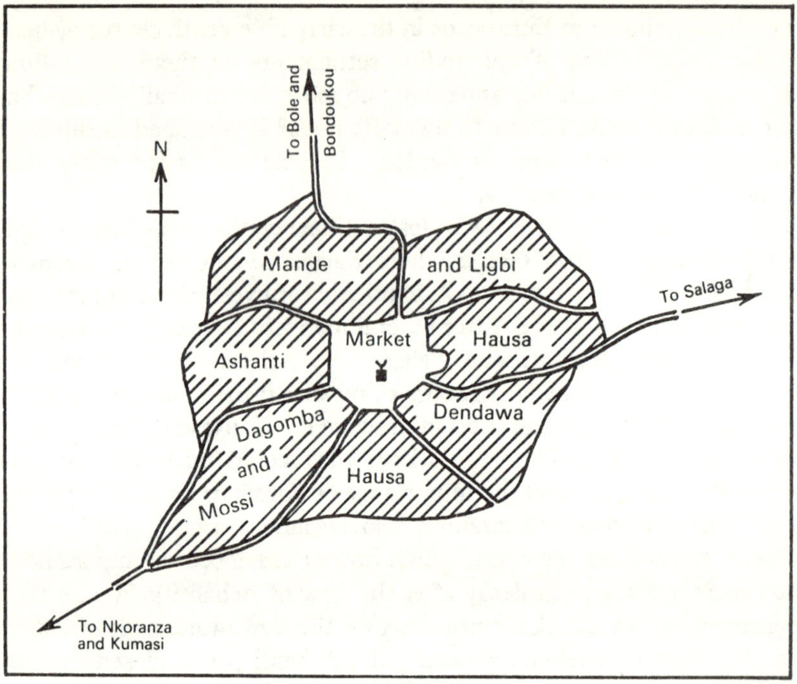


36 Kintampo in 1888 (after Binger)

1888 Kintampo's fixed population was estimated to be not more than 3,000, while the floating population numbered not more than 700 to 800.[1] The large difference in the size of the floating trading population as estimated in 1884 and in 1888 is significant; although neither estimate can lay claim to absolute accuracy, it gives a fair idea of the state of decay into which Kintampo had fallen.

Kintampo suffered another setback in 1896 when the British stopped slave trading there;[2] but this was soon more than compensated for by the selection in 1897 of the town as the British administrative headquarters for Northern Ghana. The element of political stability thus introduced into the life of Kintampo also steadied its function as a market, although by that time a great deal of trade by-passed it for other markets.

The choice of Kintampo as British administrative headquarters for Northern Ghana, a region in which it is not even now included, was not as

[1] See footnote 2 on p. 241.

[2] African (West) no. 529, *Further Correspondence Relative to Boundary Questions in the Bend of the Niger* (Colonial Office, January to August 1897), enclosure 1 in Paper no. 253.

odd as it may appear now, because Britain's sphere of influence in Northern Ghana in 1897 was rather limited, consisting mainly of parts of Gonja. Much of the rest of Northern Ghana was declared a Neutral Zone over which neither Britain nor Germany should seek political domination. It was not until 1899 that the whole of Northern Ghana, with the exception of what was formerly Northern Togoland, came under Britain (the boundaries with the neighbouring states were yet to be fixed finally). Then, clearly, Northern Ghana could no longer be ruled from Kintampo; therefore the seat of administration was transferred first, in 1901, to Gambaga and finally in 1907 to Tamale. Thereafter the deterioration of Kintampo was rapid, especially after Salaga began to recapture its trade.

In the second half of the nineteenth century Kete and Krachi were two separate settlements. Krachi, the smaller of the two and with a population mostly of Guan origin, was, as in earlier times, a famous religious centre. There was no market or trade of any description there. Traders and strangers as much as possible avoided the town owing to the stringent regulations and laws that had to be observed in connection with the shrine Dente. On the other hand, foreign ambassadors resided permanently at Krachi in order to conduct negotiations or consult with the shrine on behalf of their countries.[1]

Kete was the trading town, founded with the blessing of Dente specifically to exploit the superb advantages of location at a transhipment point on the Volta, and it grew in stature as the salt and fish trade between Ada and Salaga increased in the nineteenth century. In 1882 Kete was described as 'a young Salaga', in reference to its ever-increasing role as an international market centre.[2] The town was a large one by contemporary standards, containing an estimated number of 4,050 houses and a population of 7,000–8,000, and, as was typical of all trading towns in the parkland zone, the majority of the population consisted of foreign traders who in this case were Mohammedan Hausa. Kete was one of the bulwarks of Islam in West Africa.

After 1884 a number of factors worked together to make Kete 'a mature Salaga' and one of the largest markets in the whole of Ghana.[3] The Germans assumed political control over Kete, as well as Krachi, and established at the former an administrative station and a department store, which attracted still larger numbers of traders. Also, Kete, by its unique location, benefited from the disruption of trade between Kumasi and

[1] Lonsdale Report. [2] Ibid.

[3] A good description of Kete in the early 1890s is to be found in Heinrich Klose, *Togo unter deutscher Flagge* (Berlin, 1899), pp. 325–39.

Salaga: it emerged as the centre where Salaga merchants purchased the small quantities of kola nuts that were sent northwards from Southern Ghana, including the Volta Region. Finally, Kete took over the functions of Kintampo and Salaga as slave markets after Salaga lost its trade and slave trading at Kintampo was abolished in 1896; then slave caravans, some of which were organized by the slave raider Babatu, came there directly from Bole, Wa, Bondoukou, and Upper Volta. Indeed, the slave market for a time became the mainstay of Kete's trade, and the Germans apparently did not think it prudent to abolish it since an earlier attempt to do so nearly lost Kete all its trade.[1]

The circumstances that initiated the long process of Kete's decline began to operate in 1896, and the details of these illustrate the deadliness of the Anglo-German rivalry as the two Colonial Powers sought to oust each other from the country.[2] The British, jealous of Kete's widening sphere of influence which they considered detrimental to their own trade in the settlements lying on their side of the Volta, built a market, called British Krachi, near the village of Nsunua, on a site on the right bank of the Volta directly opposite Kete. That site was chosen because it was the only point where the Germans allowed goods to be transported by their ferry across the Volta to or from Kete. The British then enforced a series of regulations designed to kill the trade at Kete. As an opening measure, they arrogated to themselves the right to operate the ferry between British Krachi and Kete, and exercised strict supervision over craft plying between the two markets.[3] Next they enforced numerous measures all of which were designed to keep traders on their side of the Volta away from Kete. There were regulations to ensure that salt could not be shipped to Kete from Ada, that commodities from Brong Ahafo or Northern Ghana could not reach Kete, and that the Germans could not operate a ferry between Kete and any other point on the opposite bank of the Volta.

The Germans also took retaliatory measures. They enforced a regulation to the effect that all traders passing westward through Togoland should first declare their goods at Kete and obtain a pass which they had to show at a certain town about fifteen or sixteen days march north-east of Bismarcksburg, if they wished to trade outside Kete or Bismarcksburg. Naturally, the tedious journeys involved in obtaining passes at Kete and

[1] African (West) no. 529, enclosure 3 in Paper no. 253 is a letter from Assistant Inspector Parmeter to the governor, dated 'British Camp, Krakye (Right Bank), March 31st, 1897'.

[2] African (West) no. 585, *Gold Coast: Further Correspondence Relating to the Northern Territories* (Colonial Office, 1899), Papers nos. 112, 113, 121 and all their enclosures contain details of the rivalry.

[3] Ibid.

showing them elsewhere prevented the majority of Hausa and other merchants living to the east of Togoland from trading beyond Kete.

After further restrictive measures by the British which proved ineffective, the British Colonial Secretary, Joseph Chamberlain, called a halt to the suicidal struggle in 1899 and suggested the removal of all restrictions on the transport of goods on the Volta.

It was too late. The net effect of the vicious thrusts and counterthrusts by the British and the Germans on trade at Kete was ruinous, and Kete lost practically all its trade—which was considerable—from the British side of the Volta. The situation was worsened for Kete when Tamale and other towns near the Togoland frontier in Northern Ghana with good road and river connections emerged as major trading centres in the first decade of the twentieth century. Kete nevertheless continued to be of some importance, primarily as an administrative town under the Germans, and its final plunge into comparative insignificance and partial decay occurred with the departure of the Germans after the First World War.

Situated at the junction of roads from Kintampo, Kete, Salaga, and Kumasi, Atebubu underwent, but generally in a contrary direction, the full effects of the political and economic factors that altered the market status of its neighbours. Before the decay of the four big markets that surrounded it, Atebubu was a small town which functioned principally as the capital of Brong; it was little known for its trade, in spite of its central position with respect to its trading neighbours. One observer's impression of the town in 1882 was not that of a flourishing trading settlement.[1] Indeed, Atebubu itself had been adversely affected by the cessation of the kola nut trade at Salaga, for, lying on the Kumasi–Salaga trade route, it had hitherto been a minor collecting point for the commodity.

Atebubu rose into prominence as a trading town within the last decade of the nineteenth century when first Kintampo and then Kete began to lose their trade. By 1897 Atebubu was a major commercial town consisting, characteristically, of the twin units of the zongo and the original Atebubu. The latter was a small compact town about 300 yards long and about half as broad at its widest part, and contained about 41 blocks of some 140 rectangular, flat-roofed buildings grouped round interior courtyards. The zongo was said to be about twice the size of the original Atebubu.[2]

All the trading at Atebubu was conducted by the Hausa and Mande

[1] Lonsdale Report.

[2] African (West) no. 529, enclosures 1 and 3 in Paper no. 253, and African (West) no. 549, *Gold Coast: Correspondence Relating to the Northern Territories* (Colonial Office, January–June 1898). Enclosure in Paper no. 227 is 'Report on Gonja and Dagomba Countries' dated Yeji, 9 February 1898, by Capt. Kenney-Herbert.

merchants at the zongo which, like Kete's zongo before it, became an important terminus for slave caravans from Northern Ghana and the neighbouring states. Atebubu's fame came to be based almost entirely on its vast slave market. In addition to slaves the trading caravans brought some cattle, sheep, shea butter, country cloths, and gold dust (mainly from Bondoukou and Bole) in exchange for kola nuts from Brong Ahafo together with salt and European goods brought directly from the coast through Kete.

The process of Atebubu's loss of trade, which was as dramatic as its rise to fame, began from about 1900 as a result of the rebuilding of Salaga, the divergence by the Germans of traders through Northern Togoland to Kete, and the stopping of the slave trade which was the foundation of its prosperity. Atebubu's survival and importance came to depend mainly on its original status as the capital of Brong and as a Government station from 1898. But the trend towards decline was reversed after the Kumasi–Salaga trade route, on which it lies, was converted to a motor road and became the principal trade axis between Northern Ghana and Ashanti.

## FOREST TOWNS IN SOUTHERN GHANA AND ASHANTI–BRONG AHAFO

In the forest zone the growth of towns was influenced by a set of factors different from those which operated in the case of towns in Northern Ghana and in the parkland zone. The only common factor derived from the far-flung effects of the new political situation which arose through the defeat of the Ashanti by the British. Outside the political factors, the particular changes in economy that influenced the growth of towns were peculiar to the forest zone. The changes were, broadly speaking, the introduction of modern mining accompanied by the building of railways; and the rapid development of an agricultural export economy based on the cultivation of a wide range of crops.

### The influence of political development

Many towns in Ashanti were affected by the aftermath of the Anglo-Ashanti war of 1873–4, for the civil wars that rent Ashanti after 1874 resulted in the destruction, and subsequent slow development and growth, of such towns as Kokofu, Bekwai, Nkwanka, Agona, Mampong, Juaben, and Nsuta.[1] They were all, before then, comparatively large towns which played major roles in the political and economic organization of Ashanti. Only

[1] BPP, Cmd. 4477, enclosure in Paper no. 41.

Bekwai and Mampong made any substantial progress towards recovery in subsequent years, and that was due in the main to their being conveniently situated for trade in rubber and cocoa.

The development of Kumasi between about 1850 and 1914 is the most important illustration of the influence of the political factor on the growth of towns in the forest zone. Kumasi, as capital, was by all accounts the largest town in Ashanti; it was also the principal focus of trade in the kingdom. One of the earliest estimates of the size of Kumasi's population in 1817 placed it between 12,000 and 15,000, although, it was further suggested, the figure might well reach over 100,000 if all the dependants of the aristocrats in the capital, living in the suburbs and outlying farming villages, were included.[1] Another estimate in 1820 gave the figure as over 200,000, perhaps a fair measure of Kumasi's size in relation to that of Juaben whose population was estimated in that same year to be about 70,000.[2]

Kumasi, located to the south of the swamps at Kejetia and on elevated ground between the unhealthy marshes of the East Nsuben and West Nsuben valleys, was a nucleated settlement built around the palace of the king of Ashanti (fig. 37). It had a large market place, temples and sacrificial groves, and a zongo;[3] and on the whole the town appeared to exhibit a traditional functional zonation corresponding to the occupancy patterns of the different social strata of the population. Kumasi was the political and cultural centre of Ashanti. Its way of life was in no way affected by the few Christian stations established there before 1850, or by ideas of European origin, although there was some evidence of this influence in the case of the architecture of the king's palace as far back as the 1840s. The modifications to the palace were made by Dutch-trained Elmina craftsmen.[4]

Within the context of the existing political and economic framework of the country Kumasi, left to itself, would have developed into a truly unique African metropolis; but the tide of change was beginning to advance into the interior from the coast by the 1860s, and in 1874 Kumasi was pillaged and burnt by armies under the command of a British general. The destruction of the town was almost complete, for the invasion was meant to break the power of Ashanti for ever; moreover the invading armies, fired by visions of immense stores of gold in Kumasi, ransacked the town thoroughly.

[1] Bowdich, *Mission from Cape Coast Castle to Ashantee*, pp. 323–4.
[2] Dupuis, *Journal of a Residence in Ashantee*, pt. II, p. xxx.
[3] Bowdich, op. cit. pp. 234 ff. Also despatch of 15 November 1848 in ADM 1/450, NAG.
[4] H. S. Pel, *Aanteekeningen gehouden op eene Reis van St. George Delmina naar Comassie* (Leiden, 1842?), p. 15.

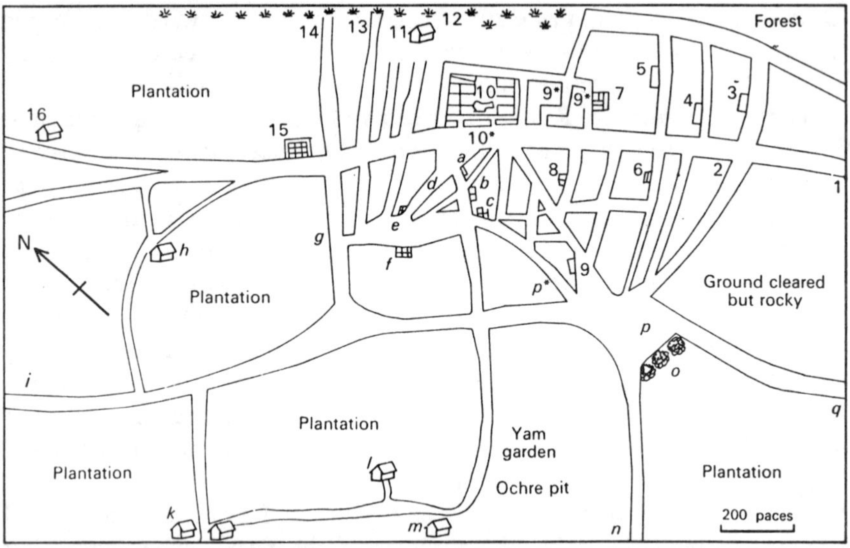


37 Bowdich's map of Kumasi, 1817. 1 Entrance from Fantee and Assin; 2 Agwabu or small market; 3 King's eldest sister's house; 4 King's goldsmith's house; 5 Appiah Nanu's house; 6 Otee's (3rd linguist's) house; 7 Odumata's (Captain's) house; 8 King's youngest sister's house; 9 Odoom Street; 9* Baba's house and the Cambos (Moor's) street; 10* Aboogawa or place of execution; 10 Palace; 11 King's wives' croom; 12 marsh; 13 entrance from Dwabin; 14 entrance from Barraman; 15 King of Dwaben's temporary court; 16 King's blacksmith's croom: *a* Himma or the King's fetish temple; *b* Apokoo's (captain's) house; *c* Adoocee's (chief linguist's) house; *d* Apirremsoo street; *e* Aboidwee's house, quarters of the (British) Embassy; *f* Adoo Quamina's (chief captain's) house; *g* Osarramandiduum street; *h* King's umbrella maker's croom; *i* entrance to Bantama high street; *k, l, m* crooms; *n* long irregular suburb and road to Dankara; *o* Sammonpome or Spirit Grove; *p* Adooebrim—the large market; *p** small market; *q* High Street of Assafo

Kumasi revived slowly: in 1884 it still bore the scars of the 1874 débâcle. Its population, caught up in the civil wars and completely war-weary, deserted the town in significant numbers, and did not return to speed up the process of reconstruction until about the beginning of the 1890s. A description of the town in 1888 contrasted sharply with pre-1874 descriptions:[1]

Kumasi was a great disappointment to me, and my disappointment increased as I walked round and examined the town. It was not merely that so little existed, but that so much had been destroyed. As it stands, or then stood, the town was nothing more than a large clearing in the forest, over which were scattered, somewhat irregularly, groups of houses. The paths were dirty and ill kept, and between the groups of houses large patches of waste ground intervened, and on these, amidst the

[1] Freeman, *Travels and Life in Ashanti and Jaman*, pp. 109–11.

tall, coarse grass that covered them, were to be seen the remains of houses that had once occupied them. These houses once stood in wide regular streets, but since the destruction of the city in 1874 the natives do not seem to have had heart to rebuild them. Yet there remained some few vestiges to show what Kumasi had been in its palmy days before the 'civilising hand' of the European was laid upon it. A few broad, well-kept streets still existed, lined by houses, the admirable construction, careful and artistic finish and excellent repair of which showed how great is the difference between the industrious, intelligent, cleanly Ashantis and the slovenly natives of the Coast countries.

Kumasi suffered further acts of vandalism by undisciplined soldiers during the British expedition of 1895–6 at the end of which the king of Ashanti was deported from the country. The suburb of Bantama was destroyed by fire, and with it perished some of the largest and most ancient buildings in Kumasi, superb examples of the unique Ashanti architecture. Kumasi's population then was estimated to be 5,500, with about three-fifths of the total Ashanti.[1] Yet another war with the British occurred in 1899–1900 to hold back the reconstruction of the town. After that war Ashanti was annexed to the British Crown, and the work of restoring to Kumasi its former reputation as a clean, well-planned town then proceeded 'under the watchful eye of the Chief Commissioner'.[2]

With the imposition of British rule over Ashanti, it was considered safe to reinstate Kumasi in its former role as the focus of trade routes from Southern and Northern Ghana, and develop it again as a major centre of trade. The process was accelerated when the railway from Sekondi reached Kumasi in 1903. Just as important in the revival of the economic status of Kumasi was the spread of cocoa cultivation to Kumasi district from about 1902, which brought great wealth to the town. The growth of Kumasi thereafter was mainly a function of its regional location and its status as a major collecting and distributing centre, and not so much of the dynamism and everything else that used to be implied in its position as capital of the great kingdom of Ashanti.

## The influence of modern mining

The beginning of modern gold mining was responsible for the rapid development into towns of many villages in the Western Region, southern and western Ashanti, and Ashanti–Akim. The rate at which the towns grew depended on the scale of mining operations. Some of the towns may not even have existed before as recognizable villages, for there were several

[1] *Colonial Report—Ashanti*, 1897.

[2] D. M. and F. G. Guggisberg, *We Two in West Africa* (London, 1909), p. 184.

instances where the towns were to all intents and purposes the sole creations of gold mining. Examples were Nsuta and Bondai.[1] Another development was the dormitory or warehouse village which served as an annexe to the mining towns, an example being Bonsa Station or Apankrom.[2] The river port of Tumentu grew in a like manner.[3] There were other towns whose growth since the beginning of the twentieth century was associated with their location in relation to that of a gold-mining town. Dunkwa-on-the-Ofin became the base from which the Bibiani gold mine, some seventy miles to the north-west, was supplied, and in 1906 it was described as a large straggling place chiefly inhabited by the carriers employed by the mining company at Bibiani.[4]

Spectacular among the mining towns with phenomenal growth rates after the last two decades of the nineteenth century were Tarkwa, Prestea, and Obuasi. The dynamics of growth, illustrated in the case of Tarkwa, were the same for all.[5]

It is possible that the early beginnings or development of Tarkwa was associated with the mining of alluvial gold in the vicinity.[6] One of the earliest and most definite references to Tarkwa was that made by Bowdich when describing trade and trade routes in Wasaw–Aowin. He referred to Tarkwa as a 'considerable town',[7] which shows that Tarkwa was already, long before the opening there of gold mines by modern techniques, a settlement of some importance.

Whatever the earlier size and importance of Tarkwa, its development into the full-grown town it became within the first few decades of the twentieth century began with the discovery and mining there of quartz gold reefs towards the close of the nineteenth century. Tarkwa in the 1880s possessed all the characteristics of a frontier town, with wooden buildings hastily erected in a haphazard manner without conforming to a planned street pattern; so that when a fire started on 3 May 1882 it spread quickly and destroyed much of the town.[8] When the houses were rebuilt immediately

[1] S. A. Darko, 'The effects of Modern Mining on Settlements in the Mining Areas of Ghana', *Bull. Ghana Geogr. Ass.* VIII, 1 (January 1963).

[2] African no. 249. *Further Correspondence Regarding Affairs of the Gold Coast* (Colonial Office, June 1883). Enclosure 1 in Paper no. 22 is Commander Rumsey's 'Report on Tarkwa District' dated 9 August 1882.

[3] Ibid.

[4] D. M. and F. G. Guggisberg, op. cit. pp. 165–6.

[5] The growth of Bibiani since the beginning of the 1930s is another illustration. See Darko, op. cit.

[6] D'Anville's map of the country in 1729 indicates that gold mining was already important in the Tarkwa Hills.

[7] Bowdich, op. cit. p. 217.

[8] The account of Tarkwa is from the monthly reports of the District Commissioners at Tarkwa published in African no. 249, *Further Correspondence Regarding Affairs of the Gold Coast* (Colonial Office, June 1883).

afterwards, they were not of more durable and less inflammable materials; neither were they in regular lines. Tarkwa's ethnically mixed population was also characteristic of new mining towns. It consisted of Wasaw, Fanti, Apollonian, and Ashanti tribesmen who gained a livelihood by working in the mines, acting as carriers, and running liquor stores. Agriculture was entirely ignored, and the town's food supplies came from the coast.

Two other factors in addition to the basic one of gold rush were responsible for the rapid growth of Tarkwa up to the end of the nineteenth century. The first of these was Tarkwa's accessibility which became more pronounced as the fame of its gold mines attracted people from many parts of the country. To Kumasi, Tarkwa was connected by several routes, the most frequented of which was that through Aboso, Kayerekrom, Adjubuakrom, Esubrerim, then through a long and nearly uninhabited stretch of forest to the African mining settlement of Akuterame, which was a day's journey from Kumasi. From the coast Tarkwa was accessible by four different routes all of which were in fairly regular use: the route from Elmina through Mansu which took 3 days of walking; the Dixcove route, about 2 days long; the 1½-day-long direct land route from Axim; and the boat journey on the Ankobra from Axim to Tumentu and thence by land through Bonsa Station. The improvement of some of these routes accentuated the value of Tarkwa's nodal position and its role as a trading and distributing centre.

The second factor that helped to account for Tarkwa's steady growth was the imposition of the rule of civil law which gave protection to life and property, and in that way encouraged permanent settlement of the population. Life at Tarkwa was fairly grim and the population was said to consist of 'renegades from the coast who, having run their course there, come here because they think they are pretty safe from the power of the law'. The British Administration appointed a Civil Commissioner for Tarkwa around the middle of 1882 but with vaguely defined terms of reference and little power in administering the law; his principal duty apparently was to submit monthly reports on the town, paying special attention to the mining industry. Nevertheless the reports of robbery and murder that reached Accra from the Commissioner within the first few months of his assumption of office were enough to prompt the Administration to appoint a new District Commissioner with clearly defined civic duties, which enabled him to bring the lawlessness at Tarkwa under control.

Throughout the first decade of the twentieth century the propulsive forces behind the rapid expansion of Tarkwa remained those mentioned above, the only addition being the railway from the port of Sekondi which arrived there in 1901 and emphasized the factor of accessibility. The factor of cocoa cultivation, which was instrumental in the growth of many towns in the forest, played a relatively minor role in the case of Tarkwa. Cocoa, for several reasons, did not succeed very well in the neighbourhood of Tarkwa, and the town did not function as a major collecting centre for the crop.

### The influence of export agriculture

The phenomenal spread and growth of the cocoa industry in the forest zone was the most important single event in the period under review, and its influence on contemporary as well as subsequent developments was so all-pervading that no aspect of the country's human geography can be fully understood without reference to cocoa. One of the many manifestations of this influence was the blossoming of many towns in both Ashanti and South Ghana. Such towns owed their rapid growth to their being cocoa buying or collecting centres, the homes of prosperous cocoa farmers, or both. The spread of cocoa was accompanied by an expansion of trade, of the road network, and the start of the 'cocoa railway' from Accra towards Kumasi, all of which in turn had considerable influence on the growth of towns.

Before the spread of cocoa cultivation, the influence of the development of export agriculture on the growth of towns could be seen throughout Ashanti and Southern Ghana, except the Western Region where commercial agriculture was not so well developed. But the rate of growth was not as great as it became after the spread of cocoa cultivation. Up to 1910 the distribution of cocoa showed higher concentrations in the Eastern Region, the Central Region, Buem district in the Volta Region, and in Ashanti-Akim, and lower concentrations in Bekwai, southern Mampong and eastern Kumasi districts of Ashanti. Western Ashanti–Brong Ahafo and the Western Region of Southern Ghana had not as yet been caught in the grip of the 'cocoa fever'. The incidence and intensity of the effect of cocoa cultivation on the growth of towns showed the same pattern as the distribution of the crop itself.

Descriptions of towns in, for example, Ashanti–Akim and Kwahu before the First World War were indicative of the atmosphere of prosperity that already surrounded many towns in the principal cocoa areas.[1] The village of Bompata, where cocoa was first seriously cultivated in Ashanti–Akim,

[1] D. M. and F. G. Guggisberg, op. cit. pp. 257–356.

had grown into a large town of about 400 compounds. The inhabitants of old Tweneduase, who apparently did not want to live too close to their neighbours in the town of Obo, had built and moved into a new Tweneduase which the Guggisbergs declared was the finest African town they had seen up to that time in West Africa. The town was well laid out and sanitary, comparing favourably with the more modern parts of Accra and Cape Coast, 'though it could have given either of them points in spacing and ventilation'. Obo was among the largest of the Kwahu towns, with an estimated population of over 9,000; also among the major towns were Abetifi, Abene, and Mpraeso, each with an estimated population of not less than 4,000. Obomen, surrounded by large cocoa farms and with a population of over 6,000, struck the Guggisbergs as being 'a very flourishing place' and was distinguished by its large craft industry whose prosperous state must have been related to the increased purchasing power made possible by cocoa cultivation. The 3,000 or so inhabitants of the old town of Asakraka were building a new town close by.

Another important result, for towns in the interior but not immediately for villages, of the increase in wealth through cocoa cultivation was the greater demand for European goods and the conscious efforts by individuals to emulate the mode of living on the coast, which had long been modified through European influence. For instance, furniture of European make began to replace the traditional type, and in this connection may be recalled the pride with which the chief of Mpraeso reportedly exhibited his imported furniture and other articles of European manufacture to the Guggisbergs.[1] There were other instances of the adoption of new ideas of living in the interior. Tiles and corrugated iron sheets began to replace thatch as roofing material; new houses were built with polished wooden doors and windows, as at Kumasi, and the spread of this idea was in some places facilitated by the Basel Mission which included excellent training in carpentry and other skills in its work. There were even some private, individual attempts at providing street lighting, as at Obo.[2]

One indication of prosperity common to most cocoa towns in the interior was the change in design and size of houses, from the simple compound houses consisting of rectangular structures grouped round an inner courtyard to huge double-storeyed constructions capable of housing a whole extended family. This urban house type, characterized by a broad open verandah on pillars surrounding the upper storey, was introduced several centuries earlier by Europeans into the coastal towns where it was initially adopted by rich Ghanaian merchants. As built by Ghanaians in both the

[1] Ibid. pp. 348–9. [2] Ibid. p. 312.

coastal and interior towns, it either stood by itself or formed one side of the traditional rectangular compound house. These period constructions are exhibited, for example, in the ridge towns of Akwapim which have long been involved in the cocoa-growing industry. The house type had appeared in Kumasi and in the principal Ashanti-Akim and Kwahu towns by 1906; it did not apparently reach these towns before the beginning of the century.

## Coastal towns

Among the most striking changes that occurred in the distribution of towns in Southern Ghana after the time of William Bosman was the break-up of most of the sub-coastal towns from which the towns on the coast were originally ruled. As Ghana's overseas trade gained greater volume and much of the country looked more to the coast than to the Western Sudan for trade, the coastal settlements grew larger and more prosperous, and in the process acquired an additional function as the political headquarters for the Colonial Powers. The vitality of the sub-coastal settlements was drained with the emigration of their population to the settlements on the coast and the loss to them of their function as principal seats of traditional rulers. By the beginning of the nineteenth century the coastal settlements completely overshadowed their parent settlements in size and importance. The latter had deteriorated to the rank of mere villages.

The growth of the majority of the coastal towns since the 1850s depended on their port functions, which in turn depended on the regularity of flow of export commodities from the interior. Although wars were not infrequent in the interior, their incidence in time and space was not so uniform as to interrupt the flow of commodities to some of the ports for any length of time.

Up to about the 1860s palm oil, rather than gold, was the principal determinant of port status. The major palm-oil ports included Ada, Prampram, Accra, Winneba, Saltpond, Anomabu, Cape Coast, and Dixcove.[1] Of these Saltpond was apparently the most important. It achieved this distinction after steamers began to call there in large numbers in the 1850s. Before then palm oil from Saltpond district was exported from Cape Coast and Anomabu; but with the increase in the district's output most of the merchants came to settle at Saltpond, and almost all the oil began to be shipped from that port.

After the 1860s the basis of port trade broadened as agricultural exports became more varied. Consequently certain ports which had up till then

[1] Despatch of 24 January 1882 in C.O. 96/137, P.R.O.

been in danger of closing down began to gain some importance. Thus was Cape Coast, which had by the beginning of the 1880s lost much of its palm-oil trade to Saltpond, able to continue as a major port because of its trade in rubber and gold. In the same way Anomabu, caught between the thriving ports of Saltpond and Cape Coast, lost practically all its port trade (fig. 38).[1]

Between 1910 and 1928 trade in cocoa was the major determinant of port status in the Central, Eastern, and Volta Regions (fig. 39). The remaining ports handled gold, timber, and other agricultural products, supplies of which fluctuated wildly. Within this period some of the cocoa ports—Sekondi, Cape Coast, Saltpond, Winneba, and Accra—became more important than others because of greater accessibility from the interior, made possible by road and rail transport improvements. Sekondi and Accra were additionally important because of their superior port facilities.[2] Ada at the mouth of the Volta also maintained its status as a major port up to the 1920s, partly because of the exploration and frequent use of the river. After 1928 Takoradi and Accra handled most of the country's cocoa, and the growth of the seaside towns came to depend on their extra-port functions.

The expansion of the cocoa ports led to most of the remaining ports losing their trade after 1910. Anomabu was closed down in 1912; then followed the port of Denu in 1916, the ports of Adjua, Shama, and Prampram in 1919, the ports of Dixcove, Atuabo, Apam, and Elmina in 1921,[3] and, finally, Axim in 1934.

Accra, throughout this period after about 1850 when the fortunes of many towns fluctuated wildly with the constant shift of locus of operation of the factors determining urban growth, was remarkably stable and maintained its position as a large and prosperous town. This feature of stability was clearly evident as far back as the late eighteenth or early nineteenth century and led to the first serious suggestion in 1818 that Accra, not Cape Coast, should be the headquarters of the British Administration.[4] As Accra was under the immediate protection of the king of Ashanti it would escape the hostilities and other disturbances to which Cape Coast was uniformly liable.[5] For many reasons Cape Coast remained the capital of British Southern Ghana until after the Anglo-Ashanti war of 1873–4, when the British began to reorganize their administration in Southern Ghana. Then

[1] Dickson, 'Evolution of Seaports in Ghana: 1800–1928', loc. cit.
[2] See above, p. 234.
[3] Dickson, op. cit.
[4] There had not apparently been any serious check to the growth of Accra since about the mid-eighteenth century. It always retained its function as a major port.
[5] Robertson, *Notes on Africa*, p. 219.

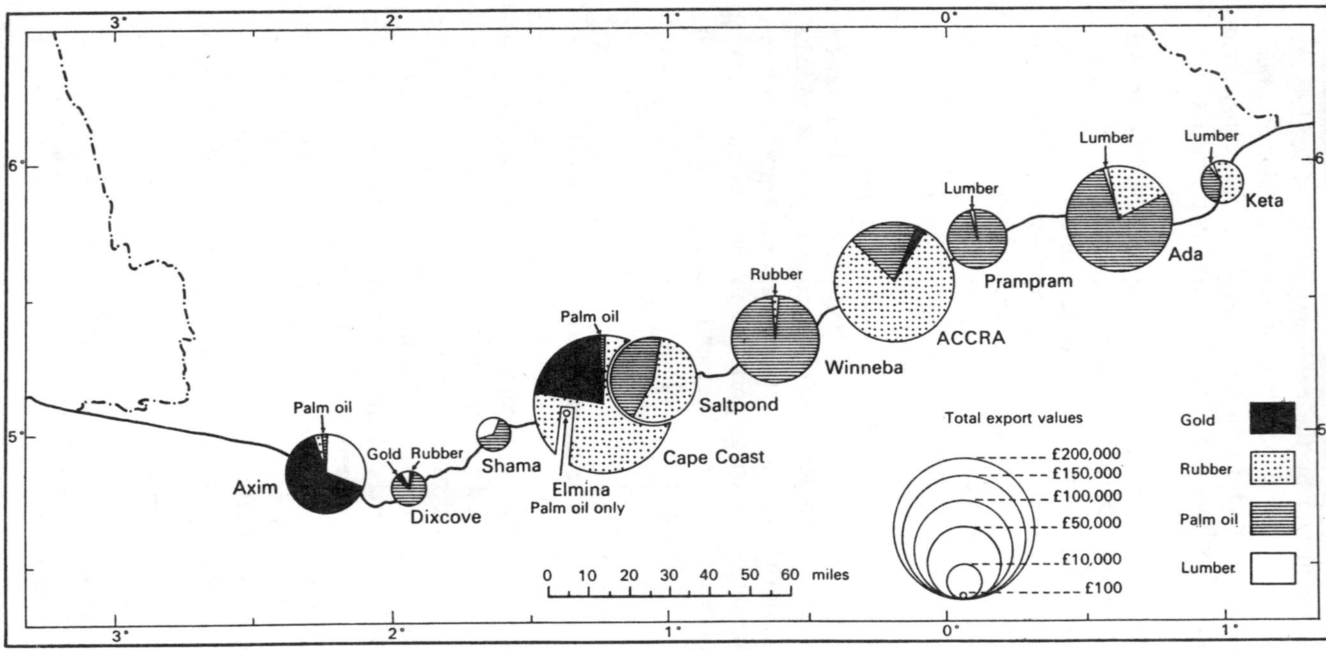


38 Export of palm oil, rubber, gold and lumber, 1895

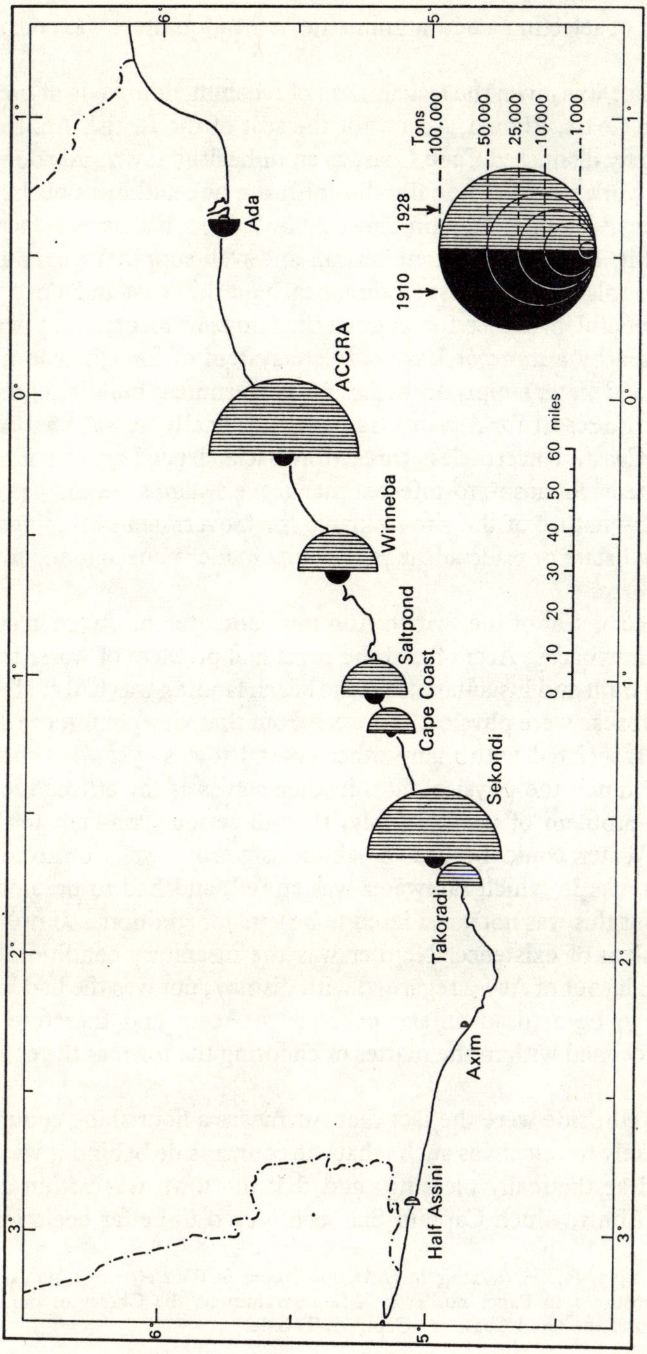


39 Cocoa exports, 1910 and 1928

the question of selecting a new administrative headquarters was considered afresh.

Captain Sale was given the task in 1875 of recommending one of the three towns, Cape Coast, Elmina, Accra, for the seat of the British Administration. He briefly dismissed Cape Coast as an unhealthy town and added that no sanitary work would materially diminish the unhealthiness of the place for Europeans.[1] Elmina, Captain Sale acknowledged, had several factors to recommend it. Built in sandstone terrain and well supplied with building stone, Elmina also had the best landing beach on the coast and a bay which offered a hopeful prospect for engineering improvement; the town was well protected by a more or less complete system of forts; it had a comparatively good water supply and a site for Government buildings; the port was a favourite resort for Ashanti traders; and, finally, it was far healthier than Cape Coast. Nevertheless three drawbacks argued against its selection: the extensive mosquito-infested mangrove swamps behind the town; the unhealthy nature of the site available for Government buildings; and the depressed state of trade at the port which made it uneconomic to build a harbour there.

The choice of seat of the British Administration fell on Accra in spite of its serious drawbacks: Accra faced the perennial problem of water supply; it was badly built and insanitary; and the beach landing was bad at all times. These drawbacks were physical and were from that viewpoint more serious than those associated with many other coastal towns; yet what mattered were not so much the physical facts in themselves as the attitude towards them. The problem of water supply, though serious, was not felt to be desperate. Water could be drawn laboriously from wells or from large household tanks in which rainwater was stored, and had to be used with economy, but this was not considered to be a major additional complication to the problem of existence. Neither was the insanitary condition or the unattractive layout of Accra regarded with dismay; nor was the bad landing considered to be a disadvantage peculiar to Accra and therefore to be seriously reckoned with in the matter of choosing the town as the country's capital.

On the credit side were the fact that Accra was a flourishing commercial town and likely to remain as such; that the countryside behind it was open, healthy and aesthetically pleasing; and that the town was within a day's journey to Aburi, which Captain Sale considered to be far healthier than

[1] BPP Cmd. 1343, *Papers Relating to H.M. Possessions in West Africa* (Colonial Office, 1875). Enclosure 1 in Paper no. 41 is 'Memorandum on the Choice of the Seat of Government of the Gold Coast' by Capt. M. T. Sale.

any place within reach of Englishmen on the west coast of Africa.[1] Accra's commercial supremacy was a matter of considerable importance to the European population, for it gave the town the necessary prestige that a capital should have. The prevailing attitude towards the hot tropical climate as one in which the health of the European broke down quickly explained the great importance attached to Accra's proximity to Aburi, in whose cooler climate sick Europeans were said to be able to regain their health rapidly. The aesthetic appeal of the open country behind Accra as well as the opportunities there for hunting and acquiring equestrian skills was also especially important to the Europeans. The tangle of bush and forest behind many of the coastal towns was an ugly and depressing sight to most European residents. Thus on balance it was considered that the advantages of making Accra the capital completely outweighed the disadvantages, and on 19 March 1877 the seat of government was removed from Cape Coast to Christiansborg, Accra.

Accra in 1877 consisted of the two townships of James Town and Ussher Town which formed one compact mass of thatched buildings arranged in a haphazard manner and separated by narrow, crooked streets.[2] A few of the buildings belonging to wealthy Accra merchants were larger, in a better state of repair, and stood out above the rest; nearer the edge of the cliff overlooking the beach were the houses of the European residents, both administrators and merchants. Osu, another unplanned agglomeration of buildings, was separated from Ussher Town and James Town by a stretch of open country.

The enforcement of a sanitation and general improvement policy, which involved the provision of street lighting by means of paraffin lamps, the cutting of drains, the opening of cemeteries, the elimination of garbage from the streets, and the provision of clean drinking water, began in 1885. The improvement measures were on the whole successful, except that for ensuring supplies of clean water. This was because the newly opened public reservoir was exposed, and its $3\frac{1}{2}$ million gallons of water soon became dirty and unusable. The site of the reservoir is where the Accra Electricity Department now stands.

Yet Accra continued to grow (fig. 40). A great deal of investment capital was channelled into the town, and the volume of trade was stepped up, as is shown by the fact that Accra in 1889 possessed the largest number of private bonded warehouses on the Ghana coast.[3] With the convergence of

[1] Reference is to Captain Sale's memorandum. See footnote on page 258.

[2] Henry Stanley, *Coomassie and Magdala* (London, 1874), pp. 77–9. Later but less detailed descriptions confirmed this.

[3] *Gold Coast Government Gazette*, 30 March 1889.

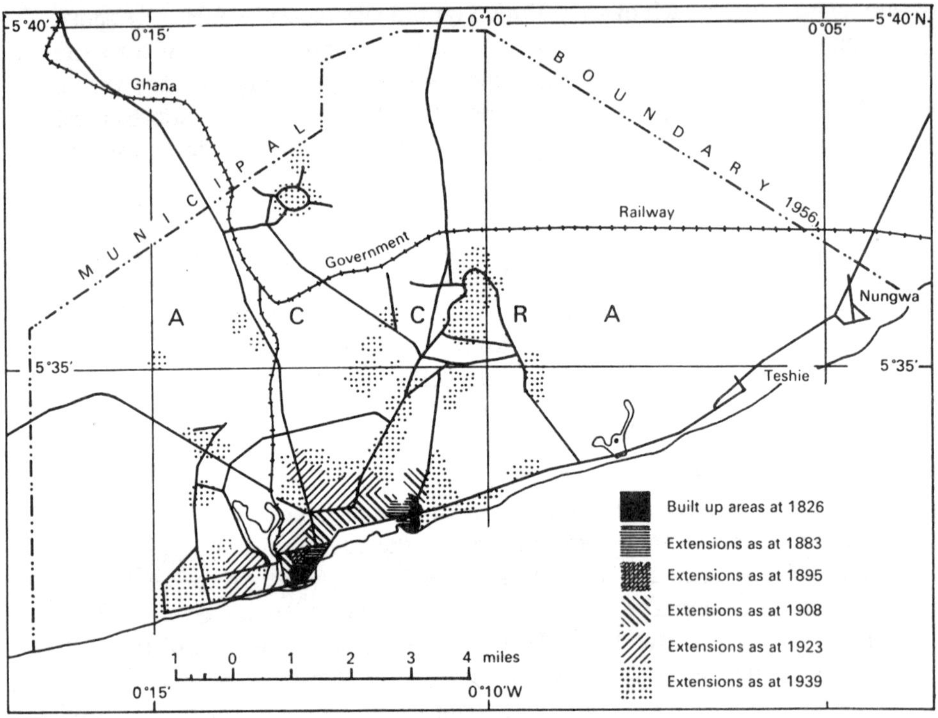


40 The growth of Accra

first 'cask' and then motor roads on the town from many parts of the Eastern Region, Accra became perhaps the busiest port on the coast.

In 1898 the Accra Municipal Council was formed under the provisions of the Town Council Ordinance of 1894, and of the eight standing committees set up by the Council, five were specially concerned with the subjects of water supply, market and slaughterhouse facilities, lighting, sanitation, and open spaces. The Council also assumed responsibility for street maintenance.[1] All the projects were to be financed with revenue from house and other rates, but since these were not easily forthcoming the Council could do little during the first few years of its existence. The James Town–Ussher Town complex remained 'an unimposing ramshackle collection of weather-beaten white-washed houses and huts'.[2] It was not until 1907, when bubonic plague raged through the town, that its inhabitants came to appreciate the need for municipal council services.

[1] Ione Acquah, *Accra Survey* (London, 1958), pp. 22–8.
[2] D. M. and F. G. Guggisberg, *We Two in West Africa*, p. 45.

From that date the totals of rates paid increased substantially every year.[1]

Throughout the first three decades of the twentieth century Accra retained its status as a major port and indeed was the premier cocoa port.[2] The increase in employment opportunities through expansion of commerce and of Government offices, the greater incentive to retail trade, the greater opportunities for better medical services and education,[3] the lure of the capital—all these and probably many other factors led to population increases in Accra. From 19,582 in 1911, the population figures rose to 41,124 in 1921 and to 60,726 in 1931.[4]

## NORTHERN GHANA

From about 1850 to 1874 much of Northern Ghana was under some kind of Ashanti political overlordship. Serious tribal wars were reduced to a minimum, and although slave dealing was still current, it was not always accompanied by desperate slave raids and the destruction of populated areas. Many towns in Northern Ghana flourished on the basis of middleman trade between Ashanti and the Western Sudan.

The destruction of Ashanti after 1874 had serious consequences for many of the trading towns in Northern Ghana, particularly Salaga which had always been strictly a traders' town. In its prime Salaga reportedly received as many as 10,000 traders a day.[5] But in 1876, three years after Ashanti's trading relations with Northern Ghana were cut off, Salaga's permanent population was estimated to be 8,000, besides a much reduced floating population.[6] By the 1880s much of the town lay in ruins, although it still appeared large (fig. 41).[7]

Decrease in trade was not the only misfortune that befell towns in Northern Ghana. In the 1880s the armies of the slave raiders Samori and Babatu began their work of destruction. Bole, the important gold market in western Gonja, was partly destroyed by Samori; so was Wa, which before its destruction by Samori in the early 1880s apparently had a population of not less than 6,000 and was about three times the size of Gambaga. It

[1] Acquah, op. cit. p. 26. [2] See below, p. 332.

[3] Korle Bu Hospital, the first of its kind in the country, and Achimota School were opened in Accra in the 1920s.

[4] The exact extent of the population increase between 1891 and 1911 cannot be judged from the official census figures, which were unreliable, but the fact of population increase was not doubted.

[5] Gouldsbury Report (African no. 95). [6] Ibid.

[7] Lonsdale Report. The best description of Salaga ever written by a European in the nineteenth century was that by Captain Binger in his *Du Niger au Golfe de Guinée*, II, 91–115.

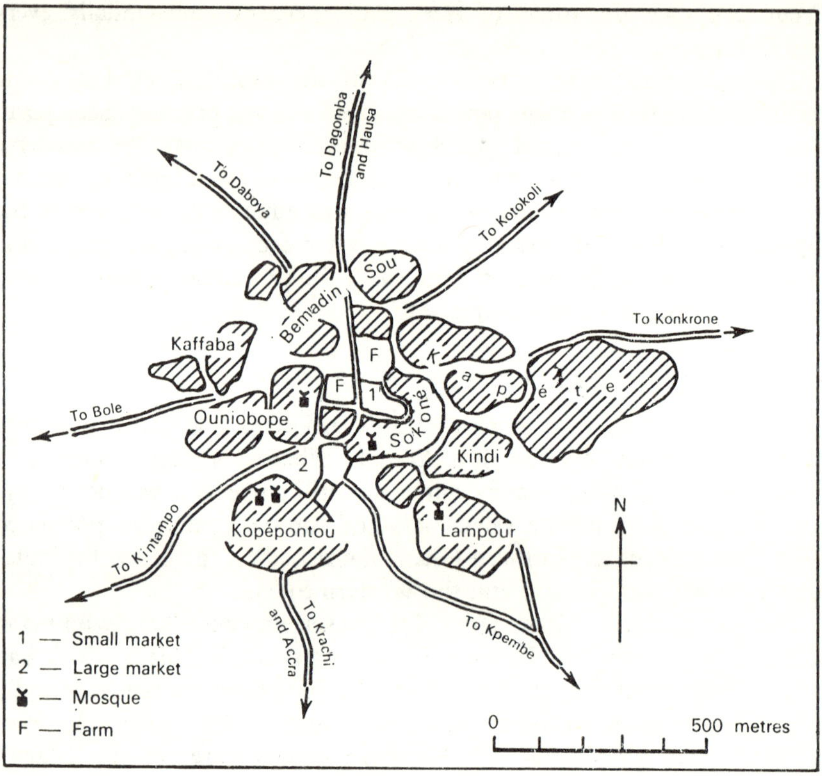


41 Salaga in 1888 (after Binger)

suffered a second raid in 1888–9 by Babatu who destroyed, among other things, its magnificent mosque. Many more towns were destroyed in Wa district, including Ducie, built on the rocky east slope of a hill commanding the Wa–Daboya trade route, and Busa which before its eclipse in 1897 was described as a large flourishing town. For some reason the town of Bulenge, which was not the strongest and largest in the district, was not raided.[1] But it was Grunsi area east of Wa which bore the brunt of Babatu's raids. Only a few of its larger settlements survived the holocaust, among which were Dasima, Tumu, and Walembele.[2] East of Grunsi the only town of consequence to suffer was Daboya, destroyed by Babatu in 1890.

[1] African (West) no. 549, Gold Coast: *Correspondence Relating to the Northern Territories* (Colonial Office, January–June 1898). Enclosure 1 in Paper no. 382 is 'Report on Wa' (June 1898) by Captain D. Mackworth.

[2] Ibid. Enclosure in Paper no. 358 is 'Report on the Country of Gurunsi' (May 1898) by Herbert J. C. Leland.

Beyond Daboya the country was safe from the slave raids. Gambaga for example continued to flourish as a major market where all Mossi caravans halted for several days. Its inhabitants numbered, according to estimates in 1888 and 1898, between 2,500 and 3,000, and this figure presumably covered both the permanent and the floating population.[1] Nalerigu was about the same size as Gambaga.[2]

The slave raids by Samori and Babatu had a dual effect. While they brought ruin to towns in the affected area, they also resulted in increased prosperity for some trading towns elsewhere which became noted for their markets for the slaves captured during the raids. Thus Bole, which escaped further harassment after its initial suffering in the hands of Samori, came to specialize in slave dealing to the neglect of its former function as a gold market.[3] Yariba grew into a fairly large town for the same reason.[4] Its population in 1898 was estimated to be about 2,000, consisting mainly of refugees from Grunsi and slave catchers from Dagomba.[5]

Another factor of significance to the growth of towns in Northern Ghana was the struggle, mainly between the British and the Germans, for political and economic domination in the region. The methods used by the Germans, especially, to further their aims were not always commendable. They undertook a number of punitive expeditions against chiefs who opposed their expansionist policy and burnt a few important towns, including Salaga in 1896, as an object lesson. The British were more subtle, and when the clouds of confusion disappeared they were seen to be in control of most of Northern Ghana while the Germans held only the narrow strip of land which became northern Togoland.

The consequences of the rise of British power for the growth of towns in Northern Ghana were complex and often contrary. Seminal to the growth of towns was the general atmosphere of peace and security established by the British after they put a stop to the slave raids and tribal wars. The opening of an administrative station, backed by a strong police force, always signalled the growth of a town. An example was Bawku whose growth into a market town did not begin until after a permanent administrative station was opened there in 1909.[6] Again, it was the British who saved Salaga. They occupied the town soon after 1896 and deliberately

[1] Binger, op. cit. II, 37, and African (West) no. 549, enclosure in Paper no. 366: 'Report on Mamprussi' (May 1898) by Captain D. Mackworth.

[2] 'Report on Mamprussi.'

[3] Binger, op. cit. II, 116.

[4] African (West) no. 529, *Further Correspondence Relative to Boundary Questions in the Bend of the Niger* (Colonial Office, January–August 1897). Enclosure in Paper no. 252 is a letter from Captain D. Stewart to the Colonial Secretary at Accra, dated Yariba, 27 March 1897.

[5] 'Report on Mamprussi.'

[6] *Annual Report on Northern Territories*, 1909.

revived it in order to draw trade away from the German markets in the Volta Region and eastern Brong Ahafo. In early 1898 the foundations of the mosques at Salaga were reconsecrated and the rebuilding of the town begun. The Hausa and other foreign merchants began to return, and by the end of the century Salaga was well on the way to regaining some of its former renown as a trading centre.[1] Also, the long-established tourist trade, conjured into being by the fame of the name of Salaga and catered for by the Gonja residents, was revived.

Tamale's growth since the beginning of the twentieth century provides yet another illustration of the effect of British rule on towns in Northern Ghana. Already, by the end of the nineteenth century, Tamale which began as a small shrine town had grown into a considerable settlement of some 1,500 compound houses.[2] Its growth was accelerated after the British transferred to it their administrative headquarters from Gambaga in 1907. With its further advantage of central location in a well-populated area, Tamale soon came to command the distributive trade in the whole of Northern Ghana. In order to give Tamale access to the Volta highway, a 27-mile cart road was opened from there to a site on the left bank of the Volta opposite Yapei, where a new town, Tamale Port, was laid out early in 1908. Within a year Tamale Port grew into a sizeable market town and supplanted Daboya as the terminus for river traffic from the coast.[3]

Contrary, nevertheless, to the continuing growth and expansion of the towns was the slowing down of trade and the general torpor that fell on Northern Ghana's economic life after the beginning of the twentieth century. Only those towns with important administrative functions continued to grow while the purely trading towns, like Salaga, deteriorated.

## TOWN IMPROVEMENT

A hindrance to physical expansion of numerous towns was the very manner in which they grew. All the towns, particularly those in Southern Ghana, needed replanning, for they consisted, as was the case over a hundred years earlier, of compact agglomerations of buildings separated by narrow, crooked and unpaved streets. The idea of redesigning the layout of some of the towns was first broached in the late 1840s and the first town to receive attention was Cape Coast, where a market place covering an acre and a half of ground was built in 1847. Around the market was planted a

[1] African (West) no. 549, enclosure in Paper no. 277.

[2] African (West) no. 549, enclosure in Paper no. 172 is 'Report on Gonja country' (January 1898) by C. H. Armitage.

[3] *Annual Reports on Northern Territories*, 1906–10.

large number of trees for ornamental purposes. The town streets were also repaired.[1] In 1850 market places similar to the one at Cape Coast were built at Christiansborg and Anomabu.[2]

The plans for urban renewal were allowed to lapse with Governor Winniett's resignation from office, until 1878 when a Towns Police and Public Health Ordinance was passed. According to the ordinance and its amended version in 1888, weeds were not to be allowed to grow anywhere in a town, and no building was permitted on any open space within the limits of a town to which the ordinance applied, except with the written permission of the governor. The keeping of livestock in certain areas within town boundaries was also prohibited. By the beginning of the twentieth century the ordinance applied to almost every town on the coast, including a few in the interior.

In 1892 a Towns Ordinance was introduced which empowered the Government to acquire land for public works; the ordinance also provided for the collection of public revenue and the undertaking of health and sanitary measures in the towns. Two years later the Government again passed a Towns Council Ordinance for the establishment of a municipal form of government in the larger towns. Non-municipal towns were still covered by the Towns Ordinance of 1892.

It was after the First World War that a large-scale and really determined effort was made to solve the problems of town planning and urban renewal. The machinery for dealing with the problems was established with the launching of the Ten Year Development Programme (1920–30) and the passing at about the same time of a Town Planning Ordinance. Attention was focused primarily on the major seaport towns of Accra, Cape Coast, Winneba, and Sekondi, and then on Kumasi, Nsawam, Koforidua, Dunkwa-on-the-Ofin, and Takoradi.[3] The growth of new towns on the Accra–Kumasi railway was also foreseen, and building sites and street patterns were laid out at every station that was considered likely to be important in the future and develop into a town. No building was permitted in the new townships without prior scrutiny of the plans; and periodic inspections were carried out to ensure that all the rules of building and settlement were complied with. Many mining towns were also rebuilt by the mining companies and provided with decent houses and public utilities.[4] Towns in Northern Ghana were entirely ignored.

[1] Despatches of 31 July and 26 October 1847 in ADM 1/449, and 5 December 1848 in ADM 1/450, NAG. [2] Despatch of 27 September 1850 in ADM 1/452, NAG.

[3] Sir Frederick G. Guggisberg, *The Gold Coast: A Review of the Events of 1920–26 and the Prospects of 1927–28* (Accra, 1927), pp. 120–30 and 290.

[4] Darko, 'The Effects of Modern Mining...', loc. cit.

# PART IV

# *On the eve of World War II*

# 12. Population and settlements

By the beginning of the Second World War nearly all the major elements of the human geography of Ghana up to the year of Independence had crystallized. It needed only the spread of swollen shoot disease of cocoa, which had been present for some time, to add the final touch to the agricultural landscape. For the rest, subsequent developments merely confirmed the establishment patterns.

According to the 1931 census the total population was about 3,160,000, of which only about 3,000 consisted of non-Africans. The total figure represented an increase of about 864,000 over that of the previous censal year, 1921.[1] Assuming an error of about 5 per cent underestimation in the 1921 figures, and an expected natural decennial increase of about 15 per cent, made possible through improved medical facilities and the cessation of tribal wars, there is still a surplus of about 287,000.[2] This is accounted for by immigration. The immigants were attracted by the better employment opportunities in the country, compared with those available in the neighbouring states where the pace of economic development was less rapid. The total population in 1921 and 1931 was distributed as follows:[3]

TABLE 4. *Population by administrative regions, 1921 and 1931*

| | 1921 | 1931 |
|---|---|---|
| Southern Ghana (excluding Volta Region) | 994,288 | 1,327,691 |
| Volta Region* | 264,780 | 369,200 |
| Ashanti–Brong Ahafo | 406,193 | 578,078 |
| Northern Ghana | 631,139 | 885,417 |
| Total | 2,296,400 | 3,160,386 |

* The figures for Volta Region are approximate. They were obtained by adding the figures for Keta-Ada and former Ho Districts

The population increases were, for several reasons, unevenly distributed (fig. 42).

[1] See Census Reports, 1921 and 1931. Also T. E. Hilton, *Ghana Population Atlas* (Thomas Nelson and Sons Ltd, 1960).

[2] A. W. Cardinall, *The Gold Coast, 1931* (Accra, 1931), pp. 146 and 147.

[3] The figures were supposed to err on the side of underestimation, but no attempt has been made to adjust them. The results would not be any more accurate than the original.

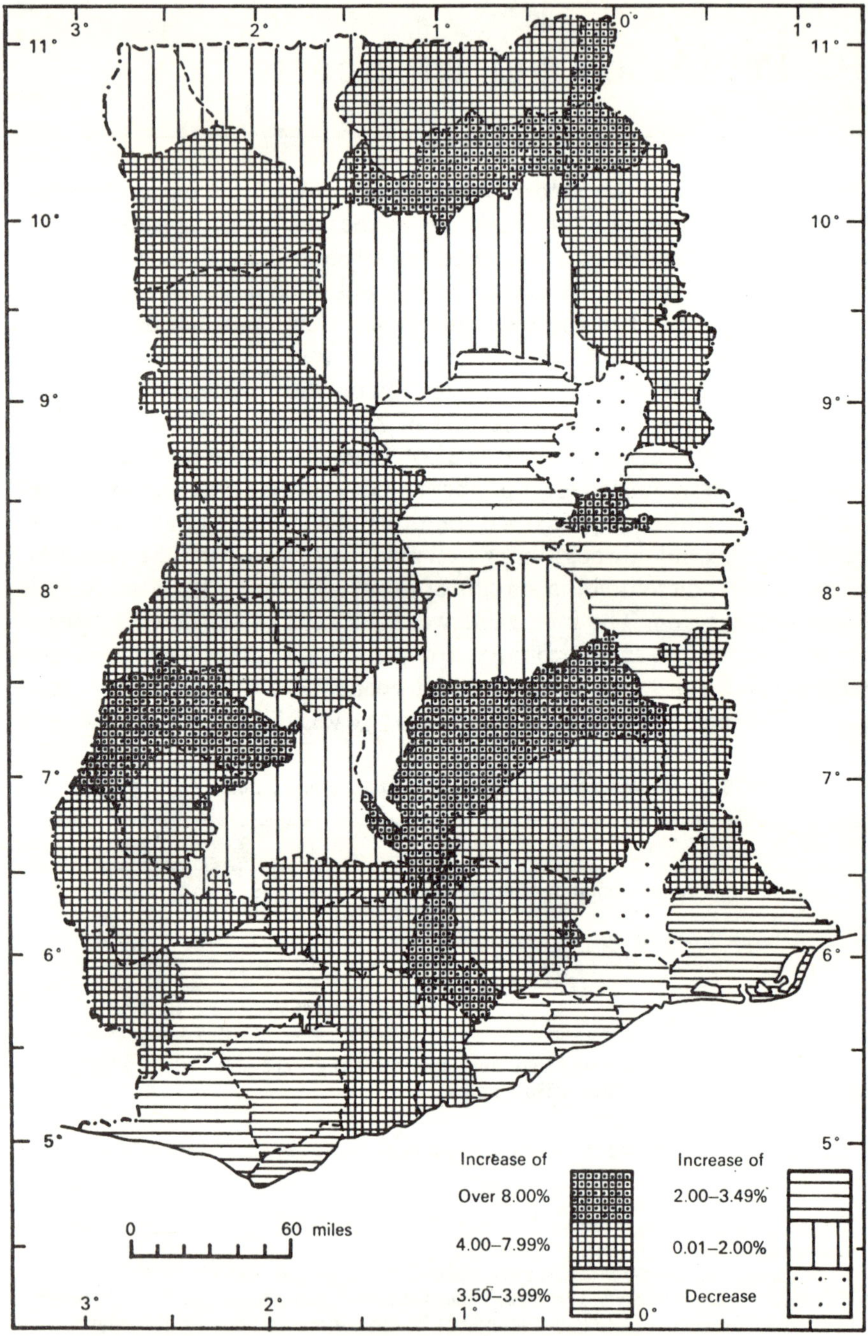


42 Average percentage increase or decrease in African population, 1921–31 (adapted from T. E. Hilton)

The distribution of the 1931 population, which was indeed fully revealed for the first time by the 1921 census, showed a threefold pattern. There was a well-populated Southern Ghana and Ashanti; a practically empty Middle Belt stretching east-southeastwards from about southern Wa to Krachi district, including the Afram Plains and parts of Brong Ahafo; and a generally more densely populated north (figs. 43*a* and *b*). The threefold pattern was a response to historical factors and was not in harmony with the contemporary political situation and the economic potentialities of the land. But within the zones of higher density the distribution of population often showed a closer adjustment to factors of physical and economic geography.

## POPULATION IN SOUTHERN GHANA

### Western Region

This Region was on the whole thinly populated compared with other forest areas in Southern Ghana. There appeared to be a direct connection between population density and the factors of accessibility and opportunities for economic development. But in the case of the western portions of Sefwi and Wasaw the extremely low population density was accounted for initially by tribal wars and the regular fights along the common boundary with the Ivory Coast in the 1880s, which drove the population from the area.[1] The opportunities for economic development in the borderlands, which had closer economic ties with the Ivory Coast than with the rest of the Region, diminished considerably when the links with the Ivory Coast were severed, following the closing of the international boundary. Elsewhere in the Western Region areas of very low population density were similarly characterized by poor transport facilities and inaccessibility from the main trade roads.

Sefwi and Aowin were among the few areas in the Western Region whose population figures in 1931 represented marked increases—61·7 per cent and 50 per cent respectively—over those of 1921. The increases were directly traceable to the improved road transport which accompanied the spread of cocoa in those areas, and the attraction for immigrants of the mining and timber industries. In the gold-mining district of Tarkwa, for example, the population density was 36 per square mile, over four times as much as the overall population density for Wasaw–Aowin. The percentage increase of population in Tarkwa district was 37, the third largest in Western Region. In these recipient areas males outnumbered females.

[1] Also, see above, p. 118. For a long time the Ashanti discouraged settlement in part of the area.

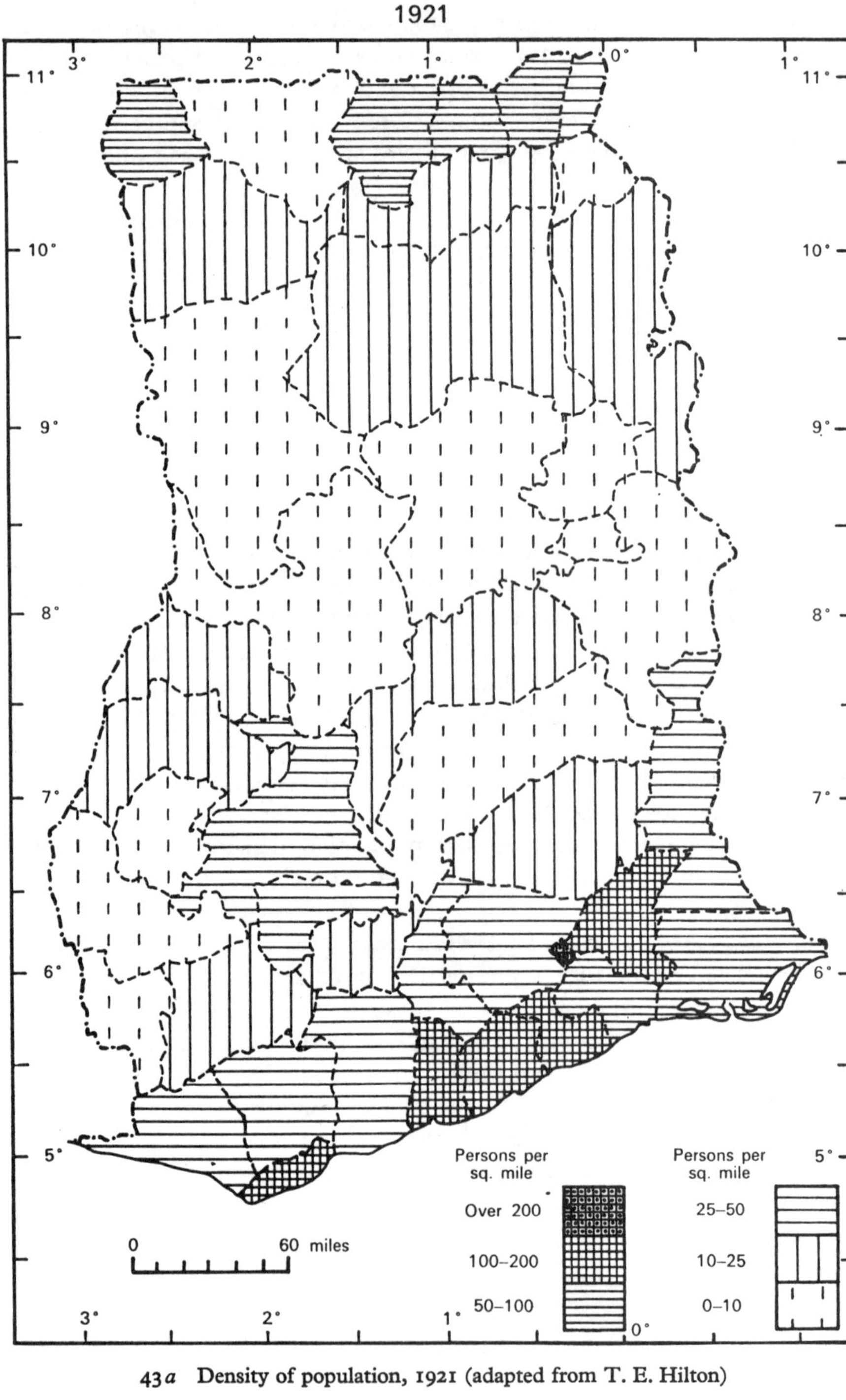


43*a* Density of population, 1921 (adapted from T. E. Hilton)

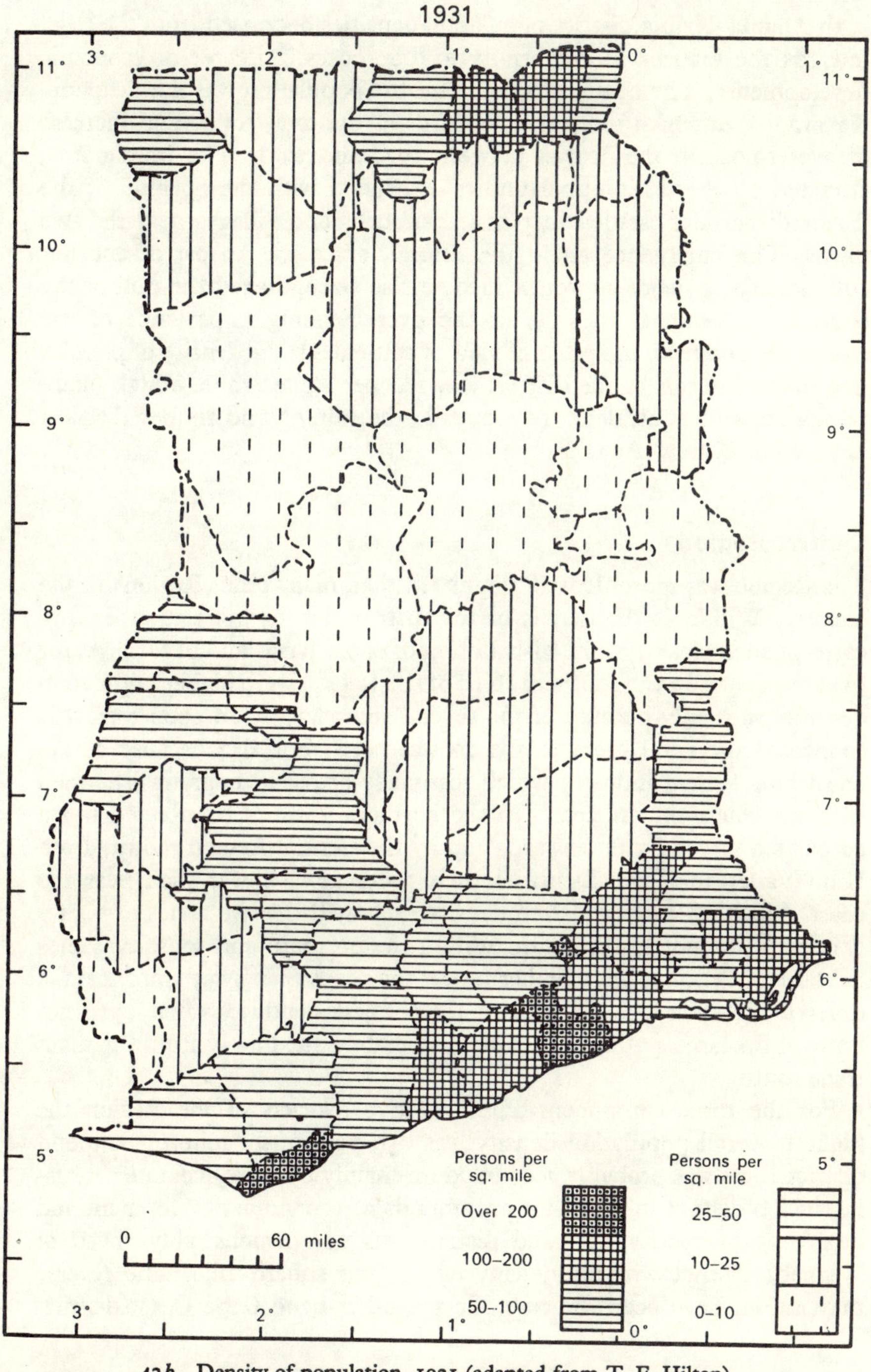


43*b* Density of population, 1931 (adapted from T. E. Hilton)



DHG

In Ahanta–Nzima district population densities decreased from the coast towards the interior in conformity to differences in degree of economic development. The centre of gravity for the population was the Sekondi–Takoradi area which received two-thirds of the total population increase of over 19,000 in the district between 1921 and 1931. The immigrants, attracted by the trade opportunities associated with the opening of the Takoradi harbour, settled in planned suburbs and villages near the two towns. The emergence along the littoral, since the 1920s, of coconut cultivation as a major source of income also strengthened the pull of the coast on settlement. In spite of the overwhelming importance of the coastal portion from the point of view of settlement, the density of population in the interior of the district was 144 per square mile, a high figure compared with equivalent areas outside the mining and timber districts in Sefwi or Wasaw–Aowin.

## Central Region

The Region was more densely populated than many other Regions in the country. Within it the details of the distribution of population density corresponded closely to the distribution of cocoa farms and of facilities for road transport. In the southern third of the Region were higher population densities, not only because of the several short lengths of good road that connected the rural areas to the coastal ports, but also because of the flourishing fishing industry which seasonally attracted migrant fishermen from elsewhere on the coast. In the northern third of the Region was a cocoa area served by fewer roads and by the Central Region railway from Huni Valley to Kade. Densities there were much lower than near the coast. A belt of low population density separated the two zones of higher density in the north and south. Within the northern and southern zones themselves densities were higher nearer the roads than away from them, a different situation from that during the previous centuries when it was not unusual for large settlements to be deliberately sited away from the main trade routes.

For the three component administrative districts of the Region the highest overall population density was 150 per square mile in Saltpond district. This was probably accounted for mainly by more accurate censusing in the district in 1931, for on grounds of economic development and degree of prosperity Saltpond district was not demonstrably ahead of Winneba district with its density of 140 per square mile. The reverse may indeed have been the case. On the other hand Cape Coast district, although it showed the highest percentage population increase in the Region, carried a lower overall population density because of the inclusion within its boundaries of large areas without cocoa. Characteristic of the major cocoa areas was the preponderance of the male population.

### Eastern Region

Eastern Region, a huge administrative unit comprising about one-third of the area of Southern Ghana, encloses within its boundaries several tribal groupings and variations in terrain and in history of economic development. One of the largest tribes is Akim, which may be conveniently divided into western Akim and eastern Akim or Akim Abuakwa. Western Akim's population in 1931 was nearly double that in 1921. In detail the distribution of the population demonstrated the strong pull of the Central Region railway and the road network linking up with it to serve the timber industries, the successful cocoa-growing areas, and the newly developing diamond-mining industry at Kokotenten.[1] The highest population densities were thus found in the Oda–Achiasi area which was also the traditional core of western Akim. In Akim Abuakwa the percentage population increase between 1921 and 1931 was 55, compared with 97 for western Akim, but the overall population density was higher in Akim Abuakwa. The reasons for the increase in Akim Abuakwa were the same as for that in western Akim.

North of Akim and reaching out into the parkland zone beyond the forest is Kwahu. It is a large unit that may be divided into northern Kwahu beginning from the northern edge of the Kwahu Plateau to the Afram Plains, central Kwahu consisting of the elevated Kwahu Plateau, and southern Kwahu at the southern foot of the Plateau and within the Closed Forest. Northern Kwahu was the most thinly populated part of the district and indeed had been, throughout the nineteenth century or before, part of the sparsely populated Middle Belt. Only those areas on the banks of the Afram or the Volta, or at the foot of the Plateau, carried higher densities of some 15 persons to the square mile. Central Kwahu, the traditional Kwahu, contained the largest settlements as it had done for over two centuries, and its population increased between 1921 and 1931 as a result of the expansion of cocoa farming on top of the Plateau. On the Plateau itself were spatial variations in population density introduced partly by the presence of uninhabited forest reserves. South of the Plateau is southern Kwahu strung along short stretches of the trunk road and the

[1] Cardinall, op. cit. p. 148.

railway between Accra and Kumasi. All the important settlements there were under twenty-five years old at the beginning of the Second World War.

Outside Kwahu and Akim, the rest of the Eastern Region consisted of the old administrative district of Accra, now Accra Region, Akwapim–New Juaben, Krobo, and Akwamu west of the Volta to which may be added, for the sake of convenience, Akwamu east of the Volta. Accra Region was dominated by the town of Accra which attracted immigrants from rural areas within and outside the Region. Away from the town of Accra, the rest of the population was concentrated at the coastal and the inland forested margins of that part of the waterless Accra Plains included within the Region. At the coast were fishing communities occupying a line of villages from about Labadi to about the Songaw lagoon, with the size of their population varying seasonally according to the migratory habits of the fishermen.

The tiny state of New Juaben with an area of about 52 square miles had in 1931 the largest population density for any administrative district in the country. This was explained by the large population in the Koforidua urban spread within which Asokori and Effiduase were included. The true rural population density was thus much lower, and was to be found mainly along the Accra–Kumasi road, where cocoa farming was the main occupation.

Rural population densities were also high in highland Akwapim. The increase in population in the district was only 8 per cent, the lowest in the whole of the Eastern Region. The main reason was that land became increasingly scarce in this cradle of cocoa cultivation after the 1920s. Besides, its attraction for cocoa cultivation was considerably diminished by the ravages of swollen shoot which had indeed begun to drive farmers, though not in large numbers, from the area to seek land elsewhere for cocoa cultivation.

Krobo and Akwamu on this side of the Volta suffered population emigration after 1921, not so much because of the ravages of swollen shoot in the cocoa areas as because cultivable land was scarce. But the emigration did not alter the long-established pattern of population distribution. The bulk of Krobo's population was, as it had been since the closing years of the nineteenth century, concentrated between Odumase and Trom (and less so between Odumase and Kpong) along the main trade route to Accra, and also along the road from this core area to Asesewa and Bisa in the north. Akwamu east of the Volta, consisting of a narrow riverine band of land, on the other hand experienced a population increase between 1921 and 1931.

To sum up: the pattern of population distribution in the whole of the Eastern Region showed two roughly parallel south-east–north-west prongs of high population and road network density. The eastern prong, broader based, extended as far as the western portion of Kwahu Plateau. Separating the two zones of high density were two similarly aligned zones of low density, accounted for by poor communications and the presence of forest reserves and, where the outermost low-density zone broadened out northward into the Afram Plains, also by a difficult and unrewarding physical environment.

### Volta Region

Like the Eastern Region, the Volta Region is an area of different tribes and varying physical environment, ranging from lowland stretches to mountain chains and from parkland or savanna vegetation in the north and south to forest in the middle. Krachi district in the north had the lowest overall population density, mainly because of the absence of good roads. The northern and central portions of Krachi district were virtually isolated and practically uninhabited, while the southernmost portion carried most of the district's population, concentrated along the motor road from Kete Krachi south to Ho. Water supply was also a serious problem in the district.

The 1931 census showed a large population decrease in the district since 1921, which was attributed to four factors:[1] the alteration of district boundaries to include Nanumba area, formerly in Krachi, in eastern Dagomba; the return of large numbers of slaves, originally settled in villages near Kete by Babatu, to their homes in Builsa and Navrongo districts; the opening in 1927 of the Krachi–Atebubu road which attracted farmers from Krachi district to settle along it; and constant emigration to the cocoa areas in the forest.

South of Krachi is Ho district consisting of the parallel north-east to south-west Togo–Atakora Ranges separated by parallel strike valleys. South of the Ranges is a lowland area terminating at the borders of Keta and Ada districts. The bulk of the population was, as in earlier times, concentrated on the tops of the mountains while the intermontane valleys and the lowlands carried a smaller population. Since the turn of the century there had been a movement of people from the hilltops to the low-lying areas, but not on a large enough scale to reverse the traditional distribution between mountain tops and valleys. A powerful incentive to descent from

[1] Cardinall, op. cit. pp. 153–4.

the mountain tops was the rapid spread of cocoa cultivation in Buem, between Hohoe and Krachi district. In the plains south of the Ranges lived a much smaller rural population which farmed the land, mainly for cassava and maize.

The 1931 population figure for Ho district denoted a significant intercensal increase. This was partly an exaggeration, for the 1921 figure was undoubtedly an understatement which resulted from incompetent and incomplete censusing by inexperienced enumerators. Yet the intercensal increase was also partly real: greater medical facilities and therefore lower death-rate, road developments in hitherto remote rural areas, and the further spread and intensification of cocoa farming which attracted immigrants to the district and stabilized the population.[1] Buem and the administrative subdivisions centred on the towns of Ho and Kpandu experienced the greatest increases in population, followed by the narrow stretch of land between Asikuma and Kpeve.

South of Ho district and fronting the sea was the remainder of the Volta Region—Keta and Ada districts. It is an area of lagoons and marshes backed inland by grassland plains, and for generations most of the population had been concentrated in the coastal sections of the district, around the lagoons and between them and the sea. The coastal section of Keta district carried higher densities, especially on the sand bar between the lagoon and the sea, in spite of the constant threat to property and life by the advancing sea. Fishermen formed the bulk of the population, and their numbers, as with other fishing communities along the coast, fluctuated owing to seasonal emigration. Behind the sand bar up to the Denu–Sogakofe road, densities were also high, but north of the road densities fell except in the oil-palm area of Dzodze and in the Todzie valley. The interior land, with poor communications, was devoted to livestock raising and extensive cultivation. Similarly in Ada district densities decreased from the coast inland. Sited on the borders of the Volta, several miles inland from the coast, were small fishing and agricultural villages, but they were not numerous enough to make the narrow riverine area one of high population density.

## Ashanti–Brong Ahafo

The administrative Regions of Ashanti and Brong Ahafo originally existed as a single unit referred to as Ashanti. About one-third of their combined area lies within the Closed Forest; the remainder is covered by parkland. Most of Brong Ahafo, which wraps round Ashanti in the north separating

[1] Cardinall, op. cit. p. 153.

it from Northern Ghana, is within the parkland zone, while about one-half of Ashanti is forest land.

Each of the two contrasting types of physical environment, forest and parkland, supported varying concentrations of population whose distribution was originally influenced by historical and political factors as well as the factor of trade opportunities, and not so much by the agricultural potential of the soil or the economic value of the vegetation cover. Formerly in the parkland of western Brong Ahafo the Ligbi, engaged in trade, lived in large prosperous settlements between the Tain River and the Ivory Coast boundary.[1] Yet by the 1930s this area had lost most of its population. The reason was the decay of the entrepôt trade of western Brong Ahafo, mainly as a result of improved communication across central Brong Ahafo linking Northern Ghana with Kumasi. This made it necessary to rely more heavily, for a basis of wealth, on direct exploitation of the parkland environment. But the utility value of this environment was comparatively lessened through the rise of cocoa cultivation which heightened the attractiveness for settlement of the neighbouring forest environment. Much of parkland Brong Ahafo and Ashanti was consequently part of the depopulated Middle Belt by the 1930s.

It was some of the forest areas of Brong Ahafo and Ashanti which showed the highest population concentrations. Between 1921 and 1931 Ahafo district's population increased by 70 per cent and Sunyani district's by 82 per cent. Although the increase in both areas was in part due to more accurate and more complete censusing, much of it was largely the result of the establishment of cocoa cultivation in the Pamu–Goaso–Sunyani triangle, and the opening of the motor road from Kumasi through Sunyani to Diabakrom on the Ivory Coast border, and through Tepa to Goaso from where branch roads reached Kukuom and Mim. Outside the new cocoa areas of Ahafo and Sunyani districts population increases, wherever they occurred, were not so high.

Increases in the rural population of central Ashanti, which equates with the old Kumasi district less Ahafo in the west, were fairly small after 1921. Within central Ashanti the rural population was clustered in the middle, along the main motor roads that centred on Kumasi; it also clustered, but to a smaller extent, around the gold-mining town of Konongo. A similar distribution pattern held for southern Ashanti, consisting of Bekwai and Obuasi districts, where the major towns of Bekwai and Obuasi, occupying central and nodal positions, attracted population. Again, as in central Ashanti and indeed in northern Ashanti, the population increase after 1921

[1] Binger, *Du Niger au Golfe de Guinée*, II, 145–6.

was small, although it was greater in Obuasi district on account of the flourishing gold-mining industry. The only area in Ashanti which had a spectacular population increase was Ashanti–Akim where the cocoa farms attracted immigrants from other parts of Ashanti.

## POPULATION IN NORTHERN GHANA

The overall pattern of population distribution in Northern Ghana, as indicated earlier, consisted of part of the empty Middle Belt in the south, succeeded northwards by increasingly more heavily populated country, and culminating in the dense agglomerations in the north-western and north-eastern corners of Upper Region. Between the two agglomerations was the relatively sparsely populated region of Tumu and of Grunsi.

This pattern correlated with differences in environmental quality.[1] The Middle Belt is a difficult terrain, soggy and impossible to cultivate in the rainy season except in elevated areas which are themselves liable to serious water shortage in the dry season. By contrast the heavily populated area of north Mamprusi is closely intersected with numerous large rivers and is well watered even in the dry season. But the correlating facts of physical geography are not basic explanations, except for the detailed etching of some of the distribution patterns within the two generalized areas of high population density. The gross pattern of population distribution is rather explained primarily by the bad cultural practices which led to soil erosion and deterioration of the environmental conditions, and by such historical factors as political stability and military strength of north Mamprusi and Wa–Lawra areas, which enabled them to escape the worst effects of wars and slave raids in past centuries. Those areas became the goal of refugees from neighbouring, less politically stable areas.

Immigration mainly accounted for the increase in population after 1921. The north-eastern and north-western areas received, from Upper Volta, northern Togo, Mali, and the Ivory Coast, significant numbers of immigrants who were seeking land for cultivation or were desirous of escaping the stringent political and administrative (tax) systems in their respective countries. In the Upper Region over 50 per cent of the immigrants settled in north Mamprusi. Other areas of notable population increases were western Gonja and eastern Dagomba: the two areas received, respectively, Lobi and Konkomba immigrants.[2]

While Northern Ghana was receiving immigrants, it was also losing a small percentage of its population through emigration to Ashanti and

[1] Cardinall, *The Gold Coast*, p. 157.

[2] Ibid. pp. 151–2.

Southern Ghana. There were several causes for this, important among which were soil erosion and exhaustion through overcultivation,[1] diseases,[2] and better employment opportunities in Ashanti and Southern Ghana. Emigration caused by soil erosion and the attraction of the cocoa farms and the gold mines in Ashanti and Southern Ghana was not new.

The most dreaded disease was river blindness, which in the heavily populated area of north Mamprusi, for example, rendered the banks of the rivers uninhabitable and effectively restricted the area of land safe for settlement and cultivation to the inextensive interfluves. But the methods of cultivation in use were not such as would support a vastly increased population density without causing serious soil erosion. Moreover, as the heavily cultivated areas receded from the banks of the large rivers, so did the problem of securing adequate water supply for dry season irrigation become intensified. In Northern Ghana as a whole, the area with the heaviest infestation of river blindness was, and still is, the Sissili valley.

Two other major 'killer' diseases that at one time or another caused depopulation of certain areas were sleeping sickness and cerebrospinal meningitis. Sleeping sickness spread quickly throughout extensive areas in Northern Ghana after the beginning of the First World War. The infection was carried by immigrants from epidemic areas generally outside the country and epidemics of the disease broke out on several occasions between the two World Wars, particularly in Lawra, Tumu, and Wa districts, and in western Gonja in the vicinity of the Black Volta.[3]

Although diseases like river blindness and sleeping sickness may be said to have caused depopulation in parts of Northern Ghana, they, strictly speaking, were able in many instances to extend their repelling presence only after those areas had been ravaged by wars. The surviving population was usually not large enough to occupy the land effectively and, as part of the normal process of living, destroy those environmental conditions, such as extensive overgrown bush, under which the disease vectors survive. Thus it would seem that the Sissili valley became heavily infested with river blindness mainly after the slave raids of the late nineteenth century which seriously depopulated the area. Similarly, the ease with which the

[1] This problem was particularly serious in the heavily populated areas. See below, p. 313.

[2] Hilton, op. cit. p. 28. Also B. B. Waddy, *Onchocerciasis and Blindness in the Northern Territories*, 1951 (in typescript).

[3] The vigorous control measures undertaken since the beginning of the Second World War practically eliminated the disease from Lawra, Tumu, and Wa districts. The epidemic that broke out in the south-western part of Wa District in 1946 and spread into western Gonja was the last of its kind. See Department of Tsetse Control, *Annual Reports*, 1949, 1951, 1952. Nevertheless the elimination of the tsetse fly from these areas only partly stayed the flood of emigration.

simulium fly (the vector of river blindness) invaded the environs of the Red Volta in north Mamprusi may be explained with reference to a primary partial desertion of the area as a result of soil exhaustion and erosion.

## RURAL SETTLEMENTS

From the point of view of siting of rural settlements, the factor of security or defence was no longer important, although the sites of many settlements still reflected the earlier unsettled times. The tendency nevertheless was for villages to be re-sited, where necessary, in order to ensure better and easier conditions of living. Consequently rural settlements appeared more frequently in better watered or more easily cultivated areas. Accessibility also became a major location factor since hostile armies no longer infested the commercial highways. Where a rural settlement was originally sited in the heart of the forest away from roads, it either moved completely or sent to the roadside an offshoot, bearing the name of the parent settlement but with the epithet 'New'.

The fundamental differentiation between nucleated settlements in the forest of Southern Ghana and Ashanti–Brong Ahafo and isolated homesteads in much of Northern Ghana still persisted. The tendency towards nucleation was nevertheless greater than before in the densely populated sections of Northern Ghana, while in the Closed Forest, particularly in the major cocoa areas, the earlier tendency for some of the large nucleated settlements to undergo partial break-up continued. Distance from the farms, which made it inconvenient to return home at the end of each day, the desire of young members of families to be independent, and other related factors led to the formation of secondary nucleated villages around the parent villages.[1] In the broad zone of transition between the Closed Forest and the savanna of Northern Ghana was a mixture of nucleated and dispersed settlements (fig. 44).

Since the beginning of the eighteenth century there were no major additions to the variety of rural house types, but there were a few changes in their distribution (figs. 44 and 45). Rural settlements in the Closed Forest and in the Akan areas on the coast still consisted of rectangular households made up of buildings of the Guinea forest type or, in the coastal villages between Anomabu and Cape Coast, of the flat-roofed variety of the Guinea forest type.[2] This variety was also to be seen in Buem where it had been

[1] W. H. Beckett, *Akokoaso* (London, 1944) and *Koransang* (London, 1945). These were examples of secondary nucleation.

[2] See above, p. 61.

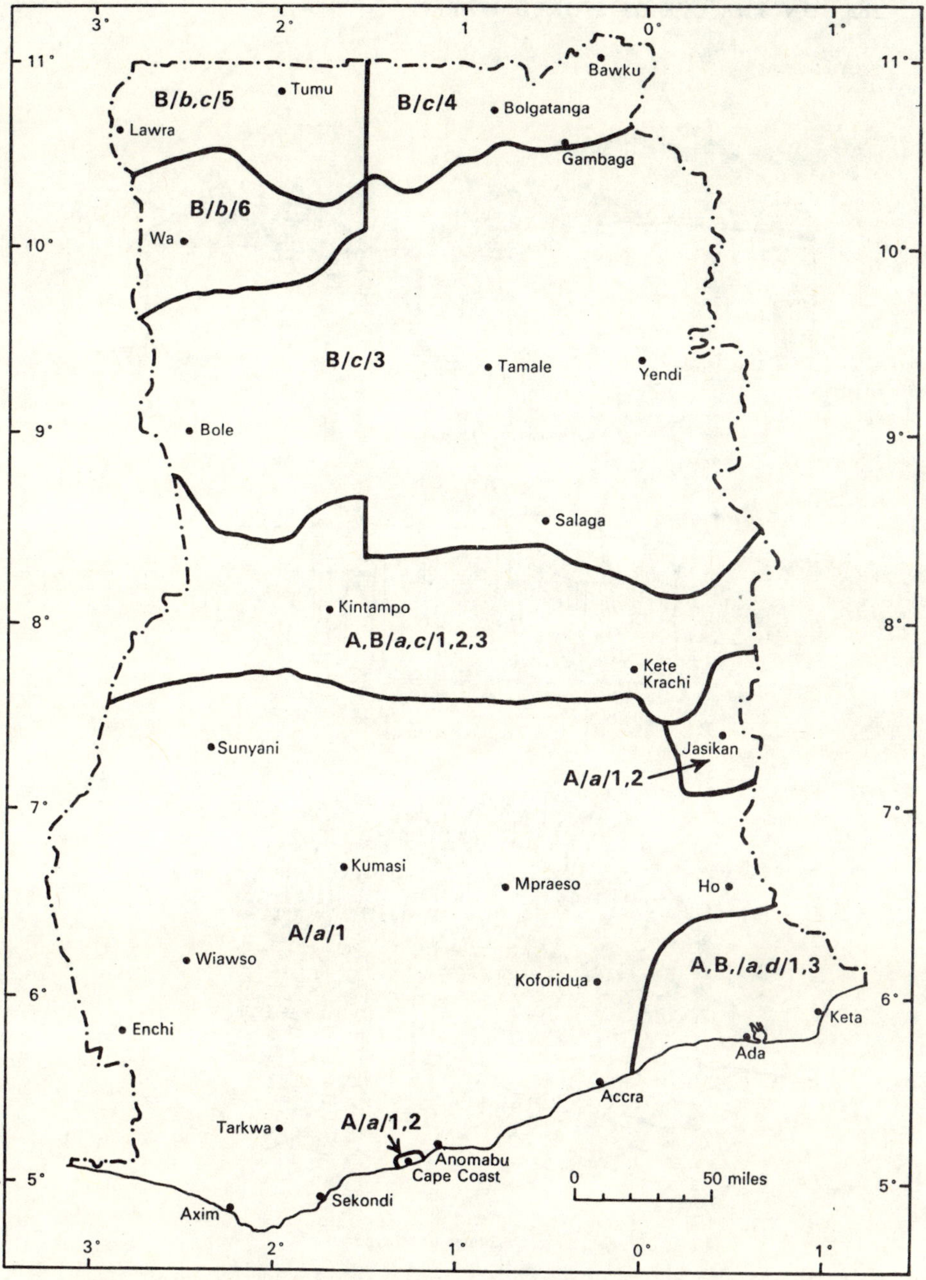


44 Rural settlements and house types, 1939. Rural Settlement types: A nucleated, B dispersed. Rural household types: *a* rectangular compound household, *b* fortress-like rectangular compound household, *c* fortress-like circular compound household, *d* circular compound household. Rural house types: 1 Guinea forest house type (G.F.H.T.), 2 flat-roofed variety of G.F.H.T., 3 round hut with conical roof, 4 round hut with flat roof, 5 much bigger and better version of 4, 6 Moroccan house type. *N.B.* There also were, and still are, round huts with conical roofs in north Mamprusi.

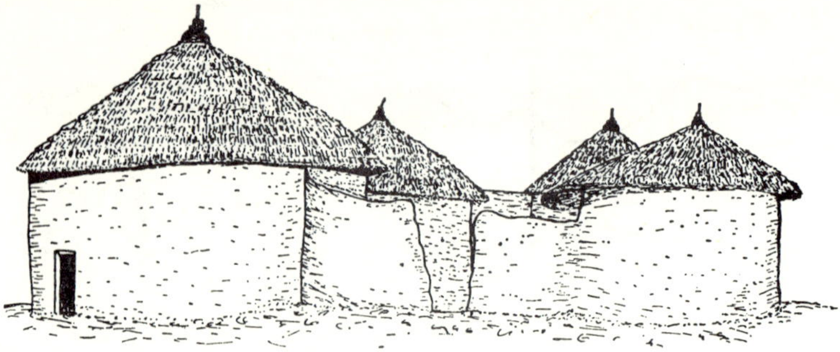

A Kusase compound household

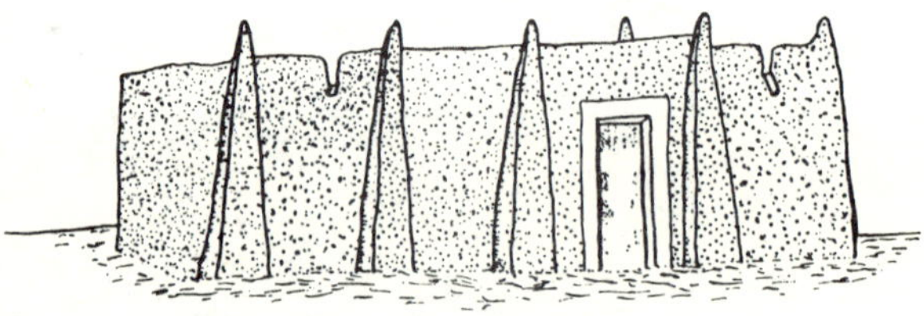

Morocco or Wa type

Guinea forest type

45 Rural house types

Lobi type or flat-roofed variety of Guinea forest type

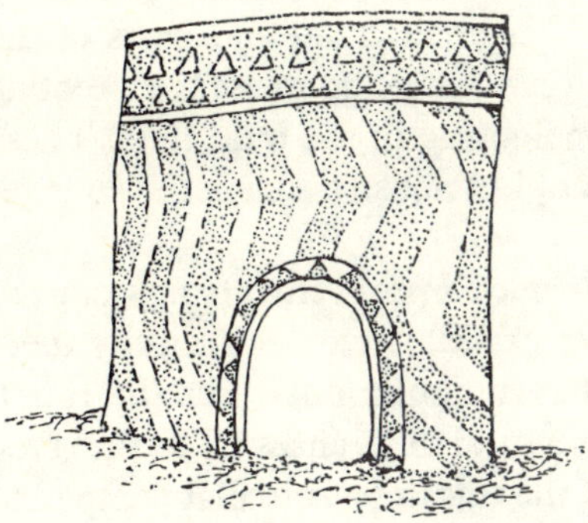

Talense type

Kusase type

Southeast coastal plains type

45 Rural house types

adopted, from perhaps the time of William Bosman, because of the threat of fire which was an occupational hazard associated with the ironworking industry.[1]

In the grasslands of the south-east coastal plains the round huts had given way to the Guinea forest house type perhaps through progressive assimilation of the inhabitants of the grassland plains into the spatially more important culture complex of the neighbouring Closed Forest. The change-over may have been complete by the end of the nineteenth century. But there were a few fishing and farming settlements in the south-east coastal plains where round huts, built by seasonal immigrants for temporary shelter, still lingered.

In many rural areas in Southern Ghana and Ashanti–Brong Ahafo, increasing affluence through farming or trade made it possible to improve the houses, as was done earlier at the turn of the century with urban houses. In Southern Ghana, but less so in the Western Region and parts of the Volta Region, galvanized iron sheets were replacing thatch as roofing material, and cement was being used for flooring in the mud huts. These changes were just as widespread in Ashanti, but not so much in the younger cocoa areas of western Brong Ahafo.[2]

Rural Northern Ghana, untouched by such improvements as occurred in the south, showed four principal types of architecture.[3] Basically there was the distinction between round and rectangular huts, but the round huts themselves showed significant architectural differences.[4] The first type of architecture (Kusase type) was seen in the traditional circular compound house consisting of cone-cylinder mud huts, thatched, with hard beaten floors, no windows, and small entrances with weather protection. This type was common in the greater part of eastern and western Gonja and Dagomba, in north Mamprusi, and in the southern areas of Tumu district. A distinctive variety consisted of round huts with flat roofs (Talense type), and entrance to a compound house in this case was usually by means of an unshaped branch of a tree notched to serve as a ladder. The type was confined to Frafra and Kusase districts of north Mamprusi. The third type was an elaborated version of the second type. The flat-roofed huts, sometimes double-storeyed, had a tendency towards the angular. They were grouped into massive compounds which had the appearance of fortresses

[1] M. Darkoh, 'An Historical Geography of the Ho–Kpandu–Buem Area of the Volta Region of Ghana: 1884–1956' (Unpublished M.A. thesis, University of Ghana, 1966), pp. 20–1.
[2] Cardinall, op. cit. pp. 204–8.
[3] Ibid. pp. 202–3. The house types have not changed since Cardinall wrote in 1931.
[4] It is not certain if these differences existed in ancient times.

and each of which could accommodate as many as 300 persons besides large numbers of cattle, sheep, and goats. Areas in which this architectural type was found were Lawra district and the Dagarti portions of Wa district. In contrast to the three types of architecture described was the flat-roofed Moroccan house type found mainly in Wa district.

In not more than three small villages in the middle of Gonja was a peculiar house type, of uncertain antiquity, not found anywhere else in Northern Ghana. It was a fairly large square flat-roofed house made of dried mud and between three and five storeys high. There was only one small door, about 5 feet high and 3 feet broad, on the ground floor. The walls, the ceiling, and the roof were very thick, with windows and roof vents pierced in the walls and the roof. This house was clearly built with considerations of defence in view.[1]

Another house type of restricted spatial distribution in Northern Ghana was the Guinea forest house type built by the Nafana, the Degha, and by later Lobi or Ligbi immigrants mainly in that part of Gonja west of the White Volta. This architectural form, already widespread in the area during the second half of the nineteenth century,[2] was probably originally introduced by Ashanti or Brong settlers.

Finally, between the Closed Forest with its Guinea forest house type and the southern boundary of the area characterized by the Northern Ghana house types was the broad zone of transition in which all the major rural house types in the country were present. This zone of transition, situated across the middle of Ghana, has persisted with varying widths and under different names as a feature of all distribution maps of Ghana, whether concerned with human or physical geography.

## TOWNS

The accelerated pace of economic development since the beginning of the century had been accompanied by an increase in the rate of urbanization. What was remarkable was not so much the rate of growth of individual towns as the conversion of a large number of rural settlements into small towns. If the towns were grouped according to population sizes of 2,000 to 3,000, 3,000 to 5,000, 5,000 to 10,000, and over 10,000, there were, according to the 1931 census, 239 in the first category, 110 in the second, 19 in the third, and 7 in the last category. The distribution of the towns, like that of

[1] R. B. Nunoo, Director of the Ghana National Museum, has expressed the opinion, in a personal communication, that the introduction of this house type post-dates the early eighteenth century.

[2] Binger, *Du Niger au Golfe de Guinée*, II, 138.

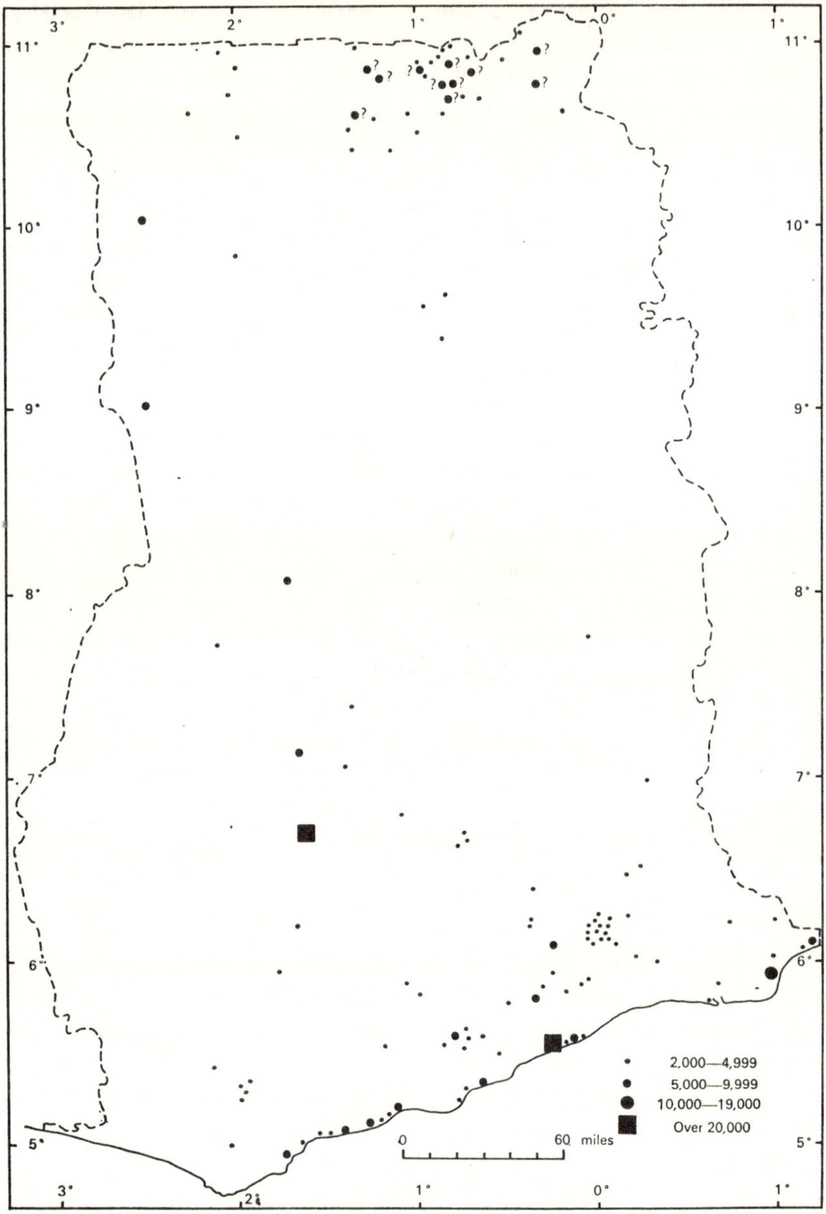


46*a* Distribution of towns in 1921

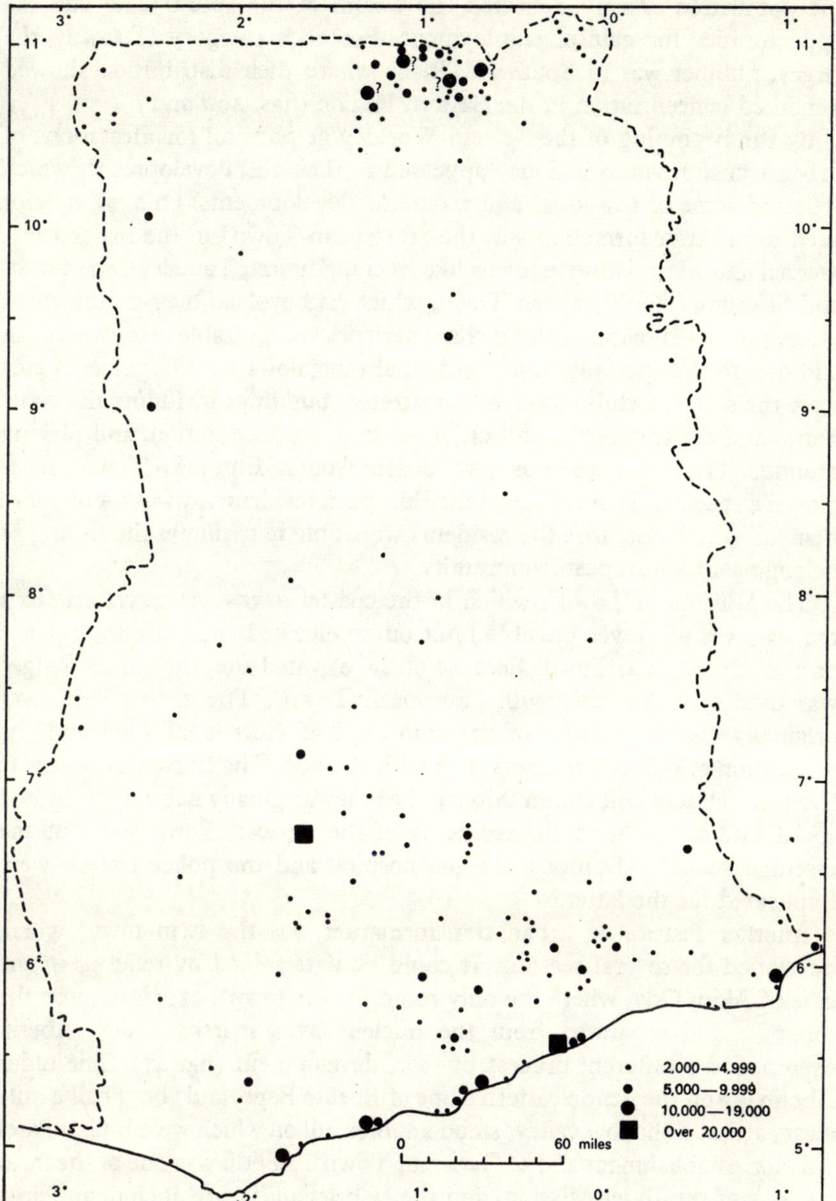


*46b* Distribution of towns in 1931

the population density, reflected the wealth of the countryside and the opportunities for gainful employment. For each category of towns, the largest number was in Southern Ghana where their distribution showed a marked concentration in the Eastern Region (figs. 46*a* and *b*).

By the beginning of the Second World War physical manifestations of urban transformation had also appeared in their full development, which reflected some of the social and economic developments. One example of such urban transformation was the 'European Town' in the major commercial and administrative towns like Accra, Kumasi, Tamale, Cape Coast, and Sekondi. The European Town, which had evolved over a number of years, possessed distinguishing characteristics recognizable everywhere. In addition to the specially built residential bungalows with large verandahs were the shops, a club house, administrative buildings including the court house and the treasury, a church, a hospital, a police station, and playing grounds. The club house was never absent from a 'European Town', for it played a special role in the life of the European residents. It was there, more than anywhere else, that the residents were able to maintain the feeling of belonging to a European community.

The 'European Town', which in the coastal towns was never far from the sea, was wherever possible built on an elevated site close to, but not part of, the African Town. Because of the elevated site, the name 'Ridge' was used synonymously with 'European Town'. The elevated site was originally chosen because of the command of view it afforded and the association of reduced temperatures with altitude. The European residents lived as a closely knit community, and as they originally had rather limited social intercourse with the residents of the African Town some of the essential social institutions like the hospital and the police station were duplicated for the latter.[1]

Another feature of urban transformation was the twin town, which developed for several reasons. It could be determined by relief as in the case of Akim Oda, where the only room for the town's expansion was the top of a hill separated from the nucleus by a marshy valley. Abetifi exemplified a different process of twin development (fig. 47). The older Abetifi lay on the gentle eastern slope of Boente Bepo, and about half a mile away, across a shallow valley, stood another hill on which were built a Basel Mission establishment and a 'Christian Town'. Abetifi was one of the head stations of the Basel Mission, and the 'Christian Town' included a large

[1] The foundations for many 'European Towns' on the coast had been laid by the end of the first decade of the twentieth century. An illuminating account of life in a 'European Town' at that time is given in D. M. and F. G. Guggisberg, *We Two in West Africa*, pp. 54–77.

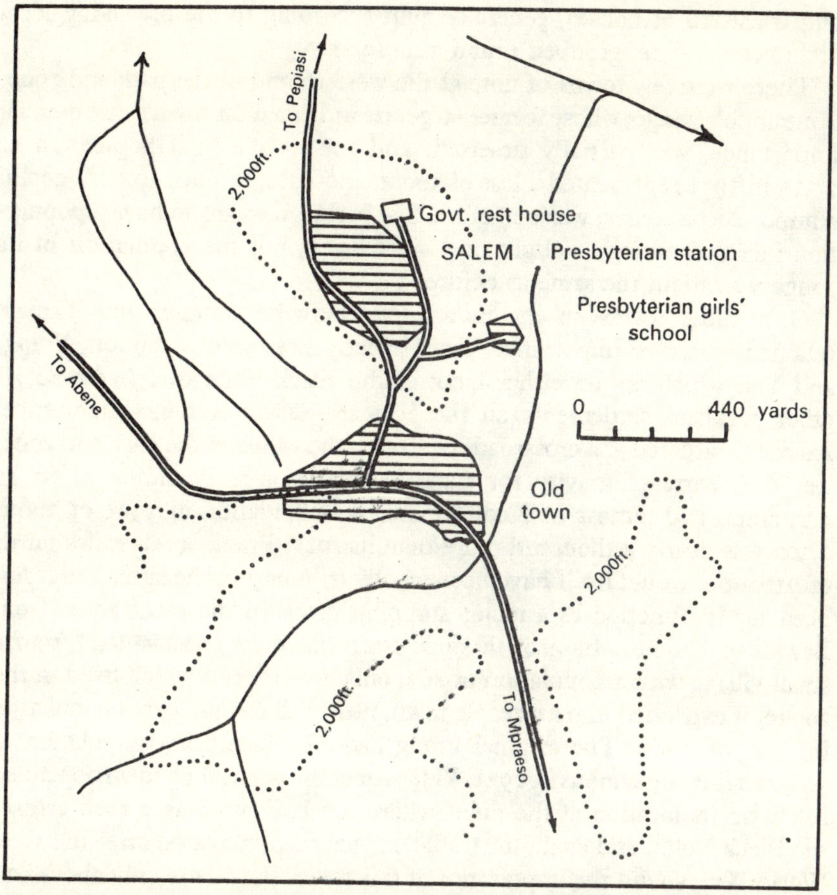


47 Abetifi: example of a twin town

double-storeyed bungalow for the missionaries, school houses for children and adults, a seminary for training Christian teachers and catechists, workshops for teaching carpentry and other skills, a fair-sized stone church, and a large number of houses occupied by the Christian converts. In civil matters the 'Christian Town' was administered together with the original Abetifi by the local chief.

There was also the long-established twin town consisting of an original nucleus and a zongo inhabited chiefly by Hausa-speaking merchants. All the important trading towns had their zongos, and that at Kumasi was especially large. Each zongo was at a little distance from the original town and consisted of houses, generally built according to the prevailing local architectural style, grouped round a mosque.

There were few towns of note at the western end of the parkland zone. Kintampo's zongo, whose former large size indicated the town's commercial importance, was partially deserted, and the town's total population of 2,315 in 1931 represented a loss of about 4,800 people since 1921. Wenchi, a minor cocoa centre, was one of the few parkland towns to have a population increase, though a slight one, since 1921; but the population of its zongo was about the same as before.

Only those towns on the motor road between Kumasi and Tamale retained whatever importance they formerly possessed. Atebubu, Prang, and Yeji which lay on either bank of the Black Volta overshadowed all other parkland settlements on the Kumasi–Salaga road in importance. Atebubu, situated at a crossroads central to the whole of the parkland zone, was the centre of gravity for trade in a large area extending as far as Kintampo and almost to Kete Krachi. Its population in 1931 of about 2,300 was nearly a thousand more than in 1921. Prang, a few miles north of Atebubu, would itself have been wholly tributary to the latter had it not been for its function as a major stopping place on the cattle route from Bawku to Kumasi. Its growth since 1921 was most spectacular. From a small village with a population of 462, only a quarter of which lived in the zongo, it expanded into a sizeable town, nearly all zongo, with a population in 1931 of 2,580. The original Prang had an insignificant population of 346, roughly the same as in 1921. Yeji's function as a trading town depended solely on its location at the point where the Kumasi–Salaga road crosses the Black Volta, and as motor traffic on this road increased after the First World War, so did the importance of this town. But it was only about half the size of Prang or Atebubu.

Kete Krachi, with a population of nearly 3,000, held on to some of its former importance, supported by its location at a major crossroads and by its function as a collecting centre for a large farming region. It was also an administrative centre and the principal town in the Volta Region north of Buem.

Towns in the forest were larger and more numerous than elsewhere in the country. Few of them experienced any significant drops in population after 1921, and they were towns which, for several reasons, were by-passed by the mainstream of economic activity. For similar reasons there were towns which were growing much more slowly than others. Their sizes depended almost entirely on their involvement in mining or in commerce.

Of the mining towns the largest were Obuasi and Aboso, with populations of 7,598 and 6,581 respectively. The remaining towns were much smaller: Tarkwa for example was about half the size of Aboso. The size of a mining town was explained not only by the extent of mining operations, as in the case of Aboso, but also by the range and importance of functions besides that of mining. Obuasi's twin props were gold mining and its function as a cocoa-buying centre, while Tarkwa's only support was its gold-mining industry. The comparatively new mining town of Bibiani, located in a relatively unimportant cocoa area, was also small. So was the new diamond-mining town of Kade, while its neighbour Oda, which was the centre of a cocoa-farming district, was much larger, with a population of about 6,000.

The largest towns were those associated with the cocoa industry. Wherever the crop flourished, towns received an inflow of merchants and others engaged in economic activities peripheral but vital to the continuing success of cocoa cultivation. In the forest of western Brong Ahafo the towns of Sunyani and Pamu, located in a newly developing cocoa area, were among the few which exhibited signs of active expansion. Sunyani's population was over 3,000, about double what it was a decade earlier, while Pamu's population of over 2,000 was about forty times as much as in 1921.

In the forest of Ashanti, again the largest towns were those located in a rich cocoa-growing countryside. The link between large-scale cocoa cultivation and the size of towns serving the cocoa area is illustrated by the case of Kumasi. Always the premier commercial town of Ashanti, Kumasi's function rested on the close ties that existed between the town and a prosperous countryside. The decade between 1921 and 1931 was one of maximization of cocoa production around Kumasi, and the town's population leaped from 26,694 to 35,829. The interactions in commerce thus formed between Kumasi and the countryside, and among individual establishments in the town engaged in various phases of production and trade, continued to generate fresh supplies of energy which propelled the town in the direction of greater commercial importance. This was so in spite of decreases in cocoa production through swollen shoot disease in the feeder countryside. Kumasi, with its nascent suburbs of Aboabo, New Amakom, and New Tafo, was at the beginning of the Second World War the second largest town in the country (fig. 48).

Kumasi's expansion had been rapid but not orderly, and therefore posed serious planning problems many of which were successfully solved. To relieve the high degree of congestion in some parts of the town, including the area on either side of the railway track and close to the railway station, new settlement sites were developed. The whole replanning programme

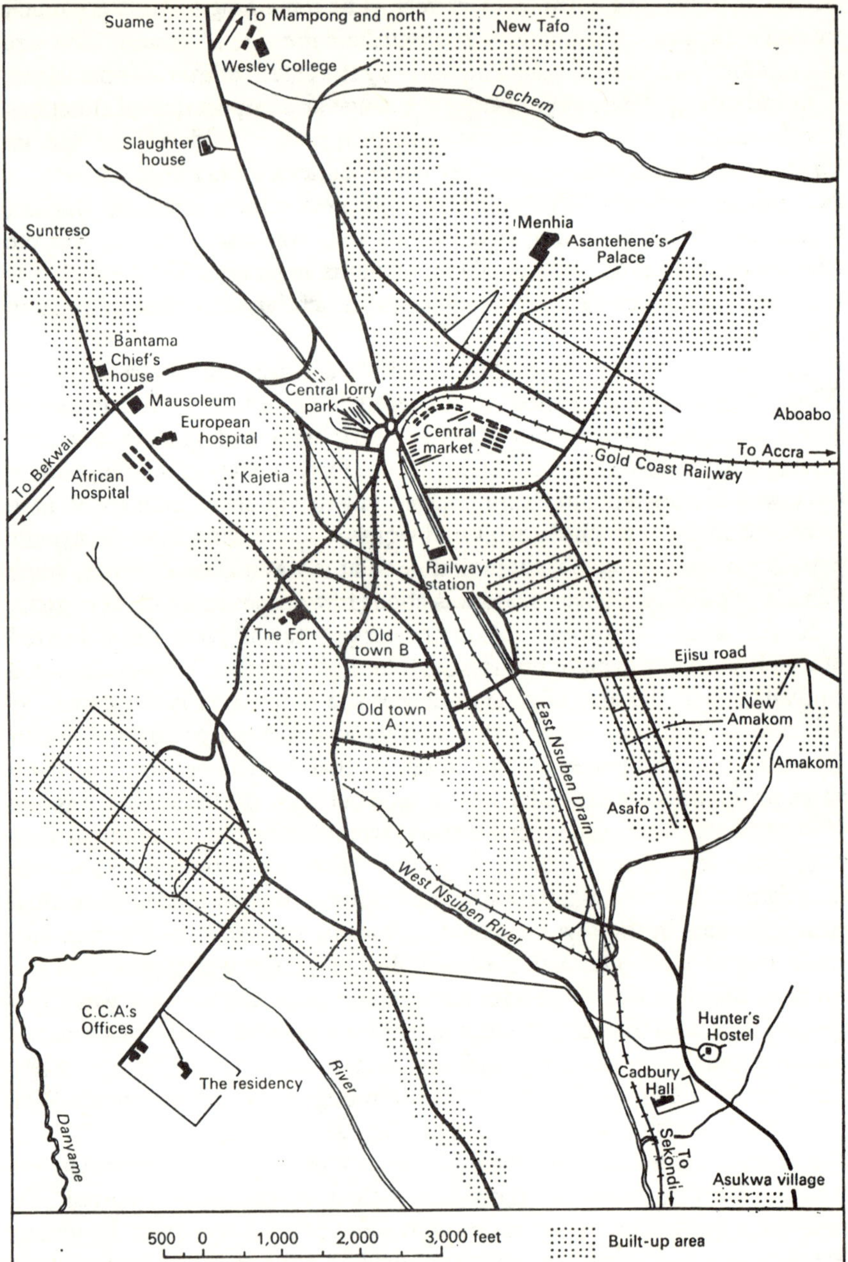


48 Kumasi, 1939

was based on a carefully prepared drainage scheme. The East Nsuben main outfall drain was constructed; then followed the reclamation of the swamps at Kejetia and the building there of a market capable of accommodating about 900 traders. The Ejisu road swamp was also drained, and the reclaimed land developed as a neighbourhood area with private houses, Government bungalows and other public utilities. The success of the planning scheme earned Kumasi the distinction of being called a 'garden city'.[1]

Outside the forest of Ashanti, the size and importance of towns in cocoa areas similarly depended on the complex of economic factors associated with cocoa cultivation. In the Volta Region Ho and Kpandu were the largest towns; but it was Hohoe, serving the new cocoa area of Buem, which had grown fastest from an insignificant settlement to a commercial town of some 4,000 people. In the Eastern Region, where devastation by swollen shoot was greatest, many towns whose growth had been on the basis of their involvement in the cocoa-growing industry had fallen into varying stages of decay. Towns on the Akwapim Mountains and several in Krobo, including Somanya, were examples. Where towns in the devastated cocoa areas had only been slightly, or not at all, retarded in their growth, it was because of their broad functional base. A case in point was Koforidua which remained large; its population of about 10,500 in 1931 was double that in 1921—notwithstanding the severe devastation of cocoa farms in the rural areas tributary to it. The town had spread out to include Effiduase and Asokori within its suburbs. Similarly, the important market and cross-roads town of Nsawam, which would otherwise have been severely hindered in its growth, had a population of about 9,000, about 3,000 more than in 1921.

In the forest of the Central and Western Regions towns were on the whole much smaller than elsewhere. This was in the main due to the restricted scale of cocoa cultivation and other economic activities. But a few towns in areas of active colonization by cocoa farmers were in the process of rapid expansion. Enchi was an example. Situated at a roadhead, it was the focus for a fast-developing cocoa area between the lower Tano and the Ivory Coast border. Agona Swedru, because of its funnel-neck position at the point where the single road from Winneba split fanwise into an expanding cocoa countryside, began to capture much of the trade from the interior that formerly by-passed it for Winneba.

Although the two basic factors of large-scale mining and cocoa cultiva-

[1] Guggisberg, *The Gold Coast: A Review of the Events of 1920–26 and the Prospects of 1927–28*, pp. 290 ff.

tion explained the importance of most towns in the forest, the influence of the associated factor of transport was also considerable. The Krobo river-port town of Kpong for example had dwindled in size after it ceased functioning as a port because of the diversion of traffic to motor roads leading directly to Accra. Akuse had lost some of its population for similar reasons. On the other hand Nkawkaw, which began as a collection of buildings around a station on the newly completed Accra–Kumasi railway, had become a major nodal point and a market town. The only motor road reaching the plateau-top Kwahu towns from the south side began from Nkawkaw. By the beginning of the Second World War, that is within about fifteen years of its foundation, Nkawkaw had grown into a town with a population of over 3,000. Juaso and New Mangoase also were examples of old towns which had grown into important market centres since their relocation in the 1920s on the Accra–Kumasi railway.

Much of the coastal savanna plain was almost devoid of towns, except the south-east plains which counted two towns, Tegbi and Dzodze, with populations between 4,000 and 5,000 and some four towns with populations ranging from about 2,400 to about 3,000. The coastal savanna plain was unimportant economically: between the forest with its cocoa farms and the coastline with its port and commercial towns the coastal savanna plain had little to attract settlement.

The major coastline towns with population over 5,000 were Takoradi, Sekondi, Cape Coast, Saltpond, Apam, Winneba, Accra and Keta. In terms of population size Sekondi was about three times as large as Takoradi, but the latter was already growing at a fast pace. Takoradi was also the scene of the most comprehensive planning project ever undertaken in any coastal town.[1] As soon as the proposals for the construction of the harbour were accepted, the preparation of a comprehensive layout plan of a new Takoradi town was begun, and the Government acquired land extensive enough to accommodate about 100,000 people. The plan envisaged a clear-cut functional differentiation of the new town, based on delimitation of commercial and industrial areas, separate African and European residential areas, a purely African suburb, recreation grounds and parks, and open spaces. The plan also provided for broad approach roads from Sekondi and Axim. Takoradi was intended to be a model tropical plan (fig. 49).

Cape Coast was larger than Sekondi, but the rate at which it was growing appeared to be slower. Cape Coast retained its importance in the spheres of administration and education but suffered a reduction of its commercial function. The amount of capital invested in new buildings in the town was

[1] Guggisberg, op. cit. pp. 290 ff.

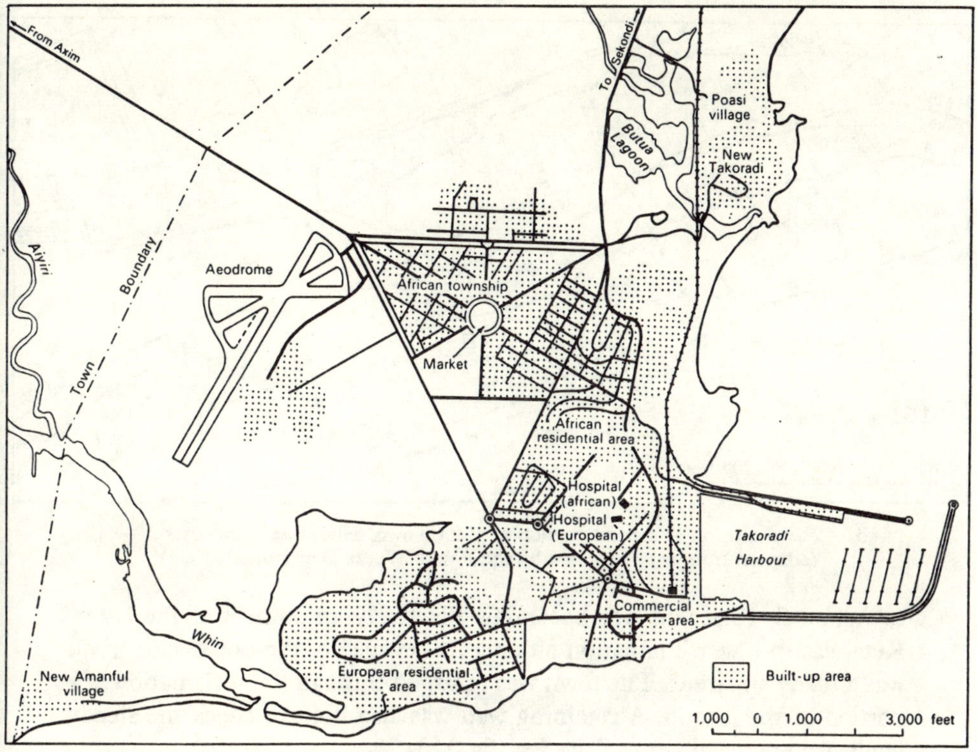


49 Takoradi, 1939

visibly insignificant compared with the investments of previous decades, and the town had begun to assume a look of ruin since the rate at which old and dilapidated buildings were replaced was very much reduced. There were some attempts to improve the appearance of Cape Coast. New streets, including a new causeway across the lagoon, and drains were constructed and an area christened Amanful laid out for resettlement of the excess population from the congested areas; but the resettlement programme made little headway in the face of stout opposition from the inhabitants.[1]

Saltpond hardly grew after the 1920s, and the prospects were not bright, for the town lost its port function in 1939. The only improvement that was seen in the town was the draining of the lagoon to make fresh land available for settlement. Apam had begun to decline after its phenomenal growth in the 1920s. Winneba was in a position similar to that of Cape Coast. The rate of expansion of the town had slowed down: the town was losing much

[1] Ibid.

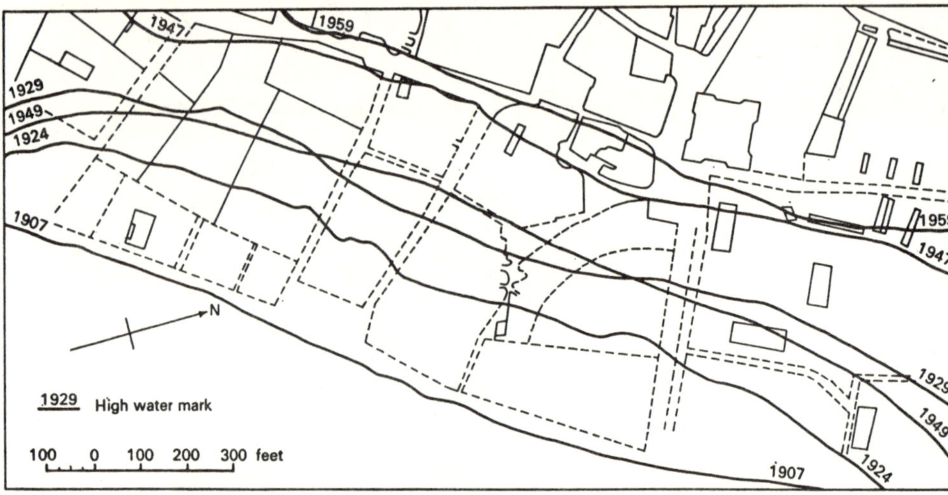


50 Coastal erosion at central portion of Keta Town. High tide contours 1907–59 (adapted from map supplied by the Public Works Department, Keta)

to Agona Swedru and was becoming effectively an outport of the latter. Keta was in a worse situation although a reversal of the downward trend was already apparent. The town was enlarged through the reclamation of a portion of the lagoon. A retaining wall was also built to check the steady landward encroachment of the sea (fig. 50).

It was Accra which showed the brightest prospects for growth. The town's population increase since the 1920s showed itself in the numerous buildings that appeared in hitherto unoccupied areas and in the outward push of the boundaries of the three original nuclei of the town towards one another. The cantonment area, which up to the beginning of the First World War was separated from the rest of the town by bad dusty roads, was linked to it by the large European quarter that developed in the intervening space. The Adabraka quarter, originally a zongo, had developed into a commercial and neighbourhood settlement area as the population spilled into it from the older parts of the town (fig. 40, p. 260). Accra's suburbia, extending in a broad arc from Chorkor through Tesano to Labadi, had already begun to develop.

Outside the European quarter Accra was a large sprawling mass of decent and slum buildings, with the latter erected hastily by immigrants from the rural areas. The need for replanning was urgent. Most of the planning problems were first tackled in the decade 1920–30. Selwyn market, built between 1920 and 1924, was the first of its kind in Accra, and it was soon followed by similar ones at Christiansborg and Korle Gonno.[1] The slum area near Selwyn market was cleared and new quarters built on Government land at Korle Bu to accommodate the dispossessed persons; but the latter refused to live in the new quarters which were subsequently occupied by the police. The whole of the Korle Bu area, then a suburb, had been replanned for orderly settlement and a causeway built across the Korle lagoon to provide an easy and effective link between Korle Bu and James Town. Achimota village had also been replanned and provided with a market. The village was meant to be part of the Achimota complex of schools, private and Government employees' quarters, shops, etc. Within Accra proper, sewage disposal systems had been constructed as well as large open drains to carry off to the sea the rainwater that on account of the flat nature of the land tended to accumulate and cause flooding. The problem of inadequate supply of drinking water had been solved by tapping the Densu river at Weija. A municipal bus service, successfully inaugurated in Accra in 1927 with six Morris motor buses,[2] dealt adequately with the problem of speedy communication between the different parts of the town.

On the eve of the Second World War occurred a catastrophic earthquake which caused extensive damage to property in Accra. To rehouse the affected households, the Government built housing estates at Korle Gonno, Christiansborg, South Labadi, Kaneshie, Sabon Zongo, and Abossey Okai.[3] It needed the building of these estate houses to almost complete the major details of the picture of Accra before Independence.[4]

A feature of many towns in Northern Ghana, especially in north Mamprusi, was the vagueness of the boundaries. Unlike Southern Ghana and Ashanti–Brong Ahafo where towns were traditionally distinguished from villages, in much of Northern Ghana there was, strictly speaking, hardly such a thing as a town. What was usually referred to as a town simply connoted the idea of the place of residence of a particular clan. *Teŋa*, the term used for a town, means literally 'land', that is, land over which the clan members are scattered 'in more or less isolated compounds, built a hundred or more yards apart'.[5] Consequently the population figures for most of the settlements listed as towns were exaggerations or understatements and not comparable, since the same enumeration unit was not adhered to. And so it would appear that only two towns, Wa and Tamale, genuinely had populations of over 5,000.[6]

[1] Guggisberg, op. cit. [2] Ibid. [3] Acquah, *Accra Survey*, p. 28.

[4] The most significant change in the distribution of use areas in Accra in post-war years was the definite emergence of Station Road as part of the central business district.

[5] Rattray, *Tribes of the Ashanti Hinterland*, I, 233, 235 and 244.

[6] Cardinall, *The Gold Coast, 1931*, pp. 158–9.

Nevertheless it would also appear that there were on the whole fewer and smaller towns in the western half than in the eastern half of Northern Ghana. The western half was impoverished as the main currents of trade followed the Yeji–Tamale–Bolgatanga road and its offshoots to the east, and all its major towns had diminished in size. Besides, these towns were not easily accessible from other parts of Northern Ghana. Thus towns like Bole, Lawra, Tumu and Lambussie had populations of only just over 1,000, and Wa, whose population doubled between 1921 and 1931, also appeared to hold little prospect for expansion. But Wa remained the most important commercial town.

Within the eastern half of Northern Ghana the conditions favouring urban growth were not evenly distributed. Salaga, surpassed by Tamale as the centre of the distributive trade in Northern Ghana, remained a small town with a population of about 4,800. It functioned merely as a food market for the immediate countryside and as a stopping place of not much importance for commercial motor vehicles that plied on the Yeji–Tamale road. Savelugu was similarly overshadowed by Tamale. Gambaga and Walewale had also lost much of their commercial function and therefore the driving force behind their growth, although Gambaga's growth was somewhat sustained by its status as an administrative headquarters.

By contrast were certain towns like Yendi and Tamale which continued to flourish. Zuarungu, Bolgatanga, and Navrongo also had population increases because of their importance in trade, administration, and education in that part of north Mamprusi.[1] The little town of Bawku similarly appeared to be in the process of expansion.[2] As a commercial centre its sphere of influence extended into neighbouring areas in Togo and Upper Volta, and its long-established cattle trade with the latter had gained in volume after the commercial motor lorry reached the town in the 1920s. Bawku had also developed strong trading relations with the rest of Mamprusi and with eastern Dagomba along the motor road to Yendi.

Yendi, unlike Salaga, had not wilted under the dominating influence of Tamale. Almost on the same latitude as Tamale but much closer to the Togo boundary, Yendi remained the focal point of trade for a large part of eastern Dagomba and part of neighbouring Togo. Its commercial function was strengthened after the completion in the 1920s of the Kete

[1] They were among the towns with ill-defined boundaries, and the exact extent of population increase cannot be determined.

[2] According to the 1931 census Bawku's population dropped from 7,710 in 1921 to 3,752 in 1931, although the evidence suggests steady growth. The census figures were obviously a result of the differences in the delimitation of the town's boundaries.

Krachi–Yendi–Bawku road which ran parallel to the Yeji–Tamale–Bolgatanga road.

Tamale, with a population of about 13,000, was by far the largest town in Northern Ghana. Tamale first achieved this distinction in the 1921–31 decade when its population more than trebled, following the completion of the first-class motor road from Kumasi and the resultant large increase in the town's trade. It was within that decade that the first foreign-owned department stores were opened in the town.[1] By the late 1930s the period of energetic growth had been replaced by one of near stagnation as the parallel development of other commercial towns like Bawku and Bolgatanga interrupted the flow of trade to Tamale. Although the seat of administration for the whole of Northern Ghana, there was little to distinguish Tamale's appearance from that of other towns. Tamale had assumed the drabness of a single-storeyed iron-roofed township.

[1] Hilton, op. cit. p. 27.

# 13. Economic geography

## PRIMARY ECONOMIC ACTIVITIES

Hunting and collecting of food crops which, as major occupations, typified a society that had not yet faced the challenge of the soil, were no longer important among the primary economic activities. The little amount of hunting that continued was strictly controlled in order to preserve certain wild animals.[1] Collecting was also completely overshadowed by conscious cultivation. One of the few non-vegetable items in the forest whose collection was still a major activity was the snail. Whole villages emigrated to the forest during the collecting season and penalties were exacted for collecting the snails at any other time.[2]

### Agriculture in Southern Ghana and Ashanti–Brong Ahafo

#### *Export agriculture*

Export agriculture in Ghana meant cocoa cultivation. The oil-palm tree was far less significant in the agricultural landscape that it had once been; cotton and gum copal had practically disappeared from, or lost much of their status as part of, the agricultural landscape; coffee was beginning to reappear on a few farms; the rubber tree only became an economic resource in time of high prices; and sisal, banana, and citrus fruits merely added to the list of unimportant export crops. Only the coconut, called *sika dua* (literally the golden tree) in the Western Region, and the kola nut trees continued to be important. But, as before, they were strictly localized in their distribution. On the other hand cocoa trees dominated the scenery throughout the forest country. The cocoa hold-up of 1937–8[3] may have disorganized cultivation, but it did not lead to any significant shift of emphasis from the cultivation of cocoa to that of other export crops. Besides, the new grading scheme introduced in 1937 was to stabilize the industry by making for better quality exports which attracted a better price.[4]

[1] *The Gold Coast Handbook, 1937*, p. 53.

[2] *Annual Report on the Gold Coast, 1938–39*, p. 39.

[3] As in the 1930–1 hold-up, farmers refused to sell their cocoa or pick the ripe pods from the trees. The situation was saved by the Nowell Commission. *See Report of the Commission on the Marketing of West African Cocoa*, Cmd. 5845, 1938, also known as Nowell Report.

[4] This grading scheme, recommended by Sir Frank Stockdale, is still in use. For a more detailed discussion of the scheme and its stabilizing effect on the cocoa industry, see Dickson, *Cocoa in Ghana*, 264–6.

In the Eastern Region, where the area suitable for cocoa cultivation was not much bigger than in Southern Ashanti, there was little room left for the spread of cocoa farms by the end of 1936. Cocoa farms covered the top of the Southern Voltaian Plateau, and were even to be found in the triangular area between the Afram and Volta rivers, although this area is distinctly unsuited to cocoa cultivation because of its dryness and poor soils. In Peki–Anum district, the limited area of deciduous forest around Kpeve, Bame, and Anyirawasi was already used up, and many cocoa farms were reported to be sited in localities exposed to the desiccating harmattan. Akwapim, western and eastern Krobo, New Juaben, and Akim Abuakwa were heavily farmed, especially near the motor roads and in the vicinity of the Accra–Kumasi railway. Companies of farmers emigrated from these heavily farmed areas in search of fresh cocoa land, and the characteristic strip farms of the Krobo and Shai appeared in many parts of the forest country, adding a touch of variety to the cocoa landscape (fig. 51). The usual practice adopted by these farmers in sharing out land was to divide up the base line, usually resting on a stream, so that each might have access to water. The width of land on the base line was measured in 'ropes' or fathoms, a fathom being the length of the stretch of a man's arms (*abasa*, approximately 6 feet), and a 'rope' usually consisting of twelve fathoms. The length of the strip was an uncertain quantity, but it usually extended to the watershed or to some conspicuous landmark.

On the other hand, cocoa farming was not so extensive in the inaccessible parts of Akim and Kwahu. The trade depression of the early 1930s hit such areas very hard, and only the most favourably situated of the farmers were able to dispose of their crop—at discouraging prices.

In the neighbouring Volta Region, the expansion of cocoa cultivation continued in the forest areas north of Ho, and output increased steadily. Cocoa from this Region found a ready market in Togo and it appears the extension of farms was not much affected by the trade depressions. Thus, by 1939, young cocoa farms filled the forest between Santrokofi and Worawora in the north, and between Chito and about Whinta in the south. In other words, there were two distinct zones of intensive cultivation, both running south-west to north-east, and separated by a relatively empty zone, between Kpandu and Misahohe, which cut horizontally across them. The southern zone, the less extensive of the two, centred on Ho and Gbogame, and was connected by a number of small, isolated farms to the cocoa areas around Peki and Asikuma. The northern zone narrowed north-eastward from about Kpandu to Ahamansu, and its development owed much to the work of immigrant farmers.

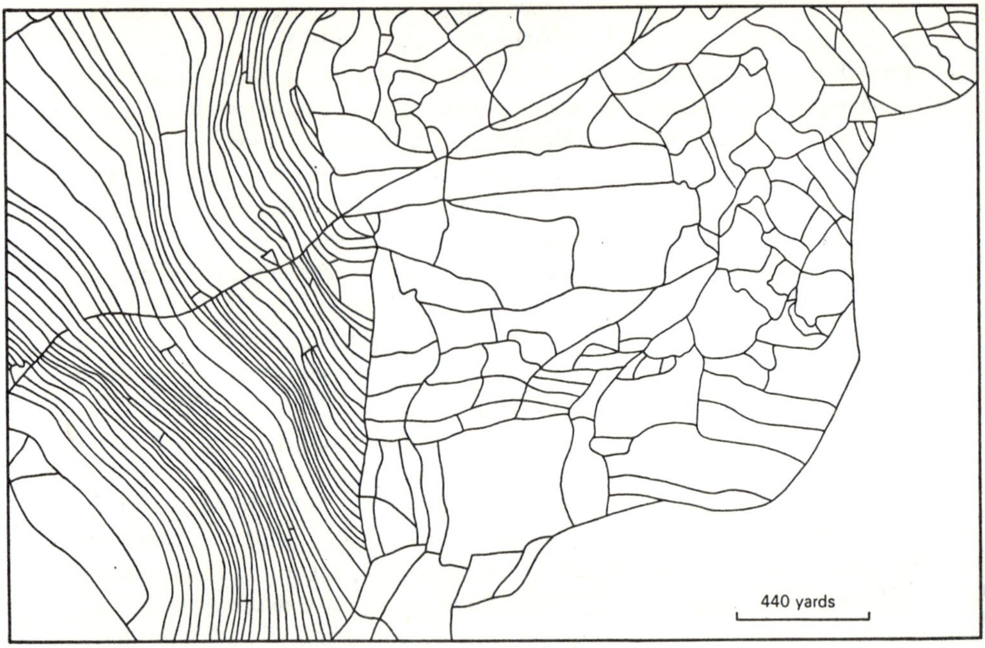


51 Cocoa farms in the Nankese area

In the Central Region, as in other parts of the country, the distribution of cocoa farms was largely related to the availability of transport facilities. There were two well-marked zones of intensive cultivation, one in the south extending from Nsaba in the east to Hemang in the west, and the other on the southern borders of Ashanti, stretching from about Akim Swedru westward to Dunkwa-on-the-Ofin. The two zones were separated by a third zone of sparse population and of less intensive cultivation. The southern zone was served by a well-developed network of roads and by the ports of Cape Coast and Winneba, while the northern zone, thanks to its restricted area, found the Sekondi–Kumasi railway and the Cape Coast–Prasu main road with its feeder extensions sufficient for its needs. The middle zone was traversed along its length by the Central Region railway, on either side of which most of the cocoa farms were located. As in all the cocoa areas, the farmers only discovered the environmental conditions best suited to cocoa cultivation by trial and error, so that it is not surprising many farms were established in the drier coastal areas. The decay of these unfavourably situated farms was only a matter of time, and by the end of 1939 cocoa cultivation in Buruata area in Winneba district, and indeed in all areas south of Agona Swedru, was fast becoming a forgotten occupation.

Western Region remained the least extensively cultivated of all the cocoa areas in both Southern Ghana and Ashanti–Brong Ahafo. An earlier agricultural survey in 1929 showed that of the 91,328 acres under cocoa in the Region, only 54,801 acres were occupied by young farms.[1] As in the Central Region, there were two distinct zones of cocoa cultivation in the north and in the south, separated by a relatively empty middle zone lying around latitude 6° N. The northern zone in Sefwi was the more intensively cultivated as a result of several factors, important among which was the influence of the agricultural station at Wiawso. The station, opened in 1915, exerted widespread influence through disseminating knowledge of the best methods of planting and preparing the crop; some of the older farms were consequently well laid out. The new farms, on the other hand, were less carefully made, for when the farmers became more familiar with the crop they found that they could establish the farms with less attention than they had given in the past.[2] There were two other reasons why the northern zone in Sefwi was more intensively cultivated. The soils in Sefwi are more suitable for cocoa cultivation than those in other parts of the Region, and Sefwi had for a long time had the advantage of road connection with the railway at Dunkwa.

The southern zone of cultivation in Wasaw–Aowin district extended north-westwards in a broad arc from about Manso Amenfi to the neighbourhood of Enchi, where it turned south-westward to about Tanoso.[3] South of Manso Amenfi, towards Prestea, deforestation had proceeded to such an extent that it was virtually impossible to establish new cocoa farms; and south of Enchi, cocoa was not widely cultivated because of the migration of the inhabitants to the timber camps and the mines in Aowin. In the northern part of Wasaw lay an empty zone. It was to develop this potential cocoa country and, equally important, to stimulate cocoa production in Sefwi, that the western railway from Tarkwa to Bibiani was proposed in 1929 (fig. 23 *b* on page 169).

In Ashanti an area of about 20 miles radius around Kumasi was one dense mass of cocoa trees, and northward and north-eastward in the open country beyond Nkoransa and Kumawu–Agogo, and along the base of the Techiman–Kintampo Heights, numerous cocoa farms had been made under the shade of riparian forests. Very definite advice was given to the

[1] Paper no. xviii in Department of Agriculture's *Year Book, 1929*. [2] Ibid.
[3] At Boinso, between Enchi and Tanoso, was a cocoa plantation belonging to the Pra-Tano Company.

chiefs in these grassland areas that time spent by their people in planting cocoa would be time wasted. To the east and south of Kumasi cocoa farms dominated the scenery, forming an unbroken chain along the railway lines and a cluster around Lake Busumtwe.[1] West and north-west of Kumasi the story was the same: new cocoa farms springing up in all directions and even trespassing into the more open country around Nsuta (south-west of Techiman), Tainano, etc. Officers of the Department of Agriculture never failed to notice the feverish activity of cocoa farmers in the Pamu–Goaso–Sunyani triangle, and an earlier agricultural survey of western Brong Ahafo in 1928–9 showed that cocoa farms in bearing covered an area of 44,172 acres, while new or non-fruiting farms occupied 134,136 acres.[2] On the western border of Brong Ahafo, cocoa farms stretched from about Diabakrom in the south to about Ntereso in the north.[3]

There was one disturbing feature about cocoa cultivation, namely, the presence of swollen shoot disease[4] which threatened to ruin the entire industry. Swollen shoot, a contagious virus disease, was first recognized in 1936 in a cocoa farm in Effiduase area in the Eastern Region, although the earliest outbreak appears to have been at Nankese in the same Region between 1910 and 1915. Further investigation showed that the disease had already spread throughout a rich cocoa belt of about 200 square miles lying in both New Juaben and Akim Abuakwa. It was to fight this disease that the Cocoa Research Station at Tafo, originally called the West African Cocoa Research Institute, was set up in 1938.[5] The research station, which began work immediately, was to save the cocoa industry.

By 1939 swollen shoot was everywhere in the Eastern Region (fig. 52). East of the Accra–Kumasi railway, the triangular piece of land between Nsawam, Senchi, and Mankrong in Kwahu, which before then was covered by one dense mass of cocoa trees, was honeycombed with swollen shoot and left with a scatter of small, isolated farms. Not all the trees died of swollen shoot, for many outside the forest zone died through being on poor soils or through over-exposure to the harmattan. Swollen shoot and over-exposure to the harmattan also took a heavy toll in the cocoa areas around Asikuma and Peki in the Volta Region, although on the whole the Volta

[1] In Southern Ashanti, the Ofin Rubber Plantations Ltd at Dunkwa-on-the-Ofin and Abomposu Estates Ltd at Obuasi had cocoa on their estates.

[2] Paper no. XV in Department of Agriculture's *Bulletin* no. 20, 1928.

[3] *Gold Coast Government Sessional Paper* no. III of 1930–1 contains a map showing, among other things, the general boundaries of cocoa cultivation.

[4] Department of Agriculture, *Annual Reports*, 1936/37 to 1939/40.

[5] Swollen shoot, although the most dangerous, was by no means the only cocoa disease. Capsids and black pod disease were also present, and failure to give them the attention they deserved was to complicate the problem of diseases in later years.

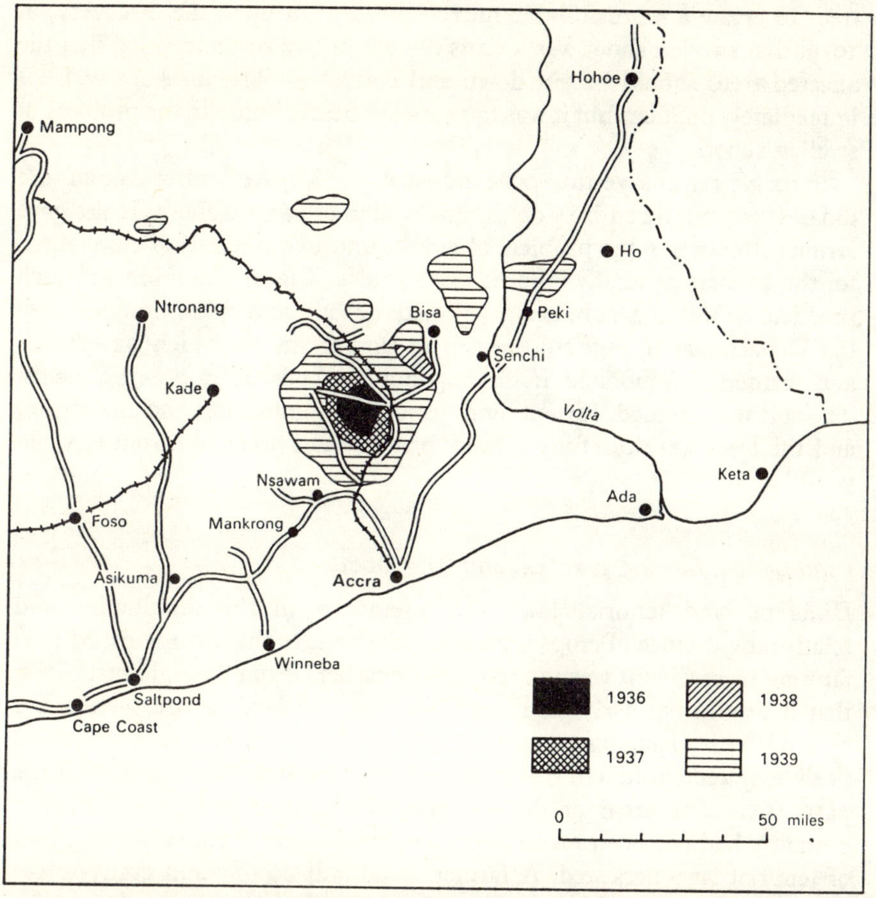


52 Spread of swollen shoot, 1936–9

Region was the area in Southern Ghana which had the least trouble from swollen shoot.

West of the Accra–Kumasi railway, in the districts of Akwapim and New Juaben, was that huge area of cocoa farms, called the Special Area, which was thoroughly infested with swollen shoot. There, hundreds of thousands of cocoa trees were felled every year in an effort to check the spread of the disease. Nowhere else in Southern Ghana or in Ashanti–Brong Ahafo was the disease so threatening and devastating.

It was at first thought, in 1937, that swollen shoot was a form of die-back resulting from unfavourable environmental, especially climatic, conditions. Thus its spread would be checked by the planting of shade trees to create a more suitable micro-climate. But upon the discovery, in 1939, that swollen shoot was a virus disease, it was recommended that the affected trees should be cut down and destroyed. The measure was not immediately popular, but it was to prove the best solution to the problem of swollen shoot.

In its efforts to save the cocoa industry, the Department of Agriculture did not concentrate entirely on the eradication of swollen shoot. It also gave serious attention to the problem of how to improve methods of cultivation, for the farmers generally ignored all the rules of farm sanitation and such practices as would ensure healthy growth of the cocoa trees. Consequently the Department of Agriculture set up unit farms on which its officials and farmers collaborated in finding out methods of improving yields. The soil was drained, turned, and enriched by mulching and manuring; and the trees were carefully spaced, pruned, and protected from sun and wind.[1]

### *Land tenure, farming practice, and farm labour*

Different land tenurial laws and alterations in the distribution and relative importance of crops were the main features that distinguished food farming from what it was in the 1850s or earlier. From the rigid institution that it was in the early eighteenth century, the land tenure system had evolved with changing economic and social circumstances into a more flexible system, although it still was not entirely free from the hold of the past. In remote areas of the country where the impact of export-crop economy had not been much felt, a modified form of the earlier rigid set of tenurial laws persisted. A farmer could still occupy and cultivate the family land free of charge, except that he had to deliver to the chief a portion of the usufruct—one-tenth in the case of cocoa and one-third in the case of rubber. Elsewhere the vital difference was that land could be bought and sold. Serious cash-crop farming required a system of land tenure which permitted individual ownership of land, for no agricultural improvement could be introduced on a long-term basis when the land would sooner or later revert to the family from which it was acquired.

On the whole the majority of food farmers adhered to the traditional farming calendar and the bush fallowing system, although they tended to shorten the fallow period in response to the increasing dearth of farm land in some parts of the country and to the need for greater supplies of food

[1] *Gold Cst. Fmr.* VI, I (May 1937), 4–5.

for the rapidly expanding towns. But there were a few areas close to the large towns where a permanent system of farming, market gardening, was practised to produce vegetables mainly for European consumption.[1] Also, there were certain heavily populated rural areas where the land, often immediately around the household, was manured and kept under constant cultivation. Onion cultivation at Keta was an illustration of a carefully organized system of fixed agriculture.[2] The onion beds were initially manured with household refuse, goat dung, and with compost from grass collected from near the Keta lagoon. Planting took place in June in soil that had been carefully turned, and after the bulbs had taken root the soil received a further dressing of cattle, poultry and bat manure. Keta district was the largest producer of onions in Southern Ghana.

Nevertheless the Keta system of farming was unique, so that for much of the country the problem of how to eliminate the fallow land remained. The problem deserved attention in view of the rapid rate of population increase. The Department of Agriculture in 1938 laid out 14 food-crop farm units—4 in the Eastern Region, 3 each in the Western Region and Ashanti–Brong Ahafo, and 2 each in the Central and Volta Regions—on which it experimented with a six-course rotation system including pasture for sheep.[3] The size of a farm unit was 4 acres, and the crops selected for the rotation trials and the farming implements used were typical of the area. If the experiments were successful, the farms would be settled by farmers who would continue to cultivate them, relying on advice from agricultural officers. But these experiments were to make no difference to the existing farming methods.

Just as unchanged was the nature of farm labour which, for the small farmer, still consisted of both male and female members of his family. But the women worked on the farms, not necessarily as labourers for their polygamous husbands, but more often because of their association with certain types of farm work. In the coastal zone, for example, the cultivation of groundnuts was left to women, although in the parkland areas of Brong Ahafo it was also the responsibility of men, especially those who had immigrated from Northern Ghana.[4] Some women were even farmers in their own right and employed male labour.

The kind of communal labour that was prevalent in the early eighteenth century had been replaced by several systems of paid farm labour: *abehyem*

[1] *Annual Report on the Gold Coast, 1938–9*, p. 37.

[2] *Gold Cst. Fmr.* VI, 3 (July 1937), 59. Hardly anything is known of the genesis of the Keta system of farming.

[3] Ibid. VII, 4 (August 1938), 63.

[4] *Annual Report on the Gold Coast, 1938–9*, p. 38.

or *abusa*, *afe*, *paa*, and *nkotokuano*.[1] Of these the oldest was *abusa*. Under this system the contract farm labourer, sometimes called *nhwesonyi* (caretaker), did all the farm work, harvested and stored the crop, one-third of which was then given him as his reward. The *afe* labourers were employed at a fixed annual wage, and it appears their function was mainly to establish new farms. The *paa* or daily-rated labourers were employed, usually for short periods only, to perform odd tasks on the farm, or perhaps to make a new farm. The *nkotokuano* labourer was more associated with cocoa than with food farming. He received a fixed amount of money for every load of cocoa he prepared, with an extra sum of money for conveying the produce to the market.

The important crops differed from those of earlier times, not so much in variety as in quality. Several new and better-yielding strains of the existing crops had been introduced by the Department of Agriculture, some of which, like those of maize and cassava, had been generally adopted not only in Southern Ghana and Ashanti–Brong Ahafo but also in parts of Northern Ghana. Again, the crops differed in their distribution and the scale on which they were cultivated. The differences were accounted for by the changes that had occurred in the size and distribution of rural population density and the vastly expanded internal market. Yams, for example, were extensively cultivated for the forest markets (fig. 53), and groundnuts were apparently cultivated more extensively than before, particularly in the Volta Region, Nzima and Keta districts, and in parkland Brong Ahafo to supply the large markets at Accra, Sekondi, and Kumasi.[2]

In the forest of Southern Ghana and Ashanti–Brong Ahafo the extent of food farming was also related to cocoa cultivation. The desire to extend the acreage under food crops was primarily determined by the nature of the cocoa market. If cocoa prices were favourable, the tendency was to substitute more cocoa trees for food crops on the farms or to clear fresh land for cultivation, while the opposite was true in times of low cocoa prices. The 1937–8 cocoa hold-up, for example, resulted in some farmers planting more land to food crops.[3]

Yet food farming was not considered to be unimportant on its own. The farmers had had enough experience of the vagaries of the cocoa market, in contrast to the steadiness of the internal food market, to realize that food farming was basic to their agricultural existence. Thus cocoa farms generally began as food farms, and it was only after the cocoa trees had

[1] Ibid. p. 68. A more detailed exposition of these contractual systems of labour will be found in Polly Hill's *The Gold Coast Cocoa Farmer* (O.U.P., 1956), pp. 8–39.

[2] *Annual Report on the Gold Coast, 1938–9*, p. 38.

[3] Ibid. p. 37.

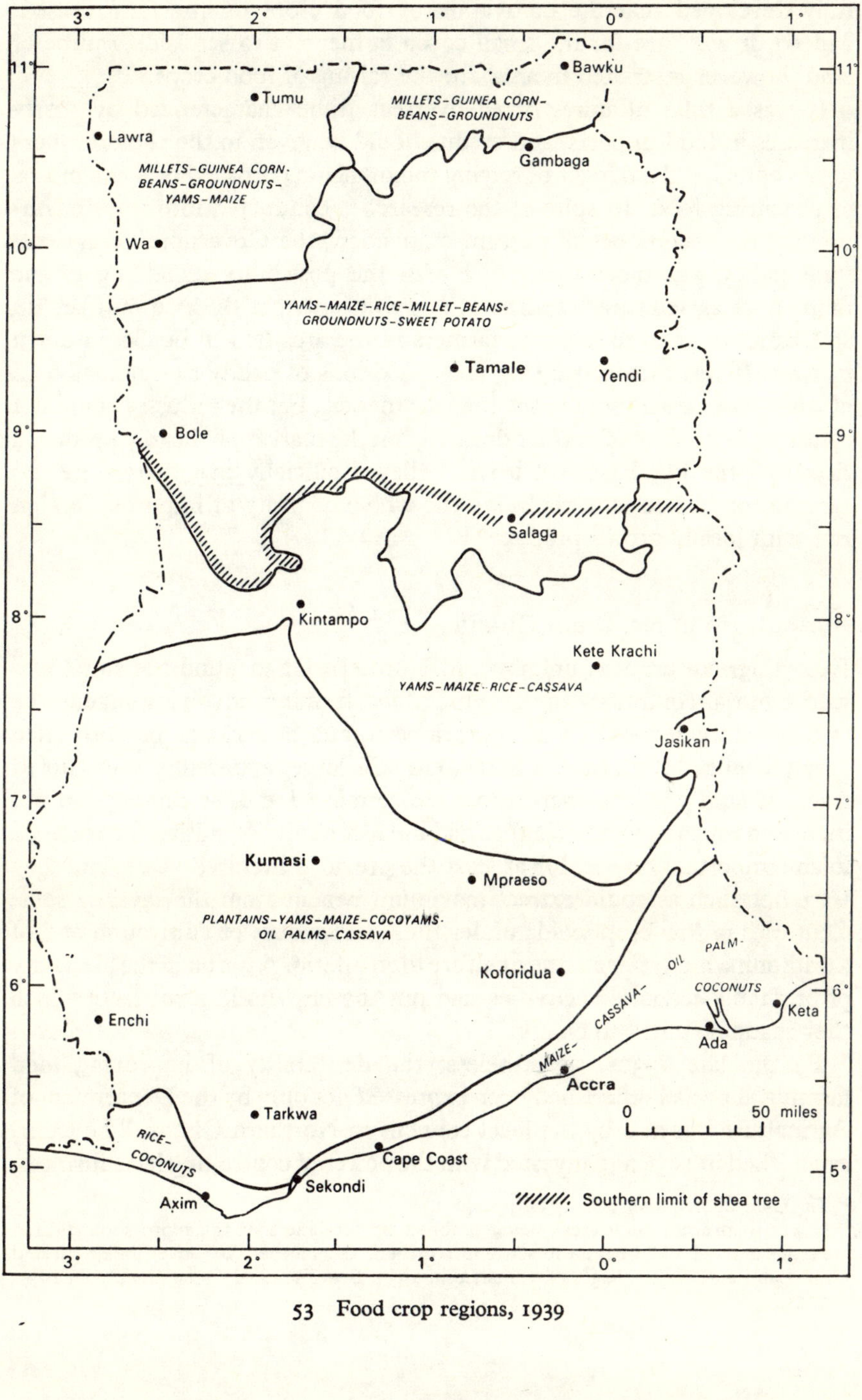


53 Food crop regions, 1939

fully developed that the cultivation of food crops on the farm ceased. Indeed, it was rare for the small cocoa farmer not to set aside a piece of land, however restricted in area, for the raising of food crops.

It was a time of unrestricted overseas trade characterized by yearly increases in food imports, and credit should be given to the cocoa farmers for recognizing the danger of relying too much on cocoa exports as a means of procuring food. In spite of the researches conducted into ways of improving the techniques of peasant cultivation, the Government's agricultural policy was more concerned with the possibility of adding to the number of agricultural exports. It is significant that the rice mill set up at Esiama in 1926 to help the farmers in the area had to be closed down in 1938. It was then processing about 400 tons of paddy rice annually, all of which were easily sold in the internal market; but the industry could not continue in the face of regular dumping on the market of cheaply produced rice from the Far East. Yet it was believed officially that there were 'no agricultural obstacles to replacing the whole quantity of imported foreign rice with locally grown produce'.[1]

### Agriculture in Northern Ghana

Export agriculture was unknown in Northern Ghana, and the social and land tenurial conditions under which food farming, involving mainly the traditional mainstays of yam, guinea corn, and millet, was practised had barely changed with time. There were still large, apparently unoccupied tracts of land whose ownership was uncertain.[2] Land, as capital, had not increased much in value. Neither had the techniques of cultivation changed in any important respect for at least the previous hundred years, and they were not such as could extract maximum benefit from the savanna soils. Centuries of low crop yields under these techniques of cultivation and of a tradition which relegated agriculture to an inferior position in the hierarchy of profitable economic activities had put the farmers in a rut from which they made no effort to emerge.

By the late 1930s, nevertheless, the desirability of improving food farming above all others had been expressed not only by the Department of Agriculture but also by the local councils in Northern Ghana. The latter, established in 1936 and invested with the power of controlling local finances,

[1] *The Gold Coast Handbook, 1937*, pp. 40–1.

[2] It was to prevent such areas being grabbed by foreigners or the more sophisticated southerners who had begun to settle in Northern Ghana that the Government enacted the Land and Native Rights Ordinance in 1931. See *The Gold Coast Handbook, 1937*, p. 152.

realized correctly that the extension of medical, sanitary, and educational facilities, which was occurring on an unprecedented scale, would be stultified in the face of recurrent food shortages.[1]

Agricultural development policy followed three lines: the introduction of crop rotation coupled with mixed farming and the improvement through these of the existing intensive cultivation such as was practised in north Mamprusi and Wa–Lawra areas; the promotion of extensive cultivation in the empty lands of Gonja; and the provision of more water for farming.

The traditional system of farming in north Mamprusi or Wa–Lawra was the 'compound type' involving continuous cultivation without a fallow period.[2] Only about 10 per cent of the land was manured, and that was immediately around the compound house, while the rest of the land was under a system of rudimentary and non-beneficial crop rotation in which cereals dominated. If there was also a 'bush farm', which would normally be at some distance from the compound farm, it was cultivated by the usual method of bush fallowing. Where the terrain was hilly and rocky, the farmers carefully removed the stones from the soil, heaped them into a series of parallel low stretches of mounds ringing the hill, and cultivated the spaces between the mounds. The hillside looked as though it had been cut into to create terraces.

As a means of food production, the compound system was superior to any other system in Northern Ghana; but it was also beset with the problem of declining crop yields, particularly in the areas that were not manured. Added to this was the problem of sheet and gully erosion in the rainy season in those areas where the ground had been completely exposed through burning of the grass cover in the dry season.

In many areas the Department of Agriculture was able to introduce measures, including terracing and controlled grass burning in the dry season, to combat soil erosion. But a careful system of rotation which had been successfully tried out with the traditional food crops in several experimental stations, and which would have provided a permanent cover for the ground, was not readily adopted by the farmers.

Neither was the introduction of mixed farming an easy process; indeed it never really got under way. The decision to introduce mixed farming was based primarily on the fact that cattle rearing as an economic venture had made, and was still making, some progress in Northern Ghana. After

[1] Except otherwise stated, this section on agriculture in Northern Ghana is based on the *Annual Reports on the Northern Territories* and the Department of Agriculture's *Annual Reports* covering the period 1937–9.

[2] Department of Agriculture, *Bulletin* no. 34: 'Agriculture in North Mamprusi', by C. W. Lynn.

preliminary trials with mixed farming at the experimental station at Tamale, unit farms were set up at Zoguiri, Tolon, Tali, Lunbungu, Savelugu, and Sambu on which the system was demonstrated. The response of farmers to the demonstrations was not enthusiastic. The whole idea of seriously incorporating animal rearing in a farming economy was still contrary to tradition. Perhaps a more serious difficulty was that in connection with the economics of mixed farming. The demonstrations did not show conclusively that the farmer would make a profit within a reasonably short time on the additional capital invested in the purchase and caring of the cattle.

The only measure that produced some results was the programme of dam and well construction which added to the limited quantities of water available for irrigation as well as for domestic purposes. The programme was launched in 1937.[1] Bearing in mind the size of the existing water supply, and assuming that each inhabitant would require, for all purposes, 5 gallons of water a day, it was decided to dig about 2,000 wells and build 56 dams. Most of these were to be located in Gonja and western Dagomba where it was felt that the possibility of agricultural improvement would be assured if enough water was made available. An additional sum of money was voted for cleaning and repairing the existing ponds, water holes, and water storage chambers hollowed out in the subsoil below a laterite cap. Indeed the water problem in Northern Ghana was partly caused by the fact that these existing sources of water, some of which, like the water storage chambers in Gonja, were ancient, had not been carefully maintained. They had been allowed to become choked with earth.

Some of these wells and dams were built before the end of 1939, and the additional quantities of water they made available were put to good use by the farmers. But since the greatest part of Northern Ghana was still without these additional sources of water supply, food farming in the region on the whole remained unchanged in its essential features.

## Livestock rearing[2]

The rearing of cattle, the most important livestock, was not as well developed as in other West African countries. Meat was expensive; it cost an average of 1*s*. 6*d*. per lb. as against 4*d*. per lb. in Lagos and 2*d*. per lb. in Kano in Nigeria. In addition to the 50,000 zebu bullocks imported annually

[1] *Gold Cst. Fmr.* VI, I (May 1937), 8–9.

[2] Unless otherwise stated, this section is derived from *Annual Report on the Gold Coast, 1938–9*, pp. 41–3.

from former French West Africa for the slaughterhouses, Ghana imported large quantities of tinned meat, more than any other country in West Africa.

There were nearly 200,000 cattle in the country, with most of them in Northern Ghana. Over 90 per cent of the animals were West African Shorthorns, and the rest Dwarf Shorthorns which were found in remote areas in the forest and in the lagoon country of Keta. In the latter area the Dwarf Shorthorns were hired out to the owners of coconut plantations who tied them to the trees to manure them; otherwise they were of little economic value. The West African Shorthorn, a mixture of Hamitic Longhorn, the Dwarf Shorthorn, and the Zebu, was a superior breed larger in size than the Dwarf Shorthorn. The infusion of zebu blood was important. It caused increased size and weight, and the more zebu a cow was, the better its market price, since meat was sold by weight only and no allowance made for quality. Also the zebu is fairly resistant to rinderpest, though not to trypanosomiasis, and is a good traveller, an important consideration in Ghana where cattle walked long distances to the market.

In addition to the West African Shorthorn were two other distinct breeds created in the veterinary farm at Pong–Tamale and confined to Northern Ghana. The White Sanga, basically a cross between the White Fulani bull (zebu) and the West African Shorthorn cow, was bigger than all other breeds and therefore the most popular. But it survived only in north Mamprusi where tsetse infestation was mild. The Ndama–Sanga, a cross between Ndama bull and Sanga cow, combined the size of the Sanga with the Ndama resistance to trypanosomiasis. It was therefore suitable for the highly tsetse-infested areas of the southern portion of Northern Ghana.[1]

These two superior breeds occurred in small numbers owing to the difficulty of rearing enough of them to distribute for breeding purposes. For the whole of Northern Ghana there were only 20 Native Authority stock farms to undertake the work of breeding and distribution, while the veterinary farm at Nungua was too new to be of service to the south-east coastal plains.

Other pressing problems were the scarcity of water in the Accra Plains and in parts of Northern Ghana, and the prevalence of the two diseases pleuropneumonia and trypanosomiasis. The water shortage problem received attention in Northern Ghana only where a number of wells were sunk. Pleuropneumonia was successfully suppressed in a few areas in Northern Ghana through the use of a vaccine produced at Pong–Tamale,

[1] J. L. Stewart and M. D. W. Jeffreys, *The Cattle of the Gold Coast* (revised edition, Accra, 1956), pp. 14–18.

but the problem of trypanosomiasis was too big to be tackled with the slender resources at the disposal of the Veterinary Department. In only a few selected areas was it possible to eliminate the tsetse fly.

## Fishing[1]

Fishing in the rivers, the lagoons, and in Lake Bosumtwe did not involve any more sophisticated techniques than were used in earlier centuries. If there was any difference, it resided in the scale of operations, since the demand for fish had increased with the population. Thus the Volta River was fished intensively along its whole length mainly by fishermen from Ada and Tongu districts, who built permanent fishing camps in such remote places as Wa and Lawra. To guard against the threat of overfishing, the Rivers (Fishing) Regulations Ordinance was passed in 1938. It prohibited the use of nets other than cast nets of not more than 15 yards in circumference in the principal rivers of the country. Of the lagoon fisheries the most important was that of the Juen lagoon which is largely in the Ivory Coast. It attracted large numbers of immigrant fishermen and was important because of its proximity to the timber camps and the mines where there was a big, steady demand for fish.

As before, sea fishing was the most important branch of the industry, but there the similarity with fishing in early times ended. The sea fisheries were sharply divided, on the basis of gear, technique, and organization, into three types: the Anlo type, found from the Togo border to the east bank of the Volta, the Fanti-Gã type between the west bank of the Volta and the east bank of the Ankobra, and the Nzima type from the west bank of the Ankobra to the border with the Ivory Coast.

The Anlo type of fishing centred around Keta. It was distinguished primarily by the predominant use of the seine net and a suitably adapted dug-out canoe with the bow built up as a high box-like structure to give the extra freeboard necessary when plunging through the surf with a heavy net on board. Some Anlo fishermen owned other kinds of net, but they generally used them outside Anlo waters. Fishing with the *ali* drift net for herring, for example, was carried on mostly off Grand Popo in Dahomey.

There were three types of seine net. The largest and most expensive was the *afafa* seine, carried in a large canoe, and used from October to January for catching horse mackerel. Next in order of size was the *yevudorga* which was used throughout the year for catching herring, mackerel, bonito and

[1] The sole reference work for this section is the *Report on the Prisons Department Fisheries Scheme, 1941*.

other small fishes. During the *afafa* season it was sometimes drawn behind the *afafa* net to trap the smaller fishes that had passed through the wider meshes of the latter. The *yevudorga* was carried to sea in a smaller canoe rowed by not more than ten men. The smallest seine net was the *nekpeli vi*, used in the same way as the *yevudorga*. Fishing with these nets required much skill and experience, and Anlo fishermen were so specialized in this that most of the seining in the Central and Western Regions was left to them.

A simple system had been evolved for dividing the seine catch between the crew and the net owner. If the owner supplied material for mending the net, he was entitled to one-half of the catch; otherwise he could only take one-third.

The Fanti-Gã type of fishing showed considerable diversity in gear and method, but the most important activity was the use of the drift net (*ali*) for herring fishing. Two other kinds of drift net were used for catching mackerel and shad. In addition to these were three varieties of bottom nets for threadfin fish, shark, and catfish and sole. The coast from about Shama to Takoradi was particularly noted for the use of the *tengirafo* net for catfish and sole, and shark nets. Cast nets had a limited use, except in and around Sekondi. Off-shore line fishing in 50–100 fathoms of water for tunny and large sea bream was important, especially in the Gã area. Fishermen in such places as Tema and Prampram used little other gear besides line and hook.

Two principal types of canoes were used for offshore and inshore fishing. The offshore canoe, with an overall length of about 25 feet and a maximum beam of 4 feet 9 inches, was bigger than ordinary. Made from *wawa* (*Triplochiton scleroxylon*), it was very buoyant and fast under sail—it normally carried a large rectangular sail of some 350 square feet. Leeboards, introduced in 1936, were also normally attached to the offshore canoe. They checked the tendency to drift sideways, but made steering more difficult. Inshore canoes resembled offshore canoes in structure and rig, but were smaller, with an overall length of 15–24 feet and a maximum beam of about 4 feet.

In the Fanti-Gã area as a whole, the total annual catch of fish was about four times as much as in the Anlo area. In view of the diversity of fishing methods and gear, several systems of sharing the catch were used. With drift-net fishing, the owner of the canoe received one portion of the catch, the owner of the net two portions, and each member of the crew one portion. In the case of line fishing, the catch was divided equally among the owners of the canoe and the fishing gear, and the crew members. Where bottom nets were used, the owner of the net, if he had rented it out, was given half of the catch as his reward.

The Nzima type of fishing was similar to the Fanti-Gã type in organization but differed from it in two important respects: the Nzima used fewer varieties of fishing nets, and an entirely different type of canoe. It was a dug-out, usually from the silk-cotton tree, but instead of the curved graceful lines of the Fanti craft, it had wall sides and a square cross-section throughout its length of about 25 feet. Its range was also limited as it did not carry a sail. The total annual catch in the Nzima fishery was about one-twentieth of that in the Fanti-Gã fishery.

A feature common to all the fishing areas was the seasonal migration of the fishermen, caused by the temporary deterioration of conditions in the home fishing ground. The migration could also be semi-permanent, in which case the emigrating fishermen visited home only at long intervals. The conditions under which the migrant fishermen could stay in a new area were the strict observance of the local traditional fishing regulations and the payment of an annual rent to the chief fisherman of that area.

Another common feature of the fishing industry was the observance of the traditional religious taboos, many of which continued to serve as a means of preserving the industry and ensuring better fishing. The prohibition of fishing on particular days of the week made time available for mending the nets and repairing other gear. But the taboo in certain fishing settlements near Accra against using the line and hook for some weeks in June and July does not appear to be traditional. It may have been imposed when the large sea bream stood in danger of being eliminated from the known fishing grounds.

In spite of the large quantities of fish caught annually, it was difficult to accumulate capital for improving the industry, for the fishermen were generally poor. A major problem was the high cost of the nets which also deteriorated rapidly. Another key problem was the seasonal nature of fishing with the associated problem of how to preserve the fish long enough to sell in the lean period. The Government Chemical Laboratory was already at work on these problems, experimenting with different kinds of curing ovens and chemicals for preserving the fishing nets. The Government was also being urged to consider the possibility of introducing fishing trawlers or propulsion motors for the dug-outs, which would then be able to follow the movement of the fish to more distant grounds.

## The timber industry[1]

A preliminary census in 1939 indicated that the distribution of timber production was roughly as follows:

| | |
|---|---|
| Eastern Region | 50,000–100,000 cubic feet |
| Central Region | 100,000 cubic feet |
| Western Region | 750,000 cubic feet |
| Ashanti–Brong Ahafo | 270,000 cubic feet |

The figures represented pit-sawn timber only and did not include the 140,000 or so cubic feet of mill-sawn timber produced partly for export by fifteen establishments whose equipment varied from a simple circular saw to more elaborate machinery. The two largest mills were operated in the Western Region by Messrs Thompson, Moir and Galloway, and the West African Mahogany Company; the other mills were operated by private individuals or by the mining companies to supply their own requirements.

Although the export branch of the industry centred mainly on the production of mahogany, the variety of other woods exported had broadened by the beginning of the Second World War to include *odum* (*Chlorophora excelsa*), other species of mahogany, and *wawa* (*Triplochiton scleroxylon*), to name only the important ones. The prospect of exporting these in larger quantities had increased with the successful advertisement of the country's timbers at the Empire Exhibition in Glasgow in 1938.

Production for internal consumption was the more important branch of the industry, for timber was needed for a wide variety of purposes. Although numerous kinds of wood were available, the *odum* tree was the most fancied for all purposes. The deeply rooted conviction that it was the only timber of any value was difficult to shake.

In spite of the large steady internal market for timber, production was subject to fluctuations related to the nature of the cocoa market. If the price of cocoa was high, there was a big diversion of labour to the easier and better paid work of harvesting cocoa. Then timber became scarce in relation to demand and its price nearly doubled. The reverse occurred when timber became more plentiful with the availability of further supplies of labour driven to the timber camps by a drop in the price of cocoa. This was the case during the cocoa hold-up of 1937–8, when the price of *odum* fell by over 50 per cent.

To stabilize timber production required the development of an extensive milling industry. The large capital that would necessarily be invested in it

[1] Department of Forestry, *Annual Reports*, 1936–37 to 1939–40.

would make it obligatory to maintain permanent and competent gangs of workmen who would keep the mills running. A start had been made in that direction with the establishment of the fifteen mills.

## Mining

Of the three minerals exported—gold, manganese, and diamonds (fig. 54), —gold was the most important, followed by manganese. Only one mine, at Nsuta, produced manganese, but its output was large enough to place Ghana third in the list of world producers. In the case of diamond mining five companies were in operation, two of them on a large scale at Akwatia and Atiankama, and the others on a small scale at Topreman, Oda, Kade, and Wenchi (in Akim). There were also a number of Ghanaians engaged independently in small-scale diamond mining. They used inefficient mining methods, and their contribution to the total output was less than 3 per cent.

There were 15 gold mines in production, including 2 in Northern Ghana: the Nangodi mine and the Dokuripe Exploration Company mine near Bole. There was also the Bremang Gold Dredging Company which operated two dredges on the Ankobra river. Finally there were several gold mines in the developing stage, and 24 mining companies engaged in prospecting for gold in many parts of the country.

On the basis of the rock material in which they were sunk, the producing mines could be divided into three groups: those located in quartz reefs in Birimian formation as at Obuasi, Nangodi, Konongo, Bondai, Prestea; those in Tarkwaian formation as at Tarkwa, Aboso, Abontiakoon; and those mines in placer deposits operated through dredging. Of the three geological formations the Birimian was the greatest source of gold; indeed rocks belonging to this formation were of far greater general economic significance than those of any other geological formation. Nevertheless the richness of ore was not the same for all the mines in the Birimian formation, so that the ore body in, for example, the Bibiani mine was nowhere as rich as that in the Obuasi mine. Next in order of general economic significance was the Tarkwaian formation. Nearly all the gold won from it came from the Banket Series which shows some similarity to the auriferous Witwatersrand conglomerates.

The prospects for the continued operation of a mine were affected not only by the richness of the ore body but also by transport costs. The producing mines in Southern Ghana and Ashanti on the whole had reasonable road connections with, or were adequately served by, railways,

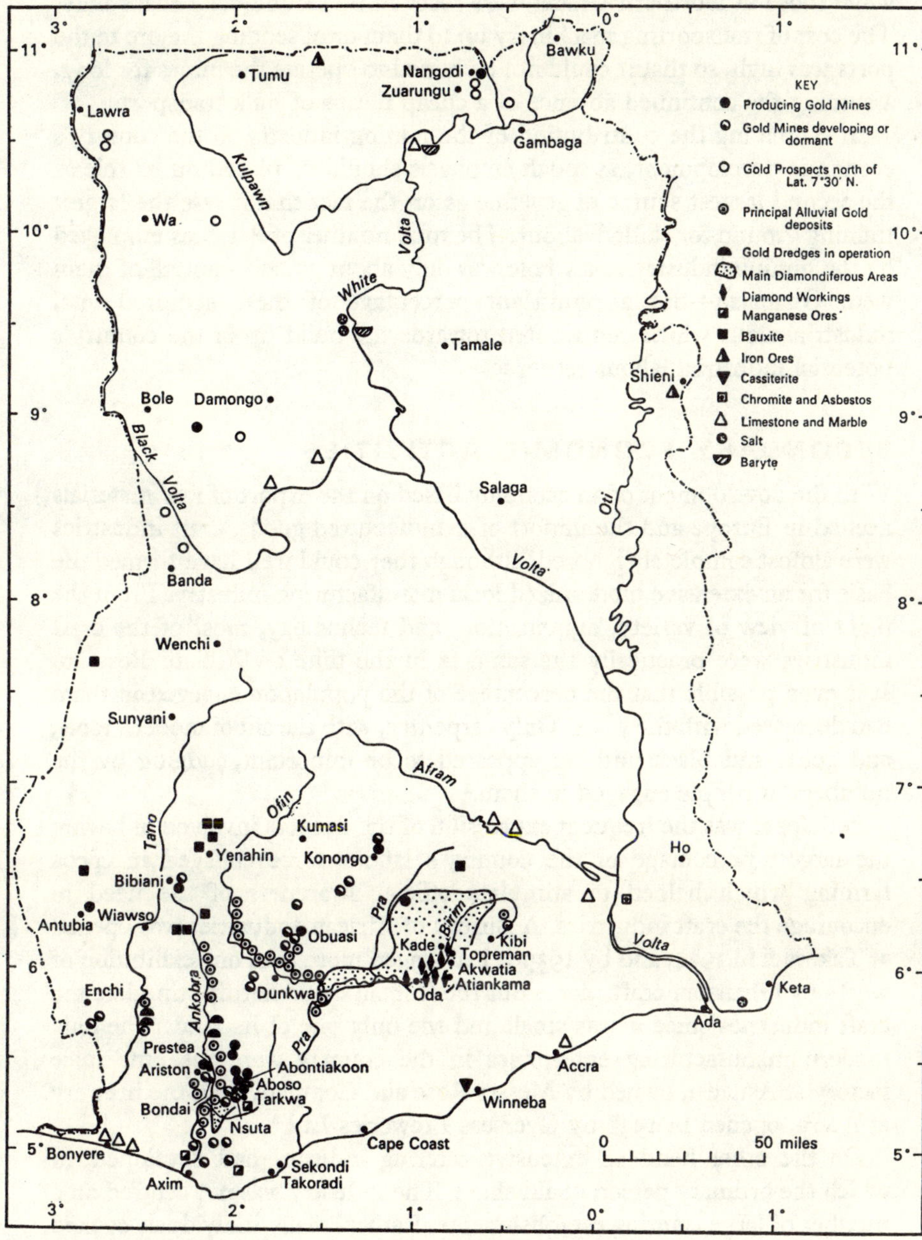


54 Mineral deposits, 1939

while those in Northern Ghana were reached by second-class roads only. The cost of transporting machinery up to them or of sending the ore to the ports was high, so that it could not be hoped to operate the mines for long, assuming the continued absence of a cheap means of bulk transport.

In estimating the contribution of the mining industry to the country's economic development, as much emphasis should be placed on its role as the second largest source of revenue as on the fact that it was the largest training ground for skilled labour. The total number of Africans employed by the mining industry as a whole was only about 39,000—not all of them were Ghanaian—but a significant percentage of these acquired vital industrial skills which contributed towards the build-up of the country's potential industrial labour resource.

## SECONDARY ECONOMIC ACTIVITIES

With the development of an economy based on the export of raw materials needed in Europe and the import of manufactured goods, craft industries were almost completely ignored, although they could well have formed the basis for an extensive modernized local manufacturing industry. From the point of view of variety, organization, and technology, most of the craft industries were practically the same as in the time of William Bosman. It is even possible that the percentage of the population engaged in them had decreased with the years. Only carpentry, with the aid of modern tools, and gold- and blacksmithing appeared to be important, judging by the numbers of people engaged in them.[1]

Perhaps it was the frequent expression of the dangers involved in having the largest percentage of the country's labour force engaged in cocoa farming which helped to stimulate official awareness of the need to encourage the craft industries. A Bureau of African Industries was opened at Takoradi in 1934, and by 1939 it had staged more than one exhibition of works by Ghanaian craftsmen.[2] But the Bureau could hardly stimulate the craft industries since it was small and the only one of its kind. The only modern manufacturing enterprises in the country were the lime juice factory at Asuansi, owned by Messrs Rose and Company, and the brewery at Accra, opened in 1931 by Overseas Breweries Ltd.[3]

On the other hand an extensive catering industry had developed, in which the ordinary person could share. The industry was not centred on a number of large catering establishments. Rather, many individuals cooked

[1] See *Census Report, 1931*.
[2] *Gold Cst. Fmr.* VII, 6 (October 1938), 111.
[3] *The Gold Coast Handbook, 1937*, p. 74.

small quantities of simple meals daily or baked, in their houses, bread, cakes, and similar items which they sold everywhere—in the markets, in the streets, at lorry parks, building sites, street and road junctions, etc. Although competition was fierce, each person made a little profit since the overhead costs were low.

## TRADE

Internal trade differed in many important respects from what it was in earlier times. The differences revolved around the fact that movement from one part of the country to the other was entirely free of interference from local politics. The country was no longer split up into a large number of independent states each pursuing a trade policy of its own. It had become united under a central colonial government whose policies overrode the traditional political differences among states. Therefore the term inter-state trade was no longer meaningful since the fiercely protected state boundaries of earlier times had given way to formal administrative boundaries that did not in any way interfere with movement. Neither was the term local trade any longer to be understood broadly with reference to trade within a state: the term had acquired the meaning of trade centred on any market and embracing all areas, in whatever administrative unit, that on balance yielded to the pull of the market.

Yet another difference was that although the traditional daily or periodic markets still existed everywhere, they no longer functioned as the sole agents of distribution. The departmental store, varying in size from the small village shop to the huge trading establishment in the town, had everywhere in the country taken over the function of distributing imported manufactured goods.

For any part of the country, the distances involved in the movement of commodities were closely related to the degree of urbanization and the extent to which a cash economy had developed. Although large market centres were few in Northern Ghana, their spheres of influence did not correspondingly extend over very large areas since the economy in most of the rural areas was rather subsistence in character, as it had been for more than a century. In the western parts of Sefwi and Wasaw–Aowin, on the other hand, the few widely spaced urban centres had large areas tributary to them since the economy as a whole was market-oriented. Contrasting with Sefwi and Wasaw–Aowin was the Eastern Region, where the existence of a large number of towns, many of them of roughly the same size, meant that supplies to and from the rural areas travelled over shorter distances.

Freedom of movement and the degree of urbanization were not the only guidelines to trade patterns. The effect of the shift of centres of production was also important. Canoes for example were no longer traded laterally along the coast; instead they moved southward to the coast since the producing centres had shifted into the interior. More important was the effect on the trade patterns for food crops which, together with fish, livestock, and imported manufactured goods, formed the major items of internal trade.

Broadly speaking, there were two areas of food shortage, Northern Ghana and the coastline with its towns. The dominant overriding directions of food crop movement were therefore north and south from the forest which produced the bulk of the country's food supply. In exchange, imported manufactured goods and the traditional coastal products of fish (dried or smoked) and salt from Ada and Keta were sent into the interior, while from Northern Ghana streamed southward cattle, shea butter, and yam. Once these broad streams of commodity flow reached the forest, they split up into numerous offshoots to reach the urban centres where they further split up into thinner streams to penetrate into the countryside.

Individual middlemen played a major role in the distribution of goods, whose prices increased with distance from the source areas. But prices were unusually high in the mining towns where, with almost the entire population engaged in mining and nothing else, there was great demand for all kinds of commodities. The mineworkers were relatively well paid and could therefore cope with the high cost of living. The same was true of cocoa farmers in Ashanti and Brong Ahafo who were rich enough to invest large sums of money in capital goods and other imported articles in spite of their high cost. The rising price gradient reached its highest point in Northern Ghana, and in this partly lay the root cause of the region's economic backwardness. It was a vicious circle: Northern Ghana was poor and depended a great deal on the south for supplies, of which imported capital or manufactured goods could only form a small fraction. But since it was expensive to invest in development projects, the materials for many of which had to be imported, Northern Ghana remained poor.

As a British colony, Ghana's overseas trade was naturally dominated by Britain, as may be seen in table 5 which shows the directions of overseas trade in 1937.[1] Next to the United Kingdom were the United States of America, Germany, and the Netherlands, all highly industrialized countries, which imported mainly cocoa, minerals, and timber in exchange for a wide

[1] 1937 was a normal year in which the characteristic features of the country's overseas trade were not distorted.

TABLE 5. *Directions of overseas trade, 1937*

| | Percentage value of overseas trade accounted for by British Empire and other countries | |
|---|---|---|
| | Imports | Exports |
| *Empire countries* | | |
| United Kingdom | 49·37 | 48·1 |
| British West Africa | 1·78 | 0.0* |
| British India | 2·54 | — |
| Canada | 1·05 | 2·9 |
| Other Empire countries | 1·08 | — |
| Total | 55·82 | 51·0 |
| *Other countries* | | |
| United States of America | 11·12 | 23·0 |
| Germany | 8·88 | 14·5 |
| Netherlands | 4·57 | 5·4 |
| France | 0·84 | 0·2 |
| Czechoslovakia | 3·07 | — |
| Belgium | 2·73 | 5·9 |
| Italy | 1·59 | — |
| Japan | 4·10 | — |
| Total | 44·18 | 49·0 |

(Source: *Annual Report on the Gold Coast, 1938–39*, pp. 52–3.)

* Ghana occasionally exported timber by sea to former British West Africa. Also, no account has been taken of the overland exports of kola nuts, which were unrecorded.

variety of manufactured goods. France was one of the least important customers among the Western European countries, and that was because its trading relations were largely with its own colonies. The same was true of Belgium, which had access to large supplies of tropical agricultural produce from the Congo.

Trade with the remaining European countries was generally conducted through Britain. Imports from these countries consisted of textiles and were not so important since there was little else from them that Britain could not itself produce and export. Through Britain they also received small quantities of Ghana's exports.

Of interest is the trade with Japan, which had been growing steadily since the beginning of the 1930s. Japan was the only Far Eastern country outside the British Empire to trade with Ghana. It imported mainly through Britain and in exchange sold artificial silk piece goods at low cost. There was a certain amount of consumer resistance to Japanese goods

TABLE 6. *Principal domestic exports, 1937*

| Product | Value (£) |
|---|---|
| Cocoa | 9,989,548 |
| Gold | 3,910,757 |
| Manganese ore | 1,025,091 |
| Diamonds | 648,057 |
| Timber (unmanufactured) | 129,748 |
| Palm kernels | 103,964 |
| Palm oil | 11,049 |
| Rubber | 33,035 |
| Copra | 23,281 |
| Lime products: | |
| Lime juice | 10,762 |
| Lime oil | 6,228 |
| Lime fruits (fresh) | 852 |
| Other kinds | 96 |
| Hides and skins | 12,711 |
| Kola nuts | 4,225* |

* The value would probably more than double if overland exports of kola nuts were included.

which were judged to be inferior in quality to those from Europe but their greatest asset, which always found a market for the goods in spite of the tendency among certain sections of the population to ignore them, was cheapness.

In contrast to trade with the industrialized countries overseas was that with the rest of West Africa, which was insignificant. Yet in the pre-colonial era trade with other West African nations had been particularly important. What was left of this was mainly with the former British West African countries. From the former French West African countries were also imported cattle and dried fish (from Mali). The whole of West Africa had, under pressure of the Colonial Powers, become a producer of primary goods to the exclusion of almost everything else. Since the products were fairly uniform from one country to the other, except in the case of those countries that were wholly within the forest or the savanna, there was not a firm basis for trade among the countries in West Africa.

Above are listed Ghana's domestic exports[1] in 1937 (table 6).

An outstanding feature, already noted, is that nearly all the exports consisted of unprocessed raw materials. The exception of lime juice and lime

[1] Information on export and import trade is from *Trade Reports* covering the years 1937–9 *Gold Coast Government Gazette, Trade Supplement, 1937*, and *Annual Report on the Gold Coast, 1938–39*, pp. 50–61.

oil was a small one. Another striking feature, fraught with dangerous implications for the country's economy, was the overwhelming importance of cocoa which accounted for over 60 per cent of the total value of exports. The remaining agricultural products were unimportant. It is true that mineral exports were also considerable, accounting for just over 30 per cent of the total value of exports, but they could not always be regarded as an adequate stand-by for the economy in case of a fall in the price of cocoa. No value was added to the minerals through manufacturing; besides the minerals themselves were liable to be exhausted with time or to become poorer in quality. Similar observations applied to timber which could not be a major source of revenue as long as it was exported largely in a raw state.

The stability of the country's economy thus depended on the maintenance of a favourable price for cocoa in the world markets, which in turn depended on factors beyond Ghana's control. Although the largest exporter of cocoa in the world, Ghana's grip on the trade was not strong or exclusive enough to enable it always to adjust supply to demand and in that way ensure a stable price. Furthermore, only three countries, the United Kingdom, the United States of America, and Germany were the principal customers, and any fluctuations in the strength of their economies were readily reflected in their demand, and therefore the price, for Ghana's cocoa. A certain amount of stability would have been ensured if the risk of changes in demand had been spread over a large number of countries.

Putting aside bullion, specie, and currency notes, the principal imports for 1937 were grouped into two classes: food, drink and tobacco, and manufactured goods (table 7).

Goods in the food, drink and tobacco category represented about 11 per cent of the total value of imports. This was a substantial expenditure for a country about 90 per cent of whose population was engaged in agriculture and fishing. Most of the items could have been produced locally but for the fact that a large percentage of the active labour force was engaged in production for export. But this did not constitute any immediate danger to the economy since the food imports could have ceased without creating any hardship. The labour force was not so committed to production for export as to be incapable of reverting wholly to food production for the internal markets, if necessary.

Of greater interest is the fact that manufactured goods represented about 53 per cent of the total value of imports. The point of interest is the composition of the goods: about 33 per cent of their total value went into textiles while not less than 50 per cent was spent on such capital goods as machinery, motor vehicles, fuel, and building materials. Ghana's economy

TABLE 7. *Principal imports, 1937*

| Product | Value (£) |
|---|---|
| Tobacco | 360,000 |
| Fish | 280,200 |
| Meat | 193,500 |
| Spirits (potable) | 201,700 |
| Flour | 181,000 |
| Rice | 179,700 |
| Cotton manufactures: | |
| Piece goods | 1,979,500 |
| Other kinds | 261,500 |
| Artificial silk manufactures | 443,000 |
| Apparel | 458,300 |
| Machinery | 1,279,200 |
| Iron and steel manufactures | 947,500 |
| Carriages, carts, and wagons | 646,600 |
| Oils | 643,200 |
| Cement | 197,700 |
| Explosives | 149,800 |
| Medicines and Drugs | 181,100 |

had developed to the point where productivity in the export sector was high enough to leave a substantial surplus to invest in the material basis for future industrialization.

Also characteristic of the economy and important for the future was the fact that Ghana enjoyed, annually, a favourable balance of trade worth about £3,000,000. The accumulated reserves of sterling were large enough to cushion the economy comfortably in time of crisis.

## COMMUNICATIONS AND SEAPORTS

### Rail, river and air transport

There were some 470 miles of railway, but they were all confined to Southern Ghana and Ashanti. The bulk of the freight carried consisted of cocoa and manganese. The passenger service was not fully patronized, and on the whole the railways were run at a loss. Rivers, as before, were not important in the overall pattern of transport, and the newly introduced air service based on the aerodromes at Accra, Kumasi, Tamale and Takoradi was a luxury that did not in any way affect the distribution of transport facilities.

## Road transport

Roads were clearly the most effective means of transport, in terms of total mileage, geographical distribution, and tonnage carried. It was roads, more than any other means of transport, which defined the areas with opportunities for economic development.

Figure 55 shows the uneven distribution of the 6,200 miles of motorable roads in the country. The Western Region, which was relatively unimportant agriculturally, had a very open road network. The transport needs of its strictly localized gold-mining and timber industries were easily supplied by a few trunk roads and the railway from Tarkwa to Takoradi. The Central Region on the other hand possessed a close network of roads behind its ports, serving a rich agricultural area. This was also true of the Eastern Region, which possessed the greatest mileage of motorable roads in Southern Ghana. The Volta Region also had a number of important roads whose alignment was guided by the nature of the relief. These roads generally followed the ridge tops and had few lateral connections. The absence of lateral road connections also characterized the plains to the south of the Togo–Atakora Ranges, where the main roads avoided the interior and kept to the frontier with Togo and to the immediate borderlands of the Volta River.

In Ashanti also the detailed distribution pattern of roads closely reflected the distribution of the dominant economic areas, most of which were also the core areas of the Ashanti nation. Mampong, Kumasi, Bekwai, and Obuasi were the dominant economic centres with Kumasi as the most important. A series of branch road networks surrounded each of the centres, but they did not extend far enough outward to link up. The existence of widely spaced clusters of branch road network was still more true of western Brong Ahafo where the dominant economic centres were far removed from one another.

Northern Ghana had relatively few good roads, and the extensive flat savanna lands were criss-crossed by bush paths which were not motorable. The paths formed a fine mesh in the densely populated north-east and north-west corners of the country, while the network was much more open in the sparsely populated sections, as in Gonja.

Although the distribution of the main motorable roads provided a good index of the degree of economic development it was the existence of feeder roads, most of which were not officially regarded as motorable even in the dry season, which determined the economic opportunities of the countryside. From the point of view of food transportation from most

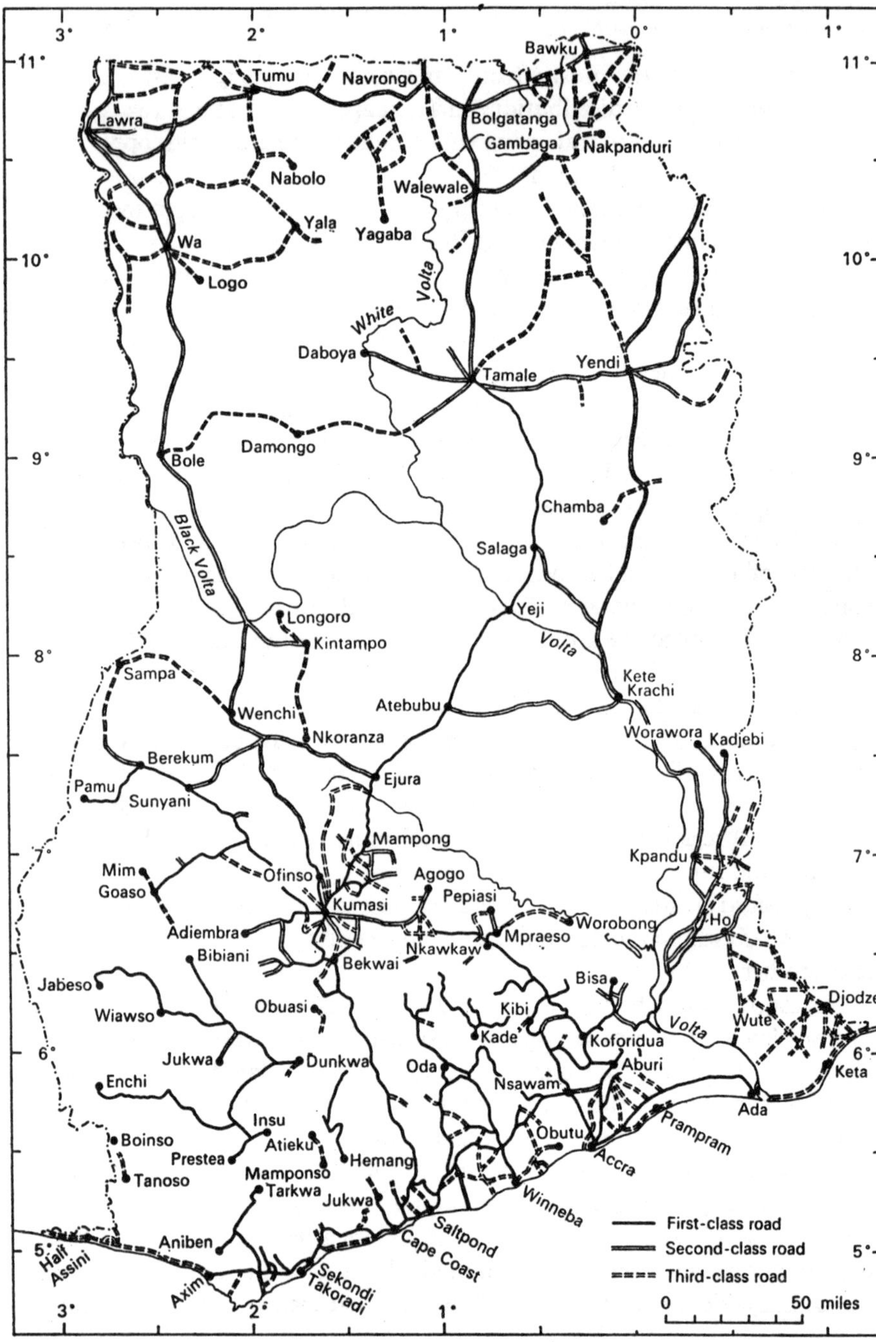


55 Motor roads, 1939

rural areas, a trunk road was nothing more than a major channel into which numerous feeder roads drained.

Six trunk roads stood out above the rest, and in only three instances did they follow the same directions as the early eighteenth-century trade routes. The remaining eighteenth-century routes had either gone out of use or were no longer important. But however different the trajectories of the later trade roads, most of them, as did the earlier trade routes, centred on Kumasi.

The Cape Coast–Kumasi trade road, which roughly coincided with the old Cape Coast–Kumasi trade route, was the only direct link between Ashanti and the Central Region. The coastal section of the Western Region also communicated with Ashanti by this road.

In the Eastern Region the busiest trade road was that connecting Accra to Kumasi. It differed from its earlier counterpart in that it passed through Aburi, Koforidua and Nkawkaw instead of passing through the Volta gorge and then proceeding through the parkland zone along the north-facing foothills of the Southern Voltaian Plateau. The road had shifted to its new position because of the intensification of economic activities in the Closed Forest south of the Southern Voltaian Plateau.

The Volta Region was linked to the coast by the road from Accra to Kete Krachi, Worawora, or Ho. Although the road was officially designated as second class, it quickly deteriorated into a third-class road in the rainy season, so that its carrying capacity was often severely limited. The difference between this road and its older counterpart was that it was no longer a three-pronged road leading to Accra, Ada, and Keta. Accra, because of its status as the country's capital and its rapid growth, which was unmatched by that of Ada or Keta, had become the sole terminus of the road.

Between Northern Ghana and Ashanti the most important trade road was that from Navrongo through Bolgatanga, Tamale, and Salaga to Kumasi. It followed exactly the same trajectory as the early eighteenth-century route. Also unchanged in the direction it followed was the Tumu-Wa–Bole–Kumasi trade road. The only significant addition to the trade roads in Northern Ghana was that from Yendi to Kete Krachi which formerly covered a longer distance by passing through Salaga.

Considering the country as a whole, the most outstanding transport problem was the fewness of the trade road links between Northern Ghana and the rest of the country. The problem stemmed from the interposition, across the middle portion of the country, of that economically negative area, the Middle Belt, where commercial motor vehicles had absolutely no prospect of picking up more freight. As a result the cost of road transport to or from Northern Ghana was high.

Elsewhere the fewness of good motorable roads was amply compensated for by the use of that unique vehicle, the 'mammy wagon'. This was an ordinary commercial motor vehicle, but unique in the sense that it was crowned with a superstructure designed to create maximum freight and passenger space but to give a minimum of comfort. More important, it was normally driven at a fairly high speed by a dedicated breed of men who did not scruple to take it over the merest suggestion of a road. Also, as long as freight or passengers were available all along the way, the cost of transport by the ubiquitous 'mammy wagon' was not high.[1] The driver, usually the owner as well, could afford to charge low rates since his overhead costs were low. So that the distributive system was on the whole more efficient than is suggested by fig. 55 which shows the distribution of roads officially considered to be motorable.

## Seaports

On the coast the main trade roads ended at Takoradi harbour and the seven surf ports which handled the country's overseas trade (fig. 56). It was not possible to leave to Takoradi harbour alone the physical handling of the overseas trade, which had undergone a vast expansion since the harbour was opened in 1928. Moreover the cost of distribution of goods from Takoradi to the Eastern and Volta Regions was obviously much higher than from ports in, or nearer to, the two Regions. In other words, exports were more cheaply sent to ports nearest the producing areas. Consequently it was Accra, not Takoradi, through which was exported the largest quantity of cocoa (fig. 57), and if Takoradi was the premier port it was because of the relative ease of access to it from the principal mining areas and those cocoa areas near, or with road connections to, the Takoradi–Kumasi railway.

Port trade at Half Assini was minimal, yet the port survived because it was cheapest to send timber, the major product from its hinterland, cocoa, and rubber down to the coast by the Tano river. The ports of Keta and Ada also survived because they exported cocoa, copra, and oil-palm products from the immediate interior.

On the other hand Saltpond, closely hemmed in by the larger ports of

[1] Cardinall, *The Gold Coast, 1931* (Accra, 1931), p. 114. The economics of running a 'mammy wagon', as described by Cardinall, held true until the early 1960s when shortage of spare parts and the unnaturally inflated cost of repairs severely reduced the extreme flexibility of this means of transport.

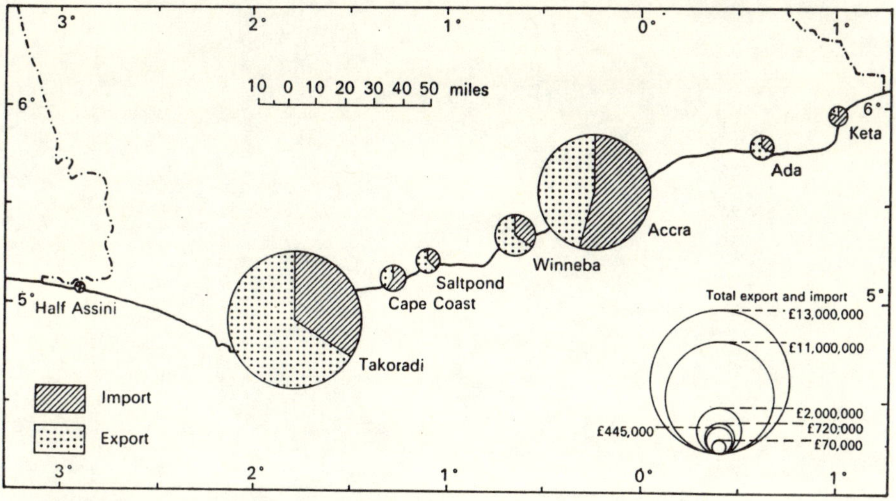


56 Value of port trade, 1937

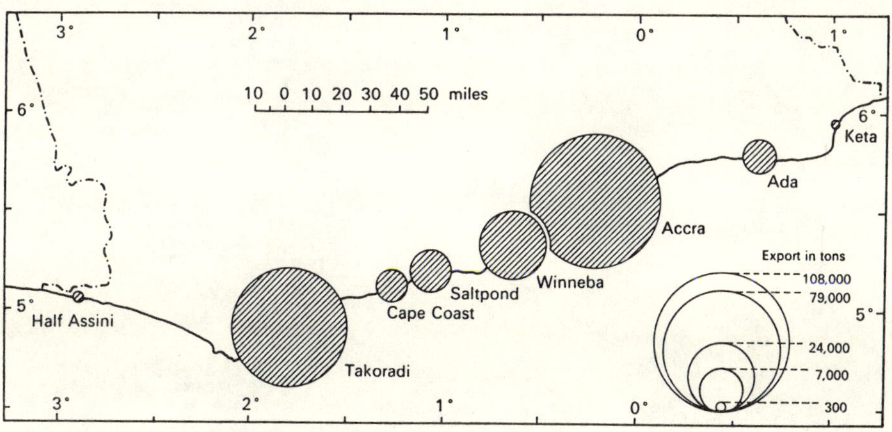


57 Cocoa exports, 1937

Cape Coast and Winneba, was clearly superfluous and was closed down at the end of 1939. The three remaining large surf ports, Cape Coast, Winneba, and Accra, existed independently of one another. They were evenly spaced; they were each served by a network of roads associated with a single trunk road from the port; and they did not compete for trade.

*Conclusion*

# 14. Man and the landscape

## THE CHANGING LANDSCAPE

Basically, the problems and contradictions implied in Ghana's human geography are related to the division of the country into two broadly contrasted physical regions: savanna and forest. The division, originally latent, was made real through the nature of man's interference with the natural vegetation. Thus were created two ecosystems, each with its own physical laws, each rewarding or yielding to man's efforts in its own way and exacting more or less severe penalties when its harmonious working was unwisely disturbed.

### The original vegetation

During the last pluvial which immediately preceded the arrival of the Saharan Neolithic, the whole country was very likely clothed with forest which may have been more open in the north and in the south-east coastal plains. In the ensuing dry phase the forest would have been thinned but not destroyed at its northern margins, probably from about latitude 8° N, through the reimposition of the tropical continental climate with its reduced total annual rainfall. The forest would similarly have been affected at its south-eastern margins by the re-establishment of the low annual rainfall.[1] So that an open forest would have remained on the coast, east of Cape Three Points, out of harmony with the anomalous rainfall amount but surviving through self-protection or the creation of a micro-climate under the tree canopies necessary for the existence of the trees.

Ecological investigations have also turned up evidence to suggest that the present savanna areas were once wooded.[2] At the margins of the Closed Forest, including the Accra Plains, the original vegetation was probably an open forest similar to the *Antiaris chlorophora* association of the Closed Forest. It was probably succeeded further north by a deciduous forest. In Northern Ghana scattered fetish groves, up to 5 acres in extent, break the

[1] The low rainfall of the south-east coastal plains is an anomaly. There is a brief but illuminating discussion of this in Glenn T. Trewartha's *The Earth's Problem Climates* (University of Wisconsin Press, Madison, 1962), pp. 106–10.

[2] For example, C. J. Taylor, *Synecology and Silviculture in Ghana* (London, 1960), p. 68, and C. Howell and F. Bourliere (eds.), *African Ecology and Human Evolution* (London, 1963), p. 37.

monotony of the grassland cover. Found in all kinds of terrain, they typically consist of deciduous woodland with a sparse grassy cover and a closed or nearly closed canopy at a height of some 60 feet. These groves, which are in sharp contrast to the surrounding vegetation, indicate that on climatic grounds there is nothing to prevent the development of a form of closed woodland throughout the region.[1] Also, a carefully conducted experiment on the Red Volta in Northern Ghana has shown that complete protection of the Guinea Savanna vegetation 'ensures rapid development towards a closed woodland or forest type of climax which would ultimately reduce or eliminate the present herbaceous cover'.[2]

Furthermore, there is historical evidence, applying to the coastal areas only, to indicate the former presence of a more luxuriant vegetation. Around the beginning of the eighteenth century, the country between Elmina and Cape Coast was described as being so densely covered with trees that the pathways were sheltered from both sun and rain.[3] Takoradi area, clothed in a forest of large trees, produced the finest and largest dug-out canoes in Southern Ghana: a single canoe was capable of carrying loads to the weight of 10 tons.[4] The town of Winneba, now backed by plains almost entirely denuded of trees, was around the middle of the nineteenth century 'very agreeably situated amongst trees', and the district as a whole ranked among the major producers of dug-out canoes.[5] Similarly, oral tradition confirms the former presence of forest on the Labadi coast.[6]

Further evidence for the former presence of forest in the savanna areas is forthcoming from place-name study. Potsin, the name of a large village situated in the grassy plains behind Winneba, means literally 'a stretch of forest'. In central Togo, close to the Ghana border, are the Kabre among whom are found the Lama. The name Lama is an abbreviation of Lan-mba which means 'people of the forest'. There are other toponyms, all of them variations of Lan, which indicate the former presence of forest in Kabre district as well as in neighbouring districts in Northern Ghana: Lao (forest), Lawda (in the forest), Landa (in the forests), Lawnoh (edge of the forest), etc.[7]

[1] J. M. Ramsay and R. Rose Innes, 'Some Quantitative Observations on the Effects of Fire on the Guinea Savanna Vegetation of Northern Ghana over a Period of Eleven Years', *African Soils*, VIII, 1 (1963).

[2] Ibid.

[3] Bosman, *Guinea*, Letter V.

[4] Barbot, *North and South Guinea*, p. 152.

[5] Horton, *West African Countries and Peoples*, p. 139.

[6] F. R. Irvine, *The Fishes and Fisheries of the Gold Coast* (London, 1947), p. 24.

[7] Cornevin, *Histoire du Togo*, pp. 39–40.

## Deforestation

Confronted with a primitive landscape of forest, man began to carve a living space for himself after he had settled down in Neolithic times to systematic cultivation of the soil. Pre-Neolithic peoples did not presumably do much damage to the natural vegetation, for theirs was a hunting, fishing and food-gathering economy which, demanding little from the soil itself, spared the vegetation that covered it.

Neolithic man, in his attack on the forest, made deliberate and extensive use of fire. His stone axes could also have been used to chop down bush or to ring-bark trees to kill them, while the hoe-like celts may have helped to clear the ground for cultivation.[1] How much deforestation was actually done by the Neolithic cultivators is not known, but it has been presumed that it was not inconsiderable. To the Neolithic cultivators has been attributed the conversion of extensive areas of virgin forest to secondary forest in Ashanti.[2]

Just as uncertain is the amount of deforestation to be attributed to the early Iron Age people. Although they were superior militarily to the Neolithic peoples, their techniques of cultivation were apparently no different. Stone remained the material for agricultural implements while iron was mainly for weapons. On the other hand the introduction of the forge and the need for fuel must have meant far greater demands on the forest.

From about the thirteenth century onwards the picture of deforestation comes into better focus. The population settles down in clan and tribal groupings and often in nucleated settlements; for the first time society is organized under a central political power vested in a chief; there is a certain measure of social stability as well as greater orderliness in the fight to wrest a living from the physical environment.[3] In other words the foundations for the country's human geography are laid, and everywhere the physical environment is being actively converted to a recognizable cultural landscape.

In Northern Ghana and in the south-east coastal plains, the result of the intensification of human occupance was more spectacular: the woodland cover was almost completely eliminated, and in its place developed parkland or savanna vegetation. This is not to say that the Closed Forest

[1] Neolithic celts probably performed a dual function as hoes and as the working ends of digging sticks for collecting wild vegetable foods.

[2] O. Davies, 'The Neolithic Revolution in Tropical Africa', *Trans. Hist. Soc. Ghana*, IV, pt. II (1960).

[3] Chapters 1 and 2.

was less heavily settled than the present savanna areas. Outside the Closed Forest the drier conditions permitted a more regular and extensive use of fire, which effectively prevented the regeneration of the original woodland cover. In the Closed Forest, on the other hand, the greater humidity prevents extensive damage through the use of fire, and a cleared area is, if left undisturbed for long enough, quickly covered by secondary bush which eventually develops into a dense forest similar to the original virgin forest.

Up to the mid-nineteenth century the process of deforestation was not smooth and continuous. Numerous tribal wars and epidemics throughout the centuries interrupted the work of destruction; the wars were particularly devastating during the seventeenth and eighteenth centuries when various states in the country were seeking to carve out empires for themselves. William Bosman drew some striking contrasts between the appearance of Southern Ghana at his first visit and at a later visit to the country, both in the late seventeenth century. Much of the coastal portions of Central and Western Regions in the 1690s wore a look of ruin and desolation. The countryside, deprived of its population through wars, lay wild and uncultivated. Yet a few years earlier the countryside as a whole was well populated and had a thriving agriculture.[1] Within the first half of the nineteenth century the greatest part of Southern Ghana still wore a look of ruin, and descriptions of journeys from Cape Coast to Kumasi contained long lists of villages in various stages of decay after tribal wars, and in the process of being swallowed up by the surrounding forest.[2]

Although the wars brought ruin and therefore preserved the forest in some parts of the country, they also encouraged deforestation in other parts of the country. When villages were attacked, the surviving inhabitants fled to quieter areas and settled there. It was in this way that many of the villages near Winneba, for example, were founded.

After the first half of the nineteenth century the process of deforestation took on a new look and became more complicated.[3] Roughly, the year 1850 stands out as marking the beginning of the period when commercial

[1] Op. cit. Letter III.

[2] For example, Dupuis, *Journal of a Residence in Ashantee*, pt. I, *passim*.

[3] It has become customary to rely on the two maps by C. F. Charter (*Cocoa Conference*, London, 1953) which are designed to show the extent of deforestation between 1909 and 1953. The problem is with the first map. It shows a shaded Closed Forest (in 1909) broken in 27 places, 20 of them in Eastern Region, by open patches in which the word 'cocoa' is written. Clearly the open patches are too few; deforestation through cocoa farming was more extensive than is shown on the map. T. F. Chipp's *Forest Officers' Handbook* (London, 1922) contains a more cautious treatment of the subject of deforestation since the late nineteenth century.

agriculture acquired greater importance in many parts of Southern Ghana. Brodie Cruickshank's enthusiastic and sympathetic review of the country's economy may suffer from exaggeration,[1] but the essential picture of a country in which trade in palm oil had replaced trade in slaves cannot be denied. The beginnings of commercial agriculture were modest, involving the cultivation of a few crops like cotton and coffee, and the preparation of palm oil and kola nuts for export. These activities became more diversified and intensified with the years, slowly making increasing demands upon the forest. Then came the last quarter of the nineteenth century when the internecine tribal wars ceased and conditions were created which led to a considerable outburst of economic activity and of deforestation. This period approximately coincided with the introduction and initial stages of cocoa cultivation.

Although cocoa cultivation made some spectacular inroads into the forest in many parts of the country within the first decade of the twentieth century, the country was still heavily and extensively forested.[2] The clearings in the forest, most of them for farms, were more numerous in the central and eastern portions of Southern Ghana and Ashanti than in the western portion where vast stretches of forest existed. Some of the clearings were extensive enough to be specially commented upon, including those on the Kwahu range of hills around Pepease, Nkwatia, Mpraeso, Apeko, Aduamo, Oho, and Tweneduase. The original forest had in each case been replaced by a dense regrowth of a more open grassland vegetation often over 15 feet high. In the Volta Region too, the speed of deforestation was gradually assuming alarming proportions.

With the accelerated economic development of the country from the end of the first decade of the twentieth century came still greater demands on the country's forest resources. The growing timber and mining industries, the implementation of vast schemes of road and railway building, the increase in the size of the population accompanied by increase in the acreage under food crops, the spread of cash crop farming of which cocoa cultivation was the most important—all these led to extensive deforestation.

The timber industry, which began in the late 1880s, took its toll of the forest cover in the Western Region, especially in Aowin, the centre of the industry. The number of trees felled for the industry was large, judging by the size of timber exports and by the fact that in the early days of the industry there were no laws to ensure the replacement of trees that had been felled. Nevertheless timber logging did not by itself cause any remarkable

[1] *Eighteen Years on the Gold Coast of Africa* (London, 1853).

[2] H. N. Thompson, *Gold Coast—Report on Forests*, Cmd. 4993 (1910).

alteration in the appearance of the forest, since exploitation was confined to a few species (of the upper age classes) which were not confined to a particular area.[1] Whatever visible damage occurred was due to the mass clearing of trees to make timber extraction tracks, camp clearings, and their associated food farms.

The mining industry also made considerable demands on the forest. Soon after 1900 the Government ruled that each mining concession should be demarcated by an 8-foot-wide avenue cut through the forest and marked with boundary posts bearing nameplates at every thousand feet. This regulation was enforced because of the large number of disputes that arose over the boundaries of overlapping concessions, and prompt compliance with the regulation resulted in a significant amount of forest destruction since the concessions were numerous. Besides, the mining operations themselves required the destruction of large stretches of forest: the demands of all the mines for fuel and pit props affected an estimated 350 square miles of forest.[2]

Road and railway building similarly involved a considerable amount of forest destruction—in 1907 about 1,500 trees were felled along the railway line between Kumasi and Eduadin (a distance of 9 miles) and 760 trees near Obuasi alone.[3] In addition, these lines of communication themselves cut up the forest into blocks and facilitated their destruction: each stretch of road or railway formed a broad front along which the forest was attacked. The eastern part of the forest was being rapidly separated from the remainder by the clearing of a belt up to 20 miles wide along the railway from Sekondi to Kumasi, and along the main north road from Kumasi to Ejura. This belt became wider and more continuous south of Kumasi, and with the completion of the Accra–Kumasi railway in 1923 the remaining forest areas of the central and eastern districts of Southern Ghana and Ashanti were almost completely encircled.[4] To supply fuel to the railways themselves required an estimated forest area of about 4,000 square miles.[5]

By far the greatest amount of deforestation was done in the attempt to satisfy the daily or normal requirements of the population. The vegetation provided material for fuel, building, furniture, canoe-making, etc.,[6] and all this required, at a conservative estimate, some 2 million cubic feet of timber

[1] Taylor, op. cit. pp. 54–5.

[2] Chipp, op. cit. p. 25.

[3] *Colonial Report, Ashanti, 1907.*

[4] Later railway construction, from Dunkwa to Awaso and from Achiase to Kotoku, cut up the forest into yet smaller blocks and facilitated the work of destruction.

[5] Chipp, op. cit. p. 25.

[6] Ibid, pp. 55 ff. There is a long list of the different tree species needed for the various purposes.

annually during the 1930s.[1] The vegetation also had to be destroyed to facilitate hunting and farming. Hunting required the use of fire to flush game, and its effect on the vegetation was more marked in the savanna areas.

Food farming was the greatest single cause of deforestation. On the basis of 11,600 square miles of forest computed to have been destroyed since 1894, it was concluded in 1934 that bush fallowing accounted for 10,600 square miles.[2] The figures lay no claim to absolute accuracy, but they confirm the fact that food farming was the most widespread occupation and, in view of the techniques of cultivation, therefore the main agent of deforestation.

There are two areas where the effect of the primary occupations on the vegetation has been most spectacular. One is the northern edge of the Closed Forest which supported a comparatively dense population and constantly received immigrants from Northern Ghana. The forest, regularly cut down to make room for new farms or nibbled at by the repeated grass fires from the neighbouring savanna, was rapidly retreating southward.[3]

Just as remarkable an instance of deforestation is Bisa area in Krobo where the inhabitants, traditionally not a forest people, use a clear-felling method when making new farms.[4] The Bisa area, situated in the Pawmpawm basin, was originally covered with deciduous type of forest of good average height and density, with only a narrow transition belt separating it from the savanna vegetation to the north.[5] By the 1920s the situation was quite different. A belt of neglected oil palms, planted in the 1890s, had replaced the forest east of the Pawmpawm Su; the greater part of the transition belt had been absorbed by the savanna vegetation which had also thrust a wedge up the valley of the Pawmpawm Su. The rest of the area was covered by a mixture of good and bad cocoa farms, groups of oil palms, patches of savanna and secondary growth, and a few scattered remnants of the original forest. The first known grassland fire on any appreciable scale in the area was in the 1927–8 dry season. It burnt out a semicircular belt on a 4-mile radius, destroying several hundred acres of cocoa and severely damaging many thousands of oil-palm trees.[6]

[1] Department of Forestry, *Annual Report, 1935–6*.

[2] Major F. M. Oliphant, 'Report on the Commercial Possibilities and Development of the Forests of the Gold Coast', *Gold Coast Government Sessional Paper*, no. I (1934).

[3] Chipp, op. cit. p. 47.

[4] Taylor, op. cit. p. 51.

[5] Department of Agriculture, *Year Book, 1928*, Paper no. IX, and *Year Book, 1929*, Paper no. XII.

[6] Ibid.

## Forest protection

While the process of deforestation generally indicated a welcome outburst of economic activity, it also posed problems which had to be solved if the land won from the forest was not to be allowed to deteriorate. Besides, it was under the shade of the remaining forest that the country's most valuable export crop, cocoa, flourished.

Up to the end of the nineteenth century, the idea of protecting the forest was hardly ever mentioned although food and cocoa farms were rapidly eating into it. Perhaps the deterioration of the cut-over areas was in some cases partly checked by the existence of fetish groves. These ancient stretches of woodland, preserved as the abodes of gods and spirits, were not intended to be forest reserves, but they served as such. They were sacred and therefore completely inaccessible to those who did not belong to the relevant religious cult. It was in the groves that were performed the secret mystic rites, and unauthorized entry into them was usually punishable by death. One of the most famous recorded examples of the seriousness with which violation of the groves was held was the incident at Saltpond in 1836, in which some local Christian converts deliberately made clearings in the town's fetish grove. Only the quick and decisive action by Government officials at Cape Coast prevented the mass slaughter of the offenders.[1]

By the turn of the century there was much concern about the rate at which the forest was disappearing in some areas. The first action taken was the passing of the Timber Protection Ordinance of 1907; but the aim of this ordinance was not comprehensive enough. It was merely to prevent the timber companies from felling immature trees. In 1909 was formed the nucleus of a forestry department whose principal aim was not to preserve the forest but to survey its commercial possibilities and superintend its systematic exploitation.

The first ordinance to deal directly with the problem of forest conservation was the Forest Ordinance, no. 15 of 1911, according to which the Governor-in-Council could declare to be a forest reserve any suitable piece of land that appeared to be unoccupied. It was not permitted to collect rubber and other natural produce in the reserves. The ordinance aroused a storm of protest, especially from members of the Aborigines Rights Protection Society, who argued that it showed a complete lack of understanding of the Ghanaian land tenure system, and that its enforcement would unlawfully

[1] W. W. Claridge, *History of the Gold Coast and Ashanti* (London, 1915), I, 467.

deprive the Ghanaian of his land.[1] The ordinance was cancelled at the request of the Colonial Office, but not before three forest reserves—the Kumawu-Agogo, Chimpor, and Banka reserves—had been established in Ashanti. The huge tract of land between the Obosum and Sene rivers was also declared a game reserve. The Germans similarly established forest reserves in the Volta Region but without opposition, since the terms of their Forest Conservation Ordinance of 1912 were more realistic and generous from the point of view of the local inhabitants. According to this ordinance, the only tracts of forest that were to be reserved were those (*a*) on dome-shaped summits, on ridges or hills, on precipitous hillsides, and at all places where the forest was serving as a means of preventing landslides; (*b*) those lying in the neighbourhood of standing or flowing water; and (*c*) those whose preservation appeared necessary for the protection of certain areas against invasion of savanna conditions. The first category did not include forests in possession of the local inhabitants. Burning, clearing, and similar activities in the reserves established within the remaining two categories might also be allowed in certain cases by the governor.[2]

Between 1912 and 1917 when the office of the Conservator of Forests was abolished, no more forest reserves were created since the Government did not have the necessary statutory powers; but sections of the population felt and expressed the need to preserve the forest. Chief Ofori Ata of Akim Abuakwa was the first ruler to publish by-laws, in 1915, controlling deforestation in his area. The by-laws prohibited the cultivation of cocoa or food crops on all the outstanding hills in the district, and included a long list of forest trees that might not be felled without permission.[3]

It was not until 1919 that a forestry policy acceptable to all was evolved. Systematic forest surveys were then begun by the re-formed Forestry Department, and between 1922 and 1926 the Department published long lists of forest reserves that it proposed should be established. The reserves were to serve a variety of purposes. Some were to protect the sources of rivers, e.g. the Atewa Range reserve was to protect the sources of the Birim and Ayensu rivers; some, like the Begoro and Dodowa reserves, were to act as barriers to further encroachment of savanna, or as shelter belts to protect cash crops; and yet others, like the Onyin reserve, were to enclose narrow strips of savanna country on which, by prohibiting the use of the land for agricultural or any other purpose, it was hoped to induce the growth of a better type of vegetation. Finally were the firewood plantations,

[1] Caseley Hayford, 'The Gold Coast Land Tenure and the Forest Bill, 1911, 1912', *Legal Pamphlet*, no. 91 (Colonial Office Library, London).

[2] *Colonial Report—Togoland, 1920–21.*

[3] *Gold Coast Government Gazettes* covering the period 1915 to 1934.

e.g. at Achimota, established to satisfy the largest domestic demand for wood. All the reserves were to be planted with trees that would ultimately be felled for commercial purposes. Reserves were also to be established by chiefs in their respective districts under the provisions of the Forest Ordinance of 1919, but since the rate at which the 'native authority reserves' were being established appeared to be slow, a new Forest Ordinance was introduced in 1927 to speed up the process.

The creation of forest reserves came up against many difficulties, of which the following cases were typical. (*a*) The proposed reserve on the Atewa Range originally covered an area of approximately 190 square miles, but later had to be reduced to 91 square miles in order to leave out, for the villages affected, practically all land suitable for cultivation. (*b*) The Apedwa reserve, proposed to cover the tops and sides of the steep range of hills between Kibi and Apedwa, was in Akim Abuakwa territory. At the time of the demarcation it was discovered that two large areas in the reserve had been alienated to people from outside the state, so that the chief of Akim Abuakwa could not insist on the inclusion of those two areas in the reserve. It was further discovered that cocoa farms had spread much higher up the hillsides than was at first realized, and that the local people were resolved that no cocoa farms should be included in the reserve. They also insisted that the boundary of the reserve should be kept at such a distance as to allow for the future extension of the cocoa farms. (*c*) The Birim reserve, as originally proposed, included a number of villages under the chiefs of Akim Abuakwa, Akim Bosome, and Akim Kotoku, and there was much difficulty in getting the three paramount chiefs to agree to any definite boundary line. The southern and eastern boundaries of the reserve were altered three times, and in the end the area of the reserve was reduced to about half of its original size.[1]

There was one universal difficulty: the local inhabitants always insisted on being allowed to farm within the reserves, a problem that was not fully solved by the introduction within the reserves of the taungya system. Under this system specially chosen forest trees, some of them, like the teak, of foreign provenance, were planted on cut-over areas within the reserves, and during the period of growth of the trees the land, previously provided with a cover of fast-growing plants, was allowed to be cultivated for the production of food crops. The system was not readily accepted, and for many years remained in an experimental stage. Between 1932 and 1939 the number of people convicted of forest offences averaged about 160 a year, and the majority of the offences were for the unauthorized making of

[1] Department of Forestry, *Annual Reports*, 1919 to 1938/39.

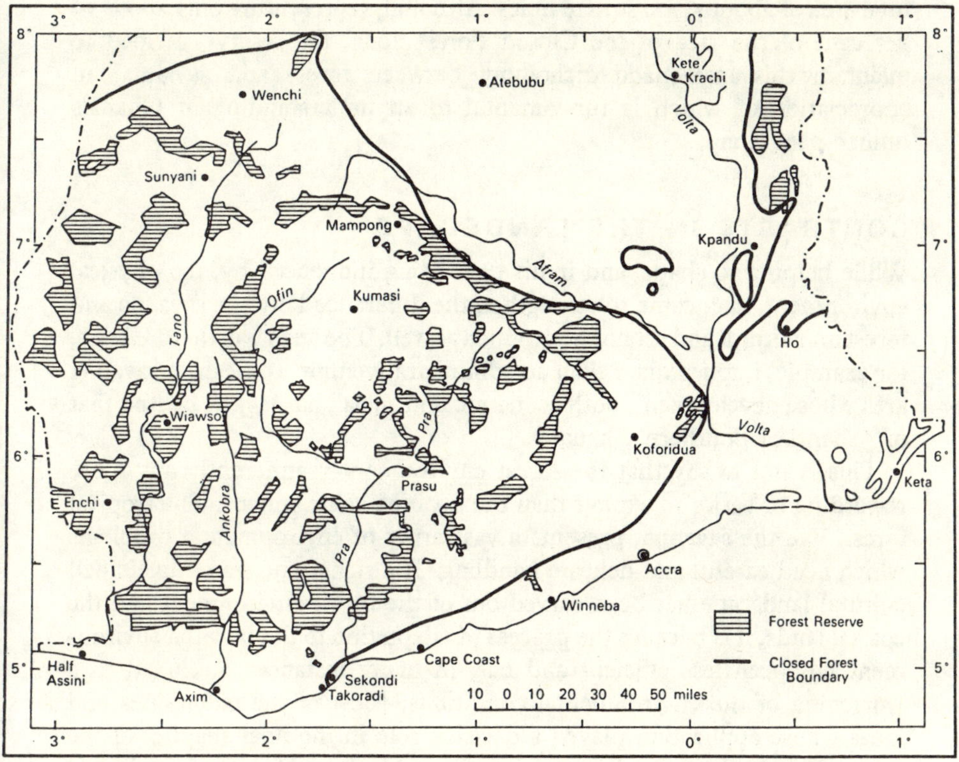


58 Forest reserves, 1939

farms within the reserves. The frequency with which the forestry laws were ignored was largely a result of the discontinuance, after the passing of the Forests (Discontinuance of Grants) Ordinance in 1932, of the practice of compensating owners of land within the reserves.

Other offences, usually unintentional, involved the setting of grassland in the vicinity of reserves on fire, which eventually spread to the reserves themselves. To reduce the risk of forest fires, grassland areas adjoining reserves were deliberately burned in the dry season in such a way as to prevent the fire from spreading to the reserves. In areas where bush fires were common, it was illegal for farmers or hunters to burn grassland except with the special permission of the District Commissioner.

In spite of the many difficulties encountered, the number of forest reserves increased so rapidly that by 1939 the programme of reservation in the Closed Forest was almost completed (fig. 58). The reserves covered a total area of about 5,700 square miles. Although representing only about 19 per cent of the area of the Closed Forest zone, the reserves helped to maintain this man-made dichotomy between forest and savanna, an appreciation of which is fundamental to an understanding of Ghana's human geography.

## CONTRASTS IN THE LANDSCAPE

While helping to shape, and in his turn being influenced by, the physical environment, man came to strengthen the difference between savanna and forest on cultural and economic grounds as well. The term Northern Ghana, for example, implies more than an administrative unit. It means a savanna area whose development, both economic and social, has lagged behind that of Ashanti or Southern Ghana.

This is not to say that the forest environment is inherently any more rewarding or easier to exploit than the savanna environment. The tropical forest, like the savanna, presents a vast array of environmental problems which need careful and delicate handling. If a richer and more diversified cultural landscape has been carved out of the forest environment and the coastal lands, it is because the process of adaptation to the savanna environment has been less efficient and has, in many instances, even led to a worsening of the environmental conditions. Most of the techniques and ideas whose application played a decisive role in the final shaping of the cultural landscape spread from south to north, from the coast northward through the forest. From looking towards the Western Sudan which up to about the end of the sixteenth century was the principal source of cultural innovations, Ghana turned round to look southward towards the coast which had come under the steady influence of Western European cultural ideas, economy, and technology. Indeed, this shift of cultural and economic superiority from the northern savannas to the forest and the coast is one of the major themes in the historical geography of West Africa as a whole. Powerful states with sophisticated economic and political systems also developed in the forest of Ghana, and one of these, Ashanti, was to set into operation new determinants which helped significantly in sketching the bold outlines of the present cultural landscape. In the northern savannas it was often the negative and destructive, rather than the positive and constructive, effects of the southern influences that were felt.

Thus Northern Ghana became a problem area inhabited by men at a generally lower technological stage and living mostly in rural settlements; an area with its population distributed in a peculiar fashion that reflected not so much the economic potential of the land as the stultifying influence of historical accidents; an area with large exposed stretches of agriculturally useless laterite and without a single major export crop; an area without railways and for the most part without good motorable roads. At the same time the forest of Ashanti–Brong Ahafo and Southern Ghana, together with the coastal lands, emerged with a sharply contrasting cultural landscape characterized by a more logical pattern of population distribution, by both towns and flourishing villages, by mines, export crops, railways, good roads, etc. Between these two broadly contrasted cultural landscapes was a zone of transition embracing the parkland of Brong Ahafo, northern Buem, and portions of the southernmost extension of Gonja.

Within each of the three major cultural landscapes there developed further areal differentiation based on the varying impact, in time and space, of the determinants of the cultural landscape. In Northern Ghana, the cultural landscape of north Mamprusi, for example, was entirely different from that of Wa area, central Gonja, Grunsi area, or eastern Dagomba; while in Southern Ghana, Ashanti, and the forest of Brong Ahafo, the cultural landscape of the core area of Ashanti, for example, was easily distinguishable from that of Sunyani region, the core area of Ewe settlement in the Volta Region, the coastal lands, or the inland portion of the Central Region. Similarly, in the zone of transition the cultural landscape of the western portion of the parkland region differed from that of the central or eastern portion. Each of these distinctive cultural landscapes was itself a composite picture including contrasting yet related smaller areal units.

It is these different areal patterns, seen against the background of the primary regions of Northern Ghana, the zone of transition, and the rest of the country, which together provided a concrete summation of the evolution of Ghana's human geography up to Independence and the basis of the country's present geographic personality.

# APPENDICES

# BIBLIOGRAPHY

# INDEX

# Appendix 1. Krobo settlements in 1882

| Divisional town on Krobo Mountain | Minor town on Krobo Mountain | Minor town's village on plain |
|---|---|---|
| Eastern Krobo | | |
| DEBIAM | Nam | Odumase |
| | Abom | Abudi |
| | Agomeh | Atuah |
| | Yoquina | Agomenya |
| PEANWOAH | Lom | Lom |
| | Waquatee | Amadam |
| | Yoquano | Yoquano |
| DOM | Memlesshi | Muchosisie |
| | Konopeah | Konopeah |
| | Colinyah | Asinty |
| | Kasanyah | Nyasso |
| AQUINOE | Konya | Otalinya |
| | Ahbutenya | Kenglish |
| | Aquinoe Wapetee | Yoquano |
| MANYA | Lomojeh | Tando |
| | Dogee | Nawasipo |
| | Mamlah | Achonya |
| SUSEE | Susee Yono | Ofuanseh |
| | Susee Wapetee | Whapeh |
| | Alamo Bonyah | Manapo |
| Western Krobo | | |
| N'YAWAY | Wokono Akoli | |
| | Harsee | Abokobi |
| | Wowekonyah | Trom |
| | Cron Teschi | Planey |
| | Lanashi | Sra |
| BONASIE | Ledenya | Adjipo |
| | Odavy | Kotokoli |
| | Noduni | Somanya |
| | Menya | Somanya |
| OGORMEH | Ogormeh | Sradom |
| | Nobiano | Cromonyah |
| | Namee | Akoli |
| BONYAH | Nakoje | Sradom |
| | Bonyayiti | Akonyah |
| | Behibiani | Saloshi |
| | Bonya | Pemoe |
| PRAOW | Praow | Pemoe |
| | Wewam | Prapom |
| | Chaco Playah | Prapom |
| OKPE | Kpteshi | Tochonyah |
| | Peam | Somanya |
| | Madam | Kpeno |
| | Quadom | Adjipo |

It would appear that the two Eastern or Manya Krobo settlements of Akuse and Kpong were not founded from towns on Krobo Mountain. In 1882 Akuse was, according to Commander Rumsey, governed by the Ghanaian merchant W. B. Ocansy, and Kpong by Mr Agbleschi, also a merchant.

*N.B.* Commander Rumsey's spelling of the names of the settlements has been retained.

Source: African no. 249, *Further Correspondence Regarding Affairs of the Gold Coast* (Colonial Office, June 1883), enclosure 2 in Paper no. 11. Commander Rumsey's list of the divisional towns agrees with that in Hugo Huber's *The Krobo* (The Anthropos Institute, St Augustin near Bonn, 1963), p. 35.

# Appendix 2. A note on statistical sources for the second half of the nineteenth century

There is very little statistical material for the study of Ghana's economic geography in the centuries preceding the nineteenth. The situation improved a little after the first half of the nineteenth century when Britain became more involved in the political and economic affairs of the country. The main official body of statistical material compiled under the British consisted of the *Blue Books* which were essentially answers to questionnaires sent out by the Colonial Office in London. The *Blue Books*, which first appeared in 1846, covered all aspects of life in the country and may be regarded as forerunners of the detailed departmental reports that are available today. All the questions in the *Blue Books* were fairly well answered, except those on agriculture and population to which the answer always was 'no information'. In 1846, nevertheless, the *Blue Book* gave some figures to show the area of land under maize, yam, cassava, and plantain. The figures were reproduced for several years in subsequent *Blue Books*, but it was frankly admitted that they were inaccurate since 'from the method of cropping adopted by the Natives' it was difficult to form 'even an approximate estimate of the large quantity of land under cultivation'.

Up to the 1870s the total export figures in the *Blue Books* did not cover the commodities shipped from all the ports, especially those ports east of the Volta river. Yet large quantities of cotton and palm oil were known to pass through those ports. Customs posts were only set up at Ada and Keta in 1877 and at Denu in 1879. Before then the Dutch kept trade records for some of the ports, but they were also incomplete. After 1887 trade figures became available, in the *Government Gazettes*, for all the ports, but if the figures are added up the totals do not often agree with those in the *Blue Books*. Fortunately the differences are not significant.

Often the deficiencies of the *Blue Books* and the *Government Gazettes* are supplied by other sources like the despatches sent from Ghana to the Colonial Office and those general works on the country which contain some relevant statistics. But these supplementary statistics themselves were mere estimates which were, in most cases, not even based on intimate field observation. On the whole, therefore, one has to depend a great deal on general descriptions and inferences in reconstructing the economic geography of Ghana in those early times.

# Appendix 3. Extracts from a letter by Colonel Nagtglas to Sir A. E. Kennedy. The letter was dated 6 March 1870*

'19. I believe it would be best to leave them entirely to themselves, to let them fight their own battles and have their own quarrels, only protecting the sea-side trade, and to drive them back from the forts when attacked.

'20. Let them if possible provide their own revenue, so that a very small part only comes from the Exchequer.

'21. Give them schools also, though as my own idea I am a great disbeliever in the civilization of Africa, as it is now.

'22. Only when a victorious Mahomedan power comes to the West Coast and Mahomedan civilization has given it its benefits, that I believe a new era will come over this part of the world.'

* Enclosure no. 2 in despatch of 23 March 1870, no. 32 in C.O. 96/84, P.R.O. Colonel Nagtglas was Governor of Dutch possessions in the country at the time.

# Appendix 4. Extracts from report on the Blue Book for 1861 *

Acting Governor Ross' *Report on the Blue Book* for 1861 is in many ways the most interesting of all such reports since about 1850. Ross, instead of commenting on the statistics in the *Blue Book*, as he was supposed to do, gave what a Colonial Office official described as 'a stormy account of the financial and moral state of the Colony'. Ross was reprimanded for this, and the Report was not published. Parts of the Report read as follows:

'2. From the time when Major Hill was at the head of the Government down to the day when Governor Andrews turned his back on the coast, three distinct agencies have been labouring to impede the social expansion, the material prosperity, the impulse and the aim of the British Protectorate in Western Africa.

'3. The bold features of the first agency are to be traced in the contradictory policy of each successive Governor for the last ten or twelve years. I will express my meaning thus: Major Hill established the Poll Tax and very fairly conjectured that its collection would afford a field of utility to the Government by throwing open a wide door of communication with the Kings and Chiefs in the interior and would likewise place the ability of founding schools, churches and other buildings and institutions necessary to the common weal within the grasp of the Executive power. No sooner was Major Hill's fiscal machinery set in motion than a second experiment was wrought to cloy the wheels and to throw them out of gear. Although not averse to the Poll Tax in its entirety, Sir Benjamin Pine was certainly opposed to it in its distribution. To the movement therefore of the Poll Tax, Sir Benjamin attached an apparatus which would not have been cumbrous had it had more room and license to work. He framed a couple of Municipal Corporations. The Municipal Corporations went through an imperfect trial just as the Poll Tax had gone through its own imperfect ordeal. Barely did Sir Benjamin's liberal English spirit of decentralization come into vogue before Governor Andrews stepped forward and displaced it with his staider notions of centralization. The two Municipal Corporations of Cape Coast and of James Town were abolished at a blow. As it was with these three gentlemen, so has the principle of the Local Government been the same in contradiction with nearly every other gentleman who had preceded them. While such principles were being tested according to the fancy of the man and according to the unstudied spur of events, the Settlements were retrograding; and, I believe, that they have now reached a point of financial and moral depression which cannot be well exceeded...

'4. The second agency resides in the total absence of an interest in the affairs of the Settlements by the mother country. The evil arising out of this agency is indirect. It is no unwonted thing to read, as I have often read, in the influential London Journals which are accepted as the mouthpieces and exponents of opinion

* Despatch of 7 July 1862 in C.O. 96/58, P.R.O.

in the whole United Kingdom, that the Gold Coast includes a tract of turbulent sea-board, unworthy of serious consideration, that it is another term for a cantle of the inaccessible African Continent famous for fevers and that Cape Coast itself courts a momentary thought only because the castle yard has had the good fortune of being the final resting place of the ashes of L.E.L. Such studious and advertised indifference begets a devout school of ignorance. It is true enough that the school may be simply suggestive of well-earned contempt; but its doctrines are not the less pernicious...Can any one wonder that the civilizing instincts of England should be so tardy in striking root among us? Who but an impracticable enthusiast would waste his charity on a region sterile, inhospitable and unworthy of concern?

That the Protectorate is girt and hampered by the jealousies and the stolid timidity of barbarism needs no straining illustration...If we affect the attributes and conscientious recompenses of civilizers and defenders, we ought also to assume the disadvantages and responsibilities which are inseparable from the vocation of pastors and masters. Our presence and our lukewarmness amount to crime...What might not be done by felling timber, by introducing cochineal, by utilizing the sugar cane for the manufacture of rum, by planting indigo, by calling afresh into tillage the coffee and the cocoa, by producing fibres, and by cultivating and exporting cotton on an extensive scale?

'5. The third agency which has been and which is industriously supplanting the motive for our tenure of the Settlements is the contiguity of the Dutch. The Dutch will neither close with us in an ordinance to levy an uniform duty on Imports nor will they part with their possessions for an equitable compensation. The explanation is easy. Their authorities carry on the Slave Trade in much of its old intensity. For my own part, I am sensible that agents are accredited and sent periodically from Elmina to Coomassie for the purpose of buying slaves...A number of half-drilled black soldiers are usually waiting at Elmina for a ship to bear them off to Java. They are the wares bought of the King of Ashantee. There is no abstruse process of thinking required to understand why the Dutch cannot conceal their repugnance to part with Settlements which in a pecuniary and strategical sense are not profitable...To yield up their Settlements which are such obstacles to our progress would be equivalent to the yielding up of Java.

'6. These, Your Grace, are the three salient agencies for ever sapping the trade, the morality and the entire ramification of the policy of our Settlements in Western Africa; and, until a counterpoise shall be invented to keep the scale of deterioration in check or to depress it altogether, I do not conceive that the expenditure lavished on our establishments ashore and afloat and that the precious blood shed without stint will be of benefit—even visible benefit—to the Protected Territories...'

# Appendix 5. Two illustrations of current nineteenth-century opinion on the effect of Ghana's hot climate on health

(i) Acting Governor Henry Connor in *Report on the Blue Book* for 1855 (despatch of 12 July 1856 in C.O. 96/38, P.R.O.):
'The effect of this climate on the health appears...like a snake preparing a victim for being swallowed. It quietly slavers him with poisonous saliva and finally gulps him unless the unhappy one has previously continued to get leave of absence and had the good fortune to get "home".'

(ii) Acting Governor Ross in despatch of 6 June 1862 in C.O. 96/58, P.R.O.:
'...but we have no Surveying Department and we have no officer who would venture into the jungle to do battle against the venomous assaults of all descriptions of vermin and who would expose himself to the more fatal effects of the sun for the sake of gratifying his taste and predilections as a draftsman.

'Some officers are indeed most skilful and, for a time, most sedulous in the use of their pencil; but the climate soon transmutes their buoyancy of spirits into melancholy, soon enervates them after the first half-year of their residence on the coast has passed, and soon sets at defiance their schemes of public utility as well even as their attempts at private amusements.'

# Bibliography


*Aborigines Protection Society*, New Series, 1890–6, IV.

Acquah, Ione, *Accra Survey* (London, 1958).

Adams, C. D., 'Activities of Danish Botanists in Guinea, 1783–1850', *Transactions of the Historical Society of Ghana*, III, pt. I (1957).

Adams, S. N., and McKelvie, A. D., 'Environmental Requirements of Cocoa in the Gold Coast', *Report of Cocoa Conference* (London, 1955).

African no. 95, *Dr. Gouldsbury's Report of his Journey into the Interior of the Gold Coast* (Colonial Office, May 1876). Also known as Gouldsbury Report.

African no. 249, *Further Correspondence Regarding Affairs of the Gold Coast* (Colonial Office, June 1883).

African no. 268, *Further Correspondence Regarding Affairs of the Gold Coast* (Colonial Office, February 1884).

African (West) no 513, *Correspondence Relating to Land Grants and Concessions in the Gold Coast Protectorate* (Colonial Office, April 1897).

African (West) no. 529, *Further Correspondence Relative to Boundary Questions in the Bend of the Niger* (Colonial Office, January to August 1897).

African (West) no. 531, *Further Correspondence Relating to Land Concessions and Railways on the Gold Coast* (Colonial Office, April 1899).

African (West) no. 549, *Gold Coast: Correspondence Relating to Northern Territories* (Colonial Office, January to June 1898).

African (West) no. 585, *Gold Coast: Further Correspondence Relating to the Northern Territories* (Colonial Office, 1889).

*Annual Report on the Gold Coast*, 1931–2 to 1938–9.

*Annual Report on Northern Territories*, 1901 to 1937/38.

*Annual Report on Central Province*, 1912 to 1929/30.

*Annual Report on Eastern Province*, 1912 to 1929/30.

*Annual Report on Western Province*, 1912 to 1929/30.

Azu, Noa Akunor Aguae, 'Adangbe (Adangme) History', *The Gold Coast Review*, II, 2, July–December 1926, 239–70.

Baker, H. G., 'Comments on the Thesis that there was a Major Centre of Plant Domestication near the Headwaters of the River Niger', *The Journal of African History*, III, 2 (1962).

Barbot, John, *A Description of the Coasts of North and South Guinea* (London, 1746).

Baumann, H. and Westermann, D., *Les Peuples et Les Civilisations de l'Afrique* (Paris, 1948).

Beecham, Rev. John, *Ashantee and the Gold Coast* (London, 1841).

Beckett, W. H., *Akokoaso* (London, 1944).

Beckett, W. H., *Koransang* (London, 1945).

Bell, H. J., *History, Trade, Resources and Present Condition of the Gold Coast Settlement* (Liverpool, 1893).

*Blue Books*, 1845 to 1900.

Binger, L., *Du Niger au Golfe de Guinée* (Paris, 1892), II.

Bosman, William, *A New and Accurate Description of the Coast of Guinea* (London, 1705).

Bovill, E. W., *The Golden Trade of the Moors* (O.U.P., 1961).

Bowdich, T. E., *Mission from Cape Coast Castle to Ashantee* (London, 1819).

Boyle, Frederick, *Through Fanteeland to Coomassie* (London, 1873).

British Parliamentary Papers, Cmd. 1343, *Papers Relating to H.M. Possessions in West Africa* (Colonial Office, 1875).

British Parliamentary Papers, Cmd. 1402, *Papers Relating to H.M. Possessions in West Africa* (Colonial Office, 1876).

British Parliamentary Papers, Cmd. 3386, *Further Correspondence Regarding Affairs of the Gold Coast* (Colonial Office, August 1882).

British Parliamentary Papers, Cmd. 3687, *Further Correspondence Regarding the Affairs of the Gold Coast* (Colonial Office, July 1883).

British Parliamentary Papers, Cmd. 4052, *Further Correspondence Regarding the Gold Coast* (Colonial Office, June 1884).

British Parliamentary Papers, Cmd. 4477, *Further Correspondence Respecting the Affairs of the Gold Coast* (Colonial Office, July 1885).

British Parliamentary Papers, Cmd. 4906, *Further Correspondence Respecting the Affairs of the Gold Coast* (Colonial Office, September 1886).

British Parliamentary Papers, Cmd. 5357, *Further Correspondence Respecting the Affairs of the Gold Coast* (Colonial Office, April 1888).

British Parliamentary Papers, Cmd. 5615, *Further Correspondence Respecting the Affairs of the Gold Coast* (Colonial Office, December 1888).

British Parliamentary Papers, Cmd. 5620–4, *Reports on Gold Mines* (Colonial Office, 1889).

British Parliamentary Papers, *Fanti Confederation* (Colonial Office, 1876).

Brown, E. J. P., *Gold Coast and Asianti Reader*, Book I (London, 1929).

Buchanan, K. M. and Pugh, J. C., *Land and People in Nigeria* (London, 1958).

Burton, R. F. and Cameron, V. L., *To the Gold Coast for Gold* (London, 1883), 2 volumes.

Butzer, K. W., *Environment and Archaeology* (London, 1964).

Calvert, Albert F., *Togoland* (London, 1918).

Cardinall, A. W., *The Gold Coast, 1931* (Accra, 1931).

Census Reports, 1921, 1931, 1948.

Chipp, T. F., *The Forest Officers' Handbook of the Gold Coast, Ashanti, and the Northern Territories* (London, 1922).

Christaller, Rev. J. G., *A Grammar of the Asante and Fante Language* (Basel, 1875).

Claridge, W. W., *History of the Gold Coast and Ashanti* (London, 1915), 2 volumes.

Clark, J. D., *The Prehistory of Southern Africa* (Penguin, 1959).

*Cocoa Conference Report* (London, 1953).

*Colonial Report—Ashanti*, 1904 to 1926.

*Colonial Report—Gold Coast Colony*, 1888 to 1939.

*Colonial Report—Togoland*, 1920 to 1937.

*Colonial Report*, Miscellaneous No. 28, 1904.

Cornevin, R., *Histoire du Togo* (Paris, 1959).

Crone, G. R. (ed.), *The Voyages of Cadomosto* (London, 1937), Hakluyt Society, Second Series, LXXX.

Cruickshank, Brodie, *Eighteen Years on the Gold Coast of Africa* (London, 1853), 2 volumes.

Dalziel, J.M., *The Useful Plants of West Tropical Africa* (London, 1955).

Danish Administration Records, Furley Collection in Balme Library, University of Ghana, Legon.

D'Anville, A Map of the Gold Coast from Issini to Alampi (English edition, April 1729).

Darko, S. A., 'The Effects of Modern Mining on Settlements in the Mining Areas of Ghana', *Bulletin of the Ghana Geographical Association*, VIII, 1 (January 1963).

Darkoh, M., 'The Economic Life of Buem, 1884–1914', *Bulletin of the Ghana Geographical Association*, IX, 1 (January 1964).

Darkoh, M., *An Historical Geography of the Ho–Kpandu–Buem Area of the Volta Region of Ghana: 1884–1956* (unpublished M.A. Thesis, University of Ghana, 1966).

Davies, O., 'The Stone Age in West Africa', *Ghana Journal of Science*, III, 1 (April 1963).

Davies, O., *Archaeology in Ghana* (Thomas Nelson and Sons Ltd, 1961).

Davies, O., 'The Distribution of Stone Age Material in Guinea', *Bulletin de l'I.F.A.N.* XXI, Sér. B, nos. 1–2 (1959).

Davies, O., 'The Invaders of Northern Ghana', *Universitas* (University of Ghana, Legon), IV, 5 (March 1961).

Davies, O., 'Native Culture in the Gold Coast at the Time of the Portuguese Discoveries', *Congresso Internacional de Historia dos Descobrimentos* (Lisbon, 1961).

Davies, O., 'The Neolithic Revolution in Tropical Africa', *Transactions of the Historical Society of Ghana*, IV, part II (1960).

Department of Agriculture, *Annual Report*, 1899 to 1939/40.

Department of Agriculture, *Bulletin*, 1–24, 26–8, 30–2, 34, 36.

[Department of Agriculture,] *The Gold Coast Farmer*, 1932 to 1938.

Department of Agriculture, *Year Book*, 1929.

Department of Animal Health, *Annual Report*, 1912 to 1936/37.

Department of Forestry, *Annual Report*, 1909, 1938/39.

Department of Mines, *Annual Report*, 1903 to 1937/38.

Department of Public Works, *Annual Report*, 1899 to 1939.

Department of Railways and Harbours, *Annual Report*, 1903 to 1937/38.

Department of Tsetse Control, *Annual Report*, 1949–1951/52.

Dickson, K. B., 'The Agricultural Landscape of Southern Ghana and Ashanti–Brong Ahafo: 1800 to 1850', *Bulletin of the Ghana Geographical Association*, IX, 1 (January 1964).

Dickson, K. B., *Cocoa in Ghana* (Microfilm Methods Ltd, London, 1964).

Dickson, K. B., 'Development of the Copra Industry in Ghana', *Journal of Tropical Geography*, XIX (December 1964).

Dickson, K. B., 'The Development of Road Transport in Southern Ghana and Ashanti since about 1850', *Transactions of the Historical Society of Ghana*, V, 1 (1961).

Dickson, K. B., 'Evolution of Seaports in Ghana: 1800 to 1928', *Annals of the Association of American Geographers*, LV, 1 (March 1965).

Dickson, K. B., 'Trade Patterns in Ghana at the Beginning of the Eighteenth Century', *The Geographical Review*, LVI, 3 (July 1966).

Duncan, John, *Travels in West Africa, 1845–6* (London, 1847).

Dupuis, J., *Journal of a Residence in Ashantee* (London, 1824).

Fage, J. D., 'Some Remarks on Beads and Trade in Lower Guinea in the Sixteenth and Seventeenth Centuries', *The Journal of African History*, III, 2 (1962).

Field, M. J., *Akim Kotoku: An Oman of the Gold Coast* (London, 1948).

Field, M. J., *Religion and Medicine of the Gã People* (O.U.P., 1937).

Freeman, R. A., *Travels and Life in Ashanti and Jaman* (London, 1898).

Fuller, Sir Francis, *A Vanished Dynasty, Ashanti* (London, 1921).

*Further Report on Economic Agriculture on the Gold Coast* (1891), Cmd. 6270.

Gautier, E. F., *Le Passé de l'Afrique du Nord* (Paris, 1937).

Geological Survey Department, All *Annual Reports, Bulletins,* and *Memoirs*, up to 1939.

*Gold Coast Ordinances*, 1900 to 1939.

*Gold Coast Government Gazette*, 1888 to 1934, and 1934 (Trade Supplement).

*Gold Coast Government Sessional Paper* no. XIV, 1922–3; no. III, 1924–5; no. IV, 1924–5; no. XXIII, 1927–8; no. III, 1930–1; no. X, 1930–1; no. IV, 1931–2; no. I, 1934; no. I, 1936; no. V, 1937; no. VI, 1945.

Goody, J., *The Ethnography of the Northern Territories of the Gold Coast, West of the White Volta* (Colonial Office, London, 1954).

Goody, J., 'Ethnological Notes on the Distribution of the Guang Languages', *Journal of African Languages*, II, pt. 3 (1963).

Gordon, C. A., *Life on the Gold Coast* (London, 1874).

Gramberg, J. S. G., *Schetsen van Afrika's Westkust* (Amsterdam, 1861).

Guggisberg, Decima Moore and Major Frederick Gordon Guggisberg, *We Two in West Africa* (London, 1909).

Guggisberg, Sir Frederick Gordon, *The Gold Coast—A Review of the Events of 1924–25 and the Prospects of 1925–26* (Accra, 1925).

Guggisberg, Sir Frederick Gordon, *The Gold Coast—A Review of the Events of 1920–26 and the Prospects of 1927–28* (Accra, 1927).

Harrison Church, R. J., *West Africa* (Longmans, 1961).

Hay, Capt. J. S., 'On the District of Akem in West Africa', *Journal of the Royal Geographical Society*, XLVI (1876).

Hayford, Casely, The Gold Coast Land Tenure and the Forest Bill, 1911, 1912, *Legal Pamphlet*, no. 91 (Colonial Office Library, London).

Hill, Polly, *The Gold Coast Cocoa Farmer* (O.U.P., 1956).

Hill, Polly, *Migrant Cocoa Farmers of Southern Ghana* (C.U.P., 1963).

Hilton, T. E., *Ghana Population Atlas* (Thomas Nelson and Sons Ltd, 1960).

Holmes, W. F., 'Notes on the Early History of Tarkwa as a Gold Mining District', *The Gold Coast Review*, II, 1 (January–June 1926).

Holtsbaum, F. P., 'Sefwi and Its People', *The Gold Coast Review*, I, 1 (June–December 1925).

Horton, J. A. B., *West African Countries and Peoples* (London, 1868).

Huber, H., *The Krobo* (The Anthropos Institute, St Augustin near Bonn, 1963).

Howell, C. and Bourlière, F. (ed.), *African Ecology and Human Evolution* (London, 1963).

Hutchinson, Thomas J., *Impressions of West Africa* (London, 1858).

Hutchinson, Thomas J., 'The Social and Domestic Slavery on Western Africa, and Its Evil Influence on Commercial Progress', *Journal of the Royal Society of Arts* (26 February 1875).

Hutton, William, *A Voyage to Africa in the Year 1820* (London, 1820).

Irvine, F. R., *Plants of the Gold Coast* (O.U.P., 1930).

Irvine, F. R., 'The Indigenous Food Plants of West African Peoples', *Journal of the New York Botanical Garden*, XLIX (1948), 586–7.

Irvine, F. R., *The Fishes and Fisheries of the Gold Coast* (London, 1947).

Isert, P. E., *Voyages en Guinée* (Paris, 1793).

Jeppesen, H., 'Danske Plantageanlaeg på Guildkysten, 1788–1850', *Geografisk Tidsskrift*, LXV (1966).

Johnston, B. F., *The Staple Food Economies of Western Tropical Africa* (California, 1958).

Jones, D. H., 'Jakpa and the Foundation of Gonja', *Transactions of the Historical Society of Ghana*, VI (1962).

Jones, W. O., *Manioc in Africa* (Stanford University Press, 1959).

*Kew Bulletin*, no. 61 (1892), p. 303.

Kimble, G. H. T. (translator and editor), '*Esmeraldo de Situ Orbis*' *by Duarte Pacheco Pereira* (London, 1937), Hakluyt Society, Second Series, LXXIX.

Klose, Heinrich, *Togo unter Deutscher Flagge* (Berlin, 1899).

Labarthe, P., *Voyage à la Côte de Guinée* (Paris, 1803)

Labouret, H., '*Les Tribus de Rameau Lobi*' (*Mémoire de l'I.F.A.N., 1958*).

Lhote, Henri, *Tassili Frescoes* (E. P. Dutton and Co., New York, 1959), translated from the French by Alan Houghton Brodrick.

Macdonald, George, *The Gold Coast, Past and Present* (London, 1898).

Mahmoud El-Wakkad (translator), 'Qissatu Salga Tarikhu Gonja—The Story of Salaga and the History of Gonja', *Ghana Notes and Queries*, no. 3 (September–December 1961).

Manoukian, M., *Akan and Gã-Adangbe Peoples of the Gold Coast* (O.U.P., 1950).

Marees, Pieter de, *Description et Récit Historial du Riche Royaume d'Ore de Gunea* (Amsterdam, 1605). The original Dutch version was published in 1602.

Mauny, R., *Tableau Géographique de l'Ouest Africain au Moyen Age* (I.F.A.N.–Dakar, 1961).

Mauny, R., and Hallemans, J., 'Préhistoire et Protohistoire de la Région d'Akjoujt (Mauritanie)', *Prehistory—Third Pan African Congress* (London, 1955).

Mensah, A. A., *The Guans in Music* (unpublished M.A. thesis, University of Ghana, 1966).

Meyerowitz, E. L. R., *The Akan Traditions of Origin* (London, 1950).

*Minutes of Evidence taken before the Select Committee on the West Coast of Africa, 1842.*

*Minutes of the Gold Coast Legislative Council*, 1870, 1901, 1928, 1929.

*Minutes of the Select Committee on West Africa, 1865.*

*Minutes of West African Lands Committee, 1912–1917.*

Moloney, Alfred, *Sketch of the Forestry of West Africa* (London, 1878).

Moloney, Alfred, Letter to the Editor, *The Times*, 11 October 1882.

Morel, E. D., 'Free-grown Cocoa', *Daily Chronicle*, 25 February 1909.

Murdock, G. P., *Africa: Its Peoples and Their Culture History* (New York, 1959).

National Archives of Ghana, ADM 1, EC 1/33–35 series, and Divisional Court Records, S.C.T. 2, 1.

Ozanne, P., 'Notes on the Early Historic Archaeology of Accra', *Transactions of the Historical Society of Ghana*, VI (1962).

Pel, H. S., *Aanteekeningen gehouden op eene Reis van St. George Delmina naar Comassie* (Leiden, 1842?).

Public Record Office, London, C.O. 96, C.O. 98, C.O. 267, and T570 series.

Ramsay, J. M., and Rose Innes, R., 'Some Quantitative Observations on the Effects of Fire on the Guinea Savanna Vegetation of Northern Ghana over a Period of Eleven Years', *African Soils*, VIII, 1 (1963).

Rattray, R. S., *Ashanti* (O.U.P., 1923).

Rattray, R. S., *The Tribes of the Ashanti Hinterland* (O.U.P., 1932), 2 volumes.

Rattray, R. S., *Ashanti Law and Constitution* (O.U.P., 1929).

Rattray, R. S., *Religion and Art in Ashanti* (O.U.P., 1927).

*Report of the Commission on the Marketing of West African Cocoa*, Cmd. 5845. Also known as Nowell Report.

*Report on Economic Agriculture on the Gold Coast* (1889 and 1891), Cmd. 5894-40 and 6270.

*Report on the Prisons Department Fisheries Scheme, 1941.*

Robertson, G. A., *Notes on Africa* (London, 1819).

Rose Innes, R., 'An Ethno-botanical Problem', *Ghana Notes and Queries*, no. 3, (September–December 1961).

Sale, G. *et al.* (ed.), *The Modern Part of an Universal History* (London, 1760).

Saxton, S. W., 'Historical Survey of the Shai People', *The Gold Coast Review*, I, 1 (June–December 1925), 127–45.

Schnell, R., *Plantes Alimentaires et Vie Agricole de l'Afrique* (Paris, 1957).

Shaw, C. T., 'Report on Excavations carried out in the Cave known as 'Bosumpra' at Abetifi, Kwahu, Gold Coast Colony', *Proceedings of the Prehistorical Society*, X (1944).

Speith, Jakob, *Die Ewestamme* (Berlin, 1906).

Stanley, Henry, *Coomassie and Magdala* (London, 1874).

Stewart, J. L. and Jeffreys, M. D. W., *The Cattle of the Gold Coast* (Accra, 1956).

Sutherland, C. H. V., *Gold* (London, 1959).

Taylor, C. J., *Synecology and Silviculture in Ghana* (London, 1960).

*The Gold Coast Handbook, 1937.*

Thompson, H. N., *Gold Coast—Report on Forests (1910)*, Cmd. 4993.

*Trade Reports*, 1899 to 1939.

Trewartha, Glenn T., *The Earth's Problem Climates* (The University of Wisconsin Press, Madison, 1962).

Villault, N., *A Relation of the Coasts of Africk called Guinea* (London, 1670).

Waddy, B. B., *Onchocerciasis and Blindness in the Northern Territories*, 1951 (in typescript).

Wagner, P. L. and Mikesell, M. W., *Readings in Cultural Geography* (The University of Chicago Press, 1962).

Wanner, G. A., *The First Cocoa Trees in Ghana, 1858–1868* (Basel Trading Company Ltd, Basel, 1962).

Ward, W. E. F., *A History of Ghana* (London, 1958).

Westermann, D., and Bryan, M. A., *The Languages of West Africa* (O.U.P., 1952).

*West India Committee Circular*, 19 March 1931.

West India Company (W.I.C.) records on Ghana, Furley Collection, Balme Library, University of Ghana, Legon.

Wilks, I., *The Northern Factor in Ashanti History* (Institute of African Studies, University of Ghana, 1961).

Wilks, I., 'The Rise of the Akwamu Empire, 1650–1710', *Transactions of the Historical Society of Ghana*, III, pt. 2 (1957).

Wilks, I., *Ghana Notes and Queries*, 3 (September–December 1961).

Wilks, I., 'A Medieval Trade-Route from the Niger to the Gulf of Guinea', *The Journal of African History*, III, 2 (1962).

Wilks, I., 'The Mande Loan Element in Twi', *Ghana Notes and Queries*, no. 4 (January–June 1962).

Wilks, I., 'Islam in Ghana History', *The Ghana Bulletin of Theology*, II, 3 (December 1962).

Wilks, I., *Ashanti Government in the Nineteenth Century* (Institute of African Studies, University of Ghana, 1964), Draft Paper no. 3, Unpublished and Restricted.

Wills, J. B. (ed.), *Agriculture and Land Use in Ghana* (O.U.P., 1962).

Wrigley, C., 'Speculations on the Economic Prehistory of Africa', *The Journal of African History*, I, 2 (1960).

# Index